£4·45.

NEIGHBOURS
AND NETWORKS

NEIGHBOURS AND NETWORKS

The Idiom of Kinship in Social Action
among the Ndendeuli of Tanzania

P. H. GULLIVER

UNIVERSITY OF CALIFORNIA PRESS

BERKELEY, LOS ANGELES, LONDON 1971

University of California Press
Berkeley and Los Angeles, California
University of California Press, Ltd.
London, England
Copyright © 1971, by
The Regents of the University of California
Library of Congress Catalog Card Number: 71-115491
ISBN: 0-520-01722-6
Printed in the United States of America

Preface

The factual material on which this book is based was obtained during my field research among the Ndendeuli people, in the south of what was then Tanganyika, between 1952 and 1954, but mainly in 1953. The book does not pretend to describe the life of the Ndendeuli in more recent times. Although I have little knowledge of what has happened since 1954, it is probable that changes of many kinds have occurred in the period which saw the end of colonialism and the establishment of the Republic of Tanzania. My account is therefore deliberately written in the past tense; and it is in some sense a piece of history. It is not, however, presented primarily in that sense, but rather as an experiment, or series of experiments, in sociological analysis where the material happens to come from the social life of a people in an earlier period. I am addressing myself primarily to anthropologists and sociologists in seeking to suggest ways by which certain kinds and sets of social relationships and institutional forms can be fruitfully examined. The concern is with the activities and interests, and the interaction and interdependence, of people who were involved in a network of relationships. These relationships were described, explained, and justified by the people themselves in the idiom of kinship. There was, however, no recognition of descent or of lineal prescriptions of their kinship relations, nor did the people operate in groups based on kinship. That is, the fundamental feature of their social organization was of a kind (sometimes broadly described as "non-unilineal") that has been little considered by anthropologists in Africa, nor has it been altogether successfully studied by them in other parts of the world.

It may be appropriate to make some apology that the ethnographic materials have remained in my files and notebooks for so long. My research among the Ndendeuli was almost directly fol-

v

lowed by several other field research projects which more immediately captured my attention and fed my anthropological interests.
To be frank, however, the material on the Ndendeuli remained
largely untouched because at that time I could not perceive how to
present it coherently. My training and experience as a social anthropologist, and chiefly as an Africanist, seemed not to have fitted
me to deal with these seemingly "unorthodox" data. It took a long
time before I was ready to devote my attention to re-studying the
data and to re-thinking my own ideas and assumptions. Unfortunately my time and energies, and my abilities of concentration,
were often claimed by other, more immediate, interests and obligations, even after I began to work on the Ndendeuli data again in
1964.

Since that time, during the development of the methodology and
the analytical framework presented in this book, I have become
indebted to many professional colleagues and friends who have
been interested, or tolerant, enough to discuss with me some of the
various issues and problems with which I have been concerned. In
particular I must acknowledge my special gratitude to my immediate colleagues, Abner Cohen, Adrian Mayer, and David
Parkin, who have given me invaluable advice, critical comment,
and much encouragement over the past few years.

Various parts of the draft chapters were presented to and discussed in a variety of seminars in my own department at the School
of Oriental and African Studies, and in a number of other depart-
ments of anthropology in England and the United States. Thus I
was able to try out many of my ideas and results before critical
audiences. Much of Chapter five, on processes of dispute settlement,
was originally presented in a paper to a Symposium on "The
Ethnography of Law" at Burg Wartenstein in 1966, and later pub-
lished (in Nader 1969) by the Wenner-Gren Foundation.

My thanks go to Joseph Gallagher who, in between school-
teaching duties in Songea, was engaged in historical research there
from 1965 to 1968. He most kindly obtained photographs and
some useful additional or corroborative data for me.

Grateful acknowledgement is due to the Hill Family Foundation
at the University of Minnesota, members of the Department of
Anthropology there, and its chairman, E. Adamson Hoebel, for
inviting me to take up a visiting professorship during the first half
of 1969. With its generously light obligations, this invitation gave
me the opportunity to devote myself to the completion of this
book.

Like all field anthropologists, I remain deeply in debt to the people among whom my research was done, and especially to those many who gave time and care to my enquiries and tolerantly endured my invasion of their lives. I was accepted in a friendly spirit, and I remember the Ndendeuli, and some particular friends among them, with affection as well as with gratitude. In fulfilment of promises made to informants, and following my usual rule, pseudonyms are used throughout this book in order to preserve anonymity.

P. H. GULLIVER

School of Oriental and African Studies
London

Contents

Figures

MAPS

Notes

---

1. Abbreviated kinship references are given throughout this book by the following conventional notation:
   F = father; M = mother; S = son; D = daughter;
   B = brother; Z = sister; H = husband; W = wife.
   Thus, for example, MFZH indicates mother's father's sister's husband.
2. In all genealogical diagrams, siblings are connected on the left-hand side, and husband and wife are connected on the right-hand side.

Part One

The Problem and Its Setting

I
The Study of
Non-Lineal Kinship

This monograph is in one sense a partial, analytical ethnography of the Ndendeuli of what is now southern Tanzania in East Africa. In this it follows the conventional mainstream of social anthropology in which the principal concern is to develop "middle range" theory and to experiment with analytical techniques and concepts within the context of the culture and social life of a single group of people. It is of course incontrovertible that much more needs to be done in comparative studies, theoretical elaboration, and the formulation of hypotheses. This may be the prime requirement in anthropology, and no doubt the major stimuli and the "high level" theoretical sophistication will come from such preoccupation. Nevertheless there is great value in trying out methods and concepts, asking new kinds of questions and pushing some old questions a little further, examining new problems, and testing hypotheses, in relation to particular and limited ethnographic data. It is also useful to contribute new ethnographic data, for the plaint that we already have more raw data than we can use is palpably false. Far too often we have too little reliable ethnographic material of the kind we need to provide answers to our new questions or to test fresh hypotheses.

In the body of this work there is no attempt to give a comprehensive ethnography of the Ndendeuli. Scattered through the monograph there is, to be sure, a good deal on the institutions and customs, the beliefs, the values, and the attitudes of these people. Much can be learned as to how they made their livelihood, arranged their affairs, dealt with their disputes, and handled individual and communal crises. But a great deal is missing, particularly in certain areas of their lives. This results partly from deficiencies of field work, from my own particular predispositions and interests,

3

and practical limitations, whilst in the field. I simply do not know very much about some features of Ndendeuli culture. A second, and more important, explanation of the partial ethnography presented here lies in the object and orientation of the monograph. It is intended to address only certain problems and to analyse a limited range of data—that is, to interpret and explain, as well as describe them, and to seek significant inter-relations. This may provide an understanding of what people did, how and why they made their decisions, and what results, intended and unintended, followed.

The dominant ideology among the Ndendeuli, and the idiom in which they overtly regularised and explained so much of their social behaviour, was undoubtedly kinship. Rights and obligations, privileges and responsibilities—and also the absence of them—were ubiquitously and continually explained and morally justified in terms of the kinship relations of people. There were virtually no specialised roles of an economic, political, or religious kind among these people. A person's closer associates, neighbours, supporters, friends-in-need were kinsfolk. Ndendeuli assumed axiomatically that kinship established both a practical and a moral relationship between people which, ideally at least, was inalienable, and indeed was the prime basis of continuity, security, and welfare. When two persons who were not acknowledged kinsmen came into significant contact and interaction, the endeavour was to discover some kind of kinship linkage (for example, the kinsman of a kinsman of a kinsman) in terms of which to operate and by which to influence each other. If no such linkage could be determined, the interaction was likely to be indeterminate, unreliable, and fruitless.

Anthropologists have become sophisticated in their accounts and analyses of non-Western kinship phenomena: these are surely one class of socio-cultural things which are undisputably their specialist province. This monograph may confirm that anthropological addiction to what superficially seem to be exotica. In fact, my concern is with the ways in which the Ndendeuli secured their economic livelihood, dealt with their conflicts and disputes, and reached decisions in matters of concern to them, especially matters relating to their living together as neighbours. These matters—how they achieved their ends—never however strayed far from the facts and the cultural assumptions of kinship.

Despite their concern with kinship, social anthropologists, particularly those specialising on Africa, have tended to concentrate on certain aspects and particular kinds of kinship phenomena, to the curious neglect of certain other kinds. That concentration, and the greatest elaboration of theory, has clearly been in reference to those cases where groups or defined categories of people are recruited, where rights and obligations are acquired, and where collective action is taken on the basis of unilineal descent. The classics of anthropological kinship literature, and not only for Africa, have been largely concerned with this aspect. People in any society are, of course, linked multilaterally by kinship traced through both males and females. But, outside of the domestic domain (to use Fortes' term), the chief concern by far has been on those situations where interests, activities, and interaction are decisively affected by unilineal descent. The concentration has been on both unilinearity and on group formation and interaction, as illustrated by descriptions and analyses of segmentary lineage systems and the development of theoretical sophistication concerning such systems; a great deal else in the literature shows the same general preoccupation. There has been some gradual change of emphasis lately, but the prevailing orthodoxy of the recent past is well indicated by the fact that a contemporary general textbook of social anthropology contains virtually no reference to, let alone a developed account of, non-lineal kinship systems outside the domestic domain.[1] It is most significant, furthermore, that there continues to be only a negative-oriented term of reference to this neglected field—"non-unilineal" or "non-lineal" kinship. I have frequently encountered a marked tendency among anthropologists, students and professionals alike, to think in lineal terms even when presented with non-lineal data. Their academic training appears to have conditioned them to rather deep-seated assumptions of lineality in kinship studies.

The Ndendeuli of East Africa recognized no lineal reckoning of descent and gave only a very minor bias to patrilaterality. They had no corporate groups, or enduring units definable in terms of actual interaction, based on kinship, lineal or otherwise. In gathering data in the field, and later in attempting to establish a reasonable framework for their exposition, I found little in the mainstream of social anthropology that was helpful—especially in that sector strongly influenced by African specialisation. My problems were greatly exacerbated because, like many other anthropologists, I was at the same time seeking to avoid the past rigidities and artificialities of structural-functionalism and presumptions of equilibria.

[1] Cf., e.g., Beattie 1964.

THE CONCEPT OF THE KINDRED: AN ASSESSMENT

One apparent way out of the difficulties was to turn to the work and thought of those anthropologists, many of whom were not encumbered by some of the built-in assumptions of social anthropology, who had studied non-lineal kinship amongst peoples in different parts of the world: southeast Asia, Oceania, Lapland, the Arctic, Euro-America, and other areas. The most obvious concept that occurred in this body of work was that of the "kindred". Although the Ndendeuli themselves had no explicit cultural concept that might be translated as "kindred", they did in practice have something essentially of that sort: overlapping, ego-centred categories of kinsfolk, as each individual maintained recognition of and active relations with a range of kinsmen traced multilaterally through both males and females. These categories were not groups; but they served, inter alia, as reservoirs from which ephemeral collectivities could be recruited and assembled for particular purposes in a variety of cultural contexts. Moreover, because these ego-centred categories necessarily overlapped, as no individual's own category was quite the same as nor yet altogether different from those of related individuals, each person was continuously kept in relationship with a much wider range of people whose interests and actions impinged on his own, directly and indirectly.

Despite Murdock's claim of "incisiveness of analysis [in] the study of cognatic kinship structures" (Murdock 1964:129), it quickly became obvious that there is considerable confusion and disagreement about this concept of "kindred", a good deal of dogmatic assertion in the teeth of awkward ethnographic fact, and, above all, rather little actual, penetrating analysis of particular ethnographic situations. Anthropology has been capable of a fair degree of useful work during this century although so many of its terms and concepts have failed to find generally agreed definition, theoretically or operationally—for example, "law", "religion", "clan", "descent", "structure". The problems have been handled by effectively ignoring such terms, by giving them particular, limited definitions, by allowing them to refer to general fields of enquiry and at the same time developing more incisive concepts referring to particular parts or aspects of the general field, and so on. Some such solution has scarcely been achieved in connection with "kindred"; disagreement and lack of refinement seem to persist. On the whole, one is forced to the sad conclusion that the concept has been a rather blunt instrument at best. This probably explains why there have been few, if any, first-class monographs in which detailed ethnographic data have been examined at length and adequately analysed in terms of the "kindred". There are few, if any, anthropological works comparable to those that have been firmly grounded on the concepts of "lineage" and "descent". That judgement may appear too severe in the opinions of anthropologists who have made most valuable contributions in the field of non-lineal kinship. Clearly, one must stand indebted to those anthropologists who have, in numerous journal articles, continued to examine the problems critically and to suggest ideas and methods from which further development must profit.[2] To make my own debt clearer, two particular examples may be mentioned. Goodenough (1962) formulated the idea of the "nodal kindred" by direct reference to the ethnography of the Lakalai of New Britain, although thorough treatment was not possible in a seven-page journal article, and the concept has not yet been further developed. Pehrson's lengthier analysis of Lapp herding groups (1957) is of a high order, demonstrating the value of careful ethnography and showing profitable lines of approach.

The inadequacy of the concept of "kindred" can be best indicated by a brief examination of the problems that have affected attempts to reach consensus in definition and, more importantly, which have prevented the concept becoming a more valuable operational tool of analysis. In reviewing the difficulties it will be possible to open the way to an alternative analytical framework by which to deal with the kinds of data concerned.

The principal areas of disagreement or lack of clarity have concerned the position of affinal kin, the genealogical limits of the kindred, the question whether or not the included kinsmen are an undifferentiated collectivity, the kindred as a social category rather than a social group, the nature of sub-units and their formation, and the implications of the overlapping of individuals' kindreds.

Some anthropologists, Freeman (1961) in particular, have insisted dogmatically that the kindred quite certainly excludes affinal kin. Freeman took this stand, firstly, on the irrelevant historico-legal grounds that the old English word referred only to blood relatives. Secondly, he pointed out, quite correctly, that in some societies affines are specifically not classified with or treated the

[2] No comprehensive bibliography is attempted here; but see, for example, the listing given by Mitchell 1963.

same as cognatic or blood kin. This is the case, for example, among both the Iban of Sarawak and the Kalinga of Luzon, where separate, distinct terminology is applied to affines. The Central Javanese similarly distinguish affines linguistically: there, affines are set apart from cognatic kin, they are always addressed with a degree of formality and reserve, and tensions and acknowledged potential conflict are evident in the relationships, in contrast with cognatic relations (Geertz 1961).

Nevertheless it would seem unwise to insist on a universalistic exclusion of affines from a general definition. Firstly, because there are many societies in which cognates and affines are, at least for certain purposes in some contexts, treated together and in which they act together within a single kinship matrix. Secondly, there is good reason to believe that at least in some cases, even where affines are formally and to a marked extent distinguished from blood kin, they are nonetheless regularly involved with cognates in kindred-like activities. Firth (1963) noted that a kindred in action is enlarged by the participation of affines. It is clear that anything we might designate as "kindred" in modern England or the United States regularly contains affines. In order to deal with this sort of case in the Faroe Islands of the North Atlantic, Blehr (1963) suggested the term "kith" to comprise an ego-centred category comprising both kinds of kin. The question of terminology per se is of minor importance only. What does matter is that we should not arbitrarily distinguish categories of a comparable sociological order merely on the grounds of the inclusion or exclusion of affines.

In any case, it is clear from Freeman's own evidence on the Iban (on which he partly based his assertion) that even there affines are involved in social action with cognates in some kindred-like activities. He described how two affinally related sets of people can be brought together in common social action focussed on their common kinsman: for example, ego's first cousins, sons of his father's brother and mother's brother, who are affinally related to each other. We cannot, and should not, neglect such affinal links even though individuals are involved as cognates of ego. But, because of achieved friendship and demonstrated mutual usefulness and trust, "in the event of the killing of a member [of one set] by some alien, his affinally related relatives of [the other] set would unhesitatingly join his kindred proper in seeking vengeance" (Freeman 1961:211). We have no full account of Iban kinship and political systems, but common sense suggests that this sort of thing occurs quite frequently. Perhaps it is even the statistical norm, so that the category of the so-called "kindred proper" does not alone usually generate the participants in collective social action of that kind. Elsewhere Freeman reported that work-parties for hunting or gathering forest produce though "largely composed of cognates . . . also commonly contain affinal kin" (Freeman 1960:73). It is perhaps significant also that marriage prescription is much narrower than the kindred proper. The Iban, and likewise the Kalinga, may and frequently do marry second cousins. "Marriage rules are predominantly concerned with alliances between cognates", Freeman recorded (1960:73). Many cognates are therefore also affines, but as such they are not excluded from the kindred. Somehow cognatic kinship and affinity are not incompatible. One suspects that cognatic kinship, and membership of the kindred, may perhaps be reinforced by inter-marriage.

Excessive emphasis on bilateral principles and preconceptions related to them have sometimes induced anthropologists to ignore important aspects of affinal kinship and the organisation of social action in non-lineal societies. For example, Pehrson's account of the Lapp reindeer nomads of Konkama (1957) has been frequently quoted approvingly as a study of kindreds in action. In a re-examination of the data, Paine came to the conclusion, however, that "a conceptual division between cognates and affines—something that his methodological point of departure sometimes led Pehrson actually to emphasize—is seriously at odds with reality as it can be observed in the manipulation of relations in the pastoralists' work-groups," [3] that is, in the nomadic bands that are fundamental to Lapp pastoral life and livelihood. On Pehrson's own evidence, ego-centred herding bands (focussed on a leader or a group of siblings) contain affines, and the latter do not appear to be differentiated from cognates with respect to band activity and co-operation, though they may be in other respects and other social activities.

All this implies, at very least, that we should take affines fully into consideration when analysing non-lineal kinship situations. It is not clear to me why among the Iban or Lapps each individual's egocentric field (referred to as the "kindred" by the ethnographers) should not include affines, just as it does among, say, the Faroe Islanders. It seems to be more efficacious to do so in analysis, even where a people themselves for some purposes culturally distinguish between the two kinds of kin. There are cases, certainly,

[3] Paine 1964:36. See also Paine 1957:201–2.

where particular politico-jural rights and obligations are specifically defined in cognatic terms only—for example, the Kalinga
of Luzon—but these seem to be numerically unusual, and might
be better treated as special cases of the more general phenomenon
of egocentric kinship organisation. There is, of course, no need to
deny the cultural distinction between the two kinds, when that
exists amongst a people; but such distinction does not necessarily
set all affines in less close relationship with ego than all cognates in
all contexts. Near affines, especially of ego's generation, may be
more important, more advantageous, and more demanding than a
second or third cousin. This is primarily a matter of ethnographic
record and not of analytical concept.

With reference to the genealogical limits of the kindred, generalised definitions have sometimes specified the inclusion of *all*
cognatic kin. The better ethnographies report a narrower range of
inclusion. Among the Melanau of Sarawak, for instance, "close
relatives" (*a sega*), who are said to comprise the kindred, include
certainly third cousins, probably fourth, but not fifth or six cousins.
Genealogically some fifth or sixth cousins are known, but they
are "distant kin" (*a suku*) or scarcely kin at all (Morris 1953:69).
Similarly among the Kalinga, cousins beyond the third category
are classified as *kapo-on*, as distinct from *mana-agi* who are nearer
cognates and members of the "bilateral kinship group", Barton's
equivalent to the kindred (Barton 1949:Chap. 2). It is frequently
reported that, in such societies, individuals in the more distant
category may move into the kindred as a result of geographical
proximity or friendly inter-personal relations with ego. Conversely,
a member of the nearer category may shift into the non-kindred
class as a result of prolonged geographical or social separation, or
of conflict and hostility.

Thus there may well be known kinsfolk not in the kindred; and
the category cannot be defined purely by genealogical limits. Although most commonly the conventional definition has referred
to simple genealogical boundaries (for example, all cognates up to
third cousins), and although this sort of thing may well be the
folk culture idiom or ideal, yet clearly the concrete situations are
less simple. The simplification overlooks a crucial factor: the need
empirically to identify the set of active inter-personal relations between ego and each of his kin. Where for any reason inter-personal
relations with kinsmen atrophy or are deliberately broken, then
those individuals shift into the non-kindred class, irrespective of
the particular genealogical link. If we are to understand the opera-

tion of kindred relationships in social organisation we should eschew generalised and ideal statements and examine the kindreds of particular individuals: who is in and who is not, and why; and whether all comparable collaterals are included or excluded together. We should also enquire whether inclusion/exclusion varies according to differently situated individuals in the society and at different times of their life cycle, and how far criteria of inclusion/exclusion relate to particular kinds of interests and activities. Very little has been done in this way by ethnographers; of course, it is no easy matter to accomplish on any scale even when some index of allocation has been established.

Instead, in the literature, the concrete situations remain vague, obscure, and ambiguous, hence the concept of "kindred" remains unsatisfactory and a difficult one to use analytically. Rights and obligations and institutionalised activities are too often described in indeterminate fashion, as if applying generally and equally to every individual of the kindred or even all kinsmen, when in fact a narrow or graded range of applicability is the case. For example, Geertz stated that in Central Java, kindred members have a moral obligation to care for a kinsman in need; but this is then qualified, for "this particularly applies to one's own parents or siblings, but it may also apply to secondary kin such as a destitute aunt or nephew if there is no one closer to take care of them" (Geertz 1961:26). What then of second or third cousins? Presumably there is no more than a vague ideal of this kind of assistance at that range. But, if so, why give it as a characteristic of the kindred? For an understanding of effective social relations rather than cultural generalities, we need a more precise and accurate analysis. Clearly, among the Kalinga a third cousin had much less obligation, materially or morally, to avenge a man's murder or to contribute to bloodwealth than a second cousin; and a second cousin had less than a first, and so on. It was considered possible to kill a murderer's third cousin in vengeance; but, Barton said, it was in "bad taste" and, presumably, less satisfactory or effective to do so. Active support of a kinsman "hardly reaches beyond second cousins", Barton stated, although he had also asserted that Kalinga include third cousins in their "bilateral kinship group" (Barton 1949).

Not all kin of the same degree of relatedness are treated the same. A man wealthy in land may be obliged to assist more distant kin who are short of land than may a man who has little land, for example. Barton noted for the Kalinga that the distribution of the proceeds of sales only extended as far as second cousins when sales were large, and then usually only to the more influential ones whom it was desired to impress or obligate. A politically influential man was likely to acknowledge a rather wider kindred: it was useful for him to extend the range of people who would support his activities and over whom his influence was acknowledged; and more distant kin might have been glad to gain his support in their own activities. Again, a second cousin living near at hand, perhaps in the same community, was treated differently from another second cousin living miles away. These examples are, of course, obvious enough, and they and their like are reported directly and indirectly in the literature; but they are most often neglected in theoretical statements or in analysis, and there has been insufficient attention to this crucial feature in field research.

This brings me to the third major point in respect of the kindred: Murdock (1949) held that the kindred is especially characterised by the fact that ego is equally associated with paternal and maternal kin. Other anthropologists have assumed that the kindred is peculiarly connected with bilateral kinship systems and the absence of unilineal descent. Freeman, for example, wrote: "A distinction must be drawn between the kindred as an undifferentiated category, as in bilateral societies, and cognatic kin as an internally differentiated category, existing in societies with unilineal systems" (Freeman 1961:204). In "pure" bilateral systems there is, of course, no differentiation between cognates in terms of lineality, but I have already indicated that there are other kinds of differentiation that are no less important (for example, genealogical and geographical closeness, political and economic advantage). It is at least naive to assume that all cognates are equal, either in principle or in concrete reality. Beyond this, however, we must note that there are cases that fall between a "pure" bilateralism and a "pure" unilineality. Then there can be some bias towards patri- or matrilaterality, such that, say, genealogically more distant kin are included from one side than from the other. Or again, unilineality might be rather strictly segregated to one area of social action (say, control of land), or it might in effect amount to little more than certain exogamic regulations and the inheritance of almost negligible property. In such circumstances, in other areas of social life, particularly in actual collective action rather than in idealised generalities, the differences between the several kinds of cognates and affines may be little more than among, say, the Lapps.

Aside from these crucial considerations, some anthropologists have considered it an error of sociological analysis to assume that unilineality (especially where it involves corporate descent groups) and kindred-type organization are mutually exclusive. Goodenough has asserted this, giving an example from Truk; and he complained that, with reference to "ego based or personal kin groups, anthropology has confined itself almost exclusively to the notion of bilateral symmetry" (Goodenough 1961:1345). Mitchell has written: "the ego-oriented network of kin, and the extended kin group as a bounded corporate unit have different system-references" (Mitchell 1963:350); and he rightly concluded that therefore kindred-like organisation is not necessarily an anomaly in a markedly unilineal society. On the other hand, Murdock is surely right in warning against the danger of confusing "kindred" with merely "kinsmen" or "relatives" (Murdock 1964:129). It begins to look as though the ethnographic, and hence theoretical, emphasis on "kindreds" in bilateral societies and failure to report on them where unilineality is marked has come from the anthropologists' preconceptions and limited interests. It seems incorrect to assume that egocentric categories and unilineal groups are mutually exclusive. We need more careful reporting in the ethnographies.

As new methods of analysis emerge with fresh concepts, and as a reaction to previous over-emphasis on unilineality continues, we must be careful that we do not set up a bilateral type of kinship organisation as a sociologically distinct category, as opposed to one characterised by unilineal descent. It is essential, therefore, that we look quite carefully at concrete manifestations of egocentric categories, and that we should expect to find various kinds of differentiation of the many relationships involved. If in fact there are undifferentiated "kindreds" in some societies, they would be only a particular variety of the more general phenomenon where the basic principles of social action and organisation are essentially the same.

Although more recently most anthropologists have recognised "kindreds" and kindred-like collectivities as social categories rather than as groups, Murdock at least has continued to designate them as "occasional kin groups". He has protested that "to regard the kindred merely as a category . . . is to deprive it of all utility as an analytic tool" (Murdock 1964:130). This is not just a matter of hair-splitting, for it raises a number of important issues. As a first step we have to distinguish the category of all those kinsfolk acknowledged by ego and who reciprocally acknowledge him, and from whom he may seek assistance of various kinds. The category may not include all known kinsfolk. This is a social category, a classifying together of certain people in relation to ego alone, a collectivity that probably never acts together as a unit at any one time, even in ego's own interests. Many of its members will not be related by kinship to each other (for example, matrilateral and patrilateral cousins), and some may scarcely know or even know of each other. It is a category from which ego can draw assistance at different times for different purposes, either on an individual basis or by recruiting some of its members as an action group or (as I prefer) an action-set. The composition of such sets varies according to context and is a matter for empirical enquiry. It may be that by repeated recruitment of more or less the same selection of members, there emerges a quasi-group of a more persistent nature in respect of some activity—for example, an economic or political enterprise. Recruitment may call for a comparatively longer-term commitment to join ego's band (Konkama Lapps) or hamlet (Lakalai) to give a semi-permanent unit—Goodenough's "nodal kindred". Such more persistent units are, however, unlikely to be exhaustive of the egocentric category, as ego's acknowledged links with other members continue in reference to other kinds of activities and interests. These other members may also be potential recruits to the more persisting units as those change over time. Thus we need to discriminate carefully between the total egocentric category and its potentiality, on the one hand, and social units organized for action which are recruited from that category, and which range from ephemeral to more persistent in nature. If there are ethnographic cases where a whole egocentric category is recruited in some matters to act in unison, this would, again, establish a special case of the more general phenomenon. Even then, such comprehensive recruitment would not occur in reference to other interests.

Finally, there is inherent in the nature of kindred-like, or egocentric, categories, the important feature that each is peculiar to a particular individual, *ex definitio*. It is true that for siblings, the designated category may sometimes be the same. This is not necessary, at least after marriage; and in reality it might be quite uncommon. Apart from affines, each sibling is highly likely gradually (sometimes precipitately) to develop his own partly idiosyncratic range of acknowledged kinsfolk who comprise his category. Geographical separation, personal inclination, personal interests and ambitions and opportunities, and individual decisions will all affect the composition of each sibling's egocentric category. Other persons start initially with more or less different categories: first cousins have a higher proportion of common kin than second cousins, but many unrelated persons have some kinsfolk in common whether they are aware of it or not. Again, the development of each person's range of acknowledged kin will produce divergencies and also convergencies.

Clearly, the categories of many individuals will contain some of the same people: in a smaller community perhaps the categories of all the men might overlap in some degree. This implies, obviously, that a person will be a member of many other men's categories. This can raise conflicts of obligations; it can also provide bridging links between otherwise unrelated, unconnected individuals (for example, men with a cousin in common, though not themselves kinsmen). More than this, it implies that some members of ego's category are themselves linked together as members of each other's categories. Thus they interact not only directly with each other, but also in respect of their common link with ego. Or, to put it in another way, some of ego's kinsmen are not merely in dyadic relationship with him, but also with each other. The field of social behaviour, predispositions to action (or inaction), interests, obligations, and so on are inter-connected in highly complex ways. To examine *the* "kindred", or a particular individual's "kindred", as if it were an independent entity (as has so often been attempted) is to miss one of the most crucial factors which directly and indirectly affect kinship relations and the organisation of action in society. The "kindred", or egocentric category, is an artificial analytical isolate. To understand it at all adequately it is necessary to examine it in the full context of contemporaneous collectivities that intimately affect its operation and significance.

Acknowledgements are no doubt in order to some anthropologists who have shown awareness of these kinds of problems connected with the kindred. Indeed, few if any of the preceding observations are original, and most are becoming accepted currency. My debt is to all those writers whose contributions have become part of the literature. Yet it has seemed worthwhile to attempt to bring these considerations together in seeking to establish a viable frame of reference in which to make an analysis of Ndendeuli kinship relations.

As Keesing has rightly concluded: "Many of us have been hoping that if we developed a detailed enough set of *Notes and Queries* type analytical terms and defined them carefully enough, we could go out and describe any society on earth in term of such

categories. . . . On the ethnographic level . . . such precisely defined terms are neither possible nor desirable. Linguists gave up
decades ago trying to describe all languages in terms of a standard
list of parts of speech; and they saw that a more and more precise
and differentiated phonetic notation did not reflect the structure
of particular phonological systems" (Keesing 1966:350–351). The
search for the defined and refined terms is illusory. It is especially
illusory when the actual phenomena to be embraced are highly
complex and are markedly variable in many significant constitu-
ents, as in the case under consideration. There is an inevitable tendency to make the desired definition more and more inclusive in
order to take account of new cases, and thus to make it more abstractly generalised. The term tends to become less and less useful, either as an analytical tool in ethnography or as a comparative
concept of sociology. We shall not get far, and we may well obscure significant features, in any attempt to compare holistically
such complex phenomena in different socio-cultural settings.

One must heartily agree with Keesing when he writes: "Let us
stop worrying whether tribe X 'has kindreds' or not, or whether
what tribe Y has is 'really a kindred' " (Keesing 1966:351). What
we need are, I think, sharper tools of ethnographic analysis, limited
but more precise concepts by which our descriptions can more accurately be given, and which encourage the ethnographers to seek
more refined details rather than to escape within the vagueness of
over-generalised terms. Such a concept as that of the "kindred"
has, in many ways, lost such usefulness as it had. It is necessary for
discriminating analysis to break down the complex phenomena. Indeed, because of the range of existing disagreement about the term,
it can perhaps be discarded altogether if that will frustrate further
diversions of attention from what are more critical matters. Apart
from its possible usefulness as a general indicator of an area of
study, its usage seems not to have produced much "incisiveness of
analysis".

KIN-SETS, ACTION-SETS, AND NETWORKS

Primarily for the purposes of making an analytical ethnography of
Ndendeuli non-lineal kinship, I now propose a number of limited
but inter-related conceptual tools. These may be useful in other
comparable circumstances where egocentric categories are important; but particular circumstances may call for other tools, and the

following ones are not intended to be exhaustive. The degree of success with which they are used, the kinds of assumptions under-lying them, and their further implications for analysis, as demon-strated in the main body of the present monograph, may persuade other anthropologists of their value and stimulate their develop-ment and augmentation. The chief intention is to provide means by which complex and detailed data can be presented as clearly as possible.

First, following Firth (1963), we can recognise the *universe of kin:* the totality of all those people with whom an ego is related by cognatic and affinal links. Secondly, within his universe of kin, ego has a *kin-set,* comprising all those with whom at any particular time he maintains an active relationship, some kind of operational link involving interaction and inter-depen-dence.[4] Generally it is not necessary, and it is probably almost impossible, empirically to identify with any certainty ego's uni-verse of kin. It is chiefly important conceptually in distinction from the (usually) rather smaller kin-set. For discriminating analy-sis, to get away from purely idealised formulations, and to examine the significance of variations from ego to ego (or over a period of time for a single ego), it is essential that kin-sets be identified in empirical terms. Some means of identifying who can be considered as belonging to the kin-set, and who does not, is needed; this may be in terms of ego's own assessment, or in actual activation of the relationship within a given period, or by some social pointer of significance. Ultimately, no doubt, no absolute finite limits can be given to the kin-set, for the boundaries are likely to be blurred; but with the emphasis on active inter-relations between ego and each member of his kin-set, a working knowledge may be ob-tained. A descriptive, statistical model can be constructed if neces-sary for general analytical purposes from the ascertained kin-sets of a number of individuals. A number of such models might be useful as a result of distinguishing different categories of individ-uals.

It may be useful to contrast this empirically derived category with the ideal category (for example, "all of a man's kin up to third cousins"). But here I wish to emphasise the importance of

[4] Mayer (1960) suggested the "kindred of recognition" and the "kindred of cooperation" for what I am referring to as universe of kin and kin-set respectively. Whilst acknowledging his suggestion, I prefer not to use the loaded term of "kindred".

seeking to discover, as nearly as possible, with which persons an individual maintains actual, active relations. This should raise issues and questions as to why, in particular or in general, certain kinsmen are included and certain others are not; this will be a step towards an understanding of what the relationship is and how it is established and maintained. Factors of geographical and genealogical distance, of past and present competition and cooperation, of conflict of obligations and interests, and the like, will call for investigation. By constructing the statistical model, we can go on to see what are the general limits of operational relations, what are the principles underlying particular geographical, genealogical, and structural skews.

The kin-set may or may not be equivalent to a "kindred"; but its significance lies in the fact that it comprises those people against whom ego can and does exercise claims, with whom he cooperates, and to whom he acknowledges obligations. They are his potential supporters in some or many of his social interests and activities. Freeman has described this kind of egocentric category as a "continuous network of relationships from which further action groups may arise" (1961:203). Geertz, on Central Java, used the analogy of "a pool of relations [which] can be drawn on for assistance" (1961:25). Pehrson, on the Lapp nomads, wrote that this kind of category provided "a wide range of alternative courses of action" (1957:96). The kin-set is, then, as it were, a supply of supporters on which an individual can and does draw. Seldom, and probably never, will all the potential supporters be drawn on together nor will they all act together in ego's interests. Many will be unrelated (either by formal kinship or in active relations) to each other; some will not know each other. The kin-set is a social category, not a social group.

Ego can seek the support of members of his kin-set individually as occasion and need arise (for advice and information, for a loan, for practical assistance, and so on). It is likely, however, that at certain times, for socially defined purposes, ego may recruit and mobilise some members of his kin-set to assist him in taking collective action on his behalf and in his interests. Such an ad hoc unit for collective action may be referred to as an *action-set*. An action-set is ephemeral, being recruited for some particular purpose by ego, and, having fulfilled that purpose, it disbands. Later action-sets recruited by the same ego for similar or different purposes will be unlikely to have quite the same composition, for much depends on the actual context at the time. Those recruited by different individuals also vary in composition since they draw on different kin-sets.[5]

The purposes for collective action in ego's interests vary from people to people, of course. It may be for economic enterprise—to cultivate his fields, to build or repair his house or boat, to engage in hunting or trading; it may be politico-jural—to defend his interests when they are injured or threatened, or when he is alleged to have interfered with the interests of another person, or to support his endeavour to gain or use influence or power; it may be religious—to perform rituals on specified occasions; or it may be to join in rejoicing over good fortune or condoling in misfortune.

Which members of his kin-set an individual can recruit, perhaps in conjunction with a de facto leader other than himself, depends on a number of considerations. First, there is the nature of the interest for which the action-set is recruited: certain requirements, say homicide, can call for larger sets than others, say birth rituals for ego's child. Some members of the kin-set may recognise only certain obligations and not others. Secondly, it depends on how far the interests of ego's kin are also involved and the advantages perceived by them. They may give help purely as an obligation to ego, with the expectation of obtaining reciprocal assistance in their future needs. But there are often other advantages and inducements: economic reward, cooperation with certain others among ego's kinsmen, political security or advancement, expression of opposition to someone who is ego's adversary, and the like. Thirdly, some kinsmen offer more useful assistance than others in particular contexts: some may be influential men, others may possess special ritual power or knowledge, or special skill, and others may have previous experience of some value in the matter in hand. Fourthly, pressures of time and the claims of other simultaneous interests of some potential recruits may preclude their inclusion at a particular time. Fifth, residential proximity often makes it easier to recruit some kinsmen rather than others. The relative urgency of action may be important, and the condition of communications. Sixthly, the actual state of inter-personal relations between ego and each of his kinsmen individually may affect recruitment: he is likely to appeal, and with more success, to those with whom he is more

[5] A number of anthropologists have used the term "action group" in more or less the same sense. I prefer deliberately to avoid the use of "group" in this connection lest it inadvertently suggest the impression of a corporate or permanent character. "Set" seems to be a more neutral word. It was used, at my suggestion, by Mayer 1966:98.

friendly or to whom he has given generous assistance. Some kinsmen may have, or feel that they have, a greater obligation to accede
to his request. Seventhly, the de facto leader of the action-set, if
different from ego, may for any of the previous reasons attract
or deter potential recruits.

Finally, some members of the kin-set may be put into an ambiguous situation when they are related both to ego and to some
other person with whom ego is negotiating—for example, over
marriage, in a dispute, in a land transaction, or in political rivalry.
Normally a man cannot act on both sides in these kinds of instances; often he may be unable to act on either. He may be compelled to choose the greater advantage, or the lesser disadvantage,
to himself. He may decide to join neither side (action-set) and
remove himself temporarily from the scene. Or he may choose, or
even be more or less compelled, to act as go-between, or conciliator, if such a role is relevant to the circumstances.

Action-sets, like the kin-set, are ego-oriented. They are not
merely clusters of kinsfolk with common interests to protect and
pursue. Obviously, in effect members of an action-set will have
their own interests in mind, but the focus, and the *raison d'être*, of
an action-set is ego's particular interest at the time. Neither is an
action-set in some sense representative of ego's kin-set. Not being
a corporate entity, it is difficult to conceive of the kin-set being
represented in the way that a descent group might be represented
by its seniormost members or by those happening to be present on
some occasion. An action-set is *not* ego's kin-set in action.

Ego-oriented action-sets are not, of course, limited only to non-
lineal kinship contexts. For example, Mayer has examined their
emergence and operation in connection with candidates for political election in India. He showed how a candidate attempted to
mobilise canvassing and voting support through all the relationship
channels (both kinship and other) available to him (Mayer 1966).
The party of supporters assembled by an Arusha man involved
in a dispute case is also an action-set. It is recruited by reference
to either determined patrilineal category or coeval alignment; but
it is both ego-oriented and ephemeral (Gulliver 1963:119ff.).

The usefulness of the concept of action-set in situations where
corporate groups do not operate is really a form of situational analysis in which we can examine impermanent, collective action. With
this concept it is possible to focus research and analysis, and to
avoid the distressing amount of vague and misleading generalisation that has occurred in even the better ethnographies dealing

with non-lineal kinship organisation. We need to know, with detailed documentation and analysis of concrete cases, how social action is in reality accomplished under those conditions, and how an individual operates within his egocentric potential.

The range of relationships is, however, more complex than I have so far admitted. An obvious feature is that an individual's kin-set does not exist in a social vacuum. Its membership overlaps in some degree with that of other individuals' kin-sets. The more nearly related those individuals are, the greater the overlap, the more kinsmen in common; but men who do not acknowledge kinship with each other may have some, even many, kinsmen in common. According to the cultural criteria concerned, full siblings may have coincident kin-sets, but this would seem empirically to be rare. Kin-sets do not merely overlap; they interlock in some way. People's relations with ego affect and are affected by their relations with one another. Their allegiance (say, in an action-set) is not wholly to ego and his interests, but to some of their co-participants and each other's interests. Moreover, by the partial overlapping of the kin-sets of inter-connected persons, there is logically a continuous *network* of relationships.

Let me try to be clear here, for there continues to be confusing disagreement about the meaning that can or should be given to the term "network". Some anthropologists speak of "ego-centred networks" in referring (within the kinship frame) to what I have called the kin-set. This is unfortunate. The kin-set is itself not a network; it is what Barnes has called (in a more general sense) a "primary star"—the actual links, expressed in terms of kinship, which ego actively acknowledges and maintains with other individuals. But probably no ego, nor any external observer, can afford to treat the kin-set in so simplistic a way, as if it existed on its own, since some of the members of the kin-set are themselves variously linked by direct, active, acknowledged kinship relations. That is, they are simultaneously members of each other's kin-sets. Thus the initial, simple star of Figure 1 (*a*) is complicated by other kinship inter-connections, as shown in Figure 1 (*b*). That may, for certain purposes of analysis, provide a convenient or useful unit; but the usefulness seems likely to be limited, and concentration on it will inevitably ignore a whole range of factors that bear on ego's and other men's opportunities, choices, and behaviour. As in Figure 1 (*c*), B, a member of A's kin-set, is not only linked as kinsman to two other members, C and E, but B's own kin-set comprises, in addition to A, C, and E, the individuals H to L. Diagrammatic

(a)

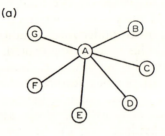

(b)

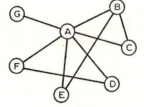

(c)

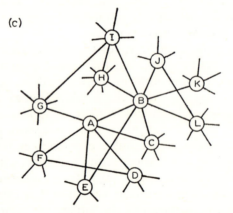

FIGURE 1: Elementary Network Models.

presentation begins to become difficult; but the chains of kinship linkages are of course extended to include those individuals comprising the kin-sets of each member of A's kin-set. Then it is necessary to include the kin-sets of the latter individuals, and so on. That is to say, a kind of graph would be produced of the network of direct kinship links that inter-connect a whole range of people. In such a graph the line between any two points would represent an acknowledged and active kinship relation of some kind.

The kin-set is therefore a simplified abstraction from this extensive network. It is important, nevertheless, partly because so complex a phenomenon as a total kinship network must be broken down into smaller units of analysis, and partly because it is quite essential to establish the empirical facts of direct, active kinship links if the wider network itself is to be understood and not melt away in vagueness.

The limits of ego's interaction with others, and of the recruitment of action-sets, do not stop at the limits of the kin-set. Action-sets may, sometimes or frequently, include not only ego's acknowledged kinsmen, but also those kinsmen's kin who are not directly related to ego. To give a simple example: A mobilises an action-set that includes, among others, his patrilateral cousin, B. To assist A in the enterprise, perhaps at A's instigation as well as to his own advantage, B might call on C, his matrilateral cousin who is not a kinsman of A. In some cases, C might himself call on one or more of his kinsmen to join the action-set, though they are not kin of either A or B. The man C assists A in fulfillment of an obligation to B; but perhaps also he wishes to obligate A for some return assistance, or because A's interests touch on his own. C may assist A in this way—as the kinsman of a kinsman—on a single occasion, or on an ad hoc, irregular basis as the circumstances make it possible and advantageous. But C may begin to join A's action-sets more regularly, obtaining reliable reciprocal assistance from A. Under such conditions it is possible that A and C may develop a direct, persisting relationship, no longer necessarily mediated by B, though reinforced by the common involvement of all three men with one another. The new relationship between A and C might, furthermore, be legitimised in kinship terms by recognising a cousin's cousin as a kinsman, or by fictionalising the genealogical link between them to bring it within the culturally acceptable range. C and A would then become members of each other's kin-sets.

The careful recording of action-set composition over a period of time would thus indicate which men, beyond the kin-set, are recruited and under what conditions. Further, it will reveal the dynamics of social interaction and the development (or atrophy) of inter-linkages. Let me emphasise that, in using the tool of the action-set, it is not merely a matter of examining who is recruited (and who is not) on particular occasions, or over a period. This preliminary should lead to enquiry as to why individual men are (or are not) recruited, and what the general principles (the rules of choice) are that underlie recruitment and the giving of assistance and support. The empirical data should instigate explanation, rather than become just an end in themselves; that again permits an avoidance of vagueness and unsupported generalisation or idealisation.

This recording and analysis of action-set formation will also provide understanding of some more persistent features of interaction and inter-dependence within the kinship network. Where there is a comparatively high degree of overlapping of the kin-sets of inter-connected men, this is not necessarily readily revealed by a genealogically based network graph—if only because that simple graph cannot indicate the operative strength of the relationships and the degree of inter-dependence. Its reality will, however, be indicated by the fact that some individuals tend frequently to be members of each other's action-sets. This will be noticeable even although each particular action-set of each particular individual also contains other people recruited in the general manner. The persons involved in such a "close-knit" or comparatively "dense" sector of the network can, following Barnes (1968:118), be referred to as a *cluster*. The cluster is not a group: that is, it is not specifically organized for common action, and seldom (perhaps never) operates as a single entity. The cluster may be no more than the observer's construct from certain noted regularities; but it is more probable that it acquires some cultural recognition. It may develop some degree of internal and external identity, and a de facto leader may emerge and act when each of its members recruits an action-set. He may then provide some kind of focus, and the cluster might be referred to as, say, "X's gang", or "X's neighbours", or "X's kin". The cluster may develop in some response to a man's ambition to become a leader; equally likely, the leader may emerge in response to the need for limited co-ordination among the men concerned. Essentially, however, the cluster represents, or emerges (however vaguely) from, the effective degree of inter-dependence, and an element of common interest and value in seeking to maintain reliable and reinforcing mutual assistance. Each member of the cluster continues to rely also on others outside the cluster with whom he is individually linked in the network, and with whom only some or even none of the other members are directly linked. Where alignments are so diffuse, and where leadership and authority are weak or absent, clusters may be of considerable significance.

Recurrent mobilisation of more or less the same body of supporters in sequences of action-set recruitment and operation, by one individual in a marked and successful leadership role, is the basis of quasi-group formation (*cf.* Mayer 1966) and of political factions. Here the focus is more definitely on the leader, action is primarily of a political kind, and the unit is more clearly delineated and identifiable. The conditions under which clusters do or do not crystallise into quasi-groups require examination. Here again these significant units are not only indicated empirically through action-set formation, but there is the possibility of analysis through time of their composition, operation, and connection with similar units, without losing sight of their source and place within the developing network itself.

The non-lineal kinship network is, or can be treated as if it were, virtually unbounded and infinite. There may be limits to the number of people involved, but for most practical purposes this can be ignored. The network is also convolute, in that individuals are inter-connected by more than one link or sequence of links—just as one can trace a route by many ways from one point to another in a real, physical net or in a railway network. At least some of the alternative sequences of inter-linking will be socially significant according to context. The kinship network is not, then, ego-centred, although for analytical purposes it may be possible and sometimes convenient to abstract and isolate that part of it which most directly involves and concerns a particular individual or a cluster of individuals.

The total open network may be subdivided, for certain purposes at least, by empirical considerations. This subdivision into partial networks is determined not by criteria directly arising out of the character of the kinship network itself, but by other factors that impinge on it. One way in which this can occur is by territorial or residential definition. A residential area is clearly distinguished from similar units by geographical boundaries, and also by a degree of limited interaction, common interests, and cooperation among the collection of neighbours. For certain purposes, though not all, those neighbours activate only those linkages in the total network which connect them together, directly and indirectly. This might occur even where people more or less casually congregate into residential neighbourhoods; but I have in mind principally those cases where residence, and accompanying economic livelihood and inter-dependence, are chosen deliberately on a kinship basis. Goodenough has outlined one such case for the Lakalai of New Britain (1962). In some cases all members of the residential unit acknowledge kinship with all other members; but this is not essential to a partial network, for many members of the closed unit might be connected indirectly by sequences of links, just as they are with other people in the open network.

In the following account of Ndendeuli non-lineal kinship I seek to use and develop the tools of analysis outlined above. Primarily they are to be regarded as tools, or techniques, though together they comprise some consistent frame of reference by which to make sense of the empirical, ethnographic data.

The account begins with a detailed study of the local groups that prescribe partial, closed networks. This procedure is followed partly because my data are more comprehensive in this respect, particularly on one local group, and partly because it seems more convenient to tackle the partial network before treating the implications of the open network. This procedure allows me to go on to examine something of the more persistent units in close-knit sectors of the partial network—clusters and factions. Throughout the analysis the concept of the action-set is used as a principal means of elucidation, most particularly to focus attention on decision-making and the effects of decision-making. The intention is to develop something approaching a decision model.[6] Such a model, fully worked out, would provide a set of "rules" for making decisions and for deciding among possible choices in recurrent cultural contexts. From such a model it would be possible to conceive of the effective units of social action and inter-dependence that are the results, the epiphenomena, of people's decisions.

Whether such a model could be comprehensively produced, I do not know. It has certain attractions, although it has not seemed possible in the production of an analytical ethnography such as the present work. Instead, although continuous emphasis is laid on decision-making and on its effects, and on the understanding of the range of choices in given social circumstances, I have not sought to produce a final synthesis of a set or sets of "rules" of decision-making. In any case, my original data are probably not adequate to meet the demands required of them in that way. Moreover, in this account I find it necessary and useful to resort to elements of both mechanical and statistical model building. As Ogan has realistically pointed out, "the three different models in combination have more heuristic value than any one of them alone."[7] It would

---

[6] See Keesing 1967:2. A similar construct, the action model, has been suggested by Ogan 1966. See also Scheffler 1965:290 ff.

[7] Ogan 1966:190. He concludes by approvingly quoting Kaplan's discussion of alternative approaches to scientific investigation: "The fact is, we need all we can get" (Kaplan 1964:30).

be a pity to set these kinds of models as antithetical to each other, when the different approaches they offer and the results they supply can be mutually illuminating in the total analysis.

For the sake of clarity, I begin with a generalised account of the Ndendeuli local group (local community) before examining the way in which one particular community came into being and developed over a period of more than two decades, as a result of the decisions and action taken by the people involved. Thereafter I describe particular events that occurred seriatim in a limited period of one year to show the situations and contexts in which decisions were taken, the decisions actually made, and their effects on the social circumstances of the collection of people involved and on subsequent events and decision-making. In some instances it is possible to give some explanation of those decisions; but often little more is possible than an account of the effective decisions themselves and some of their consequences.

A more obviously statistical, or rather numerical, approach introduces the examination of the open network through the concept of the kin-set. This is, however, superseded later by a resumption of concentration on decision-making in context. Features of mechanical model-making are introduced throughout as seems to be required for economy or clarity—for instance, to set the scene for the general nature of moots (dispute settlement assemblies), or agricultural work-parties, or certain kinship statuses. The results of the combination of aspects of different kinds of models—different approaches, different levels of generality, different ends—must be judged in their cumulative effect. The apparent neatness of diverse models cannot, in practice, be altogether maintained in the production of an analytical ethnography. We do indeed, as Kaplan said, "need all we can get" out of the various approaches available.

II

Ndendeuli Shifting Cultivators

It is no easy matter to say who the Ndendeuli are. Both histori-
cally and in modern times, the name has referred to a range of
peoples living under a variety of conditions. In the Songea District,
as in much of the rest of southern Tanzania, "tribal" designations
of peoples and territories have long been confused and variable,
and even colonial simplifications failed to produce unequivocal
identifications. A brief historical survey from about the middle of
the nineteenth century will make this clearer. It will also throw
light on the background of the Ndendeuli who are described in
this book and provide some perspective for the special study that
follows in later chapters.[1]

In the middle of the nineteenth century a people, possibly
known as the Ndendeuli, lived in scattered communities in and
around the Matagoro Hills and in the valley of the Hanga river
to the west of those hills, some twenty miles or so north-east of
the modern town of Songea. The area is about 350 miles inland
from the Indian Ocean, about 100 miles east of Lake Malawi, and
about 75 miles north of the modern boundary between Tanzania
and Mozambique. Little is known about these people. They were
Bantu-speaking and related linguistically and culturally to the
Ngindo-Ndonde peoples further east in what is now Nachingwea
District. It is clear, however, that they had no kind of centralised
socio-political system, though it is uncertain how far they recognised a social integrity among themselves. Nothing is known of
their earlier history.

In the early 1850s the Maseko Ngoni arrived in this area and,
apparently easily and rapidly, overcame any resistance to military

[1] More detailed histories are given in Gulliver 1954 and 1956, and in
Ebner 1959.

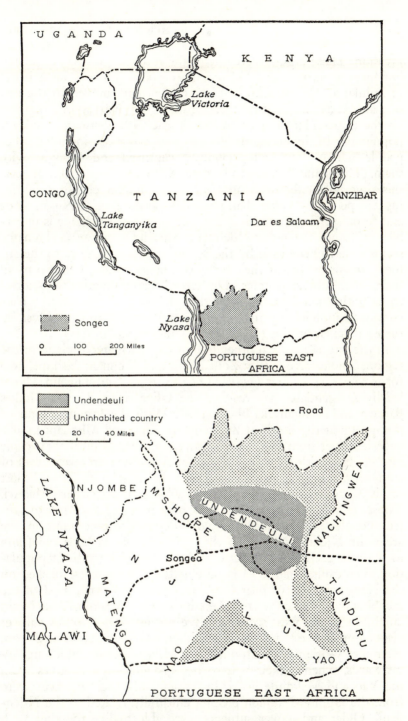

Top, East Africa, showing Songea
Bottom, Songea District, showing Undendeuli

invasion. These Ngoni were one of the refugee groups precipitated northwards into central Africa by Chaka's military imperialism in Zululand. The Maseko band had eventually moved to the east of Lake Malawi. They now established their base at Mngongoma on the upper Hanga river and made the Ndendeuli their subject population. In the same inferior category were also included other people whom they had previously captured and brought with them. The name "Ndendeuli" dates with certainty from at least this time, allegedly deriving from the common cry of the subjugated people—"What shall we do?"—in the face of Ngoni force and ferocity. Whether this is the true origin of the name is uncertain, and some latter-day Ndendeuli deny it. In any case, the name seems to have been used by the Ngoni to refer not only to the autochthonous people of the Matagoro-Hanga region, but also to all their other subject peoples. The term became practically synonymous with "non-Ngoni", even though many of the subject class continued individually to remember and to refer to themselves by their particular origins (Yao, Nindi, Pangwa, and others).

In the late 1850s, two other Ngoni migrant bands arrived in the region. These were led by Zulu Njelu and Mbonani Mshope, two former military leaders (*induna*) of the larger Ngoni group which, led by Zongendaba, had reached the Ufipa region between Lakes Rukwa and Tanganyika about 1845. With the fragmentation of that group at the death of Zongendaba, Zulu and Mbonani in alliance led their own bands of followers eastwards until they came into contact with the Maseko group. After two or three years of animosity, the two allied bands killed the Maseko leader and most of his Ngoni followers fled south to what is now southern Malawi. The Zulu and Mbonani bands took over many of the Maseko subject peoples and established two independent chiefdoms in the area: the Njelu chiefdom to the west and the Mshope chiefdom to the east, each with an Ngoni ruling class and a subject population. The capital of the Mshope chiefdom was first established on the Hanga river in or near the "Ndendeuli" country, most of the inhabitants of which were taken into that chiefdom. The Njelu chiefdom to the west seems to have recruited most of its subject class from the west and north as raiding operations continued from the military-oriented chiefdoms. The Mshope Ngoni raided mainly eastwards, whence their war-parties brought back captives from the Yao and Makonde areas, but principally their captives were from the Ngindo-Ndonde peoples culturally related to the Ndendeuli. Older and newer subjects were able to live together with minimal difficulty and to intermarry, and the name Ndendeuli was accepted by all of them. Mshope parties later raided northwards into the country of the Bena, but subjugated Bena were allowed to remain in the north of the expanding chiefdom, mixing little with the Ndendeuli, and to retain their own name.

As they expanded in size during the rest of the nineteenth century, both chiefdoms had to cope with the problems of maintaining political unity and centralised military authority. In the Njelu chiefdom with a larger Ngoni component (perhaps almost 20 percent of the population by the end of the century) this was fairly successfully achieved through the policy of allocating subchiefships to leading members of the chiefly lineage, and by allowing a degree of local autonomy and military initiative to the subchiefs (*induna*), whether of the chiefly lineage or not. The Njelu chief (*nkosi*) remained at his capital, seldom if ever leading warparties himself. Problems of chiefly succession were few and not disruptive.

The rather smaller Mshope chiefdom contained proportionately fewer Ngoni (perhaps 10 to 12 percent of the population by the end of the century), and the chiefs maintained a more autocratic, centralised control. The chief himself actively continued as the principal leader of war-parties, and he insisted that his sub-chiefs live at or very near the capital, with little opportunity for autonomy or initiative. The chiefdom was badly disrupted by a Hehe war band from the north in about 1878, when the chief was killed in his capital. The weakened chiefdom was thereafter beset by dynastic quarrels that arose, at least in part, from the highly centralised system in which the Ngoni sub-chiefs could seek to extend their power only by directly diminishing that of the chief. One contender for the chiefship provoked open conflict and, in defeat, seceded with his followers to found a new small chiefdom some hundred miles to the north in what became Ulanga District. A second contender, Palangu, remained persistently challenging the authority of the chief (his half-brother) and requiring constant control.

The net effect of this development (summarily described here) was to weaken the Mshope chiefdom, limit its predatory expansion, and concentrate the Ngoni ruling class around the capital. As the population slowly increased, and as the poor soils were exhausted under shifting cultivation, many of the Ndendeuli subject class began to drift eastwards with little hindrance, and to live in their own semi-autonomous communities with no Ngoni among them.

Although still subject to Ngoni rule, and liable to pay tribute and to supply men for military purposes, these Ndendeuli (the amalgam of autochthonous and captured people) began to move away from direct Ngoni control and influence. (Whilst such developments were prevented in the Njelu chiefdom to the west, the Mshope Ngoni seem not to have been able to prevent them in the east.) Palangu, after eventually conceding to the legitimacy of his half-brother, continued to claim semi-independent authority over the eastern part of the chiefdom. This was denied him by the chief. But perhaps as a result the chief was not strong enough to appoint an alternative sub-chief in that area. This in effect left the eastern area without clearly defined Ngoni authority. The process had gone so far by the time of the German military occupation of the region in 1897 that the colonial authorities refused to recognise the claim of the Mshope chief to legitimate authority in that eastern area. The Germans recognised the legitimacy of the Njelu chief over the whole of his chiefdom, but they allowed the Mshope chief control only in the central, western, and northern areas of his chiefdom. The eastern area, centred on Likuyu, was established as a separate unit under a German-appointed administrator (*akida*) from the Coast, on the pattern already practiced in the chiefless areas of German East Africa. It is most probable that, at the beginning of the twentieth century, no Ngoni at all lived in that eastern part of the chiefdom. Thus in effect, and formally, the Ndendeuli there were freed of Ngoni overrule.

The Ngoni of both chiefdoms had acceded peacefully to the German occupation, apparently believing that the Europeans had come as friends—as the Arab and Swahili traders had a little earlier. It was expected that, with German assistance, the Ngoni would be able further to develop their activities in military raiding and in the slave trade. Once there, of course, the Germans insisted on interfering in Ngoni affairs and on Ngoni acceptance of German superiority and the compulsory end of their military activities. After a few years the Maji Maji movement (with its magic water) offered the opportunity for revolt. The water, which originated among the Ngindo to the east, was brought to Mshope in about July, 1905. It was believed to be sure protection against German bullets and a source of strength to those who drank it. The Mshope chief enthusiastically took the water, as (it is said) did virtually all of his subordinates and subjects, and also many Ndendeuli. The resultant revolt was crushed within a few months, and there followed a year or more of severe reprisals by the German military forces. Many people were killed and injured, many houses and fields destroyed, and near-famine conditions developed. Both Ngoni and Ndendeuli scattered—Ngoni leaders to avoid arrest and execution, and the rest to get away from centres of German activity. Many fled to Mozambique or to other Districts of Tanganyika. When civil administration was restored early in 1907 and a new Mshope chief installed, and when refugees returned and settled down, many of the Ndendeuli had shifted farther east again. Some newly established communities were up to fifty miles north-eastwards, and others were some twenty-five miles eastwards. This meant further separation from the Ngoni as dispersed settlements were established in empty woodlands. It is impossible to assess how far these population movements resulted from a desire to evade German reprisals, and how far the Ndendeuli had taken the opportunity to move farther away from Ngoni-controlled areas.

After World War I the British colonial Administration continued to maintain the separate (and now extended) Likuyu chiefdom under an appointed *akida*, until in 1930 the incumbent of that office was imprisoned for peculation and other official misbehaviour. The Mshope chief raised his claim to the area, a claim that fitted well with the British colonial policy of indirect rule and "find the chief". An Ngoni nominee of the chief—his father's brother—was therefore installed as sub-chief, as local government authority within the Mshope chiefdom. This man was later succeeded by his son. By the middle of this century this man and three or four of his kinsmen living with him were the only Ngoni in the sub-chiefdom. After World War II, the colonial Administration compelled those Ndendeuli living in the far northeast to move back some thirty or forty miles westwards for the administrative convenience of concentrating the population near lines of communication. The gradual easterly drift of population was, however, allowed to continue where the people remained fairly near the main road running through the District and eastwards to the Coast.

Ndendeuli had unavailingly protested against their compulsory re-inclusion in the Ngoni chiefdom in 1930; and in 1933 dissatisfaction provoked a small rebellion which was quickly put down by the Administration. In 1950, the Administration decided to split the Likuyu sub-chiefdom into two smaller, more convenient units. The existing (Ngoni) sub-chief continued in charge of the eastern part, centred on Likuyu, and the Mshope chief assumed the right to nominate a new sub-chief, an Ngoni, to the western part, cen-

tred on Luegu. Ndendeuli protests to the District Commissioner
were strong enough to induce him to convene a public meeting at
the new sub-chiefdom's headquarters, when a popular local nominee was accepted in place of the Ngoni appointee. This nominee
was an Ndendeuli, although he sometimes referred to himself as
a Pangwa, the tribe to the north-west (Njombe District) from
which his grandfather had been taken by the Ngoni in the nineteenth century. This Ndendeuli success led to demands for the
removal of the Ngoni sub-chief of Likuyu and for his replacement
by a popularly selected local man. This was achieved in 1953.

In 1952 the Mshope chief died without an obvious heir, there
being no brother or son surviving. His brother's son, Kangara,
soon emerged as the principal claimant to office, with the support
of almost all the Ngoni and the commoners of the central and
northern sub-chiefdoms controlled by the Ngoni. A second claimant, Saidi Palangu, head of a junior line of the chiefly lineage,
gained the support only of his close kin and some of his commoners.[2] The Ndendeuli, represented by a number of influential
commoners, demanded to secede from the chiefdom. When this
was refused by the Administration, the Ndendeuli publicly supported the candidacy of Saidi on the declared grounds of opposing
the candidate supported by the body of the Ngoni. The Administration played with the idea of supporting Saidi, who was an experienced sub-chief, but quickly discovered the strength of Ngoni
opposition to this. It was caught in a dilemma. On the one hand,
the Administration wished to adhere to traditional procedures for
the selection of a new chief, which would undoubtedly have given
the office to Kangara. On the other hand, it wished to take account
of public opinion in the chiefdom. This produced a stalemate, for
Ndendeuli support for Saidi was approximately balanced by the
apparent support for Kangara in the central and northern sub-
chiefdoms. A number of public meetings were held during the
following year until eventually, at the end of 1953, the Administration agreed to the secession of the Ndendeuli and to the appoint-
ment of Kangara as new chief of the rump chiefdom. The secessionist sub-chiefdoms of Likuyu and Luegu were augmented by
the Mbunga sub-chiefdom headed by the unsuccessful Saidi, who
renounced both his chiefly lineage and his Ngoni status and became an Ndendeuli. He remained as sub-chief, but thereafter he

[2] Palangu, Saidi's father, was the chief's half-brother who had persistently
challenged the Mshope chief throughout the last quarter of the nineteenth
century: see page 31 f.

was of little interest to most of the Ndendeuli. Thus a new local government, Undendeuli, was established early in 1954.

If the Ndendeuli are taken as those people living in Undendeuli,[3] they numbered 20,436 at the Tanganyika Census of 1957. According to the Census enumeration, about 72 percent of the people specifically claimed to be Ndendeuli. Probably most (but not all) of the rest were not necessarily disclaiming to be Ndendeuli in the modern sense of the term, but they were persisting in giving their patrilineal origins as they had long been encouraged to do by both Ngoni and the Administration.

There were, however, 11,731 members of the two Ngoni chiefdoms who also specifically claimed to be Ndendeuli: 6,293 were in the Mshope chiefdom, comprising 38 percent of the total population of 16,562 in that chiefdom. There were also nearly 5,000 people in the Tunduru and Newala Districts, to the east of Songea District, who claimed to be Ndendeuli. These were presumably descendants of refugees at the time of the defeat of the Maji Maji rebellion in 1905–1907.

As already mentioned, the modern Ndendeuli are the descendants of a mixture of autochthonous peoples (possibly originally known as "Ndendeuli") and war-captives of the Ngoni drawn mainly, but not entirely, from the related Ngindo-Ndonde peoples to the east and north-east. The Ndendeuli of late colonial times, residents of the Undendeuli local government area, were the descendants of those, who, as a result of chronic weakness in the Ngoni Mshope chiefdom, had been able to move away eastwards and thus to minimise contact with and subordination to the Ngoni. Eventually in 1953 they had been able to secede formally from that chiefdom. Nevertheless in many socio-cultural characteristics— language, economy, and general culture—these latter-day Ndendeuli remained essentially similar to many of the remaining commoners in the old chiefdom.

One major difference was that a high proportion of the Ndendeuli population was Moslem, albeit of somewhat crude type, whilst the Ngoni and their commoners were converts to Roman Catholicism under Benedictine missionary persuasion. This religious difference was made much of at the time of secession. Then there were most probably no Christians in the Likuyu (easternmost) sub-chiefdom. However, perhaps as many as half of the people of the Luegu (western) sub-chiefdom were Christian, and a large minority of the Mbunga (northern) sub-chiefdom. These

[3] The prefix "u" denotes, in this case, "country of . . .".

Christians differed little from those Ndendeuli remaining in the
Mshope chiefdom, and they played a largely passive role at the
time of secessionist demands in 1952–1953. Another difference lay
in the fact that a majority of men in the southern and southeastern
areas of Undendeuli had developed tobacco cultivation as a cash
crop, but the people of the more northern areas, like those of the
Mshope chiefdom, had no established cash crop. They were primarily subsistence farmers with a high rate of labour migration. At
least one third of the men were absent from both these areas at any
one time, being migrant labourers, mainly in the Tanganyika sisal
industry (Gulliver 1955:3).

I cannot say how far and in what ways the autochtonous Ndendeuli were affected in their social lives through their subjugation
by the Ngoni and their intermarriage with captured immigrants.
Impressionistically, I consider that the changes were rather slight
on the whole, at least among those latter-day Ndendeuli whose
grandfathers and fathers had fairly early moved away from direct
Ngoni control and influence. Centralised political authority did
not bear heavily on them and they took over little of its ideology
or practice. They were able to move increasingly freely in their
regime of shifting cultivation, to follow their own inclinations in
marriage and kinship relations, and to settle community problems
and disputes by their own methods. Their wide-scale acceptance
of Islam derived from their contacts with the Ngindo and with the
Coast—eastwards—and they were able to reject Christian missionary overtures that were supported by the Ngoni. On the
whole, though, their practice of Islam was rather superficial: desultory attendance in the local community at a small hut designated
as a Friday mosque, an observance more or less of Ramadhan, and
celebration of the more important festivals. Islam had had little
effect on the rest of Ndendeuli social life. The pronounced non-
lineal character of their kinship system—the dominant organisational feature of their lives—may have been strengthened by the
arbitrary mixing of peoples by the Ngoni, and by the later dispersion eastwards, especially after the Maji Maji rebellion. Unfortunately there is no account of the kinship system of the Ngindo-
Ndonde, which might have given some indication of the original
Ndendeuli system.

Among the commoner population of the Ngoni Mshope chiefdom there had, of course, necessarily been an acceptance of organized authority, and there seemed to have been less residential movement. Local communities remained more stable in composition

and, perhaps under Ngoni influence, patrilineal kinship was a more dominant feature of social organization.

Although I worked in all three of the Undendeuli sub-chief-doms, the detailed material given in this book came almost entirely from the easternmost part of the country into which the Ndendeuli had moved only since about 1900, and where Ngoni and colonial influence had been smallest, and Christian missionary influence had been absent. In the Likuyu sub-chiefdom, covering those eastern parts, there were ten administrative headmen (*majumbe*), each of whom had a few, unofficial, unpaid assistants. Following Ngoni practice, these headmen were each responsible for a collection of people rather than an area of territory. By Ngoni custom, personal ties linked people with the political office-holder, and changes of residence did not break those ties. In the Ngoni-controlled parts of the Mshope chiefdom the norm was for a headman to move together with his commoners, when required under shifting cultivation, thus maintaining both the community and his authority in it. But the Ndendeuli, freed of control, had been moving residentially on an individual basis. The colonial Administration merely permitted the Ngoni conception of office to continue among the Ndendeuli despite its obvious inefficiency in tax collection and other administrative responsibilities. All this the Ndendeuli regarded as an external imposition; but they raised few complaints for the system meant in effect that they were largely free of administrative control. Each official headman lived, of course, in some local community, but he had no administrative responsibility towards many of his own neighbours, whilst many of his people lived scattered in other communities elsewhere away from direct contact with him. This is a measure of the superficiality of colonial rule amongst these people. Many local communities (including two of those later described in this book) contained no headman at all—that is, no subordinate official of the local government or the Administration.

The lightness and ineffectiveness of administration was admitted by most officials. In 1939 the District Commissioner wrote in his Annual Report that, although administrative responsibility under Indirect Rule rested with the chief, "the executive work devolves on the sub-chiefs. But . . . sub-chiefs confine most of their activities to court work. Even there the *jumbes* [headmen] appear to be the chief spokesmen . . . all the other work devolves on the *jumbes* who are admittedly poorly paid. But *jumbes* likewise are prone to sit in their villages and to rely entirely on their *wanyapara* [unpaid assistants]. The *wanyapara* have a legitimate complaint that they do all the work but get no pay". The work referred to consisted almost entirely of annual tax collection, recruitment of labourers for road repairs, and summoning witnesses when needed by a court. This state of affairs continued through the rest of the colonial period.

In 1953 the District Agricultural Officer reported: "It must be admitted that agriculture more or less looks after itself. . . . Agricultural staff have been walking round the fields hoping to find some Africans at home. The most extraordinary ways of doing things are suggested to him . . . and he is threatened with fines if he does not comply. There is no visual proof of the effectiveness of these new methods and it is unreasonable to expect anyone to adopt them, particularly as they seem to alter with every change of European staff".

Schools in the Songea District at that time were largely administered by the Catholic Benedictine Mission. This tended to mean rather little development of schools in the Moslem areas. Moslem parents were unwilling to send their children to Christian schools in any case, and were unwilling to have such schools in or near their communities. A few primary schools were established by the Education Department, but only a minority of children attended or reached the level of elementary reading and writing.

Despite the decades of labour migration to central and eastern Tanganyika, the returning migrants (as commonly among migrants from distant, poor, African rural areas) brought back few if any seeds of social change as a result. On the whole they could learn little as unskilled labourers in estate agriculture whilst they were away; but in any case the world of temporary employment outside was quite divorced from the home world. Songea District lay in the south-western corner of the Cinderella Southern Province, usually cut off from the outside world by impassable roads for a period each wet season. Undendeuli, despite fair success in tobacco growing in the southern parts, was one of the areas of that District least touched by the colonial Administration, missions, and trade. Politically it had turned inwards upon itself in the struggle to be free of Ngoni suzerainty and to consolidate its identity in autonomy.

Thus the modern Ndendeuli were the product of the external conquest and governance of the Ngoni in the second half of the nineteenth century. They were harshly treated by the German authorities after taking part in the abortive Maji Maji revolt, 1905–

1907, but they were largely left alone by the British colonial Administration thereafter. They were left to drift eastwards in shifting cultivation, with little or no restriction. In post-war years some settlements had been compulsorily moved and shifting agriculture migration limited, but this troubled only those Ndendeuli in the northeast of their country. Annual tax of twenty shillings per adult male had to be paid; small plots of cassava had to be maintained as an anti-famine device, though this was enforced in a desultory manner. A Cooperative Society was established by the Administration to buy tobacco from farmers and to transport and sell it in bulk. Cooperative headquarters were at the administrative centre in Songea (outside Undendeuli) and dominated by other African peoples in the District (Ngoni and Matengo). Local branches were set up in three Ndendeuli areas with locally recruited management committees; but the people had little interest in this (other than as a source of demand for tobacco), nor any feeling that they could or should participate.

SHIFTING AGRICULTURE

The Ndendeuli had, in the 1950s, an agricultural economy that was still strongly oriented to subsistence production by each household. The principal crop was maize; maize flour porridge was the staple diet throughout the year, variously supplemented by small amounts of beans, millet, cassava, ground nuts and sweet potatoes. Very few men had any livestock, seldom more than a goat or two. Tobacco had been grown as a small-scale cash crop in parts of the southern areas of the country since about 1938. Average cash income per cultivator between 1950 and 1953 was rather less than 100 shillings a year—enough for tax payment and an absolute minimum of cotton clothing of the cheapest kind. Not all men, even in the southern areas, planted and cured tobacco; perhaps two thirds of them in the southeastern area produced some tobacco for sale to the Cooperative Society. Negligible amounts of foodstuffs were purchased in the few, scattered, small stores. People expected and desired to feed themselves from their own fields, and they attempted to produce enough food to permit the sale of small quantities for cash. Some men grew small quantities of sesame or sunflowers for sale, but this was unimportant in general. This meagre economy had for three decades or more been augmented by the labour migration of the younger men, mainly to the sisal estates of central and north-eastern Tanganyika. On the average, between

1946 and 1953 men brought back savings of about 125 shillings in cash and kind after a year or so in migrant labour employment. Formerly at least one third of the men under about forty-five years of age were away at any one time in those distant parts of Tanganyika; this was still the case among the northern Ndendeuli in 1953. In some of the southern areas the proportion of migrant absentees had fallen to a little over 10 percent since the introduction of tobacco cultivation, despite, the low cash income it produced. Many men, especially when tax payments became urgent, found temporary employment in road and other public works in the Songea District for a month or two. Nevertheless, among a group of men living near Mchomoro in eastern Undendeuli (a moderately good tobacco-growing area) 35 percent had cash incomes of less than seventy shillings during 1952, and only 40 percent had obtained more than one hundred shillings in that year.[4]

Eastern Undendeuli, at an average altitude of 3,000 feet, is much like the rest of the country: undulating land quite thickly covered with *miombo* woodland—fairly low trees, few large ones, and bushes, except for grassy and gravelly patches here and there. This is "the dry *Brachystegia-Julbernardia* woodland country of south-central Africa [which stretches] with many breaks and incursions, from the Lake Province of Tanganyika into the Rhodesias", as Allan has described it (Allan 1965:210). An official report of the Department of Agriculture stated: "the soils of the *miombo* savanna are generally acid and vary from sandy granitic types to the more clayey red soils originating from gneiss. They are generally shallow, lack organic matter and are deficient in phosphates. . . . Conditions for growing crops are exacting in the poor soils, cool climate and very short season".[5] Rainfall averaged about 40 to 45 inches a year, and was usually dependable; but nine tenths of it fell between about the middle of December and the middle of April. This rainy season was followed by a marked cool season, and that by a five months hot, dry season with usually little or no rain at all. The growing season for crops was confined almost entirely to that season of rains—a crucial feature of Ndendeuli agriculture. Here and there, in favourable sites next to perennial streams, were a few scattered

[4] These figures included shares in savings sent or brought back by migrant labourers. See my *Labour migration in a rural economy*, 1955, Chap. 2, for more detailed information.

[5] The report continues: "it is believed that the dry *miombo* has intruded on what was once a vast rain forest destroyed by repeated burning of the original forest" (Tanganyika 1945:30).

plots where some rice or additional maize was grown. Only a few men possessed such plots and the food increment, though valuable, was small in total.

Agriculture depended on typical slash-and-burn techniques, using axe and bush knife (*panga*). Fields were made by clearing a patch of woodland and piling the cut vegetation on the site. Larger trees were frequently ignored for they required considerable labour to fell, and this seemed uneconomic to the Ndendeuli who contented themselves with lopping off the lower branches. The people seldom used vegetation other than that cut and cleared off the actual field site. Clearing work began in the later cool season and reached its peak in the early dry season. The work was performed principally by the men in work-parties, although women might assist if male labour were short or the work had been delayed.

The piled vegetation was left to dry in the sun and was fired in about October, before the scattered "short rains" that sometimes came at that season. Attempts by the Adminisration to obtain earlier firing had met with little success, since there were no means of enforcing official exhortations. Ndendeuli saw burning both as a means of completing the clearing work and as a method of improving soil fertility (that is, by the deposits of potash-rich ash that were left to be dug in). The clearing element was dominant in their minds, for they made no efforts to obtain, pile, and burn fresh cuttings when preparing a field for re-cultivation in subsequent years. Only such growth as appeared in the field itself—often very little—was cleared and fired.

The ground was usually too hard, after several rainless, hot months, for cultivation to begin before the first rains fell. Occasionally "short rains" in November permitted the ground to be turned over ready for sowing when the main rains came in December; but these rains were undependable, and even when they came the Ndendeuli often failed to hoe up the whole of their season's fields. Rather, they would prepare only a portion ready for early sowing, in order to obtain a slightly earlier harvest of part of their crop. The onset of the main rains varied from early to well past the middle of December. People said that they could not undertake their main sowing until it was reasonably certain that the rainy season had set in. Seed stocks were usually no more than adequate and households dared not risk failures by sowing too hastily. Cultivation therefore began with the main rains, and ideally the Ndendeuli liked to sow their seed immediately after hoeing up the soil. Since the growing season was very short, the cultivation season and therefore the amount of land planted were also limited. As Ndendeuli pointed out, it was useless to sow seed that could not come to maturity in the growing period available.

This cultivation season was only a few weeks, and during this time the people had to hoe up and sow all the land that was to produce a harvest. The Ndendeuli undoubtedly engaged in their hardest labours of the year at that period, attempting to get as much land as possible planted. When to stop further planting depended to some extent on the optimism of the individual, and each year showed at least some patches of crops that never ripened because they were planted too late. The cultivation season tailed off before the end of January.

Subsequent agricultural work—weeding and harvesting—was mainly carried out by the women and children, though men often helped with the weeding. Ndendeuli weeding was not especially thorough. Most fields were weeded once, moderately carefully, soon after sprouting was well established; but second weeding was commonly desultory and incomplete. Maize plants often struggled against a thickish undergrowth of weeds. The main harvest was taken off in about late May.

Maize was invariably planted in newly cleared fields, and it could be repeated for two to four consecutive seasons before soil fertility was reduced to an unprofitable level by Ndendeuli standards. The basis for this statement is general Ndendeuli information plus some field histories in one or two areas, but there seems no reason to doubt its validity. I have no record of more than five successive maize crops, and I was told that was most unusual. The average seems to have been two or three crops, though sometimes only a single crop was taken. After a series of consecutive maize harvests, a field, or part of it, was often used for growing beans, cassava, or sweet potatoes in the following season; but sometimes the field was abandoned altogether. Usually only a single additional crop was grown before the field was left, though cassava might stand in a portion of a field for more than one year. Each year a man aimed to clear woodland and bring new land into maize cultivation, so that there was a continuous process of new clearing and abandonment of old fields. Annual new clearing allowed this heavy work to be spread over the years; it provided a maize crop each year from new land (usually the best yield), and it allowed portions of older fields to be abandoned where fertility (even after a single year if necessary) appeared to be low. Thus between one third and one half of maize land each year was newly cleared and being cultivated for the first time.

Like many shifting cultivators, and not only in central Africa,[6] the Ndendeuli judged soil fertility in terms of actual yields. In fact the yields depended not only on soil fertility, but also on the thoroughness of clearing, burning, and hoeing, the quality of weeding, the nature of the season's rainfall, seed quality, and similar factors. Ndendeuli scarcely distinguished these, and they spoke almost as if soil fertility were the only factor, or at least by far the most important. Land tended, therefore, to be abandoned earlier than it otherwise might have been. Seldom was there a shortage of woodland to be cleared and brought under cultivation, so that Ndendeuli were disinclined to risk relative failure in old fields as against the expectation of good yields on new land. Although the labour of clearing and making a new field was physically arduous, it was done when there was little other work to do and so could be undertaken slowly and easily over a period of weeks, and when food supplies were normally at their best and men were therefore fittest.

Land that had been used and then abandoned as "exhausted" was seldom if ever cultivated again, even though it might be conveniently situated near to the hamlet. Ndendeuli said that soil fertility would have been too poor, even after years of fallow, whilst uncleared woodland was readily available. Recultivation was a risk that it was not necessary to take. For this *miombo* woodland the period for natural regeneration is usually taken by agricultural experts to be roughly twenty to thirty years.[7] For the Ndendeuli, this reckoning was irrelevant: they said that abandoned land was "never" used again, by which they meant that a man was no longer resident in the same place by the time old fields would have regenerated and become "like the bush everywhere". No rights attached to old field areas, for the people had moved on by the time that land would have been considered for recultivation. Probably all of eastern Undendeuli woodlands had not been cultivated for at least several generations. Botanical indications strongly suggest that the region had been cultivated before that, but it is rea-

[6] For example, the Iban of Borneo (see Freeman 1955).

[7] Describing conditions in the adjacent, but similar, Tunduru District to the immediate east, Allan wrote: "typical *miombo* woodland on weak, pallid sandy soils [which] are cultivated for a maximum of three years, and a subsequent fallow of twenty years or more is recognized as necessary for the restoration of fertility" (Allan 1965:212).

sonably certain that the Ndendeuli had not lived there earlier.
Therefore no question of land rights in previously cultivated areas
arose. The Ndendeuli were obviously puzzled by my questions on
this point: they did not expect to be living in the same locality by
the time that regenerated woodland would be ready for cultivation
again. They did not know who would be living there later, nor
had they any interest in the matter. Woodland was, as far as they
could see, plentiful—indeed, virtually limitless—and they assumed
that, like their fathers and grandfathers, they would continue to
move on and that they and people of subsequent generations would
be concerned only with clearing and using "untouched" woodland,
without concern about who had previously used it. The interlude
of direct Ngoni rule had little affected the Ndendeuli in all this.
They may have been constrained residentially for a couple of
decades, but not for a period long enough to interfere seriously
with the pattern of land use. There seems good reason to assume,
as the people themselves did, that the pattern of land use and movement had persisted over the generations. This assumption is not
essential to my argument, however, for the data on which my main
account is based relate to the first half of the twentieth century.

Land rights were simple. A man had a right to use the land he
had cleared until, on his own assessment, its diminished fertility
(that is, productivity) made further cultivation unprofitable. After
that the land was valueless to anyone beyond the time, most probably, when the present residents would have moved elsewhere. A
man had a right to clear woodland beyond his current cleared area
until he reached the cleared area of a neighbour. An established
household head could object if a newcomer sought to put a hamlet
so near to his own that they were likely fairly quickly to exhaust
the available woodland in between. The community organization
through which such objection was sustained is described later; [8]
but in any case a newcomer was unlikely to prejudice either good
neighbourliness or his own future cultivation potentialities by
building his own hamlet too close. Hamlets were therefore generally spaced at least a quarter of a mile apart. This left enough land
for clearing for a fairly long period without too great a dispersion
of the hamlets. On the other hand, for his own personal and social
advantage, a household head might sometimes welcome an incom-
ing kinsman to build alongside or near to him. In that event there
was some agreement that each household should extend its clearing
in a particular direction in order to avoid competition. The same

[8] See page 63 ff.

arrangement was made when a newly married son set up his autonomous household in his father's hamlet.

If there was no more woodland available between his own hamlet and that of his neighbours, a man could clear woodland elsewhere within reach so long as he did not unduly encroach upon the vicinity of any other hamlet, or upon land regarded as the area of immediate extension of a neighbour. Ndendeuli preferred if at all possible to cultivate fairly near to the hamlet, so they tended gradually to clear all around it until they reached the clearings of other hamlets. Agricultural work was easier if less time and effort had to be expended in walking to and from the fields; this was particularly important for such work as cutting, clearing, and weeding, which was commonly done in short spells as opportunity and inclination arose. "A distant field has many weeds", said one informant. More importantly, it was less easy to guard a growing crop against the depredations of wild animals when it was distant from the hamlet. These animals were numerous: monkeys, baboons, buck of various kinds, zebras, elephants, wart-hogs. Men and boys had to sleep in the fields at night in order to drive off marauders, but it was thought to be a lonely and dangerous thing to sleep far from the hamlet. During the day, unless additional special guards were kept, a distant field could not be watched from the hamlet in the course of domestic activities. There were, then, serious considerations about shifting a hamlet when the only available land began to be more than about a mile away.

Although a mile may perhaps not appear to be particularly distant—nor was it for a single journey—yet it became so in the context of many dozens of journeys to and fro during the agricultural season, several times a day in some periods. The importance of guarding the crops against animals can be gauged to some extent by the rough assessment of an agricultural officer that, despite Ndendeuli efforts, as much as 20 percent of the crops were lost to them. A small herd of elephants could devastate a whole field, and monkeys and wart-hogs were most persistent despoilers. Whilst it might be possible to criticise the Ndendeuli for inadequate guarding, it was obviously easier for them to maintain a watch on their fields near to and between hamlets.

Each hamlet, containing one or more households,[9] was therefore typically situated roughly in the middle of its own cultivation area—fields in use, abandoned land, and potential fields in uncleared woodland. The residents began clearing next to their houses

[9] Hamlet composition is considered at page 56 ff.

and gradually extended outwards, avoiding any apparently infertile land—areas where the natural vegetation indicated poor soils, stony ground, land likely to be waterlogged during the rainy season, and so on. There was, as de Schlippe has pointed out for the Azande of the Sudan (1956:205), a haphazard character to Ndendeuli farmlands. Fields and abandoned fields straggled away from the hamlet, with few or no definite boundaries and with patches of grass, secondary growth, and bits of uncleared woodland left here and there. Fields were often of no particular shape, for Ndendeuli commonly pressed on with their cutting and clearing where fewest difficulties and obstacles appeared. Larger trees usually stood uncut in the fields, together with the stumps of felled trees. Fields faded into woodland, for bush fencing was rather uncommon. Where a hamlet had been established for some years, the land immediately around would have been worked out; it was open ground, to some extent covered with low secondary growth, but it was generally re-burnt each year along with the new fields, to guard against snakes and animals that otherwise might approach the house under cover. In effect abandoned land was not necessarily left to regenerate naturally once cultivation ceased. For much of the exhausted land, regeneration did not really begin during the continued lifetime of the hamlet, and the natural process was probably lengthened by the repeated burning and the long exposure to erosion.

The important question arises: how much land did the Ndendeuli require for cultivation, and how far was residential movement necessary because of the disappearance of cultivable land within reasonable access? No agronomic survey of Undendeuli had been made and therefore it is impossible to answer these questions with any precision. Nevertheless, since I am less concerned here with the purely agronomic and more with the sociological factors, perhaps sufficiently indicative evidence can be assembled for present purposes.

The variables were numerous and scarcely quantifiable: the acreage under cultivation; the amount of land not cultivated because of assessed infertility or for any other reason; the number of successive crops of maize in each field (variable soil fertility, agricultural efficiency, standards of assessment of productivity, amount and distribution of rainfall); local densities of population; and the distances between house and field that the people were prepared to tolerate.

An abstract calculation provides some basis for the answer. My sample surveys indicated that the area under active cultivation each year was two and a half to three acres per household, of which about two acres at least were devoted to maize. With an average of two to three successive seasons of maize on each cleared field, each household would have required something like twenty-two acres of available land capable of producing an acceptable maize crop over the period of, say, twenty-five years during which time natural regeneration occurred—that is, eleven two-acre plots, where the first, used for two to three successive years, would have regenerated by the time that the eleventh had been used. It is likely that no more than one third of the land in any area was adequate for the cultivation of maize with the existing technology, though the proportion might have been smaller than this.[10] Assuming that as much as one third of Undendeuli land was ʿivable, then sixty-six acres (three times twenty-two) would have been required by each household. This would have allowed 9.7 households per square mile, with an average of 4.5 persons per household. This gives an arithmetic figure for the population density of 43.65 people per square mile, who, ideally living in well spaced-out households, could have lived on and continued to cultivate the minimal area required. But even at this abtract level it is probable that thirty to thirty-five people per square mile would be a more realistic figure in view of the probably lower proportion of cultivable land available.

The density of population in the whole of Undendeuli was about five people per square mile, but of course extensive areas were uninhabited, especially in the northern and north-eastern parts. There is no doubt that overall the country was able to carry its population at the existing levels of technology and economic standards without shifts of residence ever being necessary. That, however, is not our concern here. The question is, how far could households remain in one place, without shifting residence under the ecological conditions prevailing at the time?

First, I repeat that much of the land abandoned after cultivation (all of the land in the immediate vicinity of the hamlet) was not immediately left to natural regeneration. Thus as much as 50 percent more land per household might have been required. Secondly, not all cultivable land was necessarily utilised, or fully utilised, by the people. Standards of assessment of fertility took little

[10] A survey of 557 square miles in Northern Rhodesia (now Zambia) showed that, in not dissimilar *brachystegia-julbernardia* woodland, about 22 percent was cultivable for maize. On the best lands the proportion rose to one third, and on the poorest it was as low as 5 percent (Allan 1949:9–13).

account of poor efficiency of cultivation or unfavourable rainfall. This again added to the amount of land a household might require.

Thirdly, actual local densities of population were relatively high as the result of social and cultural factors. Over two thirds of Ndendeuli hamlets contained more than a single household,[11] as kinsfolk lived together for cooperative convenience. Nor did the people spread themselves evenly over the land; they congregated into local communities for the mutual benefit of neighbourly assistance. It was difficult to estimate local population densities since it was somewhat arbitrary where one drew the boundaries of a community. In the four local communities in eastern Undendeuli in which more intensive research was carried out, it was quite clear, however, that the local densities were well above the abstract calculation of a maximum of forty-four people per square mile. The approximate densities there were about seventy-five people per square mile—nearly twice the maximum for a sedentary agricultural population.

However approximate these figures are, the difference is so great that it is quite safe to say that, at the kind of local density actually existing at that time in Ndendeuli residential areas, the people were compelled to shift their households periodically in order to have continuous access to cultivable land. It is more difficult to suggest, even at these approximate assessments, how long a household could remain without shifting. Indeed, to pursue the matter further in this way would be invalid because of the number of practical factors that must have been involved: the actual areas of woodland available to a particular household, the efficiency of cultivation and willingness to accept both lower yields and distant fields, and the movements of neighbours, as well as the other factors previously mentioned.

For the moment I wish only to point out that the Ndendeuli were not only shifting cultivators in that they had a "continuing agricultural system in which impermanent clearings are cropped for a shorter period of years than they are fallowed" (Conklin 1961:27). They were also shifting cultivators who had to move their residence periodically, partly in order to gain acceptable access to sufficient woodland for arable purposes. For the period of fallow was generally longer than the time taken to exhaust locally available woodland. As I have very roughly indicated, had the people been fairly evenly distributed at something like twenty-five to thirty persons per square mile, there would have been no overriding ecological reason for residential movement. Their clustering

[11] See Figure 2, p. 59.

in local communities at much higher local densities made movement inevitable for most households.

The Ndendeuli saw great practical and social advantages in their local communities for these were the direct products of their own choices of residence. There were no valued land rights to be safeguarded in a country of plentiful woodland; there were no corporate groups in which membership imposed restraint; and there was no authority to control or direct movement and residence. The individual household was free to move where its head chose in terms of his perceived self-interest. A man needed and sought neighbours with whom he could cooperate on a fairly reliable basis, both in agricultural affairs and in social activities. He sought, first, some neighbours who were kinsfolk and with whom, therefore, close cooperation and mutual help could be expected. But a man's kinsfolk were scattered over a fairly wide region and the range of choice was considerable. At a personal level, some offered greater expectation of reliable cooperation, and it was preferable to choose a community in which there were at least two or three kinsmen and their households. This still left a range of choice for most men. Secondly, a man sought other (unrelated) neighbours who would at least make congenial associates, and with some of whom more regular and more advantageous cooperation might be developed, as in making up the recurrent work-parties for agricultural tasks. Where such cooperation seemed inadequate or unreliable, a man could choose to shift to some other community where, as he assessed it, the possibilities seemed to be more favourable. Since kinsfolk were scattered in a number of communities, and since unrelated men who could become cooperative neighbours were more or less everywhere, a man could move to avoid quarrels, unpleasant neighbours, and the consequences of his and their misdemeanours.

Thus, the people congregated for social purposes of cooperation and neighbourly mutual assistance and association into local groups such that local densities were greater than the land could support permanently at the existing level of technology. Many households shifted even before available land became exhausted, as men made choices in response to their perception of social conditions and social advantages. It was an easy matter to move after harvest time and before preparing new fields for the next cultivation season. The generally ready availability of untouched woodland allowed great freedom of choice, and this fact reinforced the opportunity of choice allowed by the absence of socially organized restraint of movement and association.

Part Two

The Closed Network
in the Local Community

III

Kinship in the Local Community

The Ndendeuli local community (*muji;* pl. *miji*) consisted of a more or less discrete cluster of scattered hamlets separated from similar clusters by stretches of uninhabited, uncultivated woodland and bush extending for at least a mile or two around. Each community, on a bird's eye view, was a ragged break in the rather uniform sea of *miombo* woodland. The hamlets were interspersed by stands of uncut woodland and by relatively open patches that were, or had recently been, under cultivation and where only the larger trees remained. The abandoned fields were covered with coarse grasses, saplings, and bushes as the vegetal regeneration developed.

The area and population of local communities varied, largely according to the length of time they had been in existence. A new settlement area was occupied and a new local community established in a region of plentiful untouched woodland that had not been cultivated before, or at least not for a long time. In the large-scale picture, new communities represented the gradual, slow movement of the Ndendeuli over the country as exhausted lands were abandoned and new ones exploited. New communities were established by a small group of pioneers in a few hamlets, and they normally grew over the years as more hamlets were founded by newcomers attaching themselves to the group. There was a good deal of residential movement, for individual households were free to shift as their heads saw fit; people could also leave the community to settle elsewhere where local conditions might seem more attractive. But the common pattern seems to have been that newcomers tended for some years to exceed the numbers of those who left. Sooner or later, however, people had to move on. Established communities might creep over the land, leaving behind their worked-out fields and the infertile parts, with men leap-frogging beyond their neighbours. But this process was likely to be halted or made difficult by a stretch of infertile country, or by land already exhausted by some other community and not yet naturally regenerated, or by an area in which dry season water supplies were too scarce or distant for comfortable settlement by Ndendeuli standards. Ultimately, then, available land resources began to dwindle: the number of households moving away began to exceed those of newcomers and the community began to contract. Sociological factors seem always to have been important in the developmental process as instabilities began to emerge in older communities. In rare cases, internal factions persisted to stimulate and channel conflict, leading to segmentation and abandonment of the community and its location. As a new generation of men assumed seniority in an older community, many of them might wish to develop their own particular fields of social relationships and therefore to leave the community established by their fathers. To repeat: movement was fairly easy and without restriction by the authority of individual or group; and land was plentiful. Local communities persisted, therefore, only so long as they retained tolerable supplies of cultivable land, and as they adequately satisfied men's needs for fairly reliable cooperation with their neighbours. External political factors also affected the decline of old communities and the pioneering of new ones: Ngoni overrule in the nineteenth century, and the gradual eastwards drifting away from Ngoni-dominated areas; the Maji Maji revolt and its aftermath when many Ndendeuli shifted further east; colonial administrative requirements that restricted some directions of migration and even forcibly shifted a few communities.[1]

The ecological, sociological, and historical factors interacted in a most complex way, but as a first approximation one may say that there was something like a life-cycle of a local community as it first grew in size from small, pioneering beginnings, and then later decreased again as people left for one reason or another. In this century the period seems to have been usually between about fifteen and twenty-five years. As a very general indication, a mature but not yet diminishing community might have contained fifteen to twenty hamlets. These would have comprised some forty to fifty households (domestic groups) with a population of 150 to 200 people within an area of two or three square miles.

The local community was not merely a collection of people who happened to be settled and cultivating in the same limited area. It was also a social unit with some degree of internal organization

[1] See page 33 ff.

through which its inhabitants cooperated in their economic activities, their ritual life, and their leisure pursuits. It was at least sufficiently organized that it could attempt, and often succeed in, the formulation of common policy and the maintenance of social control. Living near together, the people took advantage of the opportunities for mutual assistance: they insisted, indeed, that was the reason why they lived near together, accepting the possible dangers of witchcraft inherent in so doing. There was, however, no central principle of organization and cooperation other than, for the time being, of being co-neighbours. The local community was not bound together by the values and advantages of common descent or joint rights over property or corporate opposition to and defence against other communities. Neither did it find identity and unity as a section of an organized political system or of a wider segmentary system.

Although Ndendeuli never overtly suggested this, it is fair to say that their local communities were in effect religious and ritual congregations, as well as residential and cooperative groups. This feature will not be a particular concern in this book (at least in part because I failed to enquire sufficiently into the topic) and a brief reference must suffice here. The eastern Ndendeuli were predominantly Moslem in profession, as they had been for perhaps three decades. Some older people remained pagans, and there were many dominant non-Islamic features in Ndendeuli ritual and moral beliefs and practices. Each local community maintained a small house as a mosque, where men might congregate on Friday mornings and on other religious occasions in the Islamic calendar. Most, though not all, communities contained among their residents at least one man with some pretensions to Islamic knowledge and piety. This *mwalimu* (Swahili word for "teacher") acted as a religious leader and officiated at weddings and funerals. He also usually kept a small Koranic school intermittently for the children, where they could learn by heart portions of the Koran in Arabic. He was, however, purely a religious functionary and was rarely consulted on moral or political issues. Such issues were determined strictly by reference to Ndendeuli standards and interpreted and enforced without his intervention. I know of no case where a *mwalimu* was influential in the affairs of a local community or, in the crucial years 1952–1954, in wider Ndendeuli politics.[2]

The local community was also the social unit for the arrangement and performance of initiation of boys and girls. Members of

[2] See page 34.

the community, especially the men, participated in one another's rituals relating to the life cycle and life crises, although on these occasions attendance was not limited to neighbours, for kinsfolk from elsewhere also participated. Neighbours joined together for these ritual purposes not because of mystical necessity, but as an expression of cooperation and goodwill. Neighbours expected both the expressiveness and the instrumentality of mutual assistance in this way.

HOUSEHOLD AND HAMLET

The domestic group, or household, focussed on a married man who was its head and its representative among other household heads in the affairs of the community. This unit (*nyumba:* "house") comprised the man, his wife, and unmarried children; but this nuclear family was often augmented by dependents related to the husband or wife—widows or women separated from their husbands, and their unmarried children, and unmarried siblings or cousins. Because of their dependence on the household head, adult kinswomen occupied virtually the same economic and residential status as his own wife. He supervised agricultural operations and gave the adult labour typical of a husband. The dependent woman had her own fields and food store, but she contributed to the general food supply of the household and gave the adult female labour typical of a wife. Occasionally a widow remained in her late husband's home and worked her fields with the assistance of a kinsman living nearby. Then, temporarily at least, a household lacked a male head. This was not usual and seldom lasted for long: a woman needed not only the labour of an adult man but also his organisational capacity and representation through his participation in community affairs. It was, for example, almost impossible for her to arrange work-parties for her own agricultural purposes. She had no male labour to offer in return for assistance received, nor could she participate in men's discussions when arrangements were being made. A widow therefore became a dependent of a kinsman or she remarried; in either case she came to live in the household of that man.

At marriage children left their parents' household. Traditionally a man engaged in suitor-service to his wife's father or brother, and therefore first residence on marriage was uxorilocal. After three to five years the husband was free to choose his residence—to return to his father's community (if father and father-in-law were not neighbours), to stay with his affines, or to move to some other community where he had kinsmen. If he lived in the same community as his wife's father, it was common though not mandatory that he live in the same hamlet. During this century the transfer of money in bridewealth had gradually become more common, and in these circumstances a man was no longer compelled to take up a period of uxorilocal residence. By the middle of the century a majority of marriages were with bridewealth; but perhaps one quarter were partly or wholly by suitor-service and still involved uxorilocal residence. In any case, a young man established his own autonomous household at marriage so that wherever he lived, he and his wife were responsible for their own fields and controlled their own food supply and domestic economy.

The smallest residential cluster, the hamlet,[3] contained one or more households. In a sample of seventy-three hamlets in four adjacent communities in eastern Undendeuli, over a quarter contained a single household, and one third contained two households. Only 6 percent of those hamlets contained more than five households, and none more than seven (see Fig. 2a). No cases were recorded in my field notes of larger hamlets anywhere in Undendeuli.

Physically the hamlet was a cluster of houses and perhaps other buildings (kitchen, store, adolescents' sleeping hut, and very occasionally a hut for goats) situated within a few yards of each other. Typically a hamlet was surrounded by the inhabitants' agricultural land, past, present and future, with hamlets a quarter of a mile apart. In long established communities the land adjacent to a hamlet might have been exhausted and its inhabitants then would cultivate in a block together in some convenient stretch of woodland. In such circumstances this was not uncommon, though it was not universal, for Ndendeuli disliked their houses and fields to be much more than about a mile apart. The barrier to further agricultural expansion because of the existence of neighbouring hamlets was often good cause to relocate the hamlet nearer to available woodland.

The houses and other buildings of a household stood next to each other in the hamlet, although it was not always possible to distinguish by eye between the different households. Each adult woman had her own house, and generally adolescent sons had their own sleeping huts. Each household was primarily and principally responsible for its own houses, fields, crops, and food supplies. A

---

[3] Ndendeuli referred to this unit as *majumba* (plural of the word for "house"), or as *muji* (the same word as used for the larger community).

woman's first concern was for her own house and her own cultivation; but there was considerable day-to-day cooperation between women of a single household, dependent as each was on the male head. He perceived and administered his household as an economic unit, autonomous of other households in the same hamlet, however closely he might be related to their heads. The household head controlled the cash income and expenditure of his unit. He, and not a woman, controlled the field and tended the crop of cash-producing tobacco; and he decided what, if any, of the subsistence crops should be marketed. I state this in ideal terms, of course; but whatever might have been the influence of a wife, this economic responsibility reflected the status of the household's male head.

On the other hand, and more or less irrespective of the particular kinship links between household heads, the hamlet was in many ways an economic as well as a residential unit. Men and women continually assisted one another in all kinds of activities, from care of the sick to the minding of babies, in agriculture and in building repairs. There was a good deal of sharing and borrowing of equipment and food, and even seed and money. Men deliberately planned their periods of labour migration, their shorter spells of local employment, and other absences from home, so that if at all possible there would be at least one man at home in the hamlet who could fulfill adult male tasks and responsibilities on behalf of the women and children. The seniormost man in the hamlet—father, eldest brother, oldest kinsman—tended to acquire a certain informal leadership and to act as something of a spokesman. The hamlet was likely to be referred to by his name. His leadership was limited, however, for he had no authority and no sanctions. Usually the heads of constituent households followed an agreed common line in cases of discussion and dispute in the community, especially in their alignment with one or other of the parties to a dispute. This was not inevitable for, although being kinsmen they had some kin-neighbours in common, they might sometimes find themselves obliged to support different principals through kin-linkages not held in common.[4] In such an event the co-residents of the hamlet would have been obvious mediators in the dispute, but they could also have avoided the difficulty for themselves by not participating at all. Where co-residents of a hamlet were unable to act together on more than the odd occasion, it was probable

[4] This will be clearer later. But, for example, two cousins who were co-resident in a hamlet might align themselves on different sides in a dispute where each disputant was the affine, say, of one of the men.

FIGURE 2: The Composition of Hamlets.

Data from 73 (out of a total of 79) hamlets in four adjacent local communities in the Mchomoro region of eastern Undendeuli, 1953.

(A) *Households per hamlet*

Number of households	Number of hamlets	Percent
1	21	29
2	24	33
3	9	12
4	9	12
5	6	8
6	1)	6
7	3)	
	73 hamlets	
	189 households	

(B) *Relationships of heads of households*

	Number of hamlets	Percent
Man and son(s)	17)	44
Man, son(s), and DH	6)	
Brothers	7)	17
Brothers and ZH	2)	
Brothers and son(s)	1)	
Brothers, son(s), and DH	1)	
Cognates and affines		
same generation *	13)	33
different generation †	4)	
Unrelated men	1	
	52 hamlets	
	168 households	

* Cousins and brothers-in-law.
† Man with BS, ZS, SS, DH.

that one or another would move out of the hamlet. Such difficulty
(apart from purely personal antipathy) was most probably the
product of the fact that the men's sets of kinship linkages were
diverging to the point of weakening the links, and thus the mutual
support, between them. The prerequisite for continued co-resi-
dence in a hamlet was continued and reliable cooperation and
common alliance with other kin-neighbours in other hamlets.

The informal leader of the hamlet was generally held responsible,
by the administrative headman or the sub-chief, for the tax payments and other legal obligations of all the members of the hamlet.
This practice had no official basis under the colonial Administration, but it worked quite well in conformity with the social reality
of hamlet unity.

In those hamlets containing more than a single household the
dominant relationships between household heads were father-son
and brothers. In the sample of fifty-two such hamlets (see Fig.
2*b*), over two fifths of them contained the households of a man
and one or more of his sons, and a fifth of the total contained
households of two or more brothers. Over half of the multiple-
household hamlets contained only men who were related agnati-
cally at that close range. Sisters' or daughters' husbands were the
only non-agnatic element in another nine cases. In six of these latter cases the husband was still performing suitor-service, and in
the other three cases the husband had continued to reside with his
close affines after completing those obligations. In the remaining
hamlets in the sample—one third—the household heads were related by a variety of cognatic and affinal ties, and here agnation
was no more important than any other kind of linkage.

Although these cognatic and affinal relationships between household heads were common enough to be significant, obviously the
father-son and fraternal relationships were much more so. Ndendeuli expected and preferred a married son to establish his household in his father's hamlet, unless unavoidable suitor-service in
marriage required him to live with his affines. Even then, ideally
at least, a man should have moved back to his father's hamlet afterwards. After the father's death the sons tended to remain together
in the same hamlet, at least until a general shift of residence occurred. At the time of such a shift brothers often took the opportunity to separate. In any case a man was most likely to establish
his own hamlet when his first son married, or soon after, if that son
agreed to remain with him. This might have meant merely a move
to another site in the same community, but it could have been the

occasion for shifting to another community. This did not necessarily imply overt hostility between middle-aged brothers, but it was congruent with the gradual development by each older man of somewhat diverging sets of active kinship relations and the desire for a greater degree of autonomy of choice in social action. Few middle-aged brothers lived in the same hamlet, and the sample figures accurately reflect the small number of cases where brothers and some of their married sons resided together.

There was little tendency for anything like a localised patrilineage to develop, partly because brothers separated in this way. A second reason, however, was that not all sons remained with their fathers even apart from suitor-service commitments. Fathers had little authority over married sons, nor were there property, economic, political, or ritual necessities compelling close agnates to remain residentially near to each other. A married man could, of course, be reasonably certain of economic and other cooperation and support from his nearer agnates, but not to any appreciably greater extent than he could with his closer cognatic and affinal kin. Each household head was intent on developing a range of kinsmen, both within his local community and beyond, with whom he could maintain dependable mutual help and reciprocal assistance. This is demonstrated in the analysis of choice in social action later in this book. On the whole, though, sons were content to start their autonomous careers as household heads with the direct support of the father and utilising the kin-links that he had already established in the community. Gradually thereafter men developed their own sets of kin-linkages that became partly idiosyncratic to each individual.

The fewer large hamlets tended to comprise the households of older men with several sons, and perhaps one or more sons-in-law. But in the smaller hamlets other kinds of kinship links were equally important. When a younger man did leave the hamlet of his father or brother, he tended to associate with a kinsman in the same situation, that is, of the same generation—brother-in-law or cousin. Thus cognatic and affinal links in hamlet composition were markedly of a single generation. Perhaps three or four men out of ten were, therefore, not living with a close agnate. In later life men tended to return to agnatic links in their hamlets as sons married but continued to reside with them. But at this stage agnatic links with brothers and their sons were likely to become less important.

Thus hamlet composition was strongly influenced, though not

controlled, by the developmental process in the households that were their constituent parts. Yet there was a wide range of choice such that a man could live with some other kinsman; or he could live alone in a hamlet containing only his own household. Ndendeuli expressed no preference for this, although it was the choice, at that particular time, of 29 percent of the household heads in the sample. To live in a single household hamlet, Ndendeuli said, suggested that either a man could not find a kinsman who would agree to reside with him, or that he did not want to—that is, he was in some respect unable to follow Ndendeuli norms of cooperation. A man who lived with a non-agnatic kinsman was not thought (except perhaps by his close agnates) to be acting at all unusually or improperly because of that. But there were serious practical disadvantages for a household on its own. There was only one man to undertake male responsibilities and there was potential difficulty, even danger, if he were away from home for long. Such a man had no immediate supporter, sympathiser, and helper in his problems and difficulties such as were available to those men who shared a hamlet with a kinsman.

Informants suggested that hamlets with a single household were probably temporary. This may have been true of many cases, but certainly was not of all,[5] for two reasons. Firstly, such a relatively isolated household, with the problems of assuring reliable assistance, was likely to move away as its head sought more advantageous conditions elsewhere. Secondly, some of these households were on their own as a temporary expedient until better arrangements could be made. For example, a newcomer may have been unable to build in a kinsman's hamlet because cultivable woodland was not adequately available there. He hoped either to attract another kinsman from elsewhere to join him, or to be able to move into another hamlet when good neighbourly relations had been sufficiently established. Other single households resulted from the death of the head of a co-resident household or from his moving away independently. The remaining household would then be likely to shift soon afterwards.

On the other hand, there is good empirical evidence that hamlets did not continue to grow in size, embracing many households. A larger hamlet, even one of five households, created agricultural

[5] In the Ligomba community, described in following chapters, Mitedi (C19) had lived for at least ten years on his own. Saidi (C6) had done likewise between 1940 and 1952. They were both respected men and valued neighbours in their community.

difficulties as adjacent woodland became more quickly exhausted. People had then to be prepared to go farther and farther from their houses in order to cultivate—a situation which Ndendeuli disliked, and one which tended to exacerbate any inter-personal conflict already existing. Consequently men moved away and dispersed into smaller hamlets.

One other feature of the sample data is of some importance to the subsequent analysis of kinship relations. Only one among those seventy-three hamlets contained household heads who were not kinsmen. In this instance the two men concerned were close friends of many years' standing, ever since their labour migration together as young men. One of them had few living kinsmen and none closer than second cousin and wife's first cousin. These two men treated each other as kin, and many people assumed that in fact they were related fairly closely. Such long-lasting and firm friendship was most uncommon. Ndendeuli strongly preferred to use the recognised channels provided by their kinship links. Where friendship was important it was usually between particular kinsmen, strengthening their relationship.

COMMUNITY ORGANIZATION

In this section I briefly describe in general terms something of the internal organization of a local community and the method of recruitment of newcomers. This account is intended to be a preliminary to the detailed examination and analysis of the kinship network and social action in one particular community.

In each community there was the *mkoro mulima*,[6] roughly "the owner of the land". This man was, at least symbolically, a *primus inter pares* among the household heads resident there. He or a close kinsman of his had been the acknowledged leader of the original group of pioneers who settled, cleared the land, and first cultivated in the area. He had been, therefore, the leader of the newly founded community, and the man upon whom the other men focussed and to whom all were related by some cognatic or affinal relationship. Although all were linked with him by some direct acknowledgement of kinship, they were not all directly related to each other—and that is important. I did not obtain a firsthand account of pioneering settlement, but the general Ndendeuli accounts were adequately supported by genealogical and other

[6] The approximate Swahili synonym, *mwenyeji*, was also quite often used.

enquiry into the beginnings of a number of existing communities.[7]

As leader, this focal individual acquired the designation of "owner of the land". At his death or his departure from the community he was commonly succeeded by a son or brother, but occasionally by some other close kinsman. Informants said that it was important that the successor should be already head of his own household and a resident in the community; and he had to be generally acceptable to his neighbours. Where no satisfactory son was available there was no question of calling one from elsewhere. The role itself was not attractive or important enough in any case to warrant that, and the nearest acceptable resident kinsman succeeded instead. In the one case recorded where an "owner of the land" and his son moved away from a community, the role was taken over by his father's sister's son who was already resident there.

The "owner of the land" was not in fact perceived by his neighbours to be the owner or controller of community land, either in ideal or practice. He was, at most, merely the titular representative of his neighbours, and often he was a convenient focus for community consultations. The pioneering period, especially the first year, could be a most difficult time for the small group of households: there was much heavy manual labor, some anxiety as to the wisdom of the choice of the new location in terms both of natural fertility and supernatural propitiousness, and danger from wild animals both to the people and to their first vital crop. An able leader was invaluable at that time, and with reasonable success he could gain a useful reputation and influence. Once the purely pioneering period was over the need for leadership diminished and the normal autonomy of each household and hamlet was resumed. Newcomers would thereafter begin to arrive, some of whom would not be his kinsmen nor directly obligated to him; and they would tend to deflect from him the prime attachment of some of the original pioneers. Unless the "owner of the land" was a man of above average ability, character, and ambition, he soon ceased to be the leader of the whole community. As I shall show later, there were no authority roles in Ndendeuli communities: influence and leadership were dispersed. Even an "owner" of some reputation and influence was not a headman after the style of many villages in central Africa. For this reason I deliberately use the rather awkward, more literal translation of his named status.

[7] On the founding of Namabeya local community, see page 73; on the founding of Ligomba community, see page 84.

Public affairs affecting the local community, or some large part of it, were discussed and dealt with at semi-formal assemblies of household heads—"moots"—which were sometimes, but not invariably, held at the house of the "owner" for the sake of convenience and as an expression of unity. In each community there were two or three *de facto*, influential men who usually took the lead. They were referred to simply as *wandu wakurungwa*, "big men", whom I shall usually describe as "notables". Their role was ill defined, though public acknowledgement of their achievement was generally clear. According to context almost any man might be a "big man"—a father vis-à-vis his sons, an older kinsman to his juniors, the leader of any ad hoc set of people in an enterprise; but "notables" were "big men" in many different contexts. A notable's advice and assistance were sought by others, for it was often advantageous to have his support and influence, and his skill in debate. A notable's influence depended a great deal on his ability and shrewdness, and on the reputation he had been able to create and maintain. But it depended also on his position in the kinship network of the community—that is, on the range of kinsmen directly related to him, and others linked with him through his kinsmen. The "owner of the land" was therefore often in a good position to become a notable, for his kinship status in the community stemmed from his focal position among the original pioneers. He tended to have a slight edge over his neighbours, should he have the ability and ambition to exploit it. A few "owners" of whom I have record were or had become in practice more or less nonentities. Most "owners", however, took at least a fair share in public activities and many were acknowledged to be notables. Most notables were not "owners".

Influence and the informal leadership it allowed were delicate qualities. There were few sanctions to sustain them: principally their successful practice and the advantages they offered to other men in the community. The Ndendeuli were suspicious of and antagonistic towards a neighbour who too obviously sought personal power and who was considered to act "as if he were an Ngoni" (to use a popular pejorative phrase of the people). With the partial exception of the younger married men, household heads were considered to be equals who did not recognize any authority over them within the community. Ndendeuli were inclined to emphasize this fact, for they saw it in contrast to what they perceived to be the status-conscious, authoritarian Ngoni. They saw egalitarianism and the absence of authority as admirable traits of their own culture. Notables needed to be careful not to arouse opposition and a threat to their position by taking care that acceptable influence did not encourage impotent desire for authority. Foolishly over-ambitious notables endangered the very influence they had achieved. They made themselves liable to suspicion of witchcraft, since this was thought to be the cause and means of their evil aspiration.[8]

The "owner of the land" (whether in practice a notable or not) was not in any sense owner of the land in and around the community's hamlets. Nevertheless Ndendeuli often told me that when a man wished to join and settle in a local community he should approach the "owner of the land" and obtain his approval. In effect what this statement really meant was that newcomers should obtain the general, if often only tacit, approval of the existing residents. The reference to the "owner" symbolised the community as a whole.

A newcomer was invariably sponsored by one or more of his kinsmen who were already resident in the community. This is most important to the nature of the development of the kinship network. It must be stressed that a newcomer was related by known, direct kinship ties with at least one existing resident. Full demonstration of the sociological consequences of this crucial condition is given in the following chapters.

Almost always a newcomer's sponsorship in this way was sufficient to ensure his acceptance by the other residents. But the other neighbours should, it was firmly held, be informed about the intended newcomer, partly because they *were* members of the community, and partly so that they might raise objections should the particular residential site and area of surrounding woodland (potential arable land) selected by the newcomer and his sponsor conflict with their own immediate plans. It might have happened that an existing resident intended to start or extend his cultivation in that same area, or he might justifiably consider that the newcomer was settling rather too close so as to raise the possibility of future competition over woodland. The newcomer could then be reasonably expected to select a different site. It amounted in practice to the matter being made public so that all concerned should know and so that foreseeable conflict could be avoided. The newcomer and his sponsor [9] often did not specifically approach the "owner", especially in a larger community and if the

---

[8] The role of the notable is further discussed in Chapter Eight.
[9] There was no Ndendeuli word for the role I describe as "sponsor".

sponsor was not directly a kinsman of the "owner"; at most it was no more than an amiable formality, for the "owner" himself had no authority to accept or reject the newcomer. A newcomer was announced and introduced at any time when neighbours were met together for some purpose. Only if real objection were raised was the matter taken to a moot, and this seems seldom to have occurred. Sponsors should have been aware of the practical claims and future plans of their neighbours in respect of untouched woodland: such matters were discussed in the normal exchange of news and views between neighbours. A sponsor was unlikely, therefore, to suggest a site that would present difficulties to the newcomer or to his other neighbours.

There were no fixed territorial boundaries to a local community and no precise notion of the community corporately controlling an area of land. Although a newcomer was to live and cultivate within its ambit, he essentially joined a discrete community of cooperating neighbours, not a bounded area. In joining a community a man sought to participate in its social life and in the kind of advantageous cooperation it provided. Neighbours did not hold collective rights to land, soil, woods, or water, but to opportunities and privileges of mutual assistance and friendly interaction. A newcomer was to share in these and to add to them, and should therefore have been an acceptable person. It was probable that many, perhaps all, of the residents already knew about the newcomer; in any case what principally determined the issue was the fact of sponsorship by a resident who was his kinsman and who would therefore be held responsible for his good behaviour. Newcomers were always welcome in principle in order to swell the size of the group. Objections could be raised against the acceptance of a newcomer, or his wife, with a known reputation for trouble-making or for witchcraft (often much the same thing in effect). This very seldom occurred in strong enough form that the newcomer proved unacceptable, but existing residents did sometimes give warning that previous malpractices must not be repeated in the community. The sponsor, being to some extent responsible for the good behaviour of the newcomer, was likely to suffer along with him should he fail to meet approved standards. The sponsor was certain to be involved in any disputes resulting from the newcomer's misbehaviour.

The Ndendeuli were pragmatic in respect of newcomers. They were also good sociologists. They were quite aware that many newcomers had left their previous communities because of some kind of failure in social relationships. They also appreciated that a man who was proved a trouble-maker in one social context would not necesarily interact with a different set of kinsmen and neighbours in the same unfortunate way. He might in any case learn to improve his ways; but there was more to it than that, as a friendly informant explained to me privately. "X [the new-comer] used witchcraft when he lived in M [his old community] or so they say there. Perhaps he bewitched. Certainly he quar-relled a lot with the people there, especially with some of his kinsmen. That is bad. But here he lives near to different kinsmen, and why should he quarrel with them? Do they not like him? Yes. So even if he has witchcraft, he need not use it here. Who knows what man has witchcraft until quarrels and misfortune grow? X is friendly with his kinsmen and they will not accuse him of evil things". This kind of perception—doubtless coloured with opti-mism born of the desire to see the community increase in size—seemed to arise out of the people's experience in various local communities in which they had lived during their lifetime. They understood that different social situations and inter-personal rela-tions produced approved behaviour in one case and disapproved behaviour in another. Hence there were seldom any real difficulties about the acceptance of newcomers, and the local community had neither to mobilise nor delegate authority to deal with these mat-ters.

These procedures relating to newcomers occurred regularly after harvest time, in the cool and early dry seasons when moves could be made. They illustrate the nature of the loose organisation and self-regulating autonomy of a local community. With this in mind it is now possible to begin an examination of the kinship net-work in a local community which essentially provided the pattern and means of interaction and organization.

THE KINSHIP NETWORK

The majority, often a large majority, of a man's neighbours in his local community were not directly related to him. By "directly related" is meant a cognatic or affinal link that was overtly recog-nised by the Ndendeuli themselves. Their genealogical knowl-edge was in general relatively shallow and uneven. They recog-nised cognatic relationships up to at least second cousins through both males and females, or a combination of both, and occasionally up to third cousins and parents' second cousins. Not necessarily would all second cousins be known, and much less so in the case of third cousins. More distant kinship links might be acknowledged between residents of the same community when genealogical memory and practical recognition were stimulated and reinforced by neighbourliness and advantageous cooperation. Affinal links were usually rather more restricted, not going much beyond the closer agnates of a wife or son's wife, or of the husband of sister or daughter. Where a man remained with his affines after the completion of suitor-service, however, his range of affinal kin would be wider as, again, neighbourly contact stimulated the acknowledgement of linkages.

Within these limits, a man had several and perhaps a dozen or more resident kinsmen who were heads of their own households in the same community. This number included all those men in his own hamlet who were autonomous—for example, both an older man and his married son. I shall refer to such kinsmen as *kin-neighbours*, to distinguish them from other neighbours. The numbers of total kinsfolk in a community were, of course, much larger than that for there were also women and unmarried persons in the households of kin-neighbours. Following Ndendeuli practice, and for convenience of exposition, I assume that kin-neighbours are heads of households. The head represented and acted on behalf of his dependents in relations with other domestic groups and their heads.

An Ndendeuli man, with his household, could scarcely have come to live in a community where there were not at least two or three of his kinsmen already resident. Nor would he have wished to do so (except in the most unusual circumstances), for he recognised the need for and value of kin-neighbours to whom he could look for assistance and support. As we have seen, a newcomer was sponsored by one or more of his kinsmen in the community; and these were the men on whom he depended for considerable material assistance during the difficult first year whilst he established his farm and brought the first crop to harvest. The sponsor also mediated the newcomer's initial relations with his new neighbours so that the process of becoming an effective, accepted neighbour was eased. I have heard a sponsor explaining to a newcomer, on the occasion of a dispute, something of the personalities and relations involved. In particular, the sponsor explained his own position and expected role in the discussions and decision making. Clearly, both sponsor and newcomer assumed that the latter would conform to the former's assessment of and role in the affair. This was a first lesson, as it were, showing the newcomer how he fitted into the community.

Residents were usually ready, and often actively keen, to attract their kinsmen to the community in order to increase the number of their kin-neighbours—that is, to increase the number of people with whom they could expect to enjoy mutual assistance. A newcomer who settled down successfully could be followed by his kinsman from elsewhere, as the latter was encouraged by reports of favourable conditions. The sponsor of the first newcomer could therefore expect that further kin-neighbours would be added to his set. Often a newcomer had kin-neighbours already in the community, other than his immediate sponsor, who might well not be directly related to the sponsor himself. For instance, the sponsor might be a paternal cousin of the newcomer, but some of the newcomer's maternal cousins or affines might be already resident there. In that case the sponsor's links with these other neighbours were likely to be strengthened by the mutual connection through the newcomer. Sometimes the newcomer was accompanied by some members of his previous hamlet in the former community. Thus he brought with him kin-neighbours who could probably enter into useful relations with the sponsor.

The few men who had less than three or four kin-neighbours were not only unusual numerically, but were, as Ndendeuli saw it, in unfortunate circumstances. In the sample of 189 households in four adjacent communities referred to earlier, only two had no kin-neighbors at all at the time. Both of these men had been attracted by the possibility of becoming store-keepers and traders near the local Cooperative building on the main road that ran through Mchomoro. Both had moved in with a little capital and built small stores a year or two previously. One of them was already negotiating to marry the daughter of a resident, and through this marriage he would have immediately acquired several immediate kin-neighbours, including wife's father and brother.

Other men with few kin-neighbours were recent newcomers who had not yet had time to develop previous indirect linkages and turn them to overt acknowledgement of direct kinship (for example, a cousin's cousin). Alternatively, they had lost former kin-neighbours who had died, moved away, or become long-term labour migrants. Ndendeuli emphatically disliked being in this position. I was told a number of times that if a man's kin-neighbours remained at or decreased to only one or two, there was good reason to move to some other community where the circumstances might be more favourable. Although this was not invariably sufficient cause by itself—so far as my records show—it was certainly a contributory factor when other local circumstances deteriorated. Having few kin-neighbours meant that a man would have few direct supporters when he got into difficulties or when he wished to assemble an agricultural work-party. Thus a man with few kin-neighbours was often active in trying to increase their number, mainly by attracting kinsmen to move into the community.

The full significance of kin-neighbours becomes clear in the analysis of case studies later. Here I note only that kin-neighbours associated together more frequently and fruitfully than with other neighbours. Kin-neighbours were ideally, and most usually in practice, regular members of each other's work-parties and other ad hoc action-sets. Their hamlets were not, however, necessarily near together; this would have been impossible by the nature of Ndendeuli kinship. The range of kinship was ego-centred, and therefore to some extent the set of kin-neighbours of one resident differed from that of each of those kin-neighbours. Local aggregations of kin were consequently unlikely, if not impossible.

But if the majority of a man's neighbours in his community were not directly linked to him by acknowledged kinship—and the larger the community, the larger the number of non-kin—they were all in some way or other indirectly linked to him within a single, continuous, and often convolute, network. The explanation is simple in essence. The original pioneering group were all direct kinsmen of the "owner of the land", and therefore all were directly or indirectly (through the "owner") linked by kinship ties. All subsequent newcomers were kin to one or more existing residents and therefore they too became directly or indirectly linked by kinship to everyone else. This meant that the fields of kinship ties of most, even all, neighbours were likely to overlap and thus affect one another at some points.[10] This is a sociological feature of the greatest importance: it was integral to social organisation and the nature of social action within Ndendeuli local communities.

In a sense, a man's other associates in the community were, for him, accidental. Primarily as a newcomer he was concerned with his sponsors and with any other kinsmen who happened already to be living there. Of course, in considering a move to a new community a man did attempt to take account of what he knew or could discover about his potential, unrelated neighbours. Unless he was moving from a distant area—more than ten miles or so, and that

[10] See the simplified model given in Figure 11, page 134.

was not common—he should already have known a good deal about them. It was said, with much truth, that a man was deterred from joining a community where factionalism was rife or witchcraft accusations were being made. Although the attractiveness of his kinsmen might have been high, and he may have felt compelled for a variety of reasons to leave his present community, he was to a considerable extent a free agent. It was unlikely that he did not have a choice of other communities in which he had kinsmen resident, and to which he could move. A man's kinsmen were scattered among several local communities.

A newcomer was aware that, although they were not directly linked to him, some of his new neighbours would be directly linked to some of his kin-neighbours. He fully expected to have access to the cooperation and assistance of such men through the intermediation of his kin-neighbours—for example, the affine of a cousin, the cousin of a cousin. It was impossible that he should know the extent of the potential that was available to him in this way; indeed it was strictly incomprehensible until tested and proved in social action. Further, he was aware that as a result of these indirect linkages he would be brought into cooperation or conflict with other neighbours, through the ramifications of the network. On the other hand, it is fairly certain that a man, newcomer or not, did not appreciate that in effect every neighbour was somehow linked in kinship sequences with every other neighbour.

Where a community was well established (after ten years or so) the degree of indirectness of linkages became considerable. At that stage no man was wholly conversant with the complete network of linkages. There was no attempt to trace the genealogical connections through the entire community. There was no reason why he should, for he did not himself as a single individual make use of or refer to the whole. Nevertheless there is more than a mere academic point of logic involved here, for the network of interlinkages was effectively followed and profitably utilised in the interaction, cooperation, and conflict of ongoing community life.

Because of the overlapping and interlinking of neighbours' sets of direct, activated kinship ties, collective action—for example, the commonplace work-parties—was built up coherently through the complex ramifications of the network. Thus "unrelated" neighbours worked together in the fields of another neighbour to whom both were directly linked, or because their respective kinsmen had some other kin-neighbour in common. Similarly, action-sets in support of the principals in a dispute were recruited through those kinship sequences. Yet at the same time the disputants and their supporters were linked together in some ways, and this could significantly affect the process of the dispute settlement. To take a simple example: some neighbours could be more or less equally linked to either side in a dispute. As a result mediators were identified, though for particular reasons some of them might prefer to reject that role indirectly cast for them by the actions of others towards one another. They might choose to go with one side, thus effectively weakening the other, or they might absent themselves and remain neutral. But whatever they did they were affected by and affected other neighbours' relationships.

Although men could not trace the precise linkages through the network, they could nevertheless make use of them. It could be sufficient that a man, X, knew that a neighbour, Y, was some kinsman of neighbour Z, and that therefore Z could perhaps be recruited to X's own action-set because Y already was. Here, Y might be X's own kin-neighbour; but he could be, say, the affine of X's first cousin. The anthropologist is inclined to enquire into the precise links between X, Y, and Z that make this possible, but an Ndendeuli did not necessarily need so to concern himself. It might be quite sufficient to know that Z is a kin-neighbour of Y, and that he (X) can seek Z's assistance through Y. Only if X and Z were to begin fairly regularly to recruit each other to their action-sets would the inter-linkages be spelled out more specifically; then X and Z might become effectively kin-neighbours. But if X rarely solicited the assistance of Z, and vice versa, the kinship sequence could remain vague.

NAMABEYA LOCAL COMMUNITY

As an empirical illustration of the general points made in this chapter, there follows a brief description of the kinship network of one particular local community in eastern Undendeuli. This was one of the four communities for which comprehensive genealogical and other data were obtained in the field. To an anthropologist accustomed to reading genealogical diagrams, this summary account may be more useful than lengthy exposition. It may also be useful to compare the Namabeya network with that of the Ligomba community which is the centre of interest in the following three chapters. The Namabeya community is referred to in more detail in Chapter Eight, in the analysis of leadership and factionalism.

Namabeya was founded soon after 1939, about twelve years

before my field research, and had come to extend over two converging, shallow valleys and the slightly higher ground between them. A permanent water supply was available in each stream bed, which was important towards the end of the lengthy dry season. Although only a part of the land was considered fertile enough to warrant clearing for cultivation, there were no unduly extensive areas of uncultivable soils by Ndendeuli standards. The nearest community was three to four miles away, so that there remained considerable amounts of untouched woodland as an agricultural potential for the people of Namabeya. It had continued to be an attractive community for settlement. It had grown quite rapidly in size and in the complexity of its kinship network, as newcomers had continued to exceed by a clear margin those who had chosen to leave and to settle elsewhere.

The genealogical connections of the thirteen pioneers who first settled at Namabeya are shown in Figure 3. They focussed on Q12

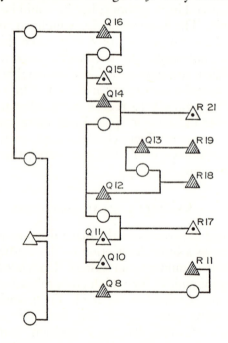

Key:

◿ pioneer who remained in the community until 1954

◿ pioneer who had moved away before 1953

Note: Letter-numbers refer to the master genealogy of Namabeya, Figure 4. The pioneer-leader and "owner of the land" was Q12.

FIGURE 3: Namabeya Pioneers, *ca.* 1940.

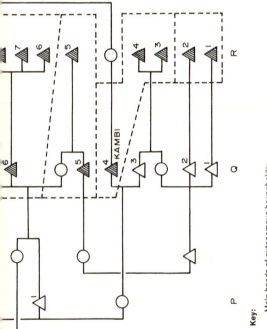

Key:

Male heads of autonomous households:

▲ resident in Namabeya, 1952-4

▲ resident who had died in Namabeya

◁ former resident in Namabeya

――― line of segmentation in 1954

- - - - - Co-members of a single hamlet

FIGURE 4: Master Genealogy Concerning Namabeya Local Community

as leader, and he became the "owner of the land". Although all the pioneers were his acknowledged kinsmen, already the sequence of indirect linkages was somewhat extended between some of those men—for example, between Q15 and R19, and between each of those and Q8 and R11. As the community grew the kinship sequences extended. Q12 found it increasingly difficult to continue to exercise leadership and influence. He remained "owner of the land", but by 1952 his role had become nominal only. This was the result, at least partly, of chronic ill health and loss of vigour, although he was by then still only in his late fifties. At the same time he had become quite overshadowed by two of his kin-neighbours, Q8 and Q16, and by two other neighbours, Q4 and R29, who were by then the acknowledged "big men" in Namabeya. Q8 and Q16 developed a marked rivalry with each other, and in 1954 the community split into two.[11] Related to both notables, but without the energy, ability, and neighbourly support accruing to either, Q12 could not take advantage of his initially favourable position in the community.

The kinship network of Namabeya in 1952–1954 is given in Figure 4, where it is shown that the sequence of kinship links runs right through the community, comprising a single network. Some of the men were linked by more than one kinship connection. This would be more obvious were it possible to present the whole of the genealogical data for all of those neighbours, but that would have necessitated diagrams of too complex a kind, nor were all the data reliably recorded. The diagram represents but one way, then, of linking all these neighbours together, though I have sought to be guided by the men themselves in selecting the pattern of linkages depicted. To take a single instance: R11 was linked with Q6 as the brother of the husband of Q6's daughter, and also as the son-in-law of Q6's two first cousins. He was, however, also the son of a female second cousin of Q6—according to Q6 himself, though R11 was vague about his mother's connection, and neither man placed importance on this linkage. This was near the limits of what Ndendeuli usually accept as direct kinship; but it might have been significant, and recognised as such, in other circumstances where, for instance, the affinal links had not existed.

In 1953 Namabeya comprised forty-two households grouped into eighteen hamlets. The approximate population at that time was 200 people, dispersed over an area of about three square miles.

[11] This development is described in Chapter Eight, page 255 ff.

THE CLOSED NETWORK

For each household head, the chain of kinship linkages extended outwards from himself, growing ever more indirect and fading into vagueness and obscurity. For assistance in some matter he might have depended on some of his own kin-neighbours who were acknowledged as such; for another purpose at another time he would have sought the assistance also of some of the kin-neighbours of his own kin-neighbours, and sometimes beyond them to more indirectly linked neighbours. Probably seldom was precisely the same set of neighbours mobilised on consecutive occasions of action-set formation. The permutations and potentialities were considerable, even in a small community. But they were limited by the accepted necessity of the obligation to reciprocate assistance received, and by the acceptance of the practical value and the moral imperative of making claims along kinship lines. A man did not claim the assistance of just any neighbour. Ndendeuli commonly asserted that kinship ascribed the right to make claims for assistance and support, and the obligation to accede to them. This was their rationale, their ideology, and it was an eminently practical one in actual social life. The sociological explanation of this, as will be more fully discussed later,[12] is that the pattern of kinship linkages provided a *system*, ready made, logically built up, which was coherent. This system could be used for the social purposes of recruiting cooperation and assistance. The linkages of cognatic and affinal kinship provided a means of identifying and systematising expectations. To establish reciprocal assistance with an "unrelated" neighbour would have raised severe problems of conflict of obligations as each of the two men had his obligations to fulfill to other neighbours. There were, of course, conflicts among kin-neighbours since, by the logic of non-unilineal kinship, each man had a set of kin-neighbours somewhat different from that of any other man. Occasions arose when a man had simultaneous but opposed demands from two kin-neighbours who were not themselves kin-neighbours of each other. Much of the dynamics within the network developed out of that repeated occurrence. Nevertheless, it was easier for a man to organize his rights and obligations to his kin-neighbours where many of them, usually his closer associates, were inter-linked also with one another. On the whole, men could time-table their agricultural work-parties so that those of inter-

12 See Chapter Seven.

connected kin-neighbours did not conflict, and so that therefore men could properly fulfill their obligations and gain their reciprocal rights. On the whole, in dispute situations a man could support his kin-neighbour unambiguously, along with others of his kin-neighbours, some or many of whom would be linked with both men. At least the lines of potential conflict were made fairly clear through this kinship idiom. Furthermore, mutual assistance between two kin-neighbours was strongly reinforced through their co-participation in assistance to other, common, kin-neighbours.

Non-unilineal kinship typically provides an open, virtually unlimited network as linkages of kin, the kin of kin, the kin of the kin of kin . . . ramify outwards, and also convolute back again. Such an open network—evident also, *inter alia*, in western, urban societies—existed among the Ndendeuli. Presumably all Ndendeuli were somehow linked, through sequences of kinship ties, with all other Ndendeuli. That would seem to be logically correct, even though it is impossible to demonstrate empirically. There were occasionally situations in which two Ndendeuli were unable to discover and establish links between themselves, though the people went on the assumption that it was generally possible to accomplish this. This assumption commonly held good since in fact Ndendeuli were very seldom interested enough to discover linkages between people who lived many miles apart, because such geographically separated people seldom came into significant contact where linkage was important.[13] Conversely, people who lived nearer together were also more likely to be more nearly linked (that is, by shorter sequences of links) as a result of intermarriage through the decades. It was also a fact that geographically nearer people knew, or knew of, or could fairly readily discover about, each other. As far as I am aware, then, and certainly as Ndendeuli held expectations and actually operated, the open network did comprise all other Ndendeuli. Of course it did not exclude non-Ndendeuli (however that term may be defined), for kinship linkages spread outwards beyond the arbitrary modern boundaries of Undendeuli. The limits of the open network were unknown and unknowable; nor did it much matter that this was the case. Some

---

[13] It did not occur to me at the time, but it would have been a useful experiment to have asked geographically widely separated men to seek to discover linkages between themselves. In a later field study, among the Arusha of northern Tanzania, a field assistant was able to demonstrate to me that he could invariably establish a linkage with any other man in his society—although he was not always able, or at least willing, to use only kinship links. Cf. Boissevan 1968:547 on tracing links in Malta.

of the sociological implications and consequences of the Ndendeuli open kinship network are examined later, in Part III of this book.

At present, however, the concern is with a bounded or *closed network*. The kinship network of an Ndendeuli local community was, at any one time, effectively a closed one because the community itself had boundaries and it contained a finite number of co-neighbours. It was truly a network in the sense that directly and indirectly all members of the community were connected with each other by kinship linkages—indeed, usually by more than a single link or sequence of links. As already demonstrated in the case of Namabeya community, the people themselves were not aware of this important fact, yet they were inevitably and frequently affected by it in their behaviour, their decisions, and their interaction. On the other hand, the boundaries of the closed kinship network were not determined by kinship criteria. They were defined in terms of neighbourhood—residence within a given geographical area comprising the territorial limits of the local community as it was separated from other communities by stretches of unoccupied and unused woodland.

Thus the closed network was a part of the total open or unbounded network. Secondly, it was closed or bounded by non-kinship criteria, though it should be noted that the residential criterion had a marked kinship element in it, so that boundedness was not entirely divorced from the facts of kinship and kinship linkages. Thirdly, the closed or bounded character of this partial network was not absolute, but only relative. In the first place, boundaries applied only to certain kinds of social activities and interests; in the second place, outsiders were not completely barred and prevented from participation or involvement. Many, but not all, interests, actions, and interactions were effectively confined to the community of neighbours: agricultural cooperation pre-eminently, but also recruitment of action-sets for other economic cooperation, in cases of intra-community disputes, and for ritual performance. Non-neighbours (that is, non-residents of the local community) might occasionally be recruited to assist a man in an internal dispute or in ritual; but much the larger number, the more important, and the more regular and dependable supporters were neighbours. Ndendeuli sometimes spoke as if outsiders were never invited to participate in the internal affairs of a community—an exaggerated emphasis of their general expectations and behaviour.

This meant that a man interacted, within the closed network, with a residentially defined and limited cluster of men who were all, directly and indirectly, linked to him by kinship. Such interaction was repetitive for different interests and in differing contexts. A man was limited in those particular matters in the range of people whom he could recruit to his assistance, and of whose alternative obligations he had to take account. He was also limited in the range of other men whose claims might overlap and conflict with, or reinforce, those of his own.

The kinship network of a community was augmented, depleted, and eventually radically changed as new neighbours joined their kin resident there, as former neighbours left, as resident bachelors married and became new household heads, and as intra-community marriage occurred. There was, however, a selection—arbitrary, to be sure—from the virtually infinite, open network involving all Ndendeuli. The particular pattern of the closed network was therefore variable within the wide range of cognatic and affinal kinship, limited only by the shallowness of genealogical memory and so of the acknowledgement and activation of formal relationships.

In the following chapters of Part II I am concerned with the dynamics of social organization and interaction that in concrete social life operated within this kind of a closed network. These chapters are largely devoted to an account and analysis of empirical events during a limited period, and mainly in a single local community, with the intention of seeking to extract and demonstrate some of the general principles of this range of social behaviour.

IV

The Ligomba Community

The Ligomba local community, located in the south-eastern part of Undendeuli, is taken as the subject of my detailed analysis of social processes within the structure of the non-lineal kinship network in a bounded community. This presentation makes the core of the book, and therefore some preliminary remarks may be helpful.

To put it quite simply: I am concerned to discover and demonstrate how the social processes actually worked, by reference to a single body of data drawn from this single community. By concentrating on one community certain disadvantages are far outweighed by the advantage of dealing with intimately inter-related, concrete data, rather than working at the level of generalisation illuminated by "apt illustrations" of indeterminate validity. Not every point that might be made in general analysis arises in the study of the single community in the limited and arbitrary period of time determined by field research requirements. Though regretting this, it seems to me to be much less important than the value to be gained from describing the series of social events and processes actually occurring in chronological connection amongst a single, interacting cluster of people. Many social anthropologists will need little if any persuasion of the advantages, and even necessities, of this course, for it involves no new departure in methodology. In particular, I have been entirely convinced by such varying examples as the accounts and analyses of Turner on the Ndembu (1957), Middleton on the Lugbara (1960), Leach on a village in Ceylon (1961), and Van Velsen on the Tonga (1964).[1]

The intention is to provide an account of social action and interaction within the bounded community as the latter gradually changed in composition through time. The account is grounded in detailed empirical evidence, although my perception and recording

[1] See also Gluckman 1961(a).

of that evidence has necessarily been incomplete. I am concerned here, as far as possible, with what particular men actually did as interacting individuals. This involves some assessment of the choices available to them in specific and culturally defined situations, the choices they in fact made, and, where possible, explanations of why they made them. The action resulting from these decisions, including the information expressed by them to other individuals, is described as well as the consequent or secondary decisions required. Then the results of these actions are examined as they affected subsequent situations, choices, and action in the social continuum. Values, expectations, and perceptions held by the participants were, of course, of great importance, and perhaps should be emphasised and analysed more carefully than is done here. But in the end my own emphasis is on what men did, as far as this could be recorded, for however faulty my own understanding I seek to give the evidence on which an understanding may be based. I have de-emphasised the search for ideal rules and modes, just as I have eschewed apt illustrations, suppositional cases, and generalised examples.

Ligomba, the changing collection of people selected for this study of social action, was not necessarily a typical Ndendeuli community. It was chosen in large part as the result of the usual, more or less accidental exigencies and fortunes of field research among an ethnographically unknown people. In part, however, the choice came from a deliberate endeavour to discover and concentrate field study in a relatively small group where, it was hoped, it would be easier to encompass and comprehend the whole. Ligomba fitted that criterion; and it happened to be conveniently situated for the purposes of other field research being carried on simultaneously.[2] By good fortune I was able to make useful initial contacts in Ligomba, and thereafter to develop good working conditions and mutual trust with many of the residents there. I believe that the general patterns of social interaction in Ligomba were essentially similar to those in other communities; but this belief is not in any case essential to my analytical argument, for I am not particularly concerned with any notion of *the* Ndendeuli local community. Few social anthropologists will be much concerned with the Ndendeuli *per se*, but perhaps many can be interested in the detailed analysis of a type of social system that has not been adequately treated hitherto.

For purposes of exposition, only fully appreciated much later,

[2] An enquiry into labor migration: Gulliver 1955(*b*).

there is a further advantage in dealing with a rather smaller community. It would be difficult, and perhaps intolerable to the reader, to deal in detail with a larger group in which the network of interrelations is more extensive, and its intricacy and the social action in which it is manifest are much more complex. Nevertheless, the data even for Ligomba are at times necessarily detailed and complicated. This was unavoidable in the course followed: so the reader must learn, and hold in mind, a fairly large amount of genealogical data, the positions of individual men, interpersonal relationships, specific events, and so on. Anthropologists have sometimes complained about the mass of detail that they must comprehend and work with in certain modern studies: for example, the monographs of Turner (1957) or Van Velsen (1964). Leach admitted, with justification, that some empirical sections of his book on Pul Eliya, the village in Ceylon, are almost unreadable (1961: 145). But he was no less justified in presenting them in that way and with careful detail. Anthropologists must necessarily be prepared to deal with highly detailed data in order to achieve understanding of complex social processes, and to get behind the screen of simplified, ideal formalisations. Standards of literary elegance and eminent readability, which reached a notable peak in Evans-Pritchard's monographs on the Nuer, must often be eschewed in the interests of a more developed and incisive sociological analysis. It is sincerely hoped that the detailed, concrete data in this account of the Ligomba community are made clear enough to be followed without too great difficulty so that my analysis and conclusions can be checked, and perhaps further deductions made. To this end, relevant parts of the total Ligomba genealogy are inserted in the text quite frequently as seems required, although the master genealogy (Fig. 5) will often have to be consulted.

Although ideally desirable, it is impossible to provide an adequate, full account of the history of the development of Ligomba from its inception down to the period of my field research. This was still essentially a pre-literate community without records, and I could find no reference to it in the official files of the Administration.[3] The period of my own field research was too limited for thorough historical investigation in the face of fading memories and retrospective interpretation,[4] nor was I sufficiently aware of

[3] The only written evidence I could discover were a few letters and records of the past employment of residents when they were labour migrants. These were useful for establishing the dating of some past events.

[4] I worked in Ligomba from early April to November, but only lived

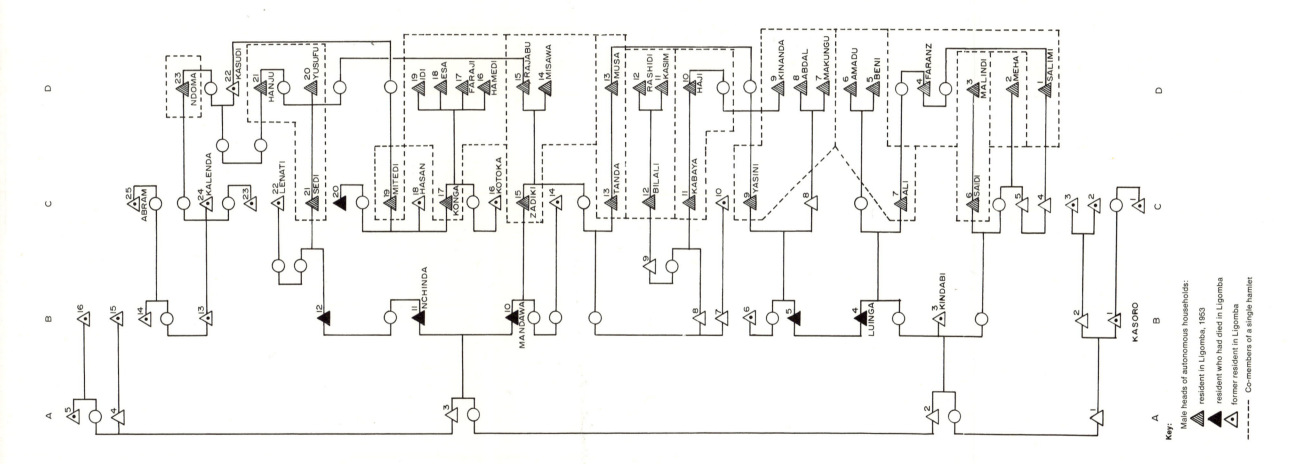

FIGURE 5: Master Genealogy Concerning Ligomba Local Community

Key:

Male heads of autonomous households:

◣◣ resident in Ligomba, 1953

◀ resident who had died in Ligomba

◤ former resident in Ligomba

▵

------ Co-members of a single hamlet

the need for this kind of work at that time. Not all the information obtained, deliberately or as a by-product of other enquiries, is demonstrably adequate, nor is its significance for subsequent events and relationships always clear enough. As a result, I have been compelled to restrict my developmental account to certain features only, largely focussing on one or two individuals from whom fuller information was obtained with some assurance of its reliability. But for at least two reasons this presentation is considered to be most important.

First, I assume dogmatically that social events and social relationships during the period of first-hand observation and enquiry were all in some sense related to and significantly affected by those earlier conditions and developments. This is a major theme of this sociological study. Secondly, I wish to avoid the possible suggestion that the kinship network and community organization of Ligomba have been treated as static conceptions either at the time of research or in the present exposition. Some anthropologists are inclined to assume that network analysis is necessarily and inherently a synchronic methodology only, presenting artificially static social systems. This is not the view taken in this book. Despite the research limitations just mentioned, even the restricted amount of developmental data and diachronic treatment may help to justify the contrary idea. It is my contention that the concept of network is, or can be, a fluid one taking full cognizance of development through time.

The account that follows relates to events and relations focussing, more or less, on two of the original pioneers who became reliable informants. One of these, Ali (C_7 in the genealogies) was my most informative and helpful informant who made himself something of a research assistant during my time in Ligomba. He was an influential resident and had been a "big man", or notable, for a good many years; thus he had been involved, as participant or interested observer, in many of the principal events that had occurred. He was more acquainted than many of his neighbours with the idea of dating events, as the result of several spells as a labour migrant, during the last of which he was a labour foreman on a sisal estate in central Tanganyika. He was willing to discuss re-

there continuously for about three months of that time. During the rest of the period I made frequent visits of several days each; further short visits were made later at the end of the same year and early the next year (the early wet season) mainly in order to record work-party arrangments during that vital time (see Chap. Six).

peatedly the history of Ligomba, and he had a memory for facts and for circumstantial detail that in total was impressive. He may have begun his association with me for ulterior motives, but later he became increasingly concerned with the success of the research itself. I have not, of course, relied on a single informant; much of what Ali told me in many sessions and on other ad hoc occasions was checked and modified by the witness of several of his neighbours. Especially useful corroboration and expansion of data were obtained from the notable, Konga (C17 in the genealogies), another original pioneer, and Saidi (C6).

This reconstruction of past events from oral information has obvious difficulties and dangers, both because of inadequate memories and because of conscious or unconscious retrospective modification of events, relations, and their interpretation. No doubt Ali was sometimes, perhaps often, concerned to present his own part in past events in the most favourable light, showing how he or his important associates acted wisely, morally, or under unavoidable pressures and provocation. I did not obtain a full account of all of the major developments that directly involved Ali or Konga, and I am fairly certain that the account that has been compiled from all the evidence collected is not absolutely reliable. Nevertheless I believe that my synthesis is logically coherent, being the product, as it were, of a consistent series of syndromes; and I think that it is adequate enough to withstand the weight of analysis and argument for which it is used. Whatever reservations there may be about the accuracy of historical data, it is essential to use these data in order to develop analysis and understanding in social anthropology. It is essential to see how earlier decisions, relations, interactions, expectations, and ideas affected later events and processes.

THE FOUNDING OF LIGOMBA

The new local community, which soon came to be called Ligomba, was begun about 1931 by fourteen men.[5] Their genealogical connections are shown in Figure 6. It is most important to appreciate that for the Ndendeuli it was no accident that these men were linked by kinship ties, for kinship was the dominant idiom in which significant co-activity and cooperation were expressed and under-

[5] It is just possible that there may have been one or two other pioneers in the founding of Ligomba who had died or moved away very soon after, leaving no near kinsmen, and who therefore had been forgotten by my informants.

stood. Kinship was the language of role expectations. Figure 6 is not a comprehensive genealogical account of any of those men, for each of them had many other acknowledged kinsmen who were not involved in the establishment of the new community. All of these men were related to the leader, Nchinda (B11), by some cognatic or affinal tie. In one way they comprised an action-set focussed on Nchinda; but this was not an action-set as that term is normally used throughout this book, for its purpose was not in-

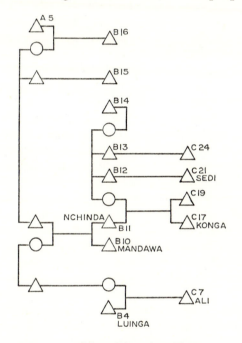

FIGURE 6: The Ligomba Pioneers. Note: B11, Nchinda, was the leader of the pioneer-set.

tended to meet the needs primarily of the focal individual. Its activities and purposes were in the direct common interests of all the participants—namely, to start new farms and to establish the men's households in new hamlets in hitherto untouched woodlands, and to establish the nucleus of a new local community.

The mixed nature of the kinship links involved in the pioneering set can be seen in their reference to Nchinda. They were as follows: one yB, two S, two WB, two WBS, one FBS, one FZH, one FZS, one MBDH, one MBDS, one WZH. But not only was a wide variety of kinship linkages involved vis-à-vis Nchinda, the leader, for an even greater range of ties is evident among the various members of this set. Moreover, some of the pioneers were only indirectly linked with one another, through Nchinda or others, and did not regard themselves as each other's kinsmen: for example, such men as B4, B12, and B16. At that time, before further members joined the community, Nchinda provided the major focus of the group for two inter-connected reasons. He was the original leader who had initiated the enterprise and taken a large part in the actual recruitment of the men and their households; and he became the acknowledged "owner-of-the-land".[6] Secondly, the men were able to relate themselves to each other, and thus to the emerging idea of community, through Nchinda.

I obtained very little reliable information concerning the relations among these men, or even of each one with Nchinda, in the pre-history of Ligomba. They were already established as heads of their own households, but they came from a number of different communities. It seems fairly certain that some at least had had little if any relationship with each other before the time of pioneering. Whatever was the reason for leaving his previous local community, each man presumably considered it advantageous to participate in the new venture and to accept Nchinda's initiative. His wife's brothers (B12, B13) and his father's sister's husband (A5) were said to have been the more influential men who, with him, joined in the selection of the location of the new settlement; but it is not clear exactly how early cooperation was organised and led, or if those four men competed for influence. Those among the pioneers who still lived in Ligomba in 1953, and other residents directly connected with a pioneer, tended retrospectively to picture the pioneers as living and working together in harmony. That is not likely to have been altogether true, however; certainly B15 moved away within two or three years as the result of some conflict with Nchinda and others. On the other hand, such a small company of men must have required a considerable amount of cooperation and toleration of each other in the first years of the community. There was necessarily a great deal of work to be accomplished, which by Ndendeuli methods could only be successful through persistent cooperation and friendliness. Woodland had to be cleared *de novo* for all arable fields and perhaps for most house sites; to build houses, timber and thatching grass had to be cut and hauled, and earth dug for mudding, by cooperative work-

[6] See page 63.

parties of the kind described later;[7] there must have been considerable burning of cleared field areas and adjacent bush and woodland that would have called for even more coordination than was usual in a well-established community in order to avoid damage to life and property. With no other community within several miles, and no settlement at all to east and south-east, there would have been large numbers of wild animals to threaten the crops in the new fields and the first harvests. Most probably, as in other new communities, the new fields would have been cleared fairly near together in order to facilitate cooperative protection. There were communal drives against herds of baboons and warthogs. All this required much coordination and leadership, at the same time as the men were coming to know and accept one another in all kinds of social activities, relatively isolated as they were from other Ndendeuli. The evident success of the new community in establishing itself on a flourishing, permanent basis indicates that organised cooperation must have been fairly efficient and conflict fairly slight, for not all such ventures were so successful.

THE DEVELOPMENT OF LIGOMBA

In this historical section I describe, first, how newcomers were introduced to Ligomba. Then I show how the ranges of kin-neighbours, the patterns of neighbourly cooperation, and the recruitment of action-sets changed through the period as men and their households moved in, became established, shifted away, or died. This will prepare the way for a description of Ligomba in 1953 and for a detailed analysis of events and inter-relationships among residents during that year.

A master genealogy for Ligomba is given in Figure 5, but relevant portions are given in other figures.

The actual dates of the recorded events are not especially important. What does matter is the chronological order of and relation between the events. A European chronology was established,[8] making use of certain key years such as the beginning and ending of World War II, and local events well remembered by the people that it was possible to date with accuracy. Eventually it proved possible to date quite firmly most events in Libomba after 1939.

The process by which a newcomer was introduced to a local

[7] See Chapter Six.
[8] The chronology was originally developed in connection with my concurrent investigation of migrant labour careers.

community, through the active sponsorship and practical assistance of one or more of his kinsmen already resident there, has already been described (pp. 66–68). Quite commonly, a newcomer had more than a single sponsor—that is, if he had more than one kinsman in the community—for it would be seriously unfriendly and unwise if they did not join in his support and so ensure his subsequent cooperation in community life. Usually, however, there was a principal sponsor, a resident kinsman who took the initiative and accepted the main burden and responsibility. I refer only to this principal sponsor except where it was impossible to identify one such person.

Events Largely Relating to Ali

The chronology of arrivals, departures, deaths, and marriages in that section of the community mainly relating to Ali (C7) was as follows (see Fig. 7):

ca. 1931—Ligomba local community founded
ca. 1933—Luinga (B4) sponsored B5 (yB) who brought with him his son, Yasini (C9)
ca. 1934—Luinga sponsored Kindabi (C3) (WB)
ca. 1936—Kindabi and Luinga sponsored Kasoro (B1) (MBS of Kindabi)
ca. 1937—Luinga and B5 sponsored B6 (WB of B5)
ca. 1938—Kasoro sponsored C2 (BS)
         Luinga died
1939—B6 left Ligomba
1940—Kindabi and Ali (C7) sponsored Saidi (C6) (ZS of Kindabi)
     Kasoro sponsored C1 (DH)
1942—B5 died
     Kindabi left Ligomba, after dispute with Ali
     C3 married and established new household
1943—Ali sponsored Beni (D5) (ZS)
1946—Saidi sponsored Meha (D2) (ZS)
1947—Yasini sponsored Makungu (D7) (BS)
     Kasoro, C1, C2, and C3 left Ligomba, after dispute with Yasini
     Amadu (D6) married and established new household
1948—Ali sponsored Faranz (D4) (DH)
     Kinanda (D9) married and established new household
1950—Faranz and D2 sponsored Salimi (D1) (ZH of Faranz)
1951—Abdal (D8) married and established new household
1952—Malindi (D3) married and established new household

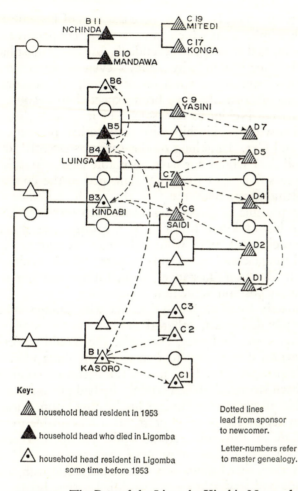

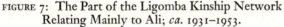

FIGURE 7: The Part of the Ligomba Kinship Network
Relating Mainly to Ali; *ca.* 1931–1953.

Events in this section of Ligomba during the period of little over twenty years can be conveniently divided into three fairly distinctive phases.

Phase 1: The feature of the earlier years was the marked activity of Luinga in sponsoring newcomers. This, it is fairly certain, was the result of deliberate policy on his part. A glance at Figure 6 shows that Luinga was only loosely linked with many of the other members of the pioneering set focussed on Nchinda. He was rather distantly related genealogically to Nchinda and to the latter's younger brother, B10, who were the sons of his wife's father's sister. Such a linkage on which to base active cooperative relations was rather unusual among the Ndendeuli, and there must have been some good, prior reason why Luinga even admitted to kinship with the two men. Apart from his own son, Ali, the only other men who might normally have been expected to become his kin-neighbours were Nchinda's two sons; but it appears that in practice he acknowledged kinship with some other pioneers, such as B12, B13, and C21. Something of this sort was essential, otherwise Luinga (and Ali) would not have been able to obtain assistance in the early years. The fact that they remained in the community is adequate demonstration of the fact that such assistance was obtained. It is possible that those last three men were acknowledged only as the kin of kin ("brothers of a brother", as it would be phrased in such case), with whom, through the intermediation of Nchinda, Luinga could reasonably expect reliable reciprocal cooperation. In these circumstances, then, Luinga was not in a particularly secure position in the new community.

Unfortunately I was unable to discover why Luinga should have joined the pioneering set, other than that he was already fairly closely linked with its leader, Nchinda. He would scarcely have left his previous community to join that new enterprise, with its incalculable prospects for him, unless the desire or compulsion to leave had been strong. Almost certainly he had got into some difficulties in his previous community; his brother's son, Yasini, once hinted at an accusation of witchcraft, but I was unable to persuade him to follow up this indiscretion, whilst Ali for once professed unshakeable ignorance that must have been feigned. All accounts agreed, however, that Luinga was a most energetic man, ambitious for influence and leadership—just as Ali, his son, became later— and he may perhaps have over-reached himself and aroused the intolerable hostility of his former neighbours.

Whatever the reasons, it is clear that Luinga found himself in a relatively unfavourable position in the new community. There were too few neighbours on whom he could rely for cooperation and support, and even those few, apart from his own son, were most probably more closely associated with other members of the pioneering set. Their reliability could not be taken for granted. Like many Ndendeuli in that sort of situation, he sought to remedy it by introducing and sponsoring some of his own kinsmen to Ligomba. With these newcomers he could expect more secure cooperation and support, since he would be advantageous to them also. Moreover, he could hope to build up an influential role among them. In so far as he was (or continued to be) ambitious after joining the new community, he was more or less compelled to introduce new supporters as neighbours unless he was prepared to come into conflict with the leading men in the pioneering set. This last he could not realistically contemplate since he was dependent on the support of Nchinda, and this effectively prevented any challenge to Nchinda's influence.

Luinga achieved considerable success in his endeavours, helped by the fact that the new community was established on comparatively fertile land and seemed to be a successful venture. He was the principal sponsor of three newcomers and joint sponsor of two others. He could justifiably expect that some of these newcomers, who had become his kin-neighbours, would in their turn attract and sponsor some of their own kinsmen to Ligomba. These new kin-neighbours lessened his dependence on indirectly linked fellow-pioneers. This effort imposed a considerable burden on his household, and on that of his son, Ali, as the latter described it. A sponsor was expected to render a good deal of material assistance in food, hospitability, and labour, and to give active support and advice whilst the newcomer was establishing his own household during the first year leading up to the taking of a first harvest. To repeat this effort and responsibility successfully in four out of (probably) five years (1933–1937 inclusive) was something of a feat, as other Ndendeuli assured me when told about it. The strength of Luinga's motivation and determination is thus emphatically demonstrated. And his success appears to have been well founded, for his new kin-neighbours are reported to have cooperated actively with him. There were no suggestions of divisive conflict among them up to the time of Luinga's death in 1938. On the contrary, Luinga was coming to be recognised as a "big man", a notable; but he died before he had sufficient time to consolidate his influence, or before it was threatened by conflict as such influence so often was.

Phase 2: The next period covered the developing conflict between Luinga's son, Ali, and the latter's mother's brother, Kindabi (B3). Soon after Luinga's death, B6 left Ligomba after only about two years' residence there. There is no clear evidence that the two events were directly related. A newcomer, Saidi (C6), was jointly sponsored by Ali and Kindabi—their first cousin and sister's son respectively. Then rivalry developed between those two aspirants to Luinga's emergent role of influence. Overtly at least this seems to have appeared as competition in respect of the relative influence each had over Saidi. Two remembered disputes were relevant. The first arose out of a petty quarrel between the young unmarried sons of Saidi and Yasini. Ali was able to intervene as an acceptable and successful mediator between the two fathers, each of whom was his first cousin. Although the matter was a minor one, Ali was able to demonstrate his public ability and to obligate both cousins more firmly to him personally. Kindabi, on the other hand, seems to have failed in the case because of a too partial support of Saidi which threatened to exacerbate the dispute against the interests of the two parties. Presumably Kindabi had intended to gain Saidi's approval and to show his influence to his other kin-neighbours.

The second dispute at this time (1941) arose out of the refusal of Kindabi's son to give a share of his migrant labour savings to Ali, his father's sister's son. Ali felt strongly enough, or perhaps strong enough, to demand a moot at which his claim could be considered publicly. In this he gained the support not only of Yasini and of B5, but also of Kasoro, C1, and C2 who might have been expected to support Kindabi instead. The reason for their choice was said by Kasoro himself, and by Ali and Saidi, to have been personal disfavour for Kindabi. That is, those three closely related men deliberately preferred Ali. Equally significantly, Kindabi failed to gain the active support of Saidi who might at least have acted in the role of favourable mediator between his kin-neighbours. But Saidi conspicuously left Ligomba on a visit elsewhere and did not attend the moot. This was typically the action of a man who did not wish to become involved and compromised in a dispute. As Saidi told me years afterwards, there was no overriding reason for his absence other than the desire to avoid his kinsmen's competition; but he had little confidence in his abilities as a mediator nor any ambition to gain influence by attempting the role, as I witnessed in other comparable circumstances later. In effect, Saidi's action strengthened Ali's position and left Kindabi virtually isolated.

At that time the "owner of the land" was Konga (C17) who had succeeded to his father's status. He convened the moot at his house, in response to Ali's request, and he acted as mediator whilst favouring Ali. The two men were second cousins, both were original pioneers, and at that time both were members of the junior generation in the community. They were close personal friends, as they continued to be in 1953.[9] In the moot both Kindabi and

[9] See pages 116–117.

his son were by common agreement censured for the asserted lack of generosity in refusing a justifiable gift to Ali. Kindabi accused Ali of spitefully making a public issue out of a private matter, and claimed that his son's savings from labour migration were required for bridewealth. Kindabi then declared that Ali was no longer his "son" nor his kinsman. Both Yasini and Konga told me that Kindabi afterwards retracted his denial of kinship and agreed that his son should make some gift to Ali. The moot therefore ended with some degree of success in a mutually accepted settlement of the dispute itself, but the settlement brought no conciliation in the wider conflict. Other quarrels followed, though none came to a moot again, and Kindabi moved his household away from Ligomba after the next harvest, in 1942.

Unless Kindabi could somehow have solved the problem of his conflict and hostility with Ali, involving their competition for influence over the same range of kin-neighbours, he was more or less compelled to leave. Essential cooperation with his neighbours was threatened, or at least it was no longer reliable, whilst his achievement of influence as a notable seemed unlikely. He did not attempt the alternative of sponsoring other kinsmen to Ligomba, but instead chose to move to another community where some of those kinsmen were already resident.

Phase 3: In the period from 1942 to 1953 the proliferation of the kinship network and the consolidation of Ali's acknowledged role as a notable continued. In contrast with his inimical relations with his mother's brother, Kindabi, Ali maintained friendly, non-competitive relations with his two first cousins, Saidi (MZS) and Yasini (FBS), as their generation emerged as the seniormost in the community. Ali sponsored his sister's son, D_5, in 1943, but he did not attempt to follow the energetic policy of his father in introducing newcomers. On at least one occasion he was unsuccessful in persuading another kinsman (his wife's brother) to join the community. This did not necessarily reflect on his ability or reputation, for men wishing to move often explored several possibilities before selecting what seemed to them the most advantageous.

Ali maintained good working relations with Kasoro (MMBS), with his second cousins, C_2 and C_3, and with Kasoro's son-in-law, C_1, whom Ali also acknowledged as his kinsman. But he received a set-back when these men decided to move away in 1947. Structurally this cluster of four neighbours had intended to become slightly separated in the kinship network after the deaths of Luinga and B_5 and the departure of Kindabi. This cannot be emphasised,

however, for they were well able to continue neighbourly cooperation with a number of people who were within an acceptable range
of kinship. On the other hand, Ali, Saidi, and Yasini were developing their principal field of cooperation amongst themselves and
their emerging kin-neighbours of the new junior generation. Ali
especially, and to a lesser extent Saidi, continued reciprocal assistance with their second cousins, Konga and his two brothers (sons
of Nchinda the pioneer leader). For some reason Kasoro was unable to attract other kinsmen to Ligomba, and this tended to put
him in a relatively weak position. This position, and that of his
three "sons" with whom he shared a hamlet, was made clear, and
their departure precipitated, by a dispute that arose in 1946.

The dispute occurred when Kinanda (D_9, son of Yasini) was
accused of the attempted seduction of the younger sister of C_1. Ali
was (or felt he was) obliged to support Yasini and Kinanda, whilst
Kasoro, C_2, and C_3 supported C_1. It appears from Yasini's retrospective account of the subsequent moot that Ali persuaded Saidi
to take the nominal role of mediator, thus perhaps limiting Saidi's
support of C_1. But in fact Ali himself so effectively took charge
of the moot that, without overtly alienating Kasoro and the others,
he persuaded C_1 to drop the allegation. C_1, however, was under
pressure from his sister's suitor, who lived elsewhere, and from
whom he had accepted gifts in order that he would tacitly allow
the suitor sexual access to the girl before marriage. This was a not
unusual arrangement, and the gifts later formed part of the agreed
bridewealth. It so happened that there were two or three of
Kasoro's kinsmen living in the suitor's local community some seven
miles away. There were, then, advantages in moving to that community, in view of their potentially disadvantageous position in the
Ligomba network. The men were certainly under no direct compulsion to move, as C_2 explained to me seven years later; but, as
Ndendeuli more or less consciously did, they weighed up the relative advantages and disadvantages as far as these could be assessed.
They probably chose wisely, for by 1953 all four men were well
established in their new community and were entrenched in its
kinship network. Both Ali and Saidi continued to maintain useful
relations with them after their move.

Thus four kin-neighbour were "lost" to the men remaining in
Ligomba. It is quite possible, though certainly not inevitable, that
had they stayed they would gradually have become separated from
Ali and Saidi—just as Ali gradually became separated from Sedi
(C_{21}) as the two men, without hostility, developed their relatively

disjunctive parts of the kinship network. In any case, compensatory accumulation of kin-neighbours occurred as other newcomers settled in Ligomba—Ali sponsored his son-in-law, Faranz, in 1948, and the latter sponsored his sister's husband, Salimi, in 1950—and as young adult men married and established new households. The last newcomer, Salimi, attempted unsuccessfully to attract a cousin in 1952 and another cousin in 1953, in a deliberate attempt to lessen his relative isolation in the Ligomba network.[10] His failure, like that of one or two other Ligomba men at this period, may have been partly the result of the comparatively disadvantageous distribution of available woodland for clearing and cultivation in the vicinity. These ecological conditions are examined later in this chapter.

During these years, Ali was generally accepted as a notable and the man whose ability, energy, and influence were most usefully available to this cluster of men. Only to a limited extent, though, was he regarded by them or by their other neighbours as their effective leader. Nor was his influence entirely restricted to their interests. This will become more obvious in the analysis of case material in the following chapters. What can be stressed at this point is that, acting as a notable, Ali met neither opposition nor competition from his kin-neighbours, as he had done earlier from Kindabi. Instead he began to come into competition with another notable, Kabaya (C11), who exercised influence in another section of the kinship network, but a section which was linked with that of the men considered here—a chief link being Yasini, Ali's cousin.

Events Largely Relating to Konga

Other developments occurred in Ligomba, of course, during this period of two decades. Ali and some of the others already mentioned were sometimes directly involved in these events, but they were indirectly affected most or all of the time by other arrivals of newcomers, by departures of residents, and by conflicts, competition, and cooperation that developed. In recording these events, I am again limited by such reasonably reliable data as could be obtained in 1953.

The chronology of arrivals, departures, deaths, and marriages in the section of the community mainly relating to Konga (C17) was as follows (see Fig. 8):

[10] The relatively weak position of Salimi is discussed further at page 209 ff.

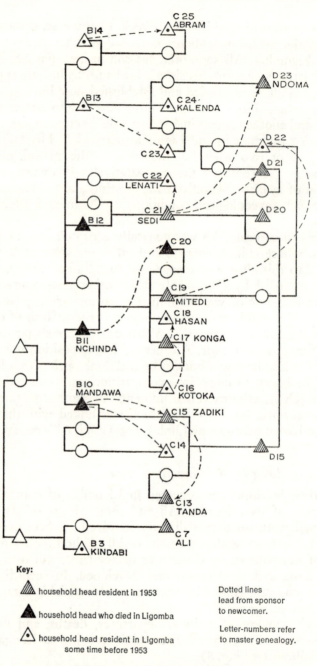

Key:

▨ household head resident in 1953

▲ household head who died in Ligomba

△ household head resident in Ligomba
    some time before 1953

Dotted lines
lead from sponsor
to newcomer.

Letter-numbers refer
to master genealogy.

FIGURE 8: The Part of the Ligomba Kinship Network
Relating Mainly to Konga; *ca.* 1931–1953.

ca. 1931—Ligomba community founded
ca. 1935—B15 left Ligomba
   Nchinda (B11) sponsored C20 (DH)
ca. 1936—Konga sponsored Kotoka (C16) (WB)
   Mandawa (B10) sponsored C14 (WZS)
ca. 1937—Nchinda died; Konga succeeded to title of "owner of the land"
   A5 and B16 left Ligomba
ca. 1938—Zadiki (C15) came to settle in Ligomba to live with his father, Mandawa
   Mandawa died
   1939—Dispute between Zadiki and Konga over Zadiki's junior wife
   Konga sponsored Hasan (C18) (B)
   B14 sponsored Abram (C25) (DH)
   1940—Zadiki sponsored Tanda (C13) (WB)
   Sedi (C21) sponsored Lenati (C22) (MZS)
   1941—Hamedi (D16) married and established new household
   B13 sponsored C23 (DH)
   1942—Tanda sponsored Kabaya (C11) (MBS), with Bilali (C12) (MBS of Kabaya)
   1943—B12 died
   Faraji (D17) married and established new household
   1944—C23 left Ligomba
   Misawa (D14) married and established new household
   1945—Kotoka (C16) left Ligomba
   1946—B13 and Kalenda (C24) left Ligomba
   Yusufu (D20) married and established new household
   1948—B14 and Abram (C25) left Ligomba, after dispute with Bilali over theft of Koranic papers
   Sedi sponsored Hanju (D21) (DH)
   Esa (D18) married and established new household
   1949—C20 died
   Mitedi (C19) sponsored Kasudi (D22) (DH)
   Lenati (C22) left Ligomba
   1950—Sedi sponsored Ndoma (D23) (FBDS)
   1951—Hasan (C18) left Ligomba
   Rajabu (D15) married daughter of Sedi, and established new household
   1952—Idi (D19) married and established new household

Three or four years after its founding, Ligomba lost the first of its original pioneers, B15, who moved away from Ligomba, reportedly as the result of some conflict with Nchinda and others. About six years after the founding, Nchinda, the "owner of the land", died after being mauled by a lion. His eldest son, Konga,

succeeded to the nominal role which by that time had come to be
of little importance. Konga's "grandfather" (FFZH), A5, moved
away soon after, together with his son. A5 had been one of the
more influential of the pioneers and it is probable that he had ambitions to become a notable. He may, but it is uncertain, have come
into conflict with Konga over the succession to Nchinda's title;
if so, this could have been one reason for his leaving. Whatever the
case was, it did not vitiate continued acknowledgement of kinship
and continued mutual assistance between the men. In 1953, some
time after A5 died, his son B16 lived about ten miles from Ligomba
and he and Konga regularly exchanged hospitality and assistance.
In contrast, by that time B15 lived rather farther away and was
scarcely considered by Konga to be any longer a kinsman.

During the earlier years Nchinda had sponsored his daughter's
husband, C20, who in part came to perform suitor-service in lieu
of bridewealth. Konga sponsored his wife's brother, C16; Mandawa (Nchinda's younger brother) sponsored his wife's sister's
son, C14. About the time of Konga's succession to Nchinda, Mandawa fell ill and became enfeebled. His son, Zadiki (C15), was
persuaded to settle in Ligomba to look after his mother and her
widowed sister. Zadiki had not taken part in the founding of
Ligomba for at that time he had been living in the community of
his first wife's father and brother, where he had settled after completing suitor-service. There, after a successful career as a labour
migrant, he had married a second wife. Both wives now accompanied him to Ligomba. Soon after Zadiki's arrival, Mandawa
died.

Fairly soon afterwards (*ca.* 1939), Zadiki entered into the first
of what was to be a long series of disputes with his cousin (FBS),
Konga. Zadiki alleged that Konga's eldest son (Hamedi, then unmarried) had attempted to seduce Zadiki's junior wife. In the subsequent moot Zadiki found himself almost isolated, for the only
unequivocal support came from his cousin, C14. Konga, acting on
behalf of his son, was well supported by his two younger brothers,
and by B13, C20, and C21, as well as by Kindabi and Ali who
might have been expected to act rather as mediators since they
were equally related to both disputants. Zadiki seems to have expected stronger support from Kindabi at least, but there is little
doubt that although Kindabi did eventually become the mediator
in the moot, he was partial to Konga's side. Ali, by his own account, was quite clear that he had supported one second cousin
rather than the other because Konga already was becoming a nota-

ble and his friendship was potentially valuable, whilst Zadiki was still something of a stranger offering fewer advantages. In the moot Zadiki's allegation was rejected by Konga's supporters who were united in condemning Zadiki's junior wife as deceitful and sexually provocative. It was on her word, apparently, that Zadiki's charge principally depended. The moot was a failure because Zadiki refused to withdraw his accusation and his demand for compensation. A second moot was arranged, but the evening before the moot the junior wife deserted Zadiki. She declared that she wanted a divorce for she was going to live with another man elsewhere. In fact, she accompanied that man who was going as a labour migrant to central Tanganyika. The men assembled for the moot at Zadiki's house next morning as already arranged. Kindabi quickly suggested that Zadiki should now agree to withdraw his allegation against Konga's son. This he did, but with bad grace, complaining that his kin-neighbours were against him and did not help him in his difficulties. He accused Kindabi and Ali of unfriendly mediation in the moot, and angry exchanges followed. B13 and C14 (on separate sides in the dispute but independently linked to each other through B13's wife) combined to act as mediators instead, persuaded Zadiki to drop his charge, and offered him sympathy and assistance in the matter of his runaway wife.

Later, those two men together with Konga's younger brother (C18) accompanied Zadiki to the moot held in the community of the father of the junior wife. A divorce was arranged and some return of bridewealth obtained. Nevertheless Zadiki was apparently not reconciled to the situation nor to his cousin, Konga, for at a subsequent beer-drink he quarrelled with both Konga and Ali, complaining because they had not accompanied him to the divorce moot. There were no immediate consequences of this further quarrel, but it seems to have set the tone for relations between these men in the following years.

Fairly soon after these incidents, probably in 1940, Zadiki sponsored his wife's brother, Tanda (C13), as a newcomer to Ligomba. A couple of years after that Tanda sponsored his cousin, Kabaya (C11), who came accompanied by his own cousin, Bilali (C12); and some time later Kabaya sponsored another cousin, C10. These events were explained by Ali years later: Zadiki had either to obtain new kin-neighbours who would reliably support him, or he must leave Ligomba. The choice may not have been quite so clear cut as that, but Zadiki faced a recurrent Ndendeuli problem—one already described in the cases of Kindabi and of Kasoro. It is

probable that Zadiki considered that he could not entirely rely on
his existing kin-neighbours in the future. The abortive adultery
case demonstrated this, and the case itself had resulted in a worsening of the situation, for his relations with both his first cousin,
Konga, and his second cousin, Ali, had deteriorated. Both men
were becoming influential and likely to be able to recruit reliable
supporters in the event of open conflict with Zadiki. As Ali pointed
out: "Zadiki could not depend on his kinsmen after that time. Yes,
they would help him and work in his fields; but if his work-party
and that of another neighbour were arranged for the same day,
then would Zadiki be able to get men for his party? No, for they
would first go with the other and Zadiki would have to wait, or
perhaps leave it for another day. He became the second man [took
second place] in affairs like that".[11] In the following years Zadiki
came increasingly to depend on his newer kin-neighbours—Tanda,
Kabaya, Bilali, and C10, and their sons who began to emerge as
new household heads.

Konga continued to consolidate his status as a notable among
his kin-neighbours, but less smoothly and with rather less finesse
than Ali. He was inclined to be somewhat authoritarian in his
role of leader, and this alienated some of his associates who strongly
resented his behaviour.

In 1945, his wife's brother, Kotoka (C16), moved away from
Ligomba after growing tension that culminated in Kotoka's protests about the allegedly peremptory way in which Konga took
the organisational lead in arranging the schedule of cultivation
work-parties in that year's wet season. Kotoka demanded (perhaps
equally peremptorily, as some later informants suggested) an earlier date in the timetable for his work-party, and he accused Konga
of arranging matters too much in his (Konga's) self-interest.

The next year, 1946, B13 and Kalenda (C24) also left. Kalenda
had (on Ali's evidence) supported Kotoka's complaints. Now
Kalenda came into a dispute with Lenati (C22), demanding payment of money allegedly owed him by Lenati. In the moot, Konga
acted as mediator between his two kin-neighbours; but he offended
both disputants (according to Lenati) by declaring the matter to
by unimportant and advocating that it should be dropped altogether. This, by default, favoured Lenati and his prime supporter,

[11] Unfortunately, no doubt because of my personal association with Ali
and also with Konga, I was unable to discuss these earlier affairs with
Zadiki. He refused to give me his own account or to comment on what
others had told me.

Sedi (C21), as perhaps Konga intended, even though he seems to have handled it poorly. Kalenda, the plaintiff, lost his temper rather violently and struck Konga. Recriminations followed as Kalenda also accused Konga of neglecting his senior kin-neighbour, B13 (Konga's mother's brother, and father of Kalenda). At the subsequent moot, Konga was supported by his two younger brothers, and by Sedi and his son and Lenati. Kalenda was supported by Abram (C25) and the two very elderly men, B13 and B14. Kalenda appealed to Zadiki for support, and Zadiki responded. Years later Konga complained to me that Kalenda had sought to stir up trouble between him and Zadiki, taking advantage of the animosity existing between those two cousins. The moot was conclusive only in affirming the conflict between Konga and Kalenda, and Konga's stronger position in the division of supporters. As a result, Kalenda and his ageing father moved to another local community where they had kinsmen living.

In 1948, Abram (C25) and his near-senile father-in-law (B14) also left. This was the direct result of his dispute with Bilali (C12) over the alleged theft of some Koranic papers (as described in the following section), and was in no way the fault of Konga. Indeed, he agreed with the quite general condemnation of Abram at the time, and he may not have been altogether sorry to see him leave since he had scarcely been a reliable associate. On the other hand, Konga's youngest brother, Hasan (C18), moved away in 1951, partly because of Konga's authoritarian tendencies. According to Hasan, the culminating quarrel arose when Hasan complained of his brother's interference in his own domestic affairs. Konga had punished Hasan's young son and reproved Hasan's wife for not controlling the boy. Informants agreed that the boy had taken and negligently damaged Konga's favourite knife and, on discovery, had been insolent to his elder "father". Yet, as informants also agreed, Konga should have left the matter to Hasan and not have assumed a tactless parental authority. Hasan declared that he was not willing to be subservient to his older brother, nor to be treated as if he were not head of his own household. He shifted to another community in the following cool season.

Despite these set-backs, and despite a disapproved inclination to high-handedness and tactlessness, Konga nevertheless retained acceptance as a notable among his remaining kin-neighbours. Clearly, in 1953, they regarded his influence and leadership as valuable. Konga had for long quite dominated his other brother, Mitedi (C19), and his four married sons were willing to follow him. Sedi

(C21) and his "sons" (D20 and the two newcomers, D21 and D23) were prepared to tolerate his unfortunate tendencies because of his useful abilities in other ways. Sedi explained to me that he had no wish to leave Ligomba (he had been an original pioneer),

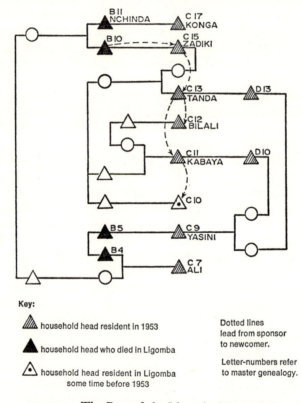

Key:

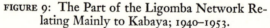 household head resident in 1953

▲ household head who died in Ligomba

△ household head resident in Ligomba
  some time before 1953

Dotted lines
lead from sponsor
to newcomer.

Letter-numbers refer
to master genealogy.

FIGURE 9: The Part of the Ligomba Network Relating Mainly to Kabaya; 1940–1953.

and therefore he needed the continued support and assistance of Konga—which, in general, he amply received. He and his "sons" also desired to maintain reliable cooperation with Konga's four sons and with Mitedi, for without this their position in Ligomba would have been insecure. All this necessitated continued acceptance of Konga himself and as a notable.

The Development of a Third Cluster: Events Largely Relating to Kabaya

By the mid-1940s, a third cluster was emerging in the community, partially distinct but interlinked with two clusters already existing in which Ali and Konga were the acknowledged influential men. This third cluster contained the newer residents who were more closely linked with one another, and were cooperating more frequently, though not exclusively, with one another than with their longer established neighbours.

The chronology of events was as follows (see Fig. 9):

1940—Zadiki (C_{15}) sponsored Tanda (C_{13}) (WB)
1942—Tanda sponsored Kabaya (C_{11}) (MBS), with Bilali (C_{12}) (MBS of Kabaya)
1944—Kabaya sponsored C_{10} (FBS)
        Misawa (D_{14}) married and established new household
1946—Kabaya's son (Haji, D_{10}) married daughter of Yasini (D_9) and established new household
1948—B_{10} left Ligomba
        Dispute between Bilali and Abram (C_{25}) over theft of Koranic papers
1950—Musa (D_{13}) married daughter of Yasini, and established new household
1951—Zadiki's son (Rajabu, D_{15}) married daughter of Sedi (C_{21}) and established new household
        Rashidi (D_{12}) married and established new household
        C_{14} left Ligomba

In this cluster Kabaya began to gain a reputation for influence and leadership, and then to be acknowledged as a "big man", or notable. He was described (in accounts given in 1953) as a man who, by his tact and intelligence, gained esteem through his ability to smooth out disputes arising from conflicts in the timetabling of agricultural work-parties—a particularly common problem during the short cultivation season each year. But he probably achieved recognition as a "big man" when he acted as spokesman for the Ndendeuli of the south-eastern region, which included Ligomba. After the war, the colonial administration compelled a number of Ndendeuli communities in the farther north-east region, near the Mbarangandu river, to move back westwards nearer to the sub-chiefdom centre.[12] The people living in the south-east feared that they too would be made to move westwards. Kabaya, formerly

[12] This was a policy to make the sub-chiefdom based on Likuyu more compact and to resolve the difficulties of administering distant communities in a region where it had been decided no longer to maintain the old road leading out of Songea District to Liwale. This policy was linked with plans to clear a vast area of human habitation at the time, creating the Selous Game Reserve.

an Agricultural Department field assistant, spoke out against such
a move at a local meeting attended by a District Officer. Afterwards he headed a party to protest to the District Commissioner
and the Ngoni chief at a meeting at the sub-chiefdom headquarters.
Most probably a compulsory movement of the south-eastern
Ndendeuli was not part of the Administration's policy; but the
people did not know this, or did not believe it, and they were apprehensive. Kabaya, among others, gained a good deal of credit
when the District Commissioner announced publicly that no compulsion would be used in the south-east.

Kabaya was also the first man to start growing and curing
tobacco as a cash crop. By Ligomba standards he became fairly
wealthy as a result; and he advised some of his neighbours when
they too began tobacco cultivation. Later he was selected to be a
member of the local committee of the Cooperative Society which
bought the cured tobacco from the growers and sold it in bulk.

Kabaya's status crystallised in 1948 when a dispute occurred between his cousin, Bilali (C12), and Abram (C25). Bilali was a
mwalimu [13] who conducted a Koranic school in Ligomba at that
time. He discovered that some sheets of paper were missing from
his house; on these he had written words from the Koran for the
purpose of teaching the children. Sedi (C21) disclosed that he had
seen one of the sheets in the house of his cousin's husband, Abram.
The wife admitted to this when visited by Bilali and Kabaya,
though Abram denied the theft and said that he had picked the
sheets up in the bush. Bilali demanded a moot to discuss the matter
and was supported by Kabaya. In the moot Kabaya acted as leader
of Bilali's action-set. Konga acted as leader of Abram's action-set
(Abram was husband of his MZD), but he was in an equivocal
position. Abram was an unpopular man, and he was generally
censured for ill-treating his senile father-in-law, B14, in whose
hamlet he lived. Abram was alleged to have stolen the sheets of
Koranic words in order to use them for sorcery (but I obtained no
details of this). Kabaya, on behalf of Bilali, and with the support
of Zadiki, Tanda, Yasini, and others was able to lead what amounted
to community condemnation of Abram, whilst Konga "was able
only to sit and say nothing" (as one informant put it). Kabaya

[13] In Undendeuli a *mwalimu* (Swahili: "teacher") was a man with some
Islamic learning, although this was often rather little. Bilali's claim to the
status came from a period of residence in Zanzibar as a labour migrant,
when he claimed to have studied under an Arab sheikh. He could recite
texts from the Koran but otherwise knew no Arabic.

virtually represented the community against Abram when he declared in the moot that Abram was no longer wanted in Ligomba. Subsequently Abram moved away, taking his old father-in-law with him.

This third cluster in Ligomba was, of course, already linked, through Zadiki, with the cluster previously described in which Konga was the principal influence. Zadiki tended to follow Kabaya's lead rather than that of his cousin, Konga, with whom his personal relations were strained. Nevertheless, Zadiki regularly needed the practical assistance of Konga and his sons and brothers in order to make up adequate agricultural work-parties; he was, therefore, prepared reciprocally to participate in the work-parties convened by those men. Similarly, his brother-in-law, Tanda, also wished to maintain reciprocal assistance with these men, for the same reason. That is, there was no decisive break in the network of actively recognised kin linkages, for it was to the advantage of a number of men to prevent this. As the sons of Tanda, Zadiki, and Konga married and established their own households, they too participated in cooperation across the potential cleavage in the community. Although there is insufficient case-material to demonstrate it, it is most probable that action-set recruitment in dispute cases similarly cut across the distinction between the clusters; actual cases recorded in 1953 justify this assumption.[14] The cross-linkage was later reinforced by the marriage of Zadiki's son to the daughter of Sedi (Konga's first cousin) in 1951.

The kinship network was further convoluted when, in 1946, Kabaya's son married the elder daughter of Yasini; and, later, in 1950, when Yasini's second daughter was married to Tanda's son. With those marriages, and the close affinal links they entailed, the network of kinship linkages took on new form. No longer was it merely a linear set of linkages (and associated cooperative relations), but it involved a kind of feed-back with a circular pattern. Yasini and his son and two nephews became closely associated with the section influenced by Kabaya, as well as with the section influenced by Ali. It is doubtful if Yasini had deliberately sought the marriage of his daughter and Kabaya's son for the advantage it might bring him in this way; but it is most probable that Kabaya had contrived it in his more perceptive fashion. Kabaya's son was well known to be dominated by his father, and the latter supplied the money for bridewealth; Kabaya was seeking to widen his influence and this was an excellent way in which to do it.

[14] See Chapter Eight, page 242 ff.

Despite my suspicions to the contrary, the marriage of Yasini's second daughter had not been deliberately arranged in order to gain the advantage of cross-linkage in the network. The marriage was in fact arranged to avoid conflict between the two fathers when Yasini's daughter became pregnant by Tanda's son. Nevertheless it was Kabaya who, in the moot, encouraged the solution and got it accepted, whilst Ali had been encouraging Yasini's original claim for compensation. It was to Kabaya's advantage in the future and he was unlikely not to have foreseen that; certainly Ali foresaw the disadvantage to his influence in the further link between Yasini and Kabaya's section.

This, then, was the state of complexity to which the kinship network had developed after a little over twenty years, by the time of my field research. There were at that time three discernible clusters in the community, in each of which one "big man" was acknowledged to be the person of principal influence—Ali, Konga, and Kabaya. It is most important to appreciate, however, that these three clusters were not clearly defined, functioning segments of the whole. Linkages of kinship and active relations of reciprocal assistance and cooperation crossed the divisions and were maintained because of their usefulness to several men. As will be seen more clearly later in the analysis of detailed case materials, alignments and action-set recruitment depended on the context of the social action involved at any particular time. Recruitment was not seen by Ligomba residents (not even, usually, by the notables themselves) as limited to what I have distinguished heuristically as clusters. Kabaya as a notable was in a state of competition with each of the other two notables; but these, Ali and Konga, aided by a strong personal friendship, had been able to avoid serious conflict. Vis-à-vis each other they had the advantage that their clusters were not so closely inter-linked as each was with that of Kabaya, so that conflicts of interest and competition for influence were weaker.

In 1953, the Ligomba local community comprised the households of thirty-two men. Since about 1931 the record was as follows: fourteen men were original pioneers; twenty-five men settled there later as sponsored newcomers; eighteen men were originally resident bachelors. The total was fifty-seven men, with their households, of whom nineteen moved away to settle elsewhere; six died in Ligomba; thirty-two remained in Ligomba (of whom four were original pioneers, eleven had settled as sponsored newcomers, and seventeen were resident bachelors who had married).

A theoretical point of some importance must be mentioned at this stage. In the development of the Ligomba local community, as far as it has been possible to describe it, a number of dispute cases were in effect critical turning points. These were the disputes between Ali and Kindabi (over a share of migrant labour savings), between Kasoro and Yasini (over the alleged seduction of an unmarried girl), between Zadiki and Konga (over the alleged seduction of Zadiki's wife), between Konga and, successively, Kotoka, Kalenda, and Hasan (in connection with Konga's alleged authoritarianism), and between Bilali and Abram (over the alleged theft of Koranic papers). Although fortuitous in a sense, they may have been partly contrived; they were certainly made use of for ulterior purposes by interested parties. There was nothing unusual in Ali's claim for a generous gift when his young cousin, Kindabi's son, returned home from labour migration; nor was it unusual among Ndendeuli that dispute should occur in the matter. Yet the way in which the claim was pressed, and resisted, must have been affected by the already existing rivalry between the two men, and had it been in their mutual interest to suppress that rivalry they could have treated the matter differently and not made it a public issue. Similarly, the kin-neighbours of the two men must have been aware that their support of Ali was likely to intensify Kindabi's isolation, and his discomfiture in seeking influence. The dispute became a test of the relative strengths of the two competing men, a time for the men involved to declare their alignments. Its direct result was that Kindabi moved away from Ligomba, whilst Ali's growing influence and claim to be a "big man" was recognised.

The dispute between C_1, supported by Kasoro, and Yasini, supported by Ali, was in itself unexceptional: young men did attempt to seduce unmarried girls. It was not possible to determine how far C_1 and Kasoro on the one hand, and Ali, Yasini, and Saidi on the other, sought to make the matter a catalyst of the state of relations and alignments in that section of the community at that time. Yet that was its effect; a direct consequence was the departure of Kasoro and his three close kin-neighbours from Ligomba, and the further affirmation of Ali's leadership. Similarly, the dispute between Zadiki and Konga was not an unusual one. It is most doubtful if Zadiki engineered it, for he was by all accounts badly upset by the implications of his junior wife's behaviour. Nevertheless, he was not unwilling to confront his cousin, Konga, nor was the

latter disinclined to accept the challenge; whilst Ali took the opportunity to demonstrate his support of Konga. The effect, although not althogether inevitable, was to persuade Zadiki of the
brittleness of his relations with Konga and others, and of the value
(even necessity) of sponsoring and linking with newcomers who
would make him less dependent on Konga.

The disputes between Konga, on the one hand, and in succession, Kotoka, Kalenda, and Hasan, on the other hand, were at one
level the result of the unwillingness of these three men to accept
what they considered to be undue influence, overbalancing into authority, exercised by Konga. Their outcome "explained" those
men's departures from Ligomba. Probably only Kalenda, and perhaps not even he, was concerned in any competition with Konga
for the role of notable. None could muster sufficient support to
overcome Konga's influence; and Kotoka and Kalenda at least
were in danger of unreliable support and cooperation thereafter.
Konga accepted the challenges to his influence and was able in
each case to obtain sufficient support from his other kin-neighbours
to sustain his role among that cluster of men.

The case of the theft of Koranic papers from Bilali's house was,
of course, a serious matter for Ndendeuli Moslems, linked as it
apparently was with the suggestion of sorcery. The alleged thief
was, moreover, a man already unpopular in the community, and
one who, by his position in the network, could not successfully
recruit supporters whose own interests were simultaneously threatened. Yet Kabaya was able to take advantage of the situation, deliberately or not, to display his leadership and his stand for moral
values, especially in relation to his own section of the community,
but also on behalf of the community as a whole.

It would be going beyond the available evidence, and beyond the
bounds of common sense, to press sociological explanation too far.
Both fortuitousness and personal characteristics played a part in
these events. On the other hand, these disputes were not the only
ones to have occurred, but they were the ones most vividly remembered by the participants. These Ndendeuli perceived those
particular events as critical: I feel certain that they saw this at the
time and not only in retrospect, for the same perception was
sometimes apparent in cases I witnessed and recorded. Some of
those men actively used the disputes for their own ends in situations of already existing conflict that had to be tackled if possible
and resolved. After the disputes were settled, as overtly at least
they were, a number of relationships were changed, new possibili-

ties opened and others made difficult, and certain necessities were shown to be unavoidable.

Of course, every event of social interaction occurs within and "uses" existing relations and affects them in some degree. Established relations are confirmed or reaffirmed, or they are shown to be less reliable or to entail other commitments. Evolving relations may be further strengthened, or weakened, as men are compelled to take action and make choices. There is no status quo, no equilibrium, but a fluid, intricate process or set of processes kept in motion by the needs and demands and interests of the people. By the concatenation of particular needs and interests, expectations, ambitions, strengths, and weaknesses, certain events (not necessarily of intrinsically great importance) come to be critical. They permit, and often demand, the redefinition and reorientation of relations as well as the affirmation of others. The further development of the pattern of the network and the influence of particular men are affected. What remains problematical is the extent to which involved persons stimulate or engineer these crises and, when they occur, how far those persons make use of them through an awareness of their significance and potentiality. The sociologist can too easily make his actors mere puppets of structural logic, which is little better than the converse of ignoring the structural significance inherent in social events. No simple or single explanation is possible.

It seems to me that Ali took the opportunity of a direct clash with Kindabi since he considered that he could win—as indeed he did. Possibly Kindabi was over-optimistic, but he could scarcely evade the challenge. In the next case, Ali preferred (on his own evidence) that no direct conflict should occur between kin-neighbours within his cluster in the community; but, when that was unavoidable, he sought first to limit the conflict and settle the immediate issue, and secondly to make his own principal loyalties clear. In the third case, Zadiki was not necessarily in direct competition with his cousin, Konga, and seems not to have coveted Konga's status as a notable. A cool assessment of the support he was likely to obtain in the event might perhaps have deterred him from pressing the allegation against Konga's son as strongly as he did. My knowledge of Zadiki causes me to conclude that he was much influenced by emotional factors: fragile marital relations with a favoured, unreliable, junior wife, and personal animosity between him and his cousin.[15] Nevertheless, as a result of the dispute

[15] Later developments in the relations between these two men are described in Case 5, page 167 ff.

however disagreeable it may have been for him, Zadiki at least
knew more clearly what his situation was; to an undefinable extent he may have sought to discover this by the way in which he
conducted the whole matter. He was "experimenting" and "testing" his status in the community's network of social relations. As
will be shown more fully later, Ndendeuli did "experiment" in this
way, though not always or primarily by deliberate choice, when
some important interest was at stake. It was much more common
for men to experiment in the context of the recruitment of work-
parties where the risks were smaller. Thus a man sought to discover whether a particular neighbour would join his work-party
if he were invited, and whether he would find it possible to reciprocate in return without raising intransigent problems of competing obligations. He sought to discover if that neighbour would
show preference to him if another neighbour held a work-party
on the same day.[16] A dispute case afforded a man a similar opportunity to test the strength of the reliance he could put on his kin-
neighbours. In the kind of fluid, ill-defined processes that make the
reality of a social network, men have a need to know in which
direction (that is, with what persons) they can expect to continue
or to develop useful cooperation and inter-dependence, and how
far they can go.

Konga's conflicts with Kotoka, Kalenda, and Hasan were in part
at least an attack on his growing leadership role—legitimate, in a
way, since Konga sought to play that role too strongly by Ndendeuli standards, but attacks which he could not, and no doubt did
not wish to, evade. He was the winner in effect since his acceptance as a notable continued among those kin-neighbours prepared
to support him. He lost the possible support and cooperation of
certain associates, but some had in any case proved rather unreliable in past circumstances.

These incidents of conflict were, then, partly political in nature,
although they also were effective in determining who cooperated
with whom in economic and other activities. Bailey has suggested
that there are two kinds of political conflict process: confrontation
and encounter. "Confrontations are messages about one's own
strength . . . assertions and claims to deter one's opponents."
They may end in withdrawal from overt conflict, but communication will have been achieved and, possibly some alteration in or
consolidation of statuses and relationships. They may, however,
develop into encounters or contests ending in "a public statement

[16] See Chapter Six, especially page 212.

of the relative strength of the two contestants" (Bailey 1968:283). They are likely, though Bailey does not emphasise the point, to end also in some more practical gains and losses involving material interests. The incidents in Ligomba's history were encounters, for although vital communications were exchanged, neither side withdrew until the contest was joined and concluded in, more or less, victory or defeat. It is certain, nevertheless, that during those years there must have been many confrontations that did not end in encounter as positions were taken up and strengths, weaknesses, and possibilities were probed and assessed. These cases were not recorded, partly because I was not looking for them. Yet for my informants, it seems fair to say, the actual encounters ending in victory or defeat were more memorable and considered more significant. Perhaps this was because of their more dramatic character; perhaps also because in an encounter there was, usually, a definite result. It would seem probable (in view of evidence given in subsequent chapters) that, at least in the Ligomba circumstances, ultimately confrontations culminated in encounters as one party at least put the matter to the acid test.

THE CHANGING RANGE OF NEIGHBOURLY COOPERATION

One aim of this account is to demonstrate that the concept of social network is not necessarily, or most valuably, a static one applying to unchanging structures. A network is more like a complex set of interacting vectors in a constant process of change. This can be further illustrated by an examination of the evolution of the range of cooperation over the years in Ligomba. This analysis relates to two men, Ali and Konga.

It was obviously quite impossible to rely on the memories of either man to provide lists of their neighbours who had on specific occasions in the past given them assistance and support in collective action. There were likely to be several occasions each year, and many of them (agricultural work-parties) were seasonally repetitive and therefore blurred in retrospect. As an admitted second best, therefore, I selected three particular years which for good reason were clearly defined in the men's minds, and asked them to list those neighbours who could reasonably have been expected to participate in their work-parties for dry season clearing of woodland and making new fields. Such a work party was almost never convened on the same day as that of another neighbour, for there was usually plenty of time in which to space out parties during the season. Thus any neighbour who wished to participate, to render assistance, and to gain reciprocal rights could readily do so. But, although all the men in the community could participate, only those actually did so who had, or wished to develop, regular cooperation with the convener of the work-party. Others might not wish or could not afford to undertake further commitments: neither would they have been invited to participate unless the convener wished to commit himself to the reciprocal obligation to return the labour and goodwill. In short, participants in a dry season work-party were those neighbours with whom a man had fairly reliable and regular relations of mutual assistance at a particular time.

FIGURE 10: The Changing Range of Neighbourly Cooperation.

Expectations of participation in agricultural work-parties in Ligomba.

(A) *ALI* C_7

1. In the first year of settlement in Ligomba *

$B_4, B_{10}, B_{11}, C_{17}, C_{19}, B_{12}, C_{21}$ *7 neighbours*

2. About 1939

$B_1, C_2, B_3, B_5, C_9, C_{17}, C_{18}, C_{19}, C_{20}$ *9 neighbours*

    (In the interval:

             B_4, B_{10}, B_{11} died

      $B_1, C_2, B_3, B_5, \quad C_9$ were newcomers

                    C_{18} was a new household head

             B_{12}, C_{21} were still resident, but non-cooperating †)

3. About 1948

$D_2, C_6, D_4, D_5, D_6, D_7, C_9, C_{17}, C_{18}, C_{19}$ *10 neighbours*

    (In the interval:

                  B_5 died

          $B_1, C_2, \quad B_3$ left Ligomba

       $D_2, C_6, D_4, D_5, \quad D_7$ were newcomers

                  D_6 was a new household head

                  C_{20} was still resident, but non-cooperating)

4. 1953 (time of field research)

$D_1, D_2, C_6, D_3, D_4, D_5, D_6, D_7, D_8, C_9, D_9, C_{17}$ *12 neighbours*

    (In the interval:

                  C_{18} left Ligomba

                    D_1 was a newcomer

         $D_3, D_8, \quad D_9$ were new household heads

                  C_{19} was still resident, but non-cooperating)

FIGURE 10 (*continued*)

1953–4: actual composition of work-parties ‡
i. Dry season, 1953—D1, D2, C6, D4, D5, D6, D7,
                                   C9, D9, C17   *10 neighbours*
ii. Early wet season, 1953–1954—D1, C6, D4, D5,
                                      D6, C9, D3   *7 neighbours*

(B) *KONGA C17*
1. In the first year of settlement in Ligomba *
B4, C7, B10, B11, C19, C21, B13, C24, B14, B15, B12   *11 neighbours*
2. About 1939
B3, C7, C9, C14, C15, C16, C18, C19, C20, B12,
                            C21, B13, C24   *13 neighbours*
   (In the interval:
                B4, B10, B11 died
      C14, C15, C9, C16, C20 were newcomers
                      C18 was a new household head
             B14, B15 were still resident, but non-cooperating †)
3. About 1948
C6, C7, C13, C15, D14, C18, C19, D16, D17, C20,
                            C21, C22   *12 neighbours*
   (In the interval:
                      B12 died
      B3, C14, C16, B13, C24 left Ligomba
             C6, C13 were newcomers
         D14, D16, D17 were new household heads
             C9 was still resident, but non-cooperating)
4. 1953 (time of field research)
C7, C13, C15, D14, D15, D16, D17, D19, C19, C21,
                            D20, D21, D23   *13 neighbours*
   (In the interval:
                C20 died
             C18, C22 left Ligomba
             D21, D23 were newcomers
         D15, D19, D20 were new household heads
             C6 was still resident, but non-cooperating)
1953–4: actual composition of work-parties ‡
i. Dry season, 1953—C7, C13, D15, D16, D17, D19,
                            C19, C21, D20, D21, D23   *11 neighbours*
ii. Early wet season, 1953–4—C13, D14, D15, D16,
                            D17, D19, C19, C21, D20   *9 neighbours*

FIGURE 10 (*continued*)

(C) *Analysis of the changing range of cooperation*

	Ali	Konga
Total number of neighbours with whom cooperation was expected		
at some time in the period	24	29
in 1953	12	13
Number of neighbours with whom cooperation was continuous		
through the whole period	1	3
since at least 1939	1	1
since at least 1948	5	4
During the period, new cooperation began with		
newcomers to Ligomba	11	10
newly married residents	5	7
By 1953, of neighbours who had formerly cooperated at some time during the period of 22 years		
number who had died	4	5
number who had left Ligomba	4	7
number who were still resident	4	4
Number of neighbours in Ligomba in c. 1931		14
Number of neighbours in Ligomba in 1953		32
Number of men resident in Ligomba at some time during the period, including those in 1953		57

(NOTE: By "neighbour" is meant the head of a household resident in the community.)

* Ali and Konga, like other informants, stated in generalization that all pioneers participated in each other's work-parties. But they said that they neither expected nor obtained the labour of all their pioneer-neighbours. Those listed here were said to have been relied upon.

† "Non-cooperating" does not mean hostility necessarily between the men concerned. It means that they considered themselves no longer able to continue their earlier commitment to reciprocate assistance.

‡ Work-parties were usually rather smaller in the early wet season when many parties had to be fitted into the restricted period for cultivation. Expectations of assistance were therefore more limited, and it was not considered unfriendly if a man could not join a man's party at that time, although it might have been so construed if a neighbour failed to join a dry season work-party.

The results of this enquiry for Ali and Konga are given in Figure 10. They obviously cannot be assumed to have any fine accuracy, for both defective memory and retrospective reconstruction are likely to have interfered. On the other hand, I do not rate possible inaccuracies too high since these data fit quite well with my other information from Ligomba. In any case, they are valuable at a general level, even though they do not reveal the whole developmental process. No doubt some changes occurred during the intervals between the arbitrary years taken for the enquiry.

It is clear from the data that expectations of neighbourly cooperation changed a good deal during the period of a little over twenty years. Neighbours died or moved away to other communities, newcomers settled in Ligomba, and young bachelors married and established new households. Thus some earlier possibilities of cooperation were closed and new ones became available. New patterns of cooperation developed, and these it must be remembered were not limited only to participation in agricultural work-parties.

For Konga, there were three men who remained within his range of regular cooperation during the whole period: his brother Mitedi, his first cousin Sedi, and his second cousin Ali. For Ali the only man permanently in regular cooperation was Konga, although his first cousin, Yasini, came into that category after his arrival in Ligomba about two years after its founding. With the special exception of the link between Ali and Konga themselves, these were cases of close kinship, within the same generation, unaffected by rivalry or conflicting interests. Konga and Mitedi had almost the same range of kin-neighbours over the years, and therefore were virtually compelled to remain in close cooperation. Failure to do so would probably have meant that one of them (presumably Mitedi, being the less influential) would have had to leave the community to escape intolerable conflict. This had not occurred, mainly because Mitedi had remained content to follow Konga's lead. In the case of Konga and Sedi, those two first cousins had been able to retain close association of great value to each other. Sedi had shown no ambition to become a "big man", he had continued to tolerate Konga's achievement in that role, and had followed and taken advantage of Konga's leadership and ability. Much the same had been true in the persisting cooperation between Ali and Yasini. Latterly, Yasini acquired additional significance because of his structural position between Ali and the competing notable, Kabaya. He became an object of their competition for influence, as Work-Party Case 1 demonstrated (pp. 203–206). Thus Ali had become especially concerned to maintain the regular cooperation with Yasini.

The persisting cooperation between Ali and Konga was more unusual and was organisationally significant. Although not rare, it was comparatively uncommon for second cousins to remain actively cooperative into their late imddle age, for each tended to develop and depend on his own particular range of kinsmen in divergence from the other. This continuity was rather more remarkable since both men had been notables for a decade or more. In practice, as already noted, the spheres of influence of each man had been fairly distinct following the early enterprise of Ali's father in Ligomba. Competition between them, therefore, had been structurally minimised. They themselves had been the chief link between the two sections of the network and had been able to control conflicts. In part their continuous relationship rested on close personal friendship and its accompanying readiness to toleration. This was a non-structural feature of importance, though its strength had not been too severely tested because of the men's structural separation. This relationship later became disadvantageous to the third notable, Kabaya, with whom both men were inter-connected in competitive relations, even to the point where they made common alliance against him. It seems reasonable to conclude, by contrast, that Kabaya could not have had a close, friendly association with either Ali or Konga because he was put into structural opposition to them.

Even Ali and Konga no longer expected to maintain comprehensive cooperation with each other. That had become impossible as the range of commitments of each had diverged. Both men recognised this equably. For instance, at that hectic time of year in the early rainy season, when everyone was preoccupied with planting his fields as speedily as possible in order to gain full advantage of the rains, neither man expected to participate in the other's work-party. Each had more pressing obligations to closer kin-neighbours. But in the dry season, when there was little pressure on time and effort, the two old friends had continued to join each other's clearing parties. In 1953 on this occasion, when Konga appeared at Ali's work-party, there was good-natured joking about old men looking for beer and who would join anyone's party to obtain it (that is, the beer provided at the end of the work). Konga took this with good humour; but he pointed out that, "I have always helped my brother, Ali. Is it not right to come and work for your brother? If I did not do so there would be no brotherhood, nor kinship, and he would not want to help me another time".

In contrast to that sort of persisting relationship, the data in Figure 10 show that some neighbours who had once been expected to cooperate were later not expected to do so any longer, although they continued to be neighbours within the community. This was not necessarily a consequence of hostile relations. Four cases are shown for each man, and some others also occurred that are not revealed by the arbitrary dates used for the collection of the data. This was a quite normal result of the development and growth of a local community: at one time it was convenient and mutually valuable for two neighbours to cooperate, but later it became increasingly difficult and perhaps quite impossible to continue the working relationship as each man acquired commitments of greater priority with other, newer neighbours. Thus in the early years it was advantageous for Ali and Sedi (C21) to reciprocate assistance; later it became less so, and eventually to give assistance to each other would have interfered too severely with the newer commitments each had taken on. The two men had remained on friendly enough terms as neighbours but without any longer recognising particular obligation to each other. Much the same was true in the case of discontinued cooperation between Konga and Saidi.

In this connection, the case of Ali and Mitedi (younger brother of Konga) is particularly significant. These two men, according to the account of them both, had fairly regularly given each other assistance and support for many years, but this they no longer did at the time of my 1953 enquiry. Ali continued to cooperate with one brother, Konga, but not with the other, Mitedi. As Ali explained, Mitedi was scarcely considered to be his kinsman any more. In relating his genealogical knowledge to me, he had stopped at Konga, saying that Konga could tell me the rest. "The kin of Konga are not my kin," he explained—not even Konga's own brother. In this case, too, there was no hostility between the two formerly cooperating neighbours—formerly acknowledged kinsmen—merely the disappearance of positive cooperation. The personal friendship with Konga, and the advantages he offered as a notable to Ali, did not apply to the younger brother.

The reverse kind of process might occur when two neighbours developed cooperation where it had not formerly been the practice. This was so between Yasini and Kabaya; it was initiated by the new affinal links through the marriage of their children. But this brought Yasini into new cooperation with Bilali and others, who were kin-neighbours of Kabaya. In itself this was no more than the creation and operation of new affinal ties; yet it introduced new features into the pattern of the evolving kinship network—new lines, direct and indirect, along which inter-action could develop. It created new possibilities, and it raised threats to the continuation of already existing relationships, requiring their modification or even abandonment. For example, Yasini's opportunity and desire to cooperate with and support Kabaya and Kabaya's close kin-neighbours produced inevitable conflicts of interests when at the same time he wished to continue cooperation with Ali, and with Saidi and others. Occasions arose (some of which are described later) when kin-neighbours on Kabaya's side wished to hold a work-party at the same time as, say, Ali or Saidi. Formerly two such men had been able to operate simultaneous work-parties be-cause their respective ranges of kin-neighbours had not overlapped —that is, they were not calling on the labour of the same neigh-bours. This was no longer the case, so that Yasini (and his son and two nephews also) had to be much more active in timetabling organisation in order to avoid the invidious conflict. Even so, they were sometimes compelled to make difficult choices, for it was usually impossible for them to work in both parties on the same day. Similar conflict could, and did, arise when action-sets were recruited in dispute cases between kin-neighbours on either side of Yasini.

The precise ways in which the kinship network was utilised and activated by the co-neighbours involved in it was the product of multiple choices made by them and their efforts to render compati-ble the obligations to their neighbours with whom at any one time cooperation and reciprocal assistance obtained. The problems of seeking compatibility, or minimising the conflict of interests and obligations, is examined in some detail in Chapter Six, in the ac-count of agricultural work-party organization. Before that, how-ever, it will be shown that the neighbours whom a man could recruit for his assistance were not a fixed set even within the short period, let alone over a period of years. Whom among a man's neighbours he could recruit depended very much on the circum-stances at the time: This is demonstrated in Chapter Five by an examination of some successive dispute cases that occurred during 1953.

This incomplete account of the development of Ligomba local

community through two decades is primarily intended to suggest, if not adequately document, the fluid changing patterns of cooperation and interaction, of conflict and competition, which comprised the social process within the kinship network. Each man attempted within the scope of his ability and perception to gain what advantage he could out of the available opportunities for cooperation, and was limited by the possibility of making congruent those commitments to his neighbours with whom he sought reciprocity. Such congruence was achieved in actual practice partly by reasoned choice and partly by the severely practical tests of feasibility that were effectively imposed as situations arose in terms of the needs for action-sets for collective action of various kinds.

LIGOMBA IN 1953

Ecology

This local community was established, in about 1931, in a broad and shallow valley through which flowed a stream said to be perennial. Its flow was reduced more or less to a trickle by the end of the dry season, but it provided a permanent supply of water for domestic purposes in what was, for at least two or three months of the year, an arid country. This seems to have been a major factor in the choice of settlement area by the original pioneers. As far as could be discovered, neither the pioneers nor any other Ndendeuli had knowledge of any previous inhabitants of the area. It is extremely unlikely that there had been any since well before the Ngoni conquest in the middle of the nineteenth century, for the autochthonous people had lived at least forty miles to the west. At the time of settlement, the Ligomba pioneers were in the vanguard of a general drift of the Ndendeuli eastwards.[17]

The community was initially settled in dispersed hamlets in the upper, south-western part of the valley. By 1953 almost all the cultivable land had been exhausted, in the opinion of the people themselves, and nearly all the hamlets had been shifted away. Some had disappeared as people left the community; others had been moved down the valley to new sites more convenient to still untouched woodland on cultivable land. Newcomers had tended to settle in the lower valley. Thus the geographical focus of settlement and cultivation had shifted some three miles north-eastwards, although one or two earlier households remained within the original

[17] See page 33.

area, taking up land left uncleared by those who had moved away; these households had come to form the southern edge of the settled area.

To the north of this broad valley was a low wide ridge of gravelly soil and thin woodland considered by the people to be useless for cultivation. Beyond the ridge and also on the southern, undulating edge of the valley, untouched woodland stood on acceptable soils; but both areas were said to be too distant from the permanent water supply to make them attractive for settlement or for clearing and cultivation from hamlets sited tolerably near the stream. Like many shifting agriculturalists, the Ndendeuli disliked to have their arable fields far from their houses; a distance much more than a mile between house and field was considered unacceptable.[18] Thus not only were the flanks of past and present settlement considered unattractive by these standards, but there was limited opportunity for further expansion downstream where the valley narrowed through broken, infertile country for a mile or two. By 1953 there was therefore the prospect of a shortage of convenient, cultivable woodland for new fields, as the people of Ligomba assessed the situation. This assessment was, of course, relative to the free abundance of woodland in other parts of the country that were open to settlement. Land had not at that time yet become scarce enough to inhibit cultivation, nor had there been any disputes over access to woodland. In general, households continued to extend their clearing outwards; but some of them had reached the stage of being unable to clear and cultivate in the vicinity of the hamlet, and were working in blocks beyond a neighbouring hamlet. People complained that cultivation had become less easy and less attractive. It was foreseen that conditions would become positively unattractive. It was said that potential newcomers had already been discouraged from joining the community because of these poor prospects: certainly both Salimi (D1) and Kabaya had failed to persuade kinsmen to move to Ligomba when, for good reasons, each wished to augment his kin-neighbours in the community.

It is possible that the community had reached the end of its expansion. The period from 1950 (when the last newcomers joined) to 1953 was probably the longest in which no newcomers had settled since the community had been founded. At least one or two men had talked of shifting elsewhere, though none at that time had made any definite plans as far as I knew.

[18] See page 45.

The people themselves were aware of this developing situation, and this must have affected community life. It is difficult to assess its significance, if only because I did not actively investigate the matter at the time.[19] It is possible—and I cannot now put it more strongly—that awareness of the prospect of a shortage of land had increased the effort to minimise conflict in order that threats to continued unity should not increase. If households had to shift in the fairly near (though not immediate) future, some dissatisfied men might decide to leave at any time—that is, men would have had less reason to tolerate conflict, unpleasantness, and difficulties in obtaining adequate cooperation. Older men generally had less desire to move, and less potential advantage; and a general exodus would almost certainly have meant the loss to them of some of their current, valuable kin-neighbours. No Ndendeuli would have expected the whole community to shift en bloc to another area: it was unlikely to happen. More probably, households would form into small clusters, each separately joining other already existing communities or perhaps becoming the nucleus of a new pioneering enterprise. Thus the kinship network of Ligomba would be shattered. One line of policy in the circumstances might then have been to delay any trends towards dissolution of the existing community by the prevention or limitation of destructive conflicts. Thus men would have been prepared to exercise special toleration and to damp down conflicts with particular care. They might well have attempted to deter more strongly than usual any neighbour who decided to move away. All this, therefore, might go some way to explain the marked efforts at containing conflict and reaching compromise settlements of disputes, as described in the following chapters.

If this had been the case, however, surely the men concerned would have expressed such notions and necessities during the course of moots and at other times. There would probably have been an especial emphasis on the need for continued unity. My field notes do not show this to have been the case; neither is there hard evidence that moots and other discussions were essentially different from those recorded in other Ndendeuli local communities. Moreover, on reflection I consider that, had the ecological pressures been keenly felt at the time, household heads would probably have begun to separate into something like small cliques, preparatory to

[19] I am grateful to Dr. Richard Werbner who pointed out to me, after a seminar discussion in 1966, the need to consider the possible effects of ecological pressures on social processes in Ligomba.

the eventual break-up of the community.[20] There was no firm sign
of this either. In summary, my conclusion is that whilst the life
span of the Ligomba local community was foreseeably coming to
an end, within the context of Ndendeuli shifting cultivation, this
fact had not at that time come seriously to affect men's attitudes
and behaviour, or their relations with one another. They had not
yet begun to take serious and positive account of the trend. Ligomba
was not an actively decaying community.

The Kinship Network

In 1953 there were thirty-two households grouped into thirteen hamlets scattered irregularly, but seldom more than about
half a mile from the stream. These hamlets contained a population
of 143 people.

As the master geneaology (Fig. 5) shows, all the household
heads (and by extension, all members of their households) could
be presented in a single, extended network without a break in acknowledged kinship links. That this was so was the logical result
of the processes of the creation and growth of the community
working through the idiom of kinship. To reiterate: all the original
pioneers were directly related to the "owner of the land" who led
the initial settlement, and thereafter all newcomers were sponsored
by kinsmen who already resided in the community. The implications of this fact comprise a most crucial feature of my analysis of
social action and social processes.

I must emphasize quite clearly that this genealogical diagram
or model is the *anthropologist's construct*. It has been compiled by
synthesising all the pieces of kinship information remembered by
Ligomba men and women, and given to me largely in response to
direct questioning. *It can, unless treated with due caution, produce
a serious distortion of the reality it purports to illustrate and explain.*

In the first place, by omitting kinsfolk who live elsewhere, it
appears to over-emphasise intra-community linkages at the expense
of the total fields of acknowledged, operative kinship. Each household head had a majority of kinsmen living elsewhere, including

[20] I obtained no first-hand evidence on the process of the break-up of a
"normal" local community; but Ndendeuli accounts suggested that this
was the kind of thing that occurred. The factional segmentation of the
Namabeya community (described in Chap. Eight) was certainly a rare
way for a community to break up. The clusters, typical of any established
local community, did not usually provide the basis for segmental fission.
See page 253 f.

some of his genealogically closer relatives and also those (not necessarily the same ones) with whom he maintained close association. It is impossibly unwieldy to give comprehensive genealogies for each household head, and I can only assert this dogmatically. Of course, to a considerable extent and for many social purposes, members of a local community faced inwards, as it were, in relation to one another: this the diagram can indicate, together with the particular nature and variety of formal links involved. That is a raison d'être of the diagram. Nevertheless it presents merely the inter-linkages of these thirty-two men who happened to be co-neighbours in Ligomba. No implication of stability or permanence should be read into this genealogy; nor should it be assumed that the particular set of kinship linkages concerned are in any inherent way of patterned significance for Ndendeuli society.

Secondly, although I have sought to show the more significant kinship linkages—or rather, the ones stressed by the men themselves—some neighbours were linked by other kinship paths that could be important in some context. That is, the diagram tends to be over-simplified, though not dangerously so, I think.

Thirdly, an anthropological model such as this can distort by the very way in which it is constructed and oriented by the symbols and lines and their physical juxtaposition on paper. To make my point clear: this genealogical diagram was finally constructed by starting at Nchinda (B11) (the pioneer leader) and working outwards from him to include all the others. This may seem unduly to emphasise some linkages and underemphasise others. Nchinda was no longer the focus, or rather not the only focus, in Ligomba. To be frank, it proved no simple task of draughtsmanship to accommodate all Ligomba men in one straightforward diagram because of the complexity of the inter-linkages, and yet it was sociologically imperative to achieve this in the light of the empirical facts. There are other and no less valid ways of making the representation that would have provided a quite different visual impact. For example, as the diagram is constructed, the linkage between C9 and C13 may seem to be more distant than it was, or more distant than that between C9 and C11. Spatially the diagram suggests this, though genealogically it is not correct. Similarly, some second cousins are close together, and some widely separated, but this is no necessary reflection of actual relationships but merely diagrammatic convenience. It has been my constant endeavour not to be improperly influenced by the purely spatial relationships of the diagram itself in making my analysis. Nevertheless, the point needs to be made explicitly in order to warn readers of the possible misconception inherent in the set form of the model to which constant reference is made in these chapters.

Fourthly, Ligomba residents themselves had no such working model of their community and its kinship network. None could, nor would have wished to, describe all the linkages in the network. They did not work with anything so definite and coherent as a model in their own minds. They would have agreed, however, that neighbours were inter-connected in various ways, and that such linkages afforded both possibilities and limitations for social action. I am here providing a bird's-eye view of what the participants saw only partially and, very largely, each from his own standpoint.

From this overall genealogy it can be seen *prima facie* that few men had more than a dozen kin-neighbours, and none had less than two. That is the empirical range, and with one notable exception there is fairly even distribution through the range which precludes any attempt to speak of an average number of kin-neighbours.[21] The exception concerns the cluster of nine men, C_{15}, C_{17}, C_{19}, and their sons, each of whom had more than a dozen kin-neighbours—though the range was not coincident for all of them. These men, as it happens, were agnates, descendants of the pioneer leader and his brother. A number of points must be made immediately on this matter in order to prevent misapprehension later.

In an Ndendeuli local community the pioneer leader or "owner of the land" was not necessarily associated with several or many of his agnates. For instance, in Namabeya the only local agnate of the "owner of the land" was his son though he had other agnates resident elsewhere. A great deal depended on the composition of the set of pioneers, the kinds of kinsmen accompanying the leader. In logical conformity with the absence of lineal emphasis, there seems to have been no particular pattern about this, either in fact or intent. The composition of the original set arose out of the context of cognatic and affinal kinship at the time. There was no reason, thereafter, for an Ndendeuli to give preference to particular kinds of kinsmen when sponsoring newcomers. Accidents of births and deaths were significant: thus Konga (C_{17}) not only had four adult sons but all chose to live with him after marriage. On the other hand, it was common enough to be characteristic that the nearer kin of the first "owner of the land" did have relatively large numbers of kin-neighbours, for they moved into a kinship network

[21] The same general conclusion can be drawn for the Namabeya local community; see Figure 4, following p. 74.

that originated solely in its focus on that person. He was most likely to have had more kinsmen than any other member of the pioneer set, and thus started with some advantage.

In Ligomba, as in any other local community, there were other residents with a relatively large number of kin-neighbours—for example, Ali (C7), Yasini (C9), and Sedi (C21). It has already been shown how Ali and his father deliberately fostered that number. Thus the ability in a developed community to call on many kin-neighbours for assistance and support was not at all limited to the surviving close kin of the original leader. Nor, therefore, was the potential of influence and leadership limited to them, either in practice or ideal. In Ligomba, Konga (C17) had in fact made use of his opportunities, but his younger brother and patrilateral cousin had not.

This particular cluster of agnates in Ligomba did not exhaust the total of acknowledged patrikin of these men. Konga's younger brother, C18, had formerly lived there, but he left in 1951. A younger brother of Zadiki (C15) had never lived there since marriage, and there were a first cousin and several second cousins elsewhere who had never been Ligomba residents. These patrikin were scattered widely, and neither the whole nor the particular cluster in Ligomba in any sense comprised a corporate group by acting together, appearing as a separate, identifiable unit, or controlling common property and interests. On an individual basis, each of these men invariably associated with his local cognates and affines in collective social action. Each was subject to the demands from his other kin-neighbours who, of course, sometimes pulled in different directions in respect of alliances and mutual assistance. These agnates, and indeed any other genealogically defined cluster of neighbours, did not necessarily have their houses and fields close together. They did not form residential sub-groups within the community. Most importantly, neither this agnatic cluster nor any other provided in effect or ideal any kind of kinship core for the community. Other residents did not perceive and identify their membership or status by reference to any single focus. Only in the very first years of settlement could this have been the case, before the diversifying range of newcomers began to expand the network.

In short, this agnatic cluster in Ligomba enjoyed no particular privilege, and it had neither structural nor organisational significance—just as the "owner of the land" was neither headman nor necessarily leader in a mature local community. Were all this otherwise, it would imply an emphasis on agnation that the Ndendeuli did not express nor demonstrate in action. It would, in fact, ignore what is quite crucial to the sociology of the Ndendeuli: the moral and practical equality of different kinds of kinship links and the virtual disregard of categories of patrilineal, matrilineal, and affinal. It would ignore also the essential character of the inter-locking kinship network, both through directly acknowledged kinship and sequences of indirect linkages.

The Ndendeuli would no doubt have been puzzled by my insistence in this matter, for it was self-evident to them, if they considered it at all. Ligomba people saw no cluster of agnates, for to do that they would have had to use notions of lineal descent and lineal categories. This they most certainly did not; and they were scornful of those peoples they knew of, such as the patrilineal Ngoni and matrilineal Yao, who did impose artificial limits (as it seemed to them) on the range of social relationships.

My insistence on this largely negative point arises because of the emphasis in the history of social anthropology—especially in Africanist studies—on unilineal criteria of kinship ascription and in the recruitment of groups. As a result of this emphasis many anthropologists appear to find the greatest difficulty in thinking and working in non-unilineal terms when that is required, although most of them live in a non-unilineal world. Unilineal criteria have been shown to be crucial in many societies described by social anthropologists, even in local groups wherein diverse cognatic and affinal relationships are numerous. But Ndendeuli kinship was most emphatically non-unilineal in character as it provided linkages on which to base, or through which to explain, working social relationships and channels for social action. The sociological processes among Ndendeuli were not directly comparable with, for example, the well-known case of the Nuer in southern Sudan. There, as Evans-Pritchard has described, in territorial section, village, and camp, the people recognised and stressed the primacy of agnatic kinship, and also of particular patrilineages that he designated "aristocratic". The local members of an aristocratic lineage provided both the genealogical core and the operational focus of collective action in a residential or territorial unit. So dominant was the agnatic ethic that matrilateral kin and "sisters' sons" were gradually absorbed into the patrilineage with which they were associated, and their links eventually came to be regarded as agnatic.[22] This appears to have been a quite logical process among the Nuer, for to them an agnatic link was more significant, practically, mor-

[22] Evans-Pritchard 1951: 16 ff. and 151. It is possible, however, that Evans-Pritchard unduly emphasised the agnatic factor in his analysis.

ally, and emotionally, than any other tie. Thus unity of social action was both expressed and systematised through lineal categories and agnatic incorporation. Clearly this was not the case among the Ndendeuli: there was no point in transforming one kind of kinship into another, for there was nothing to be gained. A mother's brother's son, father's sister's son, and wife's brother were "as good as" a father's brother's son in respect of rights, obligations, and reliability of expectation. They were "equivalent" to each other in social action. The dominant characteristics of Ndendeuli social organisation were the ego-centred sets of kinsmen and their complex involvement in networks.

The people of Ligomba were not a group of kinsfolk, and they did not claim to be such. They were, and saw themselves as, a group of neighbours amongst whom the fact of living near together as neighbours was the prime consideration. Each man had a random cluster of his own kinsmen among his neighbours, and some of the others were positively acknowledged and treated as kin of his kinsmen. But a man did not perceive the sequences of kinship linkages that logically connected him and all of his neighbours in what the sociologist calls a network. Of course, men did recognise and take advantage of some of the indirect linkages, when seeking wider cooperation, or alliance and support towards achieving some aim in social action, as subsequent case materials demonstrate. With their common interests as neighbours, engaging in more or less everyday, face-to-face interaction, men did not remain oblivious to the local kinship connections of their own kin-neighbours; but this awareness was limited.

For example, Ali (C7) did not regard D10 or D13 as a kinsman; but he was aware that each was a son-in-law of his own first cousin, Yasini (C9). Their hamlets were not far from his, and he saw them frequently. He participated with both of them in work-parties in Yasini's fields and in other action-sets convened by Yasini. The latter's support of his son-in-law in some situation might well bring in Ali on his side. But Ali scarcely knew nor, I think, cared about the exact genealogical position of either man. There was no especial reason why he should. By his experience in Ligomba he knew that one son-in-law, D13, and his father were closely associated with Zadiki (C15), and that the other, D10, and his father were closely connected with Bilali (C12). When pressed by me he was able to explain the former but not the latter; but obviously he regarded such details as irrelevant to himself.

That is a fairly straightforward case. It was not so between, say

D2 and D21 or between C6 and C12. A glance at the Ligomba
genealogy shows that those inter-linkages were highly indirect.[23]
For obvious reasons, neither of these pairs of neighbours could or
even wished to trace the connection. However, D2 was able to
explain that D21 tended to be associated with such neighbours as
C17, C19, C21, and D23 in community affairs. Saidi (C6) explicitly
denied any connection at all with Bilali (C12), insisting that they
were merely unrelated neighbours. I suggested to him that some
linkage must exist: this was after both men had been members of
an action-set convened by Yasini (C9). Saidi admitted to his own
participation on the valid grounds of supporting his own first
cousin, Ali, whom he knew to be first cousin of Yasini. I pointed
out that Bilali was similarly linked with Yasini, and thus with
Saidi himself; but he was quite impatient with my argument, which
appeared to him beside the mark. In practice the logic of the network, and men's choices within it, brought neighbours into alliance
or opposition without a detailed comprehension of it.

In making this point I do not mean to suggest that Ndendeuli
had no appreciation of the structure and dynamics of their own
community. They knew well that action-sets ("the people of so-
and-so") were composed of neighbours recruited overtly by kinship criteria; but beyond the linkages directly concerning themselves they were largely uninterested in precise details. Thus when
occasionally Saidi and Bilali did come together in collective action,
they were recruited to the action-set through the activation of
quite different sequences. There was no need for either man to
know the other's sequence or to know that they were therefore
sequentially linked. No wonder, then, that Saidi dismissed my
over-logical argument as "the nonsense of Europeans". The argument was no doubt "nonsense" for his particular, practical purposes; but it is not nonsensical for the structural analysis of the
processes of social relations and social action in an Ndendeuli community.

In this chapter I have attempted to describe and show the significance of certain past events, and to introduce some of the analytical

---

[23] There are a number of different sequences of kinship links by which
the connections could be traced between these men in fact. But, for
example, by one sequence D21 was linked to D2 as the latter's mother's
mother's father's sister's son's wife's brother's son's daughter's husband!
Cf. the master genealogy, Figure 5, *facing* p. 82.

features that are developed in the following chapters. In the first place, I have given some outline of the background to and history of the growth of the kinship network in the local community as it operated in early 1953. I have drawn attention to some of the reasons for the existence of certain patterns of cooperation, and for the existence of certain tensions, conflicts, areas of competition and of alliance, which in 1953 significantly affected events, the way in which they were treated, and their consequences for the participants. It is assumed in all this that it is not possible adequately to understand the nature of social action at a particular time without knowledge (however imperfect) of what had gone before.

Secondly, I have tried to show how *all* the co-neighbours of the local community had inevitably become inter-linked within a single, operational network of some complexity. The idiom of inter-linkage, and the idiom in which rights and obligations between particular persons were expressed, was kinship. This close kinship network was the result of the territorial definition of the community, the mode of recruitment by the sponsorship of kinsmen, the overt use of kinship ties in particular forms of co-operation and social control, and continuous interaction in all kinds of face-to-face activities. Within this framework of kinship there was an absence of unilineal concepts and of corporate kin groups. The character of kinship was inherently non-lineal, both in idea and in action. Distinctions between cognatic and affinal kin were comparatively unimportant in terms of the definition of rights and obligations, loyalties, and conflicts.

Thirdly, I have introduced the notion of the necessity of the compatibility of the range of obligations and interests within each man's set of active relations with certain neighbours—those relations being based on, or at least expressed in, direct and acknowledged kinship links. This is a logical consequence of the non-lineal network as each man's range of active cooperation differed, more or less, from that of each of his neighbours. Absolute compatibility was, of course, impossible, but some kind of workable pattern had to be developed. This was in part the conscious aim, and certainly the effect, of the men's choices in sequences of actions. To some extent men experimented with the possibilities open to them in the network in order to discover what would in practice work with minimal conflict of interests. Each man (that is, household head) encountered the necessity to have several kin-neighbours on whom he could reasonably rely for material assistance and for support in times of disputes. I indicated the problems confronting a man who finds himself insecure for lack of such dependable supporters: some men left the community to seek greater security elsewhere, and some sought to remedy the matter by sponsoring newcomers who would become cooperating kin-neighbours.

Fourthly, I emphasised the fluidity and the changing character of the kinship network—and more precisely, of the operative relations between neighbours expressed in terms of kinship. The concept of network is not, or at least need not be, a static one. Indeed its nature and some of its intrinsic processes can only be perceived diachronically.

Fifthly, the network tended to divide into vaguely discernible parts, or what I have called "clusters". These clusters were never discrete, for the cross-linkages between them kept them coalescent. In so far as they were distinguishable, however, this was because of a high degree of compatibility that persisted between the sets of kinship linkages of the various men involved: that is, collective activities tended to include the men of a single cluster without too marked conflicts of interests, although never entirely so. The social visibility of clusters was enhanced by emergence of a "big man" in each. This notable was the principal influence and leader among that set of neighbours, though his influence was not restricted to them alone; nor did he have sanctions by which to enforce his leadership. Notables might compete for prestige and influence in general within the community, but competition between them tended to be greatest at those points in the network where clusters were inter-linked and where therefore conflicts of interests were apt to be greatest.[24]

In order to examine more closely the dynamics of this network, I present some extended case materials in the following two chapters with particular reference to two kinds of collective action: the treatment of inter-personal conflict and dispute, and the organisation of work-parties for agricultural purposes. Description and analysis focus on fairly readily recorded, specific social events. Faced with a seemingly inchoate social system, and without the guidelines of corporate groups, specialised roles, and lineal categories, I was compelled to anchor my research enquiries to something determinate in order to avoid persisting confusion and vagueness. I also wish to show the essential sociological connections between chronologically successive events in the context of ongoing

[24] The concept and significance of the cluster is discussed further in Chapter Eight.

community life. The procedure, at least in this case, has a disadvantage now impossible to circumvent or rectify. The concentration on particular events of cooperation and conflict ignores the mesh of everyday activities and interaction within this small community—casual gossip, leisure activities, petty borrowing and lending, casual visiting and hospitality, small acts of assistance and animosity—the give and take of neighbours. I am also unable to give enough of the background activities that accompanied the principal events concerned—the visiting, gossip, exchange of views, private pressures. All these, as any field anthropologist can testify, are not easily observable; but I must confess that their full significance did not occur to me at the time, and so no systematic attempt was made to gather such data. No less unfortunate, though perhaps more unavoidable, my records largely ignore relations between women neighbours, and between men and women. Women were obviously important in disseminating gossip, and no doubt they influenced the actions of their male kin. Much of all this must have affected the events described. Precisely what the effect was is unknown, but an important dimension of social organisation is left unassessed.

Nevertheless, concentration on the two major features of community life in Ligomba reveals a great deal of the dynamics of social organisation. The social reality of the closed networks becomes apparent; and some of the tools of analysis are tested. By concentrating on these events it is proposed to get away from over-vague generalisation coloured by ideal and formal conceptualisation.

V

Processes of Dispute Settlement

Disputes between neighbours, and differences of opinion and action affecting the interests of neighbours, were almost invariably treated within the local community. There was neither intervention by nor subsequent appeal to an external authority or influence. While it was quite possible for a man to take his neighbour before the official court of first instance, held by the sub-chief on the authority of the colonial Administration, and to take complaints to the sub-chief or to the District Officer for advice and perhaps investigation, very few people from eastern Undendeuli (or from other areas) took advantage of these possibilities.

Firstly, these official institutions were controlled by non-Ndendeuli and represented alien authority to the people. The sub-chief was an Ngoni and an appointee of the Ngoni chief. He and his official court were remnants of the resented Ngoni overlordship persisting precariously on the western edge of the sub-chiefdom.[1] Ndendeuli wanted as little contact as possible with any Ngoni authority. In any case, the court was the best part of a day's walk from eastern Undendeuli. It was difficult and time-consuming, requiring at least two journeys to the court, to get a defendant before the sub-chief. The headquarters of the Administration were even less accessible, over fifty miles away, and offered no direct judicial facilities. The people saw little reason to accede or appeal to either external authority, and neither sought to compel the use of the official judicial mechanisms except in certain limited instances (for example, homicide, infringement of administrative regulations such as tax evasion).

Secondly, Ndendeuli ignored the court because it involved

---

[1] The last Ngoni sub-chief lost the office late in 1953 when Undendeuli was becoming independent of the Ngoni chiefdom: see page 34. I have no data on the courts since that time.

authority per se. They were aware that the court could give an enforceable decision on any legitimate matter put before it; but they regarded that as an arbitrary procedure, and one that failed to take proper account of the complex of kinship and neighbourly relations within which the dispute arose. Authoritative judgement by an external, third party inevitably, they believed, ignored the full range of interests that needed to be taken into account—including the interests of other concerned neighbours, who should then (by Ndendeuli standards) be fully involved in the process of settlement. Following a court judgement, the disputants had still, on their return home, to tackle the problems (often the reality behind the overt dispute itself) of readjustment to the requirements of continued community life.

Thus, for the Ndendeuli, authoritative judgement was not merely arbitrary, but dealt with only a part of the whole matter. It was a wrong method; it was inconvenient at a practical level; and it related to the resented aliens, Ngoni and European. It is possible—I can put it no stronger than that—that the Ndendeuli had been induced to rely even more firmly on local community autonomy and indigenous methods of dispute settlement than otherwise might have been the case.

Within the local community [2] a disputant sought to recruit active supporters in his own interest through the kinship relations of the community's network. At the same time he was subject to pressures and limitations exercised by his opponent and the opponent's supporters because of the relations interlinking them and his own supporters in that same closed network.

Non-resident kinsmen of a disputant were not excluded from appearing in his support and speaking on his behalf. On the whole such outsiders participated only occasionally, and they seldom took a prominent part. They were unlikely to appreciate the full complexities of neighbourly interlinkages and of the interests of those other than the disputants. They were aware of their disability: men told me that they were reluctant to make suggestions during the course of discussions that affected the lives of men (many of them unrelated, even strangers) in another community. A disputant who invited outsiders (his own kinsmen, of course) was sometimes considered to be unable to recruit sufficient support from among his neighbours, and to admit to a weak case in consequence.

[2] In this chapter I am concerned only with disputes between members of the same local community. Disputes between members of different communities are considered in Chapter Ten.

A greatly simplified model may serve as an introduction to the nature of the social processes concerned. In a dispute between neighbours A and E (who are not directly linked and do not regard each other as kin), A expects the support of his kin-neighbour B; and B may seek the support of his own kin-neighbour C (who is not kin to A) to the side of A. But C might similarly be expected to give his support in the affair to D, another kin-neighbour of his (and not kin to B) on the side of E who is kin-neighbour to D. Thus A and E are connected: their fields of social action impinge on each other's and are mutually limiting. C is placed in the structurally intermediate position where, perhaps, he may be compelled or wish to act as mediator in the dispute; whilst B and D may seek to influence one another and to prevent their own cooperative relations (via C) from undue disruption. Very roughly, the basic situation is illustrated in Figure 11: there, all arrowed lines represent actual inter-personal relations, with unin-

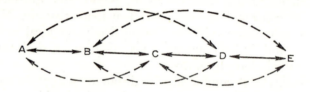

FIGURE 11: Simplified Model of the Network.

terrupted ones denoting direct, acknowledged kinship links, and interrupted ones denoting indirect linkage (such as the cousin of a cousin).

An actual dispute situation would, of course, have been far less simple. It is certain that A and E, and indeed any others of these men, would have been linked in other effective ways through the kinship network. Thus more neighbours would have been involved, and the impingements of the fields of action of A and E would have been considerably more complex. As I have already suggested, a dispute between neighbours was not a self-contained, isolated social event, for it occurred in the context of the continuum of community life and could affect the relations of other neighbours. A or E, or both, might have supported C on some recent occasion, and they both perhaps had participated in C's work-parties and he in theirs. Similarly, A and D, B and D, and B and E, may occasionally, or even more regularly, have engaged in mutual assistance. All would hope and expect to give and obtain assistance in the future. A real dispute situation would probably have been affected by other factors that could have been as significant to the eventual settlement as the overt dispute itself—for example, the contingent interests of other neighbours, the desires and efforts of particular neighbours to demonstrate or enlarge their influence and prestige, rivalry between men on opposing sides, and particular cordiality or animosity between individual neighbours involved resulting from their structural positions and past encounters.

Matters of public interest and concern, including disputes, were open to discussion whenever men came together in any number: at a beer-drink, a feast, a ritual performance. A rather more formal treatment of a dispute, deliberately and obviously putting it into the public arena and effectively declaring it to be a dispute rather than a private disagreement, was obtained by convening a special assembly of neighbours. Ndendeuli referred to this simply as *mkutano*, "a meeting". I shall refer to it as a "moot". In a moot the principal disputants, each with his action-set of supporters, confronted each other to discuss the matter in dispute and to seek some means of reaching a settlement. A moot could be convened by one of the principal disputants, or by a neighbour: a man linked to both disputing parties, or a notable linked to one side or the other. A moot was usually held on neutral ground—at the house of an intermediary neighbour, of a notable, of "the owner of the land"—though in less serious cases it might meet at the defendant's house.

Each disputant recruited his own action-set,[3] although a younger man (who was nevertheless head of his own autonomous household) might sometimes leave the responsibility to his father or other senior kin-neighbour. The members of the action-set advised their principal, sat with him in the moot, spoke on his behalf, cross-examined speakers on the other side, and assisted him to negotiate his case. Though it was an arranged arena of dispute, a moot was fairly informal as men sat on the verandah or under the eaves of the house and on the ground in front. There was generally a certain amount of moving about during the course of the meeting so that the two action-sets were often not distinguishable by eye. Those participants who were structurally intermediate tended to sit in the middle of the gathering, or at one side, thus demonstrating their lack of definite allegiance to either set. Neutral neighbours, if any, usually sat at the edge of the group. There were few rules

[3] The general concept of action-set is considered at page 18 ff.

of procedure; and there was no one to act as chairman, let alone
as arbitrator or judge. The matter in dispute was commonly first
described by the plaintiff, with the defendant afterwards replying
with his own account; but not infrequently the defendant started
off, rebutting what was already a well-known complaint and perhaps making a counter-claim. Thereafter discussion was free, open
to anyone present, even occasionally to the neutrals, though on the
whole the discussions tended to be dominated by the principal
disputants, one or two of their more influential and able supporters, and any influential intermediaries. Often two or more
men spoke at once, especially when discussion became heated;
but for the most part each man was allowed his say, as ideally he
should have been. A speaker remained seated, and he could be
interrupted or questioned whilst he was speaking. The participants
would have known each other well, of course, for they were
neighbours who met frequently in all sorts of circumstances. There
was an assumption of equality amongst them, all heads of their own
households, and a willingness to let each man give his opinion and
to listen to him with tolerance and respect, even when emotions
ran high. Discussion was sometimes disorganized and rambling
(even allowing for the widest range of relevance), but only the
worst irrelevancies were summarily checked by the impatience of
the audience. Men were not obliged to speak, though unless they
were clearly neutral they needed to indicate their support of their
own principal and their agreement to the final settlement.

In the following account and analysis of actual dispute cases in
Ligomba a number of special terms are used to refer to the roles
of the participants. *Plaintiff* and *defendant*, referred to in common
as the *principals* in the dispute, were the men who respectively
brought and rebutted the claim or complaint. They were the actual
men who had suffered or allegedly caused the injury or offence
that was the subject of the dispute, or the heads of households of
the injured and the offender if the latter were women or minors.
Sometimes, however, the role of principal might be taken by a
"father"—a kin-neighbour of senior generation.

A neighbour who was more or less equally related in the kinship network to both principals is referred to as an *intermediary*
(for example, C in the preceding diagram). This is a purely structural designation resulting from the relative position of the two
principals in the particular case. The actual role of an intermediary
varied. He could choose to be actively partial to one of the principals, for whatever reason of his own, though seldom entirely

opposing the other principal. Or he could decide to avoid embarrassing participation by deliberately absenting himself from the community temporarily [4] and thus remaining inactively neutral. Or he could become a *mediator*. Primarily a mediator attempted to act as broker between the principals, and he played on his links with each as demonstration of his goodwill to both; but he could be active in suggesting and pressing positive means of reaching an agreed settlement. At most, however, he was a conciliator. He did not seek to act as an arbitrator, for he neither could nor was expected to give a decision and a settlement. He had no sanctions at his disposal, and was a prime exponent of the compromise. Not every dispute precipitated a mediator, although most did of which I have record. Sometimes the mediator was obvious from the start (even convening the moot), but in other cases one or more might emerge as negotiations developed.

The two or three men in the local community who were consistently acknowledged to be "big men"—*notables*—demonstrated and developed their influence and leadership in the processes of dispute settlement more than in any other circumstances. They were consulted by principals who were linked with them in the network, and they usually took leading parts in a moot. Their status was achieved mainly by virtue of their ability and success in giving advice and influencing the public discussions.

The particular role of a notable during a dispute case depended on his position vis-à-vis the two principals and their kin-neighbours. If he were closely linked to a principal in a more or less regular cooperative relationship, then he would be included in the action-set. In that event he probably shared with the principal the leadership of the set; but he sometimes assumed the effective initiative in the promotion or defence of the interests involved in the dispute. If, however, a notable were an intermediary—sometimes, even, a neutral—he acted as mediator. Thus according to circumstances, notables might have been leaders of the two action-sets, or one could have been a leader whilst another acted as mediator. Then rivalry between notables for influence—general prestige, or influence over certain neighbours—was often important, affecting the trend of negotiations between the principals. Nevertheless a notable's skill could lessen conflict between neighbours and improve the efficacy of a settlement of the dispute.

[4] The stock excuse, almost always patently obvious, for non-attendance at the moot was the need to visit some kinsman elsewhere.

SOME DISPUTE CASES IN LIGOMBA

From this brief, general introduction to the processes of dispute settlement, there now follows accounts of seven actual cases that occurred in Ligomba during 1953, and that were recorded and discussed in the field. Apart from a number of disputes arising out of conflicts of timing in the organization of agricultural work-parties, and described in Chapter Six, these were the only inter-personal conflicts that were made public during that year: that is, they were the only inter-personal quarrels, disagreements, misunderstandings, and difficulties that were removed from private negotiation and put into the public arena. They became "disputes" in the technical sense. Other differences between individuals were settled, or left unsettled, without acquiring the status of a dispute.

These seven disputes were empirical events in the arbitrary period of my field research, and therefore they do not necessarily show all the analytical problems that might be desired; and they may have left uncovered some problems that I have not perceived. Nevertheless in the examination of the kinship network these actual disputes do demonstrate a good deal, and provide the opportunity to base generalised analysis firmly in empirical data. In an Ndendeuli local community almost any two or three consecutive disputes were inter-connected because of the interconnectedness of neighbours within the closed network. I wish to indicate how the resolution of one dispute could affect the course and resolution of subsequent ones by affecting the nature of relations between the people. In this way the dynamics of the network and of the social life of the community can be understood. I assume that all social events were influenced by conditions of cooperation and conflict that had previously developed—some a long time previously. This assumption, and its sociological implications, can only be partially validated by Ndendeuli data; but a start can be made in dealing with the short time-span for which my records are more reliable and detailed. For this reason the following dispute cases are presented in the chronological order in which they occurred.

Case 1: The Persistent Thief (March)

This case, which began just before my research period in Ligomba, was really the culmination of a series of disputes involving the same man. It ended during the time I was there, with the virtual expulsion of this man from the community, through his exclusion from the cooperative activities of his neighbours. The skeletal genealogy in Figure 10 shows the relevant part of the kinship network.

In 1948, Kasudi (D22), then living elsewhere, married the daughter of Mitedi (C19), giving a cash bridewealth of 105/-, rather below the roughly average amount in Undendeuli at that time. The following year, after quarrelling with his father in the community where they shared a common hamlet, Kasudi moved to Ligomba. Here he was sponsored principally by his father-in-law, Mitedi; but he also had the support of his first cousin, Hanju (D21), who already lived there. This was an advantageous move for Kasudi: he escaped further quarrels with and a partial subservience to his father, and he acquired a potentially favourable position in the Ligomba kinship network through his links with Mitedi and Hanju.

Kasudi soon turned out to be a petty thief, an unreliable member of work-parties, and frequently a troublesome person at beer-drinks where he easily became drunk and quarrelsome. He was a poor neighbour. By 1952 he had trouble recruiting work-parties, and was the last household head to convene his work-party in the early rainy season that year. Nevertheless, both Mitedi and Hanju continued to support him, as did Ndoma (D23), a recent newcomer and Kasudi's sister's husband. To a lesser extent Sedi and his son, and Konga and his sons, supported him too, largely in deference to Mitedi, as they said. They argued lenience when his petty thefts were discovered. Mitedi in particular was described by several of the men as being especially tolerant. He had no sons of his own and only the one daughter, and he hoped therefore that Kasudi would "stay in Ligomba like my son" (his own words to me). There had been some idea of the two men's households sharing a joint hamlet, before personal relations between them began to deteriorate.

In the dry season of 1952, Kasudi's wife (Mitedi's daughter) left him and went to live at her mother's brother's house in a community several miles away. According to Mitedi, his daughter had been mistreated: he alleged that Kasudi had beaten her severely a number of times, that he had often left her to do the main work in the fields without help, and that Mitedi himself had been compelled to provide money for her clothing when Kasudi refused. Finally the only surviving child had died suddenly, and Mitedi implied witchcraft by Kasudi, though without making an open accusation. Kasudi held that any difficulties were the fault of his

wife and that Mitedi had not used his paternal influence to improve the marriage. He also alleged that although his wife had gone
to her mother's brother's, she was in fact living with another man
in that community.

The wife refused to return, and Mitedi seemed to have been
unable or unwilling to persuade her. Kasudi therefore demanded a
divorce in a quarrelsome scene at a beer-drink at which he
threatened violence against Mitedi. The latter was agreeable to the
divorce, and he asked his brother, the notable Konga, to convene a
moot at his house when the matter could be dealt with. Kasudi
agreed to Konga's invitation and the moot assembled a day or two
later, with the following action-sets:

Action-set of Mitedi
            Konga   (B)
Hamedi and Faraji   (BS)
             Sedi   (MBS)   (8 men)
           Yusufu   (MBSS)
           Zadiki   (FBS)
            Tanda   (WB of Zadiki)
Intermediary [5]
        [Ndoma]   (MBDS of Mitedi; ZH of Kasudi)
Action-set of Kasudi
            Hanju   (MZS)
               F   from another   (4 men)
             ZHF   community

In the moot Mitedi agreed to Kasudi's demand for a divorce, and
said that his daughter agreed also. Kasudi's request for the return
of part of the bridewealth was, however, firmly rejected. Mitedi
argued, with the support of Konga and the others, that the fault
lay with Kasudi and that two children had been born of the union.
Kasudi's two senior kinsmen from elsewhere gave him only mild
support for his claim. His only Ligomba supporter, his cousin
Hanju, spoke in his defence and asked his neighbours for tolerance.
This account is based on information given me some months later;

---

[5] The men in the *intermediary* position, as given above and in subsequent cases in this chapter, were the more important neighbours who were
thus structurally identified in the particular context of each dispute. An
intemediary's linkages from the principals or other member of the action-
sets are noted in round brackets. Where the intermediary's name is given in
square brackets (as in the case of Ndoma above) this indicates that the
man absented himself from involvement in the moot. If the man's name is
not in square brackets, then he acted as mediator.

I could not assess the divergent allegations of responsibility for the marital breakdown. Mitedi refused to agree to any return of the bridewealth, but he declared that the agreed divorce should stand. The moot ended inconclusively, with no final agreement.

The degree of Kasudi's estrangement in the community was, however, made manifest. Only one neighbour had joined his action-set, and he had looked for assistance outside the community. His other kin-neighbour (apart from Mitedi), Ndoma, deliberately did not attend the moot, presumably preferring not to be involved

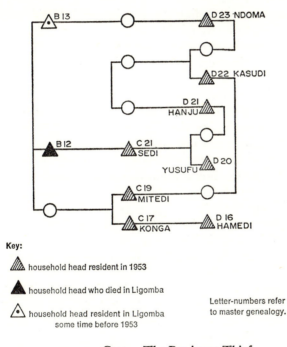

Key:

△ household head resident in 1953

▲ household head who died in Ligomba

△ household head resident in Ligomba some time before 1953

Letter-numbers refer to master genealogy.

FIGURE 12: Case 1: The Persistent Thief.

in what for him, a young newcomer, was a difficult dilemma. At the end of that year, in the early wet season, Kasudi was unable to recruit a normal work-party to hoe and plant his field. Both Hanju and Ndoma, with their wives, went to help with hoeing for an hour or two on one day; but neither considered it politic to invite Kasudi to join their own work-parties for fear of offending their other kin-neighbours who had announced their intention not to include him.

In March 1953, Kasudi was accused of stealing a small bag of

maize from the house of Saidi (C6). Saidi's wife had just brought
it home from her sister's house where she had been to beg food.
The wife had seen Kasudi, but no one else, near her house when
she went to fetch water, and the maize was gone on her return.
Saidi consulted with his cousin, the notable Ali, and on Ali's suggestion they both went to discuss the matter with Mitedi and
Konga. As a result Konga and Ali convened a moot to be held at
Konga's house. Within less than a day virtually everyone in
Ligomba knew of the meeting, though not all household heads
attended. Kasudi did not attend. He was absent from Ligomba,
visiting kinsmen, according to Hanju; and I did not discover
whether or not he knew of the moot beforehand. Ndoma also absented himself again, almost certainly for the same reason as before.
The participants in the moot were largely kin-neighbours of Saidi
and of Mitedi.

After a brief account of the alleged theft by Saidi, there was a
lengthy, often repetitive, discussion of Kasudi's earlier misdemeanours up to and including the divorce moot. There was a general
consensus in condemnation of Kasudi. Mitedi said that people
should no longer exchange assistance with him; and then he asked
Sedi directly that he should no longer give support to Kasudi. Sedi
replied that although he had formerly cooperated with Kasudi, as
other neighbours had, he had already decided to do so no more.
Sedi's son, Yusufu, added that he too was no longer prepared to
cooperate with Kasudi. This was, of course, no news to the assembled men; but the procedure made the situation clear, and it
prepared the way to bring open pressure to bear on Kasudi's remaining supporters in the community, especially Hanju. Mitedi
and Konga sought to complete the isolation of Kasudi without
alienating Hanju—as Ali explained to me in reference to the discussions held before the moot was convened. Konga, the notable,
took the initiative by asking Sedi about his son-in-law, Hanju.
There was a pause as the men turned to Hanju who had so far remained quiet, taking no part in the discussions. He had made no
attempt to defend Kasudi. Now he stated that he and Sedi were
"good kinsmen", cooperating together and living in the same hamlet. "Sedi is my father, my big man, and I follow him to his
brother", he said: that is, he was prepared to follow the lead of
Sedi in supporting Mitedi against Kasudi. Note that Hanju was
perceiving the principal conflict to be that between Mitedi and
Kasudi, and not the particular dispute concerning Saidi. Although
not specifically denying further support to Kasudi, his first cousin

and hitherto his kin-neighbour, Hanju's brief statement was accepted as tantamount to that, or at least sufficient for the purpose of the leading men in the moot. Konga then claimed to speak for all the men there—probably rightly so, for Saidi did not raise the issue of the theft—by declaring that no one wanted Kasudi as a neighbour and that no one would cooperate with him again whilst he remained in Ligomba. Konga reiterated Kasudi's past misconduct and current unpopularity. He referred to the exceptional nature of the situation where a man had become so estranged from his neighbours, saying that the whole fault lay with Kasudi and not with his neighbours. There were calls of agreement to Konga's points by the rest of the men. The moot ended in euphoric unity.

No further action was taken in the matter. It was no one's responsibility to inform Kasudi, let alone to order him to leave. But nothing more was required in fact, for it had been made virtually impossible for him to remain since he was cut off from the normal, and essential, system of cooperation and mutual help. He could not leave immediately because he had a standing crop nearly ripe in his field. He eventually removed his possessions in June; and he left Undendeuli soon after to become a labour migrant.

There had been little consideration of the alleged theft from Saidi's house, though that had been the immediate cause of the moot. It was summarily agreed that Kasudi was the thief, but there was no discussion of compensation to Saidi. Neither was the matter of Kasudi's bridewealth raised again. It is possible, at least Saidi hinted so, that Mitedi and Konga had been concerned to distract attention from the bridewealth issue by directing and emphasising the common censure against Kasudi, and by getting rid of him in disgrace. I had no proof of this, however. No return of the bridewealth was made, and Mitedi's daughter remarried later that year.

Hanju's dilemma was solved. Clearly he could no longer go against general opinion; in particular, he could not jeopardise further his most valuable relations with his wife's father and brother with whom he shared a hamlet and regularly cooperated, and through whom his relations with other valuable neighbours were established. Hanju could not continue close cooperation with Kasudi, although under other circumstances Kasudi might have been an important kin-neighbour, linking Hanju more securely with other neighbours such as Mitedi, Konga and his sons, and Ndoma. Hanju was not censured for his persisting support of Kasudi; all the comments which I heard afterwards agreed that Hanju had acted properly in supporting him until such time as

Kasudi was finally estranged from all his other neighbours. By implication, Ndoma, Kasudi's other kin-neighbour, was included in the general refusal of further assistance to Kasudi.

This was, in my experience, an unusual case, for men were rarely quite so alienated from their neighbours that they were effectively excluded from community life. An Ndendeuli might move because he considered that he could not obtain reliable enough support and cooperation in his community, but this was generally a matter of voluntary choice to try some other community that appeared to offer better prospects. In this case, the men of Ligomba came more nearly to acting as a unit than on any other occasion that I recorded. Nevertheless the community cannot be said to have acted as a firmly organized group. Leadership and initiative lay with the interested parties: the final immediate plaintiff supported by a notable, Ali, and the aggrieved father-in-law supported by his brother, Konga, also a notable. Only fifteen of the twenty-eight household heads actually present in Ligomba at that time attended that final moot. The third notable, Kabaya (C11), and some other more senior men, did not attend—not even those who had earlier suffered from Kasudi's thieving and trouble-making. Kabaya said that it was no concern of his for Kasudi was not his kinsman, nor kin of his kinsmen. A man's behaviour and his status in the community were the concern of those actively associated with him and those affected by his misconduct. Kabaya agreed with the action that had been taken in the final moot, for he thought that the community was well rid of Kasudi; but he saw neither necessity nor possibility of action by the community as a whole.

Summary and Analysis of the Case. (a) Divorce moot: There was complete agreement that divorce should occur. There was final disagreement on the matter of repayment of bridewealth. No settlement was reached. No mediator emerged.

(b) Theft moot: The defendant was not present. There was agreement that the defendant had committed the theft; that he had committed numerous offences against his neighbours; and that further cooperation should be denied to him. There was no final disagreement, and settlement was intrinsic in the total agreement attained. The defendant later acceded and eventually left the community. There was no mediator. The implicit significance of the second moot was the effort to evict a chronic thief and a bad, unreliable neighbour. A possible implication was the desire to avoid further discussion and repayment of bridewealth by the defendant's father-in-law.

Case 2: A Bridewealth Claim (June)

In June 1953, Rajabu (D15) returned to Ligomba after more than a year away as a labour migrant. The day after his return he visited his wife's parents, Sedi (C21) and his wife, and presented them with a blanket and a length of cheap cloth. He apologised that he offered them no more, saying that he had managed to bring little home with him. Sedi appeared to be satisfied; at least he commended Rajabu on these gifts in the hearing of others. A day or two later, however, Sedi made a demand for money from Rajabu as an additional contribution to bridewealth. Rajabu

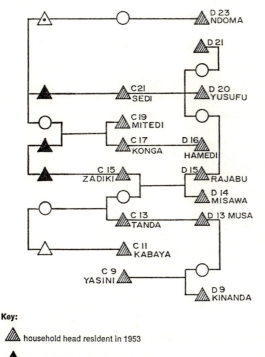

FIGURE 13: Case 2: A Bridewealth Claim.

claimed that he had completed all bridewealth obligations before he had left home at the end of 1951, and that Sedi had then been satisfied with the transaction. In support of this he said that Sedi had not at that time made further demands for future payments, and that his daughter (Rajabu's wife) had continued to live in her house in the hamlet of her father-in-law, Zadiki (C15), whilst Rajabu had been away (that is, her father-in-law had assumed responsibility for her). Sedi denied that this was any proof of completed bridewealth; it was merely a demonstration of good and proper affinal relations. He repudiated any idea that he had ever expressed final satisfaction with the bridewealth. A stalemate followed as Rajabu was fully supported by his father, Zadiki. After these private discussions, Sedi consulted with his kin-neighbours and then asked for a moot to consider his persisting claim. His request was negotiated by Konga (C17) (his first cousin, FZS) who was also first cousin of Zadiki (FBS), and the moot was held at Konga's house.

The action-sets were composed as follows. Sedi recruited and led his own set. Rajabu was a young man about twenty-four years old who had been absent from Ligomba a great deal in labour migration since becoming an adult; his father therefore acted as principal in the case and recruited the action-set, whilst Rajabu, though present, took little part.

Action-set of Zadiki

Misawa and Rajabu	(S)	
Tanda	(WB)	
Musa	(WBS)	
Kabaya	(Tanda's MBS)	(8 men)
Yasini	(Musa's WF)	
Kinanda	(Musa's WB)	

Intermediary

Konga	(FBS of Zadiki; MBS of Sedi)
Hamedi	(FFBS of Zadiki; FMBS of Sedi)
[Mitedi]	(FBS of Zadiki; MBS of Sedi)

Action-set of Sedi

Yusufu	(S)	
Hanju	(DH)	
Ndoma	(FBDS)	(5 men)
MBS—non-resident		

Konga and his son attended the moot; they were equally related to both principals, therefore equally obligated formally and in an obvious position to act as mediators. Mitedi, no less intermediary, preferred to opt out of what he judged to be a too difficult position. He left Ligomba on a temporary visit the day before the moot was held. Konga took the lead as mediator. It was a small moot and, as it turned out, the only one required to settle the dispute. Because of the fairly close and interconnected kinship linkages, the action-sets were limited, nor was there any need for either principal to appeal to more distantly related neighbours. The only others present were two neutral neighbours who joined the moot after it had begun, apparently attracted from their fields nearby where they were working. Bilali (C12) arrived towards the end of the proceedings. None of these men took any part in the moot.

Zadiki, the effective defendant, opened the moot. He argued that the request for more bridewealth was really a demand for a larger share of the savings Rajabu had brought home after his period of labour migration. On the intervention of Tanda (C13), the gifts to himself and his wife were admitted by Sedi; but he claimed that these represented the obligation of any young son-in-law on his return from abroad. Sedi insisted that he had a right to more bridewealth and that Rajabu was in a position to give it. Rajabu called out that he had brought home very little, but Sedi refused to listen to this. The amounts of cash previously given in bridewealth were described by Zadiki and admitted by Sedi after some minor argument. But Sedi refused to admit Zadiki's assertion that the completion of bridewealth had been acknowledged at any time. He restated his current claim, but set no specific figure to it. After further discussion, Zadiki was forced to admit that his son had brought some money savings home, but he said they were small and were needed for other purposes by his son and himself. Zadiki was supported in this by Tanda who also raised the point that Sedi and his wife had been given generous gifts when Rajabu had returned home from his previous spell of labour migration. Sedi conceded this, and also the overt implication, pointed out by Zadiki and Kabaya, that Rajabu had shown himself to be a good son-in-law. Kabaya stated baldly that Sedi had no claim at all against Rajabu and Zadiki, and suggested that he was showing himself to be a poor father-in-law by persisting with this claim. Kabaya continued to review the discussion so far, and the evidence produced, in order to show the absence of a basis for Sedi's claim. He was followed by Yasini (C9) who mainly reiterated the substance of the argument of Tanda and Kabaya.

This intervention by Yasini brought a crisis to the discussion, for Yusufu (Sedi's son) enquired aloud what interest Yasini had in the matter. Yasini replied that he was supporting his "brothers"; and Tanda elaborated that by saying, "Is he not the father of my son's wife? my brother, then? He goes with [supports] me because I am a brother of Zadiki. It is right that we are here, and I and Zadiki invited him". Kabaya called out that Yasini was his brother too. "We go with our brothers, yes", retorted Sedi, "but is it not true that Yasini has not yet received all the bridewealth for his daughter? Where is the rest to come from? Who gives Musa [Yasini's son-in-law] the money for bridewealth, for he has not been to the Coast [that is, has not been a labour migrant] for a long time? Is Musa getting money from Rajabu so that he can give bridewealth to Yasini?"

After further discussion it appeared that Sedi's suggestion was correct, although it was never explicitly admitted by Zadiki and his supporters. I am uncertain how much of this was previously known by Sedi and how far he was probing on the basis of suspicion, for nothing of this aspect of the matter had been raised before. The explanation—not fully detailed in the moot—was that two years previously, on returning from labour migration, Musa had lent money to Rajabu, his first cousin, to use for bridewealth payment to Sedi. Now, on Rajabu's return from employment abroad, he was expected to repay the loan so that Musa could himself complete his own bridewealth payments to Yasini.

Until this stage Konga had taken no part in the proceedings of the moot; but now, with the details of the case fairly well established and at least tacitly agreed by both sides, he began to take the initiative in negotiating an acceptable settlement. It became clear that he was not an entirely neutral mediator for, though cautiously, he leant to the side of Sedi. It was he who finally stated that Sedi's allegations were substantially correct—Zadiki's side remained silent, thus apparently acceding to that statement; and he added that this indeed was a proper claim for bridewealth, though he went on (somewhat ambiguously) to say that Sedi had a right, as a father-in-law, to a larger gift than he had so far received since Rajabu returned home. In all this Konga was not giving a ruling on the dispute, but he was affirming what had overtly and covertly been agreed by the two parties in the moot. Konga then commended Rajabu on his desire to repay his debt to his cousin, Musa, but he declared—cutting across remonstration by Zadiki to the same opinion—it was equally commendable to be generous to a father-in-law who had given his daughter. There was a good deal of general discussion by speakers on both sides on the relative strengths of the conflicting claims of the father-in-law and the creditor cousin of Rajabu. In the end, mainly I think because of Konga's insistent advocacy quietly backed by Hamedi, it was accepted that the bridewealth debt was more important in this instance. It was agreed that Rajabu should give Sedi another twenty-five shillings in bridewealth, and that Musa should receive fifty shillings. Konga asked Yasini directly to agree to this; and this he did, implying that he was prepared to accept for the moment a bridewealth instalment of fifty shillings from Musa—a smaller amount than he had been expecting. With Yasini's agreement, Zadiki could now scarcely withstand Konga's request for his agreement also. But Zadiki demanded that Sedi should state there in the moot that no further bridewealth obligation lay against Rajabu. After some attempt by Sedi to avoid so committing himself, he eventually agreed to this. Rajabu went off to his house, less than a mile away, and returned to hand over the twenty-five shillings to Sedi. The moot ended at this point as the assembled men together drank some beer provided by Konga.

The significance of the role of Konga in this moot and settlement was emphasised to me afterwards in conversations with Yasini and my field assistant, and also with Ali who had not attended the moot. These informants explained that Konga (and Hamedi) could have thrown their weight on the side of Zadiki and argued that Sedi had already received an adequate bridewealth,[6] whereas Rajabu owed a genuine debt to Musa who had a need for the money for his own bridewealth payment. But Zadiki and Konga, though first cousins, had long been atagonistic to one another:[7] they still continued to participate in each other's work-parties and were often co-members of the same action-sets in other matters, but their relations were largely formal and without warmth. Each man was suspicious of the good faith of the other. On the other hand, Konga was concerned to maintain close cooperation with Sedi and his kin-neighbours. Strictly logically, Konga should, or

[6] It was agreed in the moot that Sedi had received 185 shillings in cash previously from Rajabu. This was about an average sum for Ndendeuli bridewealth, so that in itself it gave no real basis for a further instalment.

[7] See page 98 f.; also Case 5, page 167 ff.

at least could, have given equal support to both principals. As far as I understood the issues in dispute, and in the opinions of my informants, there was no clear-cut solution. Had Sedi not already received an average-sized bridewealth, for instance, there would have been a better case for his claim at this time; but this was not so. Of course, other factors also affected the settlement. Had Yasini been more insistent in his undisputed bridewealth claim against Musa, or had Tanda been a more influential person, or a better speaker, or had Zadiki been more stubborn rather than being prepared in the end to placate his son's father-in-law, the actual settlement could have been rather different. Fathers-in-law commonly attempted to obtain generous gifts from the savings of returned labour migrants, but they did not invariably succeed, especially where other valid debts could be proved. In this instance Sedi did succeed and without endangering his daughter's marriage, though he did nothing to improve his affinal relations and he put his son-in-law in a somewhat difficult position between himself and Zadiki. The role of Konga nevertheless seems to have been crucial, and his generally accepted influence and his persuasive skill in discussion gave him an advantage. Yet he had no wish to alienate his cousin, Zadiki, entirely. There was useful cooperation between them and between each man and the other's kin-neighbours in the community—a break with Zadiki would have almost certainly have meant a break also with Tanda, for example. Konga's support of Sedi had to be tempered with these considerations, and consequently he made much show of backing Zadiki's demand that Sedi should declare the end of his bridewealth claims against Rajabu. Fairly skillfully in the event, Konga managed to bring off something of a personal success that enhanced his reputation for ability and influence in Ligomba.

I should note also that a moderately successful settlement of the actual dispute was achieved, in that the various claims of the men concerned were mutually adjusted and community life was able to continue. However, as will be seen later, in Case 5, relations between Zadiki and Konga were not made any easier as a result of this case and its settlement; whilst relations between Zadiki and Sedi were less cordial than previously, and this became important in Case 4.

Summary and Analysis of the Case. There was agreement that the plaintiff's claim was for additional bridewealth and not merely for a gift; that good affinal relations had existed hitherto; on the amount of bridewealth previously transferred; that the bridewealth debt took priority over the debt for a loan of money from a kinsman, and the repayment of that debt was not critically urgent; and that the defendant did have the money with which to make a bridewealth instalment. The final disagreement was over the amount to be paid in bridewealth, and whether or not such payment should be regarded as a final instalment. The settlement was that twenty-five shillings should be paid, the repayment of the other debt should be reduced by that same amount, and that no further bridewealth claim would be legitimate. The mediators were Konga (first cousin of each principal) and his son. The implicit significance of the case lay in the relationship between the fathers of the two spouses concerned in the bridewealth, and between the defendant and the mediator.

Case 3: A Compensation Claim (August)

During the early dry season, Yasini convened a work-party to cut and clear a piece of woodland and make a new field. Including himself, thirteen men participated in the day's work—a fairly large party. At the beer-drink that followed in the mid-afternoon, these men were gradually augmented by other neighbours, until a large majority of Ligomba men were present. There was plenty of beer, and it was a highly convivial affair as these parties were at that time of year. A number of men grew intoxicated, among them Malindi (D3) and Rashidi (D12), who began to quarrel. Fighting broke out between them but this was stopped by some of the others, and Malindi moved away as if to leave the party. As he left he shouted abuse at Rashidi, who ran after him and started the fight again. The two men were finally separated, but Malindi was now in a bad state—his clothes were torn and his face and arm were bloody—and his father and his cousin, Meha, took him home. There it was found that his arm was broken, in addition to cuts, bruises, and torn clothing.

Next day his father, Saidi (C6), sent a younger adult son as a messenger to Rashidi to demand compensation. The latter denied responsibility for the fight, saying that Malindi had begun it by grossly insulting him. The messenger, Malindi's younger brother, after some altercation threatened to take up the fight anew. He had to leave hurriedly to avoid assault by Rashidi and his brother.

Malindi's father, Saidi, consulted with his cousin, Ali, as he usually did at times of trouble. Ali advised that renewed direct negotiations with Rashidi were not feasible, and with Saidi's agreement he went to see Kabaya (C11), another notable and first cousin of Rashidi's father. The two men agreed to try and arrange a moot, and Kabaya persuaded Rashidi to concur. The moot was held the second day afterwards at the house of Konga (on neutral ground). I was unable to attend and obtained rather conflicting accounts of what occurred. Certainly the moot broke up fairly quickly as threats of renewed violence were made. Saidi continued to insist that his son should receive compensation and that therefore another moot should be held.

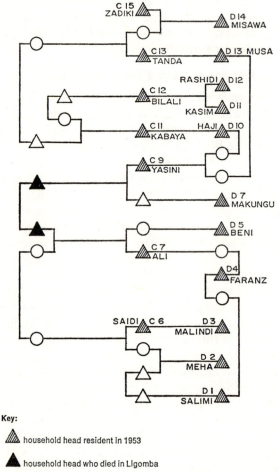

Key:

△ household head resident in 1953

▲ household head who died in Ligomba

Letter-numbers refer
to master genealogy.

FIGURE 14: Case 3: A Compensation Claim.

The people of Ligomba expressed much disquiet about this dispute and the way it had gone, for threats of violence had been flung around rather indiscriminately. The two notables, Ali and Kabaya, who were of course already rivals for influence in the community, had quarrelled over the failure of the moot, each blaming the other's side. Neutral opinion condemned Malindi's younger brother as a foolish youth stirring up trouble; his father was also blamed, first for using him as a messenger, and then for allowing him to be present at the moot where, as an unmarried man, he scarcely had the right to participate. But Rashidi and his elder brother, Kasim, were also thought to be at fault in the continued threats of violence, whatever the truth about Rashidi's behaviour at the time of the fight at the beer-drink. Saidi's demand for a second moot was therefore generally welcomed. After three days—during which time work-parties for D6 and D13 were postponed because of the persisting affair—a moot assembled at the house of Yasini. The two notables were unable to cooperate in convening this moot and the initiative was taken by Yasini and his elder nephew, Makungu. By this time Konga was absent from Ligomba attending the funeral of an affine in another community, so that his house was no longer available as a neutral place for another moot. But in any case, Yasini told me, the fight had occurred at his beer-drink at his house, and Rashidi had been a member of his work-party earlier that day. On further discussion it was clear that Yasini saw himself put into the role of mediator in the dispute because of his structurally intermediate position between the disputants in the network.

The action-sets at the second moot were composed as follows. Rashidi was principally responsible for his own set, though Kabaya shared the lead with him. Since Malindi was still incapacitated, the opposing action-set was recruited by his father, Saidi, though the lead was largely taken by Ali.

In addition to the three intermediaries—Yasini, Makungu, and Abdal—three other neighbours (C19, C21, and D21) also attended although they were in no way involved and appeared only as interested spectators. Amadu, Ali's sister's younger son, did not attend, although he had joined in the first moot; he was deliberately absent on a visit elsewhere.[8] Neither did the younger unmarried brothers of Malindi and Rashidi attend: they were among those who had previously threatened further violence. Of the other

[8] Amadu and Malindi were personally hostile to each other and seldom exchanged support.

Action-set of Saidi
Malindi	(S)	
Ali	(MZS)	
Beni	(Ali's ZS)	
Meha	(ZS)	
Salimi	(Meha's FBS)	(8 men)
FBS	non-residents	
MBS		

Intermediary
Yasini	(Ali's FBS; Kabaya's SWF)
Makungu	(BS of Yasini)
Abdal	

Action-set of Rashidi
Bilali	(F)	
Kasim	(eB)	
Kabaya and Haji	(FFZS and son)	(9 men)
Tanda and Musa	(Kabaya's FZS and son)	
Zadiki and Misawa	(Tanda's WB and son)	

heads of households then at home in Ligomba, only D15, D19, D20, and D23 were absent from the moot.[9] With twenty household heads present, and two outsiders, it was the most comprehensively attended moot that I witnessed in Ligomba—the result partly of the relative distance between the two principals in the kinship network,[10] and partly of the concern and interest aroused by the affair as it had developed.

Here I give only a summary version of the proceedings in the moot. In the field and in the records I made at the time, I was not especially concerned with the quasi-judicial aspects but rather with the interaction of these neighbours in the kinship network. Moreover the moot was most informal: often more than one man spoke at the same time, and verbal interchanges between the two sides were too rapid or oblique to be recorded properly. I discussed the whole moot afterwards with my assistant and several of the participants in an attempt to verify my understanding of it; but their and my afterthoughts may have affected my description of it.

In effect the proceedings of the moot fell more clearly into two parts than happened in many moots, and it was this case in particu-

[9] Absent from Ligomba at the time on what seemed legitimate grounds were D9, D4, D14, C17, D16, D17, and D18; that is, they were not deliberately avoiding the dispute.

[10] Cf., for example, the limited action-sets in Case 2, when the principals were fairly close in the network.

lar which gave me the first clue on the pattern of the processes of dispute settlement among the Ndendeuli. There was a good deal of overlapping of the two parts, nevertheless, and as far as I am aware there was no explicit recognition nor attempt to distinguish and separate them by the actual participants themselves. First, there was elucidation of the facts, and secondly there was negotiation of the settlement. The moot began with Saidi, the effective plaintiff, describing his son's injuries and attributing them to Rashidi's drunken ferocity. He asserted that the whole blame for the fight lay with Rashidi, and he noted, what was patently true, that Rashidi had suffered little or no damage in the fighting. He ended by demanding sixty shillings in compensation because, he said, his son's injuries prevented him from working at a time when men were engaged in preparing their fields for next year's cultivation. The only immediate response to this demand was an expletive from Rashidi signifying rejection. Instead, Rashidi, his father, and Kabaya, in turn put the responsibility for the fight on Malindi. It was by now well known that Malindi had insulted Rashidi by calling him impotent: this was not seriously questioned in the moot for many men had overheard Malindi's words. Saidi remained silent when the notable, Kabaya, finally stated this to be the case, and Ali only argued that nevertheless this did not absolve Rashidi from responsibility for the injuries he had caused. Rashidi claimed that his blows had not in fact broken Malindi's arm, but that the latter had tripped over a tree root and broken it in falling. He admitted, on Ali's insistence, to causing the other, minor injuries and tearing of Malindi's clothes, but excused himself on the basis of the intolerable provocation of Malindi's insults. Kabaya spoke in support of this.

Ali then made a long speech in support of Saidi, showing that Malindi and Rashidi had quarrelled on previous occasions, with Rashidi invariably at fault. He said that Rashidi was well known as a trouble-maker, especially at beer-drinks; and he gave examples that brought some calls of agreement from his own side of the moot. Rashidi's denial of this was, unfortunately for him, spoiled by Ali's direct appeal to a member of Rashidi's own action-set. Ali was able to extract the grudging agreement from Misawa (D14) that Rashidi had quarrelled with him at a beer-drink some weeks before. Perhaps emboldened by his success, Ali reiterated what he considered to be Rashidi's poor reputation and then went on to suggest, indirectly but fairly obviously, that Rashidi used witchcraft and was a bad neighbour in Ligomba. Amid murmurs of disapproval of Ali's innuendo, Yasini now intervened for the first time. He deprecated the introduction of suggestions of witchcraft, and he appealed to "all my kinsmen" (on both sides) for amity and a speedy settlement. Bilali, the father of Rashidi, indignantly denied any association of witchcraft, saying that if there were witches in Ligomba they were not among his kinsmen. He admitted that his son had previously quarrelled with Malindi and with Misawa, but he explained this away as "merely the affairs of young men and beer", and not serious matters relevant to the present dispute. Meha (ZS of Saidi) declared outright that he knew nothing of witchcraft in Ligomba, but added that Saidi's claim was fair and that Rashidi was a quarrelsome man. Another member of Saidi's action-set, Salimi, remarked that though he was a newcomer to the community he did not think that his neighbours practiced witchcraft or else he would not have moved to live here. Kasim began hotly to deny the imputation that his brother might be a witch, but he was interrupted by Yasini who declared that no one believed Rashidi to be a witch and that it was quite wrong to talk about it at all among kinsmen and neighbours. This statement received general commendation from all sides, whilst Ali remained silent.

Yasini continued to speak and for once everyone listened without interruption. He suggested that although Rashidi was to some extent guilty because he had twice attacked Malindi, yet he was badly abused by Malindi without justification. Rashidi's wife had a child, Rashidi's child, he said, and a man could not be expected to take such an insult quietly at any time. Here there was some inconclusive discussion, begun by Yasini, of a recent case of impotency slander in a nearby local community. Then Kabaya broke in to demand that this discussion should cease as it was irrelevant, for Rashidi was not impotent. Yasini accepted this statement on behalf of the moot, and no one attempted to contradict him.

After a brief pause, Saidi revived his demand for compensation of sixty shillings for the admitted injuries sustained by his son. Yasini turned to Mitedi (C19) and Sedi (C21), saying that he thought sixty shillings was too much. These two men, both neutrals to the dispute, signified agreement but said nothing. Kabaya said that no payment at all was necesary, nor would it be right. Meha said that some compensation was justified, but he suggested no figure. Saidi then asked what Rashidi would be prepared to give. After some confused cross-talk, Zadiki gained the moot's attention by saying that although he agreed with Kabaya that no compensation should be given, yet because of neighbourliness a small "friend-ship payment" might be made for Malindi's broken arm. Tanda, brother-in-law and close friend of Zadiki, supported this, saying that some small payment would demonstrate the generosity of Rashidi and his father. Kabaya also agreed but said that the pay-ment must be a small one. Saidi rejected this, but Yasini asked Rashidi what he would be prepared to give. Rashidi remained silent, but Zadiki suggested twenty shillings. Kabaya said this was too much and suggested five shillings, the cost of the fare on the lorry to Songea (the township of the District) where Malindi had gone to be treated by the European medical officer. Ali said that this was too little, as did Saidi and Meha. Yasini urged toleration on both sides. It was important to settle the matter, he said. "We are all kinsmen here, and neighbours. Let us cut this case in peace. Look! Have not Amadu and Musa put off their work-parties be-cause of this dispute? We all want to go out and cut woodland and drink beer together. But truly, Malindi went to Songea on that lorry to be treated by the European doctor, and so we should pay his fare". He asked Saidi to agree to five shillings, but Saidi would not. Meha asked for a little more. After further discussion it was agreed that a sum of twelve shillings should be paid. Several members of Rashidi's set, including Kabaya, expressed their ap-proval, as did Yasini who urged Rashidi to make some payment immediately. At last Rashidi produced two shillings, to which was added another shilling by Kabaya, and fifty cents each by Kasim and Musa. On Yasini's personal persuasion, Bilali produced twenty cents which, he said, was all he had. This money was handed over to Saidi by Yasini with the comment that the rest would certainly be paid soon after. Yasini's wife then brought out some beer, and the moot ended in overt amiability over the drink.

As far as I knew, only another two shillings were in fact handed over to Saidi—at a beer-drink some days later. Most probably no more would ever be paid, in the opinion of several of the men whom I questioned.

There are a number of points to be made about this case. The action-sets of the two principals were fairly clearly defined as the men sat on or near the verandah of Yasini's house, for they clus-tered more or less on opposite sides of the doorway. The support of members of a set was also made clear—perhaps deliberately—by their early remarks at the commencement of the moot. Of course men were well aware of the relevant alignments in any case, but loyalties were expressed and emphasised in this way. The two kinsmen of Saidi who were not residents of Ligomba took little part in the proceedings beyond occasional brief comments in support of remarks made by Saidi himself.

The first stage of the moot—the elucidation of the facts of the dispute, their relevance, and the degree of agreement—was monopolised by the principals and their more influential neighbours: Saidi and Ali on the one side, and Rashidi, his father, and Kabaya, on the other. The second stage—negotiation of compensation—was initiated by Yasini and supported by less involved members of the action-sets: Zadiki and Tanda on the one side and Meha on the other, whilst the principals remained silent or made a show of intransigency, but finally agreed to their supporters' compromise.

One of the original disputants, Malindi, scarcely contributed to the proceedings at all. He left the initiative to his father, as he had already done in the matter of recruiting the action-set prior to the second moot. He had been away from Ligomba at the time of the first moot, visiting the hospital in Songea. The other disputant, Rashidi, took a leading part, however. The explanation of this difference seems to lie in the character of the two men and in their relations with their fathers. Rashidi was a rather aggressive person, whilst Malindi was a quieter man of little forcefulness. That both were still young men was not in itself especially significant, for even older men of mild disposition would allow an influential kinsman to take the lead in dispute proceedings. In this instance neither of the fathers was a particularly prominent man in the community, and both were prepared to share the lead with a notable in their action-sets—Ali and Kabaya respectively. It so happened that each of these notables was first cousin to a disputant's father (that is, clearly a kin-neighbour); but that is less important than that each was an acknowledged man of influence, each had the ability and the ambition to assume leadership, and each sought the opportunity to demonstrate and enhance his influence. These two men were rivals for influence and this stimulated them to take the lead in opposed action-sets that emerged in the dispute. In the event, though Kabaya's achievement was not particularly marked, Ali's reputation was rather diminished by his unwise and undiplomatic reference to witchcraft. In this case Ali became a definite liability to Saidi, which was one reason for the repudiation of the witchcraft suggestion by other members of Saidi's set.

The structural position of intermediary imposed on Yasini was quite clear. Yasini himself recognised this and took the role of active mediator once the moot showed the extent of the difference between the principals. He could not remain a passive neutral, although he was not directly related by kinship to either principal. On the one hand, through the marriages of his daughters he was closely linked with members of Rashidi's set, and he and Rashidi and his father generally participated in each other's work-parties during the dry season. He was closely associated also with the notable Kabaya. On the other hand he was equally closely linked with the other notable, Ali, his first cousin and long-time associate; and he had reciprocal obligations with some other members of Saidi's set. However, Yasini was not a man of forceful character, and he seemed to have little ambition for gaining influence in the community at large. Because of this, I think, he made an effective mediator in the circumstances since he sought no marked advantage of his own. It seemed to me, and to my informants, that Yasini was not altogether impartial: rather, he leaned to Rashidi's side. The injuries to Malindi were moderately serious since he could not work in his fields at that busy time of year; and he might perhaps have obtained a larger compensation despite his demonstrated fault in provoking fighting. Yasini was partly responsible for the particular settlement that was in fact achieved.

The way in which Yasini played his role of mediator is typical of Ndendeuli processes of dispute settlement. He remained quiet until the stage of real negotiation began, and then, apart from appeals to goodwill and for concord in the community, he acted in effect as spokesman, stating what he conceived to be the feeling of the moot and opening the way to the next phase of discussion. Thus after discussion had run on in each instance, he stated that the suggestions of witchcraft were both wrong and irrelevant, that the imputation of impotency was false, and that sixty shillings was too high a compensation though some payment was justifiable. He finally urged Rashidi not only to agree to the sum of twelve shillings but also to make a part payment straightaway. These were critical steps in the movement towards an agreed settlement, although Yasini was supported by the other members of the moot in each and was generally only emphasising their suggestions.

I should also note Yasini's attempt to involve the manifest neutrals, Mitedi and Sedi, in support of compromise and agreement. This was not, as it turned out, either important or necessary; but it might have been had the disputants proved more intransigent.

Sedi told me afterwards that he did not regard the dispute as any affair of his, nor that of his kinsmen, and therefore he wished to remain passive. But he had been interested enough to attend the moot and he might possibly have been pushed into the role of assisting the mediator had the dispute continued. Sedi commented to me that had Konga not been absent from Ligomba then that notable would probably have attempted to take an active part, even although he was not at all involved. "Konga likes to have power [strength] and to show that he is a big man, a man to whom people listen", he said. Thus in the opinion of Sedi at least, Konga might well have been led by his ambitions to ignore his prescribed status as neutral in this dispute. It is unsatisfactory to resort to conjecture in analysis, but the significance of Sedi's opinion is not unimportant to an understanding of the social processes involved.

There was virtually a complete failure to pursue the allegation of impotency made against Rashidi—an acknowledged cause of the fighting. As we have seen, Yasini blocked this line of discussion after both Rashidi and his father had said little beyond blank denials. As a result of later enquiries, I became almost certain that Rashidi was impotent, and that his wife's child had been fathered by his elder brother. Ligomba informants were unwilling to discuss the matter and my enquiries were obviously unwelcome; but my field assistant reported that most men believed the allegation to be true. If this was so, it explains why a more spirited defence was not made and perhaps it helped persuade Rashidi and his father to accede more readily to the compensation demand in order to prevent further discussion. They, and Kabaya also, did not want the matter publicly discussed for fear of ridicule and shame. On the other hand, whether true or not, it still remained provocation for the violence, and there the fault lay with Malindi.

This matter was related to the way the witchcraft issue was treated. Here, the notable, Ali, overreached himself and weakened his side's case. There seemed to be no justification for the suggestion—even so obliquely as Ali put it—in the history of Rashidi and his kinsmen. Such accusations were made against people alleged to have committed other offences, and often against a person who was repeatedly a trouble-maker. But such accusation was a grave matter and put a dispute onto a more serious and more intractable level. It was likely to be efficacious only where a dispute was prolonged and where the balance of opinion ran strongly against one principal; more often it occurred where a dispute was one of a closely interconnected series of conflicts between the same people. It was difficult for Ndendeuli to achieve acceptable agreement and reasonable reconciliation after such an accusation had been publicly made; commonly one or other of the parties sooner or later withdrew from the community. This seems to have been empirically true; but in any case Ndendeuli thought and said that an accused witch and his accuser could not continue to be neighbours and that a dispute between them was likely to go unsettled. The witchcraft accusation raised the possibility, by implication, of a breakdown in intra-community relations and of a failure to settle a dispute. Ndendeuli certainly believed in and feared witchcraft as such; but they implicitly associated it with the failure of normal social control.

Consequently, Ali's indirect accusation was felt by most men, on either side, to be both irrelevant and dangerous, tantamount to suggesting that the dispute could not be settled and that the principals could not remain neighbours. Ali should have perceived this—indeed I am sure that at other times he did, for I discussed witchcraft with him on other occasions—and it may be surmised that he was too preoccupied with his efforts to demonstrate his influence and leadership, and to score against his rival, Kabaya. His mistake was unfortunate, too, in another way for it offered the opportunity to Rashidi and his supporters to make heated, lengthy, and self-righteous remonstration and denial, allowing the impotency allegation to be more easily ignored. Fellow members of Saidi's action-set—Meha and Salimi—were virtually compelled to repudiate Ali's imputation, whilst Saidi did much the same thing by remaining silent. Thus, unintentionally no doubt, Ali weakened the case he was promoting and damaged his personal reputation. He also endangered his relations with Yasini who, equally closely linked with both notables, was here put on the side of Kabaya. As I shall show later, competition between Ali and Kabaya over and through Yasini was persistently significant in Ligomba affairs.

Finally, I note that although compensation of twelve shillings was agreed to, only six shillings and twenty cents were actually handed over. People did not expect the rest to be paid. It seemed unlikely that Saidi would reopen the case by making a public issue of the outstanding amount; he probably had little wish for this once Malindi's injuries healed satisfactorily, and his supporters had little to gain by encouraging it. Yasini told me that the matter was ended: it should not be raised again or the whole dispute would be

renewed, he explained. But he too had no wish to see the matter
discussed since it might affect his own neighbourly relations ad-
versely. No one had anything to gain, therefore, by insisting on
full payment of the agreed sum, and general opinion was against
anything that might threaten good working relations among neighbours. Sedi suggested to me that possibly the unpaid debt might be
raised if Malindi and Rashidi, or their near kin-neighbours, became
involved in another dispute. His surmise may have been correct;
and the chance of some other dispute was not fanciful, for although
the moot had successfully ended in agreement and settlement, yet
the insult of impotency, the suggestion of witchcraft, and the bitterness of the quarrel and of earlier quarrels, all lingered. They
were potentially fertile ground for further trouble. On the other
hand, however, as community life went on and fresh disputes and
conflicts brought rather different alignments of support and opposition, this particular conflict became less and less likely to have
the makings of a persistent cleavage in Ligomba such as might produce factions. Too many other people, in addition to Yasini,
bridged the gap between the two sides with their own neighbourly
relations to allow cleavage of this sort to develop. In this kind of
network system, persisting factions were both empirically and logically unlikely, as each successive dispute tended to produce its
own particular set of ephemeral alignments.

Summary and Analysis of the Case. There was agreement that
the defendant was responsible for the injuries, but that the plaintiff
was largely responsible for causing the fighting; that the defendant
had some reputation for violence; that the allegation of impotency
in the defendant was not true; that the defendant was not involved
in witchcraft; that the plaintiff's injuries prevented him from
working at a busy time of year; that the defendant had incurred
the cost of going to hospital; and that other neighbours' work-parties
had been postponed because of this dispute. The final disagreement
lay in the degree of blame to be put on either principal, and the
amount of compensation to be paid by the defendant. The settlement was that twelve shillings compensation should be paid: contributions to this were made by the defendant's action-set, but
eventually only just over half of it was paid over. The mediator
was principally Yasini (passively supported by his nephews), with
compromise suggestions coming in the end from Zadiki, a less
closely linked member of the defendant's action-set. Rivalry between competing notables was a significant factor.

Case 4: A Creditor's Claim (September)

About three weeks after the end of the previous case, a small moot was held at Konga's house to discuss the clash of arrangements for the work-parties of Musa and Sedi, which, it had been belatedly discovered, had been set for the same day. Thus some men (for example, Zadiki and his sons) had obligations to join both parties on the same day. There was nothing unusual about this since, there being no central organisation of work-party schedules, some conflicts of dates were to be expected. They could be ironed out in a friendly moot attended by interested persons. This moot was attended by Kabaya (C11), though he was but peripherally involved. In the course of the subsequent casual gossip over beer, he learned that a young, unmarried son of Sedi had just returned from employment abroad; and therefore he took the opportunity to request Sedi to repay the loan of a goat Kabaya had provided over a year ago for the bridewealth of Yusufu, another of Sedi's sons. Kabaya was unusual in this part of the country in maintaining a small flock of goats from which he made a modest profit by occasionally lending or selling an animal. Sedi and his son had wished to impress the wife's father and to avoid suitor-service (since bridewealth had been owing some time), and had therefore obtained a goat on promise of payment in cash in the near, but unspecified, future. Now Kabaya expected to be paid since, he argued, Sedi's younger son had brought back some money after working as a labour migrant. At first, Sedi attempted to deny that his son had brought back any money, and he declared that he himself had had no opportunity to earn money. Kabaya grew indignant, saying that the son must have brought something back, enough to repay this debt. He grumbled that Sedi had made no attempt at all to pay what he owed, and recalled that this was the second time he had asked for his rightful claim to be met after more than a year. Sedi showed no sign of regret or apology, but on being pressed he offered five shillings to Kabaya as part payment. He also remarked that the goat had been an old and poor animal, that it had since died and the father-in-law was much displeased in consequence. At this point Kabaya lost his temper; he dismissed the denigration of his goat, rejected the part payment offer, and left the house shouting that he would not let the matter drop, and that Sedi was a thief.

Negotiations for a moot were conducted between Kabaya and

the notable, Konga, and it was agreed to hold it at Konga's house.
The action-sets, each recruited by the principal, were as follows:

Action-set of Kabaya

Yasini	(SWF)	
Kinanda	(SWB)	
Bilali	(MBS)	
Tanda	(FZS)	(7 men)
Musa	(FZSS)	
Zadiki	(Tanda's ZH)	

Intermediary

[Misawa]	(Tanda's ZS; Konga's FBSS)
[Rajabu]	
Ali	(Yasini's FBS; Konga's FMBDS)

Action-set of Sedi

Konga and Mitedi	(FZS)	
Hamedi and Faraji	(FZSS)	
Yusufu	(S)	(8 men)
Hanju	(DH)	
Ndoma	(FBDS)	

It might perhaps have been expected that logically Zadiki, as
structural intermediary in the context and not directly related to
either principal, would have acted as mediator instead of appearing
as a member of Kabaya's action-set. There were, however, good
reasons for his choice. First, Zadiki had long been a close friend
and constant associate of his wife's brother, Tanda, and through
him had regular cooperation with Kabaya whom he regarded as his
kin-neighbour. But additionally, this alignment was strengthened
because of his poorly suppressed antagonism towards his cousin,
Konga, which had made him more dependent on Tanda and
Kabaya. Moreover, Zadiki apparently felt no need to support Sedi:
although Case 2 had been settled and accepted by both Zadiki and
Sedi, clearly they were not altogether reconciled to one another.
Zadiki saw no reason to act as mediator in Sedi's dispute, neither
did he choose the course of opting out of the moot, as he could
easily have done—presumably wishing to mark his support of
Tanda and Kabaya. On the other hand, Zadiki's sons, especially the
younger son, Rajabu (son-in-law of Sedi), were put into a dilemma
by their father's action and by the context of the dispute itself.
Both chose to absent themselves from Ligomba for a few days.
Consequently there was no overt mediator participating in the

moot. This seems to have offered an opening to the notable, Ali, for he attended the moot and sat, at first, with Kabaya's set; and it was Ali who came to take the role of mediator. He had not been invited by Kabaya, nor presumably in view of their rivalry did Kabaya wish to have him there. In the moot itself Ali did not disguise his partiality for Kabaya's claim as legitimate creditor, although he was not so committed as to prevent his acting fairly successfully as mediator. In this role he also made use of his personal and long-standing friendship with Konga (his second cousin) in order to gain a workable compromise and reconciliation between the principals. As a result of his careful intervention, Ali also succeeded in preventing any eruption of antagonism between Zadiki and Konga and Sedi.

The moot was not protracted, and with the successful insulation of Zadiki there was no particular complication to prevent agreement being negotiated. The facts of the case were too obvious to everyone to produce any real difference of opinion, and the proceedings were largely devoted to the determination of some payment by Sedi to Kabaya. Eventually Sedi paid twenty shillings before the assembed men: he had the money already in his pocket and had evidently come to the moot prepared to pay something. He promised to pay another four shillings later, though no time limit was fixed for this. It was admitted by Sedi that he knew little about goats or the particular goat in question. He had, he said by way of apology, merely repeated the complaints about its poor quality that had been made by his son's father-in-law. All the men in the moot agreed euphorically that fathers-in-law invariably complain about the bridewealth they obtain (though of course several of them were themselves fathers-in-law), and this was the mood in which they drank together the beer Sedi supplied.

As the moot ended, the question remained, at least for me as observer, why Ali should have participated uninvited and assumed the role of mediator. My Ligomba informants were not puzzled, however, as I discovered in later conversation with Yasini, Konga, and Tanda. According to them, Ali wished to participate in any public issue in the community, for "he is a big man". Although this was not altogether true—Ali had not attended the moot in Case 2, for example—it is most relevant. Notables gained and retained their acknowledged prestige and influence by their successful participation in moots. It was further suggested that Ali wished to try and recover some of the reputation he had undoubtedly lost as a result of his ill-judged tactics in Case 3. That he was successful was clear.

Konga actually complimented him in the moot, though that was an old friend speaking and meaning to be helpful. More significantly, Kabaya was obliged, at Yasini's tactful prompting, to express gratitude for Ali's intervention and assistance. As a principal disputant in the moot, Kabaya was of course in no easy position to take a lead in the negotiations towards a settlement, and he had necessarily to accept and be glad of Ali's help. He could not in fact have found a better mediator, and I believe that he was relieved that tensions between Zadiki and Sedi were prevented from interfering in the settlement of his own affairs. Yet Kabaya disliked admitting an obligation of gratitude to Ali, and no doubt he had no wish to be the means by which Ali was able to restore something of his reputation in Ligomba.

There was more to Ali's action than this, however. He was a rival of Kabaya not only in a general sense, but in particular for the allegiance of their mutual kinsman, Yasini. Ali understood that in this case, as doubtless on previous occasions, Yasini was unreservedly obliged to support Kabaya, as a kin-neighbour should. But this tended to draw Yasini away from Ali himself, and therefore he seems to have chosen to join with Yasini in assisting Kabaya, rather than allowing a separation between them. He said to me afterwards: "Is not Yasini my brother? Therefore I must help him and go with [support] him. I cannot leave him on his own when he goes to help another neighbour. We are one, brothers together, and we are nearer together than he and Kabaya.[11] I went with him when he helped Kabaya in order to show how near we are, and to show that we are brothers and neighbours". There is no reason to suppose that on this occasion Kabaya had deliberately attempted to emphasise his association with Yasini or to weaken the ties between the latter and Ali. He had every right to expect Yasini's support in the dispute with Sedi. Yet in effect he seemed to threaten Ali's position. In the event, then, Ali was able to emphasise both his tie with Yasini and his capacity for influential leadership, and both to some extent at the expense of his rival notable; but he accomplished this without overtly antagonising Kabaya.

Summary and Analysis of the Case. It was agreed that the de-

[11] There was no Ndendeuli dogma in fact that made a first cousin "nearer", genealogically or in terms of rights and obligations, than a daughter's husband's father. But in any case Yasini scarcely wished to distinguish the strengths of his valuable ties with either of his "brothers". A test case arose some months later on this very matter: see Work-Party Case 1, page 203 ff.

fendant owed a debt to the plaintiff for a goat; that there had been no payment to date, despite a previous request by the plaintiff; and that the goat had been a satisfactory animal. The final disagreement concerned the size of repayment to be made and whether the defendant had the immediate means to pay. The settlement was an immediate payment of twenty shillings and the promise of a further four shillings later. The mediator was Ali (first cousin of plaintiff's SWF; second cousin of defendant's first cousin) who at first had joined the action-set of the plaintiff.

Case 5: A Cousins' Quarrel (November)

Towards the end of the dry season, Hamedi (D16) and his father, Konga (C17), were visited by the father of Hamedi's wife.

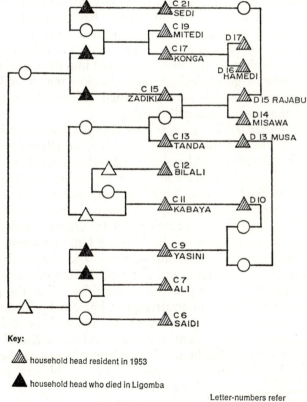

Key:

▨ household head resident in 1953

▲ household head who died in Ligomba

Letter-numbers refer
to master genealogy.

FIGURE 15: Case 5: A Cousins' Quarrel.

A small beer-drink was arranged by Konga which, in addition to the visitor, was attended by Konga's sons, and by Saidi, Ali, Mitedi, Sedi, and Yusufu.[12] Next day, whilst the visitor was still in Ligomba, Zadiki (C15) came in great indignation to complain to Konga because, he said, he had not been invited to the beer-drink. He alleged that Konga had ignored him—an unfriendly act—and had made him appear unimportant to the visitor. Konga claimed that he had sent one of his grandsons to Zadiki's house with news of the beer-drink, and that he had assumed that Zadiki had chosen not to attend for some reason. Zadiki insisted that he had had no knowledge of the event (or he would certainly have attended) and asked why Konga had not made sure that the message had been conveyed. He declared that a young grandson was neither a reliable nor a proper messenger. Konga tried to dismiss the matter as an unfortunate accident, but his complacency seemed to irritate Zadiki further. He began to rail against Konga, his first cousin, enumerating past occasions when Konga had failed to extend invitations to him or to help him in other ways. He referred to Case 2, saying that Konga should have supported him then. Zadiki eventually left after a good deal of recrimination which ended in a shouting match in which Hamedi joined (annoyed, he said, because his father-in-law was still there).

Two days later Zadiki returned to Konga's house, again in an angry mood. He had two complaints. First, he alleged that some of Konga's young granddaughters (daughters of Hamedi and Faraji) had insulted his wife at the water-point, upset a pot of water, and cracked the pot. This had happened the day after his earlier visit. Second, he had heard through the women that, after he had left on the previous occasion, Idi (youngest married son of Konga) had amused the others by likening him to a strutting cock and had caricatured his walk and gestures. Zadiki now demanded apologies for both incidents, and the replacement of the damaged water pot. Konga tried to pass the whole thing off as the playfulness of young girls and a poor attempt at humour by his son (who had the reputation of being a clown). He ignored the claim for a new pot. Another angry scene occurred, and when Zadiki left the house he shouted out that he would not leave the matter there. Nor did he, for he obtained the support of kin-neighbours, including the notable, Kabaya, in seeking a moot.

The development and persistence of antagonistic relations between these two first cousins, Zadiki and Konga, have been de-

[12] This was in effect an action-set recruited by Konga.

scribed in the preceding chapter,[13] where it was indicated that they
had been important in the evolution of the Ligomba kinship network. To reiterate summarily: not long after settling in Ligomba,
in 1939, Zadiki had been embarrassingly defeated in a dispute with
Konga who had gained the support of most of their common kin-
neighbours. At least partly to gain kin-neighbours less committed
to Konga's sector of the network, Zadiki had sponsored Tanda as
a newcomer, and the latter had soon sponsored Kabaya and Bilali.
As it turned out, Kabaya, an able and forceful man, became a serious rival of Konga, and of Ali, for influence and leadership. Zadiki
became a supporter of Kabaya—not invariably, of course, but
quite commonly—and he tended to seek the advice and help of
Kabaya.

Relations between Zadiki and Konga had remained poor. There
had been some minor disputes between them during later years.
Yet it continued logically in the interests of both cousins that at
least a minimum of cooperation and neighbourliness should continue. Moreover, it was in the interests of their kin-neighbours also
to maintain working relations through the linkages provided by
the two men. Those most concerned were the sons of Zadiki and
of Konga, as well as Tanda and his son on the one side, and Mitedi
and Sedi and his son on the other. Some of these men had been
frequent members of each other's action-sets for years, including
the period of field preparation not long over that year; and they
wished for such cooperation to continue in the following wet
season.

Yet the tension, the potential conflict, persisted. Only a little
earlier that year (Case 2) Konga as structural intermediary between the principals Zadiki and Sedi had shown himself in the
opinion of several men, including Zadiki himself, to favour Sedi
when acting as mediator. The residue of resentment between Zadiki
and Sedi following that case had affected Zadiki's role in Case 4,
when he had joined Kabaya's action-set in opposition to that of
Sedi, instead of becoming a mediator. Konga was a member of
Sedi's set on that occasion, and Zadiki's decision then was certainly
affected by that, when otherwise two first cousins under such circumstances might have allied together as mediators.

The present dispute, then, arose out of the history of relations
between the two men and their current positions in the kinship
network of the community. One might say that it, or something
like it, had been imminent for some time. Konga was probably to

[13] See page 98 f.

blame for initiating this latest phase, for he did not make sure that
his cousin was properly invited to the beer-drink. This may or may
not have been deliberate. The affair of the water pot was a petty
matter that no doubt could have easily have been settled privately,
but Zadiki was angered by it and seems to have seized the opportunity to use it against Konga. The latter showed little sign of
wishing to accommodate his cousin in the matter. In addition, according to one reliable informant (Saidi), Kabaya had encouraged
Zadiki to insist on a public apology and reparation. On this evidence, Kabaya sought to embarrass his rival, and Zadiki seemed
only too glad to take his advice. Kabaya arranged the calling of the
moot, which was held at Tanda's house. At the moot the action-sets
were composed as follows:

Action-set of Zadiki
           Misawa   (S)
            Tanda   (WB)
             Musa   (WBS)   (7 men)
  Kabaya and Haji   (Tanda's MBS and son)
            Bilali   (Kabaya's MBS)

Intermediary
         [Yasini]   (Kabaya's SWF; Ali's FBS)
         [Rajabu]   (Zadiki's son; Konga's FBSS)

Action-set of Konga
Hamedi and Faraji   (S)
           Mitedi   (B)
             Sedi   (MBS)   (8 men)
            Ndoma   (MBDS)
     Saidi and Ali   (FMBDS)

   In this context, Yasini (C9) was not linked at all closely with
either principal; but he was forced into the position of structural
intermediary as a result of invitations from Kabaya and Tanda on
the one hand, and by Ali on the other, to join their respective action-sets. He left Ligomba the day before the moot to visit a kinsman; and the men at the moot assumed, no doubt rightly, that he
had chosen to opt out of a difficult situation that promised no
advantage and potential disadvantage to him. Nevertheless, a more
ambitious man might have taken up the role of mediator in this
context. Rajabu, Zadiki's son, was also put into an ambivalent
position: he clearly should have supported his father, but he under-
standably had no wish to act in a set opposed to one in which his

father-in-law, Sedi, participated. As in Case 4, Rajabu decided to absent himself, despite the displeasure of his father; but, because of his relative juniority and unfamiliarity with his neighbours, he was not (unlike Yasini) a potential mediator.

My account of this moot depends on information from my field assistant and informants in Ligomba, as I was unable to attend. Zadiki began the moot by lengthily repeating his complaints that Konga had allowed him to be insulted in the ways already mentioned; and he went on to refer to previous occasions when, he alleged, Konga had failed to meet expectations. Zadiki spoke with growing indignation. Konga replied in similar tone, ignoring Zadiki's complaints and raising complaints of his own against Zadiki's past behaviour towards him. The notable Kabaya spoke in support of Zadiki, and the notable Ali followed in support of Konga. Bilali also supported Zadiki's allegations and directly attacked Ali.[14] Emotions began to run high as tempers rose, but gradually an alliance of Tanda and Musa on the one side and Mitedi and Hamedi on the other led to a settlement and overt reconciliation. As these men continued to insist on a conciliatory solution of the dispute, they were joined and supported by Sedi and Ndoma, and then by Ali. Eventually Kabaya openly counselled Zadiki to accept an apology from Konga and his son, Idi (who had caricatured him). As Idi was not present at the moot (on his elder brother's advice), his apology was expressed on his behalf by that brother, Hamedi. Zadiki also agreed to drop his complaints against Konga.

On the face of it, the moot was inconclusive in that neither the immediate nor the deeper, long-term issues were tackled. Probably it was impossible, or at least not desirable, that they should have been, however, for a real settlement of these and the establishment of friendly "brotherly" and neighbourly relations was out of the question because of the personal antagonism between the two men and their structural pulls in opposite directions. Much would depend on future circumstances, of course, but some basis seems to have been laid for the continuance of some kind of working relationship between the two cousins. The emergent, *de facto* mediators in the moot were concerned to head off continued discussion

[14] Both Saidi and my field assistant believed that Bilali's attack was the result of Ali's earlier suggestion of witchcraft against Bilali's son in Case 3. This may have been true since Bilali was not normally an outspoken participant in moots, and on this occasion his obligations to support Zadiki were not especially strong. Bilali may also have wished to show his close association with Kabaya, the notable.

of the immediate dispute because of the danger that might arise. Sedi told me later that he and others wished to stop the quarrelling, not exacerbate it. The issue of the damaged water pot was not taken up at all by the moot, though Zadiki had made it a complaint in his opening statement. Zadiki must tacitly have acceded to this.

The moot did achieve the major result—at least for the time being—of preventing the crystallisation of hostility not only between Zadiki and Konga, but also between their respective supporters. There was no breakdown, even temporarily, of neighbourly cooperation in Ligomba: this was especially important as the wet season was to be expected soon, with all the needs for agricultural cooperation of that critical season of the Ndendeuli year. Men on both sides wished to continue reciprocal assistance and to avoid the threat to this end that might have come from some overt schism between Zadiki and Konga. On the occasion of this moot Tanda, for example, was specifically on the side of his brother-in-law, Zadiki; but he had fairly well-established conventions of reciprocal assistance with Konga, Mitedi, and others that were most valuable to him. Sedi had an additional reason for urging a settlement, for he could scarcely afford to allow a worsening of relations with Zadiki, his daughter's husband's father, unless it proved quite impossible to avoid making a choice between Konga and Zadiki. In brief, too much was at stake for a number of the men for them to want anything other than the opportunity to continue their working relations. These considerations were far less important for such men as Ali, Kabaya, and Bilali, since their own working relations in the community were not threatened in this way.

All three Ligomba notables were involved in this particular dispute, though Konga's role in the case was of course limited to that of defendant rather than of leader or mediator. Kabaya sought to lead on Zadiki's side, perhaps in some personal opposition to Konga, and to Ali, but his influence in the circumstances was limited in effect by the self-interested determination of those others more intimately involved to prevent a thorough-going showdown and to preserve neighbourly, cooperative relations. Ali supported Konga; but more perceptively, perhaps, than his rival, Kabaya, he fairly quickly joined with the conciliators. Unlike Kabaya, he did not show that he needed to be persuaded and convinced of the satisfactoriness of their advocacy. Kabaya's reputation was not helped, whilst that of Ali was, if anything, strengthened.

Summary and Analysis of the Case. There was agreement that

relations between the principals were poor, and marked by previous conflicts; that first cousins should be friendly and cooperative,
and so therefore should these principals; that a decisive break between the principals was unacceptable to their kin-neighbours because of the subsequent threat to the latters' own cooperative
relations. The final disagreement lay in the degree of culpable animosity, by the defendant. The agreed settlement was that the defendant and his son should apologise in the moot to the plaintiff.
There were no mediators, but gradually kin-neighbours on either
side joined in propagating the compromise. The implicit significance of the dispute and its handling was the state of relations not
only between plaintiff and defendant, but also between their sets
of kin-neighbours: the moot gave the opportunity for a thorough
examination of these relations by those concerned.

Case 6: An Errant Son-in-Law (December)

Yasini (C9) had left his house repairs until late in the dry
season, and as a matter of urgency (for the first rains might soon
come) he called on his local "sons" (own son, nephews, and sons-
in-law), a few days after the previous moot, to haul and put in
place two new wall posts for his house. One of the sons-in-law,
Musa (D13), did not turn up next day and the work was done
by the others under Yasini's supervision. But Yasini grumbled
about Musa's absence, and the following day he refused to accept
Musa's excuse that he had to go and visit his mother's brother in
order to obtain medicines for his sick mother. Yasini then raised
the matter of Musa's bridewealth payment. In Case 2, Yasini's willingness to accept a smaller instalment of bridewealth than he had
at first been promised had been important to the settlement of that
earlier dispute between Zadiki and Sedi (cf. page 149). At that
previous moot he had agreed to receive only fifty shillings instead
of the sum of seventy-five shillings; but in fact he had since received only a part payment of forty shillings, and had agreed to
wait for the remainder. Now he firmly demanded the outstanding
ten shillings. Musa said that he no longer had any money, nor, for
the moment, could he obtain any. This Yasini refused to accept.
He declared that he would no longer be lenient to his young son-
in-law; he also complained of the latter's failure to help him as he
should and alleged that Musa had ill-treated his daughter (Musa's
wife).

Consulting with his first cousin, Ali the notable, Yasini was encouraged to persist with his claim and complaints. Ali sought to

convene a moot on Yasini's behalf. This was easily arranged and was held at Konga's house, where the action-sets were composed as follows:

Action-set of Yasini
Kinanda	(S)	
Ali	(FBS)	
Saidi	(Ali's MZS)	(6 men)
Makungu	(BS)	
Haji	(DH)	

Intermediary
[Kabaya]	(Yasini's DHF; Musa's FMBS)

Action-set of Musa
Tanda	(F)	
Zadiki	(FZH)	
Misawa and Rajabu	(FZS)	
Konga and Mitedi	(Zadiki's FBS)	
Hamedi and Idi	(Konga's S)	(12 men)
Sedi	((Konga's MBS; Rajabu's WF)	
Bilali and Kasim	(MBS and son of Musa's FMBS)	

In this context, Kabaya was structural intermediary and, especially as he was a notable, he might have acted as meditor. He chose to opt out, however, by absenting himself from Ligomba, whilst his son, Haji, joined the set of Yasini, his wife's father. As far as I could determine, Kabaya did not wish to act as mediator between two sets that would be—and in fact, were—led by the notables Ali and Konga respectively. He might have gained prestige by negotiating between these notables, but probably he foresaw what was likely to happen. Ali and Konga were life-long friends as well as kin-neighbours (second cousins); they often supported each other and had contrived to avoid the rivalry and hostility that commonly existed between notables. In this moot they cooperated together in effect as mediators after starting off as leading advocates for their own principals. Had Kabaya been present he would have been squeezed out and made to look superfluous; and so, wisely from his point of view, he absented himself.

The moot was neither difficult nor prolonged. It amounted less to a demand for the acknowledged bridewealth debt to be paid than to a general complaint by a father-in-law against his son-in-law. Musa was clearly in the wrong for Yasini had been abundantly tolerant and helpful in Case 2, and since that time as well. After Yasini's opening statement to this effect, Musa made a brief defensive reply in which he concentrated on his inability to pay anything yet to Yasini. He made some play with his imminent obligation to cultivate his fields when the new rains soon began, in order to provide food for his wife (Yasini's daughter) and child (Yasini's grandson). His father-in-law, he protested, could not expect him to go off and find work to earn money when he had to work for his wife, as a husband must. He denied any ill treatment of his wife. Konga spoke on his behalf but (it seemed to me) without marked conviction. Ali followed with a summary of Yasini's complaints, and then suggested a public apology by Musa to his father-in-law and at least some token payment of bridewealth. Musa remained silent, but Konga expressed readiness to accept that suggestion, though he made the point that no one really thought that Musa had mistreated his wife. He then turned to Musa and asked him to agree on condition (though it was more tactfully expressed) that Yasini withdrew his allegation of ill treatment of the wife. Yasini murmured agreement to this; and Ali added that as soon as he could Musa should find temporary work in order to earn money for bridewealth. After a little more discussion all this was affirmed, and Musa gave fifty cents to Yasini. Ali and Konga ended the moot by praising the good sense of Yasini and Musa and the good relations between them. The whole moot lasted little more than half an hour.[15]

Why, then, was Musa's action-set so relatively large (twelve men), and why did it contain so many indirectly linked neighbours? The dispute was not a difficult one to settle, and Musa showed little sign of unwillingness to come to terms with his father-in-law. Informants were clear about this. Following the previous case by only a week, these men who at that time had been on opposed sides had managed, as I have described, to produce a working settlement; they now wished to emphasise their association together. They were (as Sedi told me) less concerned with Musa's case than with their own neighbourly inter-relations, and they took this accidental opportunity to demonstrate their ability and willingness to engage in successful common action. Even Zadiki and Konga sat together in the same set in the moot. Perhaps Yasini and Musa were fortunate that among and between their respective supporters there was no additional antagonism to complicate their own straightforward dispute.

[15] The affinal relations of Musa were, however, not altogether improved. He remained somewhat casual in his obligations to Yasini, and to his brother-in-law, Kinanda, as shown later in Work-party Case 5, page 212.

Summary and Analysis of the Case. There was agreement that bridewealth was owing and that a promise to pay had not been kept; that the defendant had failed to fulfill his obligations to work for the plaintiff, his father-in-law; that the defendant had a prior obligation at that time to cultivate his fields rather than to go away to work and earn money to pay his debt; and that the defendant had not ill treated his wife. The final disagreement was on the amount to be paid and the time of payment, and on the degree of failure of the defendant to meet his other obligations to the plaintiff. The settlement was that the defendant should pay a token instalment of the bridewealth debt and the remainder later, that he should apologise to the plaintiff and seek to fulfill his obligations in the future. There were no mediators, but notable Ali (FBS of plaintiff) and notable Konga (cousin of defendant's FZH) joined in conciliatory negotiation. The implicit significance of the moot was the desire of the plaintiff's father-in-law to gain public recognition of the inadequate behaviour of his son-in-law, and the opportunity afforded to a cluster of neighbours to reaffirm their friendly association.

Case 7: A Refusal to Lend Seed to a Kinsman (December)

The last dispute to occur that year was of a rather different order. Most men in Ligomba were, I believe, scarcely aware of it before it had been settled. My assistant and Ali told me, one day in mid-December, that they had heard that Misawa (D14) had refused to make a loan of bean seed to Kasim (D11) when the latter had requested this in preparation for the impending cultivation season. Such a request was not unusual when a household was short of seed at that time of year, if a kinsman or his wife could be persuaded that some of theirs could be spared. Apparently Misawa's refusal on this occasion had led to a quarrel between him and Kasim. Something of this had been overheard by other neighbours, and Kasim told Saidi (meeting him on the path immediately afterwards) that he (Kasim) had a case against Misawa and would call a moot. He did not specify particulars of the case, however.

Next day a moot was held at Kabaya's house, attended (as far as I could ascertain) by Kabaya, Tanda, Bilali (father of Kasim), Zadiki (father of Misawa) and their sons, including the two disputants (D10, D11, D12, D13, D14, and D15).[16] There had been little or no spreading of news about this, but afterwards it was

[16] See the genealogy in Figure 14, page 152.

generally understood that Misawa had agreed to make a loan of seed to Kasim. To me there seemed to be some unusual degree of secrecy, or at least privacy, about this case; but Ali and Saidi commented that "it is the affair of the neighbours of Kabaya, and they are not our kinsmen". Yet both men had, I discovered, been curious enough to find out what had occurred. Their story, more or less corroborated by Konga later, was as follows.

The seed beans stored away by Kasim's wife had been spoiled by insects and there was an urgent need to obtain another supply. It was decided, for some reason unknown to me, to beg some from Misawa's household. Usually this kind of transaction was conducted between and by wives, but it happened that Kasim's wife had injured her foot on a large thorn. So Kasim himself went to Misawa's house. According to his own account (given in the moot), he found the hamlet deserted except for Misawa's wife and one or two small children.[17] Kasim made his request, which was parried by the wife, and then he stayed on talking to her in her house. Rajabu, returning home at the time, heard the voices inside the house, and immediately went back to call his elder brother Misawa, who was at Tanda's house. Misawa hurried home and accused Kasim of seduction of his (Misawa's) wife. This was denied by both Kasim and the wife, but Misawa refused to accept their innocence. He struck his wife who ran away, and he threatened Kasim. The latter protested his innocence, saying he had merely come to beg seed, but Misawa ordered him to leave and declared that he would not lend him seed. Returning home, Kasim told his story to his father, Bilali, and to Kabaya who happened to be visiting there. After some discussion Kabaya said that he would arrange a moot, and he went off to find Tanda and Zadiki.

The moot next morning was not composed of confronting action-sets, and apparently much effort was made to reconcile the two disputants. Kasim insisted on his innocence, but Misawa pointed out that to sit in a woman's house (unless it be of a sister) when her husband or other male kin are absent was sufficient proof of seduction or at least the wish and intent. In this he was, by Ndendeuli standards, essentially correct. Kabaya and Tanda both declared that, though Kasim had been foolish and provocative, they did not think that he had done any harm nor had he intended to do so. They urged Kasim to apologise and Misawa to accept this. Misawa eventually agreed after his father, Zadiki, had shown

[17] This was the hamlet shared by Zadiki and his two married sons, Misawa and Rajabu.

readiness to accept Kasim's innocence when this was supported by Kabaya and Tanda. Finally Kabaya persuaded Misawa to make a small loan of seed to Kasim, to which Kabaya himself added an additional amount from his own store.

Whether or not Kasim had had intentions upon Misawa's wife seemed not to be known to my informants. The significance of the case was nevertheless fairly clear to them. This dispute, unlike the previous ones that year in Ligomba, occurred between men who were not only kin-neighbours but who had a significant number of kin-neighbours in common. Relations among these men comprised a highly inter-connected section of the Ligomba kinship network, and all of them tended to look to the notable, Kabaya, for advice and leadership. It was most important to them, therefore, that a dispute between two of their number should not disrupt the high level of reliable cooperation and mutual dependence among them all. For Kabaya in particular it was important to restore amity and confidence and continued good working relations amongst what amounted to his "followers". Thus a moot was held uncommonly quickly; other neighbours were not invited who otherwise might have been asked to give their support to one or other of the disputants, and the moot was not divided into action-sets. Kabaya, supported by Tanda, succeeded not only in persuading Misawa and Zadiki to accept Kasim's innocence, but also in persuading Misawa to make a small loan of seed as—I would interpret it—a token of restored good will. Kabaya himself was sufficiently concerned that he augmented the loan of seed by some of his own. The result certainly seemed to justify Kabaya's ability, for in the following cultivation season this cluster of kin-neighbours actively and amicably participated in each other's work-parties as usual.

Thus this was a crisis situation for these neighbours, and for Kabaya's status as a notable. The membership of the rapidly convened moot served, in effect, to identify those men who considered themselves to be particularly closely inter-linked. I note that Yasini, his son and his two nephews were not invited, indicating his equivocal status in this respect. Neither were Konga and his sons, and Mitedi, invited, though they were kin-neighbours of Misawa and Zadiki. No doubt in view of his past experience with them, Zadiki had little desire to seek their aid and to be further indebted to them; but had the small moot not reached a settlement, he might have needed their support in an action-set. I note also, and with emphasis, that this was not simply a matter of quickly settling a dispute between two close kinsmen. Genealogically Misawa and Kasim were not closely related: they had a second cousin in common. It was a matter that involved a whole cluster of highly interconnected kin-neighbours.[18]

THE SIGNIFICANCE OF MOOTS IN THE LOCAL COMMUNITY

The processes of dispute settlement within an Ndendeuli local community, as demonstrated in the foregoing cases, followed the mode of negotiation, not that of adjudication. Principals to a dispute, each assisted by their socially relevant supporters, sought to exert what strength they could against each other: appeals to and interpretations of norms and values, special pleading, skill in argument and in confusing the argument, bargaining (directly and indirectly) by offers or denials of other advantages and interests, the involvement of the interests of others who might then bring their pressures to bear. Sooner or later mediators emerged, but they could rarely be more than brokers and spokesmen; they had no formally constituted status nor were their sanctions at their disposal. These Ndendeuli processes were what may tentatively be called "politico-jural", in distinction from "judicial". That is to say, they operated in the realm of political activity, being concerned with the distribution of power, competition for power, and the use of it to defend or promote men's interests and rights. There was no adjudication by a third party with the hint or full strength of authority behind him. There cannot, of course—and I stress this—be any absolute dividing line between processes of negotiation and processes of adjudication, between politico-jural and judicial modes of dispute settlement. There are significant sociological characteristics common to both that are of great importance for comparative analysis. But the contra-distinction of the two modes is heuristically useful at least.

Although politico-jural processes of negotiation were not controlled by direct, overt authority or disinterestedness, they were not by any means wholly unrestrained, pragmatic struggles for power and ascendancy. This was particularly evident in two respects: the virtual absence of a resort to physical force, and the permeation of norms, values, and role expectations throughout the negotiations. The resort to physical force was inhibited partly by socio-cultural dispositions and partly by the constraint of the external (at that time, colonial) government. It is, I think, impossible

[18] The significance of the cluster is examined in Chapter Eight.

to determine the relative weight of significance for these two factors, internal and external. Without at all gainsaying the passive weight of external governmental influence and power here, it must be noted that (rationalising or not) the Ndendeuli perceived a resort to violence (which did occasionally occur) as the antithesis of neighbourliness, of the possibility of reliable cooperation, and of peacefulness. They said, and sometimes showed intrinsically in behaviour, that resort to violence, even in a good cause, was both a weakness and a grave fault. As they put it, serious violence, violence to gain one's ends, precluded the possibility of living together in a single community. It precluded minimal trust both between those who were kin and those who were not. It introduced an uncontrollable element. It was related to the illegitimacy of witchcraft. Moreover, in practice the man who used violence was likely to increase the number of his opponent's supporters beyond those who otherwise were obligated to give him assistance. Even were such a man to move away to live elsewhere (as he would probably have to do), he would find difficulty in establishing adequate supporters again, and might be assessed an unacceptable newcomer in other communities. I have good record of one such case where the offending man was successfully refused membership in four local communities in this way: he ended up living a precarious existence in a fifth community, with one kin-neighbour and poor prospects of developing further links of cooperation. In other societies under colonial rule, where self-help violence was also made illegal and punishable by the colonial authorities, violence did nevertheless sometimes continue as *one* means of social control—for example, in Karamoja in eastern Uganda. But in Undendeuli, with a light and inefficient colonial Administration,[19] resort to violence, or real threat of it, was empirically rare.

It is clear from the cases described that the men involved, both as principals and supporters, made continual reference and appeal to norm rules, values, and reasonable role expectations.[20] Whatever the other pressures they were seeking to exert, men claimed the legitimacy of their actions by their alleged conformity with accepted norms; and they attempted to demonstrate the illegitimacy of an opponent's actions in the same way. They inferred a hierarchy of norms such that their behaviour should be measured against a superior one rather than an inferior one. (For example, in

[19] See page 37 f.
[20] For brevity, I shall hereafter refer simply to "norms".

Case 2, it was agreed that a man ought to repay a debt, but that an obligation to give bridewealth to another party overrode the debtor's obligation.) A disputant could be persuaded to concede (at least tacitly) that his behaviour had been wrong and that he was in some degree responsible therefore. Because of this he could be required to rectify the consequences of his conduct. It is an extremely complex matter to analyse the real significance of this in the processes of dispute settlement. Was the common reference to norms merely the language and idiom of negotiations within which pragmatic bargaining strength was mobilised, tested, and assessed against that of an opponent? To a marked extent this seems to have been the case, as it is the case in much political competition in other societies. Both strength and weakness in the political arena seem to need rationalising justification by appeals to ideals and ideology. Yet this is not a wholly adequate explanation. The norms did provide a starting point, a base line for negotiations, and an approximate definition of the field of argument. In a marriage dispute, to give a crude example, the Ndendeuli argued about bridewealth, and they had some consensus of the amount of bridewealth that should and would be transferred. They argued within the rough limits of expectation of between about one hundred and three hundred shillings. Certainly they did not regard, say, one thousand shillings as within the realm of the possible, nor did they raise such unknown norms as the payment of dowry. There was more than this, though, for within the general area of consensus, and during the negotiations, there was further reference to other norms: for example, obligations to give bridewealth were subject to a man's other obligations to plant his fields or provide clothing for his wife and children. That is to say, the area of consensus could be widened, and the area of disagreement narrowed. Pressures of varying kinds were certainly used in this process, as well as appeals to norms; but it was when the final area of disagreement was reached (for example, could or could not the man afford to give bridewealth? Was or was not the father-in-law being extortionate?) that relative bargaining strengths played their principal parts.

This is not a full analysis of a problemmatical aspect of dispute settlement, and is intended here to be suggestive only. Nevertheless it does, I contend, throw light on the nature of the processes involved in intra-community dispute among the Ndendeuli. In this present account I am not primarily concerned with making a contribution per se to the comparative sociology of law. I am, however, concerned to explicate the processes of interaction that underlie decision-making among men enmeshed in a closed social network. Both the principals in a dispute and their respective supporters were inter-related in complex ways. The relations between two neighbours and their inter-actions necessarily involved their several relations with many of their other neighbours within the closed network; and they involved the several relationships of those other men with each other. There was much more than a culturally posed value in reaching a settlement, there was a practical utility. Within the network context, this was the utility of disrupting as little as possible the sets of inter-linking cooperative relations of the various men concerned. This required, even if only implicitly, at least minimal agreement as to the "rules of the game"—the norms of various kinds—and a serious attempt to keep near to them and to eschew resort to political strength. Hence there was the process of seeking consensus and of narrowing down the area of disagreement. It required also at least some degree of willingness to give way, to compromise, to be tolerant and charitable. This willingness, expressed by Ndendeuli as the value of good neighbourliness, was a *de facto* recognition of that requirement if men were to continue useful, practical cooperation. I do not predicate any mystique of group unity; nor did I discover it a principal concern of individual men to preserve the group. The unity of an Ndendeuli local community was too nebulous, and corporate constraint was virtually absent. Rather it was that individuals had, and realised they had, to take account of the future of their relations with certain other neighbours who simultaneously were individually taking account of their own sets of neighbourly relationships. Thus ultimately the pressures on a disputant were not only those of his opponent's party, but also those of his own party. So often in the later stages of a moot, suggestions for a compromise settlement came from members of an action-set, reaching over the reluctance or intransigency of the principal himself. This was well demonstrated in the conclusion of Case 3 (p. 157), but it occurred in other cases too.

As a result of my interests during field research, and the kind of analysis outlined above, this account of Ndendeuli intra-community, intra-network processes has been primarily concerned with what Gluckman has distinguished as "the social processes which largely determine the outcome of a dispute". In contrast with that concern, he noted, is the "analysis of the processes of ratiocination by which negotiations proceed." [21]

It will be clear that settlements of Ndendeuli disputes were typically compromises between conflicting claims. This is a function of the mode of negotiation, and of the network in which disputants and their disputes were enmeshed. Even where one of the principals was quite clearly almost wholly in the right and almost wholly with the monopoly of bargaining power, he often made some show of toleration to his opponent. He showed, as Ndendeuli put it, "friendliness" or "neighbourliness". Where the balance of rights and of bargaining strength was more nearly equal, a compromise solution in the final area of disagreement was inevitable if the matter were to be settled at all. The settlement had to be one to which parties would agree. Each might have wished for something more favourable to himself, but both were, eventually, prepared to accept the compromise. Continued insistence on obtaining the full claim might result in no solution at all; and it might even rally the obstinacy of the other party. Furthermore, such persistence (even were it successful) could be to the man's own disadvantage, and to that of his supporters, in creating conflict and animosity in relations thereafter between the various men involved. This could not, in any event, always be avoided. It was not, for example, in Case 2 when the fathers of the spouses in the bridewealth dispute were left in some animosity. But as far as possible the compromise was an attempt to prevent as much subsequent conflict as possible. This general desire was, of course, one of the bargaining strengths open to an otherwise weaker party.

A characteristic feature of Ndendeuli norms was that they were phrased in general terms in which rights and obligations were not spelled out in detail. For instance, kinsmen should help one another in certain ways, but to what degree, or which kinsman had priority, was seldom made clear. At marriage, all Ndendeuli agreed bridewealth should be given or suitor-service performed (or some combination of both), but the size of bridewealth or the length of suitor-service was not defined. It was a matter, one informant explained, of how much a father-in-law could obtain and how little a son-in-law could give. Ndendeuli were most interested in what others did in these circumstances, but they avoided drawing induc-

[21] Gluckman made this point, in a personal communication in 1965, when distinguishing between his own analysis of Lozi dispute cases (Gluckman 1955) and my analysis of Arusha cases (Gulliver 1963). But see Gluckman 1961(*b*).

tive conclusions on particular details. With reference to Case 2, for instance, no Ndendeuli was prepared to give a definite answer to the question whether Rajabu owed his father-in-law, Sedi, a further instalment of bridewealth. They agreed that an answer was only possible in the full context of the past and present relations between the disputants and their supporters. Even then, an Ndendeuli was wary of saying which way the settlement would actually go since the way in which the moot proceedings went would have some bearing on this. It was not a matter of determining the matter by reference to norms—though they would have some bearing— but principally by reference to the complex of social relations involved, as that complex had developed, and as the participants perceived that it would develop in the future.

This vagueness, or generality of enunciation, of norms *may* be related to the sociological requirements of compromise settlement in the negotiation mode of politico-jural processes. Both seem to be inter-connected with a corresponding vagueness in the definition of kinship relationships. This is a tentative hypothesis only. There must be more to it than that, if only because other peoples practicing mainly the mode of negotiation do in fact enunciate their norms and expectations more precisely and clearly, even though in typically compromise settlement of disputes they are ready to ignore or explain away the necessary divergence from those norms.[22] All that I am able to say here is that there is at least logical conformity between the mode of negotiation, compromise settlement, vaguely enunciated norms, and vaguely defined kinship relations among the Ndendeuli.

Ndendeuli dispute moots were not entirely concerned only with attempts to reach a settlement of the overt matter in hand. Their significance was wider than that, and due account must be taken of this aspect for an adequate understanding of interaction in the community. In the first place, there is the elementary point that the overt matter in dispute might not be the real point at issue. The overt matter might have been either the final straw that brought developing conflict to a head, or a timely excuse for one principal to force the other to come to public discussion on some other matter. This is a common feature of dispute cases in most societies, and it needs no particular emphasis here.

More importantly, the real issue underlying the overt outbreak of dispute might have been the desire on the part of one or both principals to have a full examination of the relationship between

[22] The Arusha are a case in point. See, for example, Case 21 concerning a bridewealth dispute, in Gulliver 1963:243-51.

them, and between them and others. Thus in Case 5, the overt dispute over the broken water pot was virtually ignored, whilst the participants in the moot got down to what was in effect a critical and constructive survey of the relations between the two cousins and between their overlapping sets of kin-neighbours. In Case 6, the father-in-law desired primarily not so much to obtain the bride-wealth owed to him, but to gain an affirmation that his son-in-law had been neglecting his obligations and his due respect for his senior. The father-in-law also wished to gain recognition, publicly, that he himself had acted properly in his dealings with his son-in-law. In this he gained his ends effectively and was prepared to leave the matter of the bridewealth payment until later. It is, noted in reference to earlier dispute case material,[23] difficult to say how far a man took advantage of an overt offence to press the more significant matter, and how far he "manufactured" a dispute in order to provide the public excuse for a moot. In Case 5, Zadiki the plaintiff was, I felt certain, genuinely troubled by the broken water pot and the insulting caricature of his behaviour, as well as by the apparent failure to be invited to the beer-drink or to get any apology afterwards. Nevertheless, in other contexts he might perhaps have allowed the matter to rest, once his immediate irritatation died down. In the particular circumstances the offences were, to him, yet another example of his cousin's animosity and prejudice. He welcomed the opportunity to "let off steam", to seek public sympathy, and to attempt some re-assessment of the whole cluster of relationships involved. Although it is impossible to prove, it is highly likely that he wished to justify himself before his kin-neighbours, and indeed before all of his neighbours, in a righteous case. He wished to bring pressures on his cousin so that he would conform to normal expectations in the future and, perhaps, to justify any slackening of performance of obligations by him to his cousin. Thus a moot, in discussing all the social relations involved and past performance by parties concerned, did this partly because these matters had some direct bearing on the dispute itself, but also because these relations and role performances were of great importance *per se*. Furthermore, neighbours other than the principals were able to understand more clearly, and therefore take account of, the cluster of relations where these affected their own interests and future expectations.

A moot sometimes provided an opportunity to examine not only a particular dispute but also the general area of social life concerning similar disputes. Matters of concern to many or all men, par-

[23] See page 107 ff.

ticularly matters where change was occurring and opinions and choices differed, were thus open to consideration as men exchanged views and ideas. For example, the size of bridewealth was at that time tending to increase as the amount and turnover of money grew, and as bridewealth was increasingly preferred (at least by sons-in-law) over suitor-service. On several occasions I watched a moot develop a general discussion on bridewealth, almost to the neglect of the particular case in hand. No definite conclusions were reached (or, I think, expected to be reached) in these and similar instances; but clearly men took the opportunity to examine a matter of common concern, and in this way new perceptions were spread, and new idea and new possibilities, whilst older ones might be reinforced or weakened.[24] This kind of discussion could occur on almost any occasion when men came together, but moots with their semi-formal character provided perhaps the best opportunity as men focussed their attention on a specific issue. Actual choices by men that cumulatively produced or checked social change were made individually, but the general climate of opinion tended to be created in these public discussions in moots.

A more general significance of moots is that, obviously, they necessitated neighbours taking sides, or at least making choices, if they were associated with either or both principals. They were, therefore, compelled to express their alignment and obligation in favour of one side and against the other; or an intermediary expressed his dual obligation to both principals, or to neighbours linked to the principals. In making these decisions, men declared to themselves and to other neighbours where they stood. Often a man wished to do this, welcoming the chance to express and fulfill obligation and to acquire credit that would be useful to him in the future. He may have wished to express his hostility, or at least opposition, to the other principal or to members of the latter's action-set. But even where the necessity of decision was painful, it was important to a man's future place in the network of relations of reciprocal assistance. These decisions helped to clarify alignments and expectations. Although a man was giving support to a neighbour in the latter's need—*the raison d'être* of the action-set—he was also acting in his own interests and to his own advantage as

[24] This did not occur in Case 2 largely because, as far as I could understand it, the two fathers-in-law and their respective kin-neighbours were closely inter-linked in the network in Ligomba. There was no desire, indeed a positive disinclination and disadvantage, to prolong the dispute settlement in that context.

far as he could. The most obvious example occurred in Case 4 when Ali joined, uninvited, the action-set of Kabaya—partly to express his close connection with his cousin, Yasini, in some competition with Kabaya for Yasini's prior loyalty, and partly so that Ali could participate in the moot and gradually assume the prestige-providing role of mediator.

This example raises the political aspect of moots, which went beyond the politico-jural processes of dispute treatment of disputes. Men, and most particularly notables, could and did use moots in order to try and increase their acknowledged influence and their reputation for leadership and forensic skills. Notables often competed with one another in the arena provided by a moot, as I have shown where Kabaya contended with Ali or Konga, his rival notables in Ligomba. On one occasion (Case 6) Kabaya chose to withdraw when the odds were high against him because of the expected alliance of Ali and Konga: he did not wish to have his weak position publicly demonstrated relative to theirs in the context of that particular dispute situation. The decisions and actions of notables could affect the process of a moot as they sought their own individual advantages as well as those of the principals and their kin-neighbours.

In conclusion, I reiterate that moots were politico-jural institutions, the means of dealing with intra-community disputes by the processes of negotiation. Moots were also occasions for examining the development and readjustment of neighbourly relations and expectations within the changing network, for expressing as well as fulfilling obligations, for acquiring entitlement to future claims for assistance, and for seeking to further influence and prestige. In addition they were forums in which neighbours could exchange views and discuss established and changing institutions and roles. The specific ways in which men behaved and operated in moots was a direct consequence of their inter-linking within the closed kinship network. At the same time their actions and alignments in turn affected the development of the network. Later disputes were significantly affected by the ways in which neighbours had performed in previous disputes. That is, a full understanding both of the dynamics of the network itself, and of any particular dispute, necessarily requires a recognition of the nature of the flow of events and relations up to that time. Each of the seven cases demonstrates this in its particular way, and this has been the reason for the serial manner in which they have been presented in this chapter.

VI

Economic Cooperation

The preceding chapter examined the treatment of inter-personal disputes, where the raison d'être of social action was conflict brought into the public arena. Yet quite clearly, conflict was not the sole element to be considered: cooperation was intrinsically involved at the same time, and in two ways. First, there was co-operation among the members of an action-set on behalf of a principal in the dispute. But there was, secondly, a wider field of cooperation. Among the Ndendeuli there was no breaking of relations between neighbours who temporarily belonged to different action-sets within the one community. There was no feud-like situation during the course of a dispute case. Rather there was a form of cooperation between the sets, specifically at first between various individual members of the opposed sets, in order to deal with the conflict and reach some kind of settlement. This cooperation, though not usually apparent in the earliest stages of a dispute case, gradually became more important as the moot continued. It was often initiated by a mediator. Thus conflict produced and necessitated cooperation if social action was to be adequate.[1]

The present chapter is concerned with situations and processes in which the raison d'être is cooperation in the basic economic tasks of producing a harvest and maintaining a livelihood. In so far as this cooperation was efficiently planned and executed, conflict should not have arisen; but complete efficiency was impossible in practice. Difficulties occurred where decisions had to be taken concerning the relative priorities of men's interests and commitments in respect of one another, and in relation to limitations of time in which to accomplish all that was required to be

---

[1] By "adequate" I do not mean that a fine reconciliation of the disputants was necessarily achieved. As I have shown, this might not occur. But some treatment of the open dispute was achieved, some resolution obtained, and perhaps some realignment of working relations.

done. Agreement could not easily be reached. Apart from attempts to weigh interests and claims and to allocate priorities, men would take advantage of the opportunities to express their conflicts and competition (arising out of other interests) by pressing the superiority of their own claims vis-à-vis those of another neighbour.

Thus, on the one hand, inherently conflict situations entailed cooperation; and, on the other hand, essentially cooperative interests and action entailed conflict. Conflict and cooperation were two sides of the same coin of social interaction. It is, then, too simple to suggest that overall cooperation and social cohesion are necessarily increased, or at least maintained, by the successful treatment of conflict. Certain areas and links of cooperation may well be damaged as a result of conflict resolution, and new conflicts may be set in train. The inter-relationship of conflict and cooperation is, I think, a most subtle one in any society—more subtle, perhaps, than some so-called conflict theorists in sociology have admitted. The seeds of the one are contained in the operation of the other in a complex dynamic process.

THE WORK-PARTY SYSTEM

A great deal of the more laborious tasks in Ndendeuli agriculture was performed through cooperative action in arranged work-parties. The three main tasks were the preparation of new fields, hoeing and planting, and weeding. These were regularly recurring tasks and provided the most frequent and important occasions on which action-sets were recruited for work-parties. In addition, but more irregularly, parties were recruited to construct and repair bush fencing around the fields, to cut and haul timber and grass for building, repairing, and thatching houses, and occasionally to hunt and chase away predatory animals that threatened the crops.

Ndendeuli said that in the smallest local communities—mainly the newly established ones—these work-parties comprised all of the residents, there being so few of them. Although I have no adequate first-hand knowledge of such a community, it appears that this common assertion was more a declaration of idealised unity and harmony among the pioneers than a factual statement. In a new community, numbers of people were small, a large proportion of them were directly linked by kinship, and inclinations to amicable cooperation were strong. Nevertheless, even there the size of most pioneer sets and the indirectness of some of the kinship linkages seem to have precluded comprehensive work-

parties. It is fairly certain that they did not occur in the first years
at Ligomba.[2]

The four local communities on which I concentrated in the
field were all well established and obviously too large to operate
comprehensive work-parties. The smallest—Ligomba—after more
than twenty years contained thirty-two households in fifteen hamlets; the largest of the four contained sixty-four households in
twenty-six hamlets, and the youngest—Namabeya—contained
forty households in eighteen hamlets. In all of these, work-parties
never comprised even a majority of residents. This was partly
the result of the attenuated nature of the kinship network so that
comprehensive cooperation was less easily arranged and less clearly
supported, but it was primarily a matter of numbers and convenience. This was true particularly when hoeing and planting
were concerned, with only a short time available at that season of
the year. All cultivation parties had to be fitted into a period of a
few weeks, after which time it was a waste of effort and seed to
plant more.[3] If work-parties were too large some men would have
had to wait too long for their turn in the rota. Numerous smaller
parties allowed each participant to hold his own party before it
was too late in the season. Even so, men whose fields were hoed
and planted towards the end of the season were likely to be put at
a disadvantage. Attempt was made to compensate for this unavoidable condition by varying the order of work-parties from year to
year so that relative advantages and disadvantages might be roughly
balanced over a period. Despite this, complaints were common
among younger household heads, newcomers, and those with fewer
kin-neighbours that they were too often compelled to take a late
date for their cultivation parties.

A typical cultivation work-party contained seven or eight men—
ranging from four to twelve men in my records—together with
their wives and older children. Work-parties for cutting and clearing new fields usually contained more men, but seldom women
and children.

It was straightforward for the men of a single hamlet to arrange
their several work-parties on different days during a work season.
It was less easy, and probably not altogether possible under the
circumstances, for other neighbours to avoid clashes of arrangements. It was an obviously unfriendly act to convene a work-party
on the same day as that of a kin-neighbour: it reduced the number

[2] Cf. Figure 10 (A), and footnote, page 114.
[3] See page 42.

of people available for each party, it prevented each convener assisting and reciprocating with the other, and it presented their common kin-neighbours with a serious problem of choice. If at all possible, no two men should have held their work-parties on the same day if some of their neighbours were potential members of both. Men disliked and often resented being put into a position where they had to choose to assist one neighbour rather than another. In a moot when a dispute case was being considered, this kind of choice was often unavoidable, as I showed in the previous chapter; but the dilemma should have been avoided in work-parties by prior discussions. Even if a man's choice was quite clear in terms of comparative obligations, he preferred not to express it in practice. In any case, a man lost the opportunity to assist the convener to whom he had, at that time, a lesser obligation, and therefore such reciprocity as did exist between them was further weakened.

The season for the preparation of new fields was much longer than that for hoeing and planting, so that the organisational problem at that period was fairly easily dealt with amongst neighbours anxious to avoid conflict. It is probable, in fact—though my evidence is not adequate enough—that when clashes of dates did occur they arose out of conflict and rivalry between the conveners, and were more or less deliberate. In the early wet season, when cultivation had to be concentrated into a few weeks, the problems were much greater and, with Ndendeuli techniques, they were never altogether solved successfully, despite frequent and lengthy discussion and tolerant accommodation by most neighbours. My evidence, given later in this chapter, shows that work-party arrangements at this season were affected by the structural relations within the kinship network, and also by particular interpersonal relations. Neighbours certainly took advantage of organisational clashes to attempt to strengthen their positions relating to other neighbours with whom they were in competition. They sought occasionally to establish a situation in which they believed that they could defeat a rival in competitive claims against other neighbours.

There was an element of chance, varying from year to year, whether or not a man encountered difficulties in the arrangement of his work-party. Human errors in consultations and planning, and neighbours' conflicts founded partly on other issues, were commonly aggravated by weather conditions. Parties had to be postponed, or they were interrupted before the work was finished, by heavy downpours that made cultivation temporarily impossible. The whole arranged programme often had to be held over for a day or two, thus requiring further consultations and reorganisation. This was a time of much strain for the Ndendeuli, so that men were liable to be inconsiderate and even to act against their own best interests in seeking temporary advantage. Working conditions were frequently disagreeable in the wet, cold, and mud. The actual labour was heavy, especially so since it followed a period of inactivity in the latter part of the dry season. Food was sometimes becoming scarce. Everyone was aware that their livelihood depended on rapid and successful planting. Pressures were great, and men were not in their most amenable frame of mind. It was not surprising that under these conditions difficulties occurred and that the inevitable problems were not always handled as carefully as they might have been at other times.

A work-party was convened and recruited by the head of a household for his own fields. When necessary, a party was arranged by some close kinsman on behalf of a woman whose husband was dead or absent in labour migration or for other reasons. The convener called on the labour of his kin-neighbours and of other indirectly linked neighbours (the kin of kin) with whom he had mutual obligations. With kin-neighbours, the obligation was implicit in the acknowledgement of kinship; but both with them and with other neighbours the recognition of the reciprocal basis of cooperation was marked and overtly emphasized. With indirectly linked neighbours a man sought to establish a working convention of reciprocal assistance. Where such a convention began to be well established, it was associated with the development of the acknowledgement of direct kinship between the two neighbours. Some men could have relied more or less entirely on their kin-neighbours who were numerous enough to make up adequately sized work-parties, but few, if any, did so. This was partly because a man desired to develop relations with other neighbours, relations that would be useful in other situations when it was necessary to recruit action-sets (for example, in dispute cases). Also, many men could not recruit a large enough work-party from among their kin-neighbours alone; therefore they were assiduous in nurturing links of reciprocity with other neighbours. In Ligomba, for example, the fairly recent newcomer, Salimi (D1), had only two unequivocal kin-neighbours, but he had developed more or less regular cooperation with a number of other neighbours who were kin of those two but had not at that time yet begun fully to acknowledge him as a kinsman.

It is important to note that an Ndendeuli did not choose merely to cooperate with those neighbours who happened to live geographically near his own hamlet. From the purely economic point of view, residentially near neighbours might have sufficed, and communication and coordination of arrangements might have been easier on a localised basis. But agricultural cooperation in work-parties was not an isolated piece of social organisation: it was an integral part of the whole continuum of community life and interaction. It not only utilised the linkages between certain neighbours, and the rights and obligations entailed, but it added to and consolidated them. A man and his household worked for and obtained the labour of those on whom he could exert justifiable claim and who had recognised claims on him. He cooperated with such neighbours in many other activities as well as in agriculture. He had to take some care not to spread, even dissipate, his rights and obligations too widely and freely, for otherwise they would become too dispersed, too fragile, and inadequately reinforced by other sets of rights and obligations, so that they did not form a dependable pattern. It would have been arbitrary and incongruous to seek agricultural labour on the mere basis of residential proximity when that would implicitly deny, or at least neglect and weaken, links that were already available and valued. Ndendeuli remarked that a man could rely more on kin-neighbours than on others; and this was strictly true in the full context of activities within the local community. The lines of acknowledged kinship channelled and brought together in coherent fashion all the kinds of cooperation and assistance that a man needed. To put it in another way, and one emphasized in this analysis, the kinship network provided in effect an understood means of social organisation: that is, a recognised pattern through which rights and obligations, and expectations, could be coordinated. A degree of choice and opportunity for manipulation remained to the individual, but the field of choice was narrowed down to manageable proportions. Social life was thus given a fair degree of predictability and stability as the many and varied activities, and the relationships involved, were fairly well integrated together. Patterns might—indeed did—change over time as men made new choices, and as alternative choices became newly available; I am not positing equilibrium and changeless stability. Analytically, this was the real value and justification of kinship relations among the Ndendeuli, although they themselves expressed it more simply and categorically by saying that a man ought to help those who were his kin, and that a kinsman was more to be relied on than an unrelated person. They appealed to and depended on the overt facts of kinship per se rather than on the underlying sociological factors revealed by analysis.

For a cultivation work-party, the people assembled early in the morning, fairly soon after sunrise, at the home of the convener or at his field. In the field the men lined up along one side with their hoes, and then worked across it together in a sweep to the far side. A single sweep might cover the whole field if the hoers were numerous or the field narrow, but usually two or three sweeps were required. Wives and children followed behind the men, picking out stones and refuse. Others behind these, usually led by the convener's wife, carried out the planting. As commonly reported for this kind of African work-party, these were times of some pleasure as well as hard physical labour. Whether or not the work could have been accomplished as satisfactorily if each household had cultivated its own fields separately, Ndendeuli believed quite firmly that it could not. They said that a main reason for congregating into communities was to obtain such necessary neighbourly cooperation. This cannot be the whole explanation, of course, if only because local communities were much larger than was required simply for labour requirements; but it had some validity, and certainly so in the eyes of the people.

Some informants explained that a man must be prepared to brave the potential witchcraft of other people by living with or near to them in a local community in order to obtain the benefits of cooperation with neighbours. This was a culturally standard explanation. Two reliable informants, at different times and places, commented that because of witchcraft fears Ndendeuli could not live close together in compact villages, as did the Yao people to the south in similar country. "But we cannot live alone in small hamlets because we need the labour of other people", said one of these men.

Although at other times informants gave me other explanations of their communities, this explanation was common enough to illustrate the acknowledged importance of the work-party system among the people. Certainly there was both pride and pleasure in helping each other and working together.[4] Often there was a song or chant leader to coordinate and stimulate the men's hoeing, and the women and children sang together at their own tasks. With

[4] As so often when praising their own institutions, Ndendeuli made disparaging comparisons with alleged Ngoni practices. In fact the Ngoni followed a somewhat similar kind of work-party system.

perhaps a pause for a little beer, the work-party would continue until the task was completed (one or more fields, according to size) or until about mid-afternoon. Then the workers retired to the convener's house where they were served with beer and, if supply permitted, often some porridge. Beer-drinks in the early wet season were neither heavy nor prolonged. Men knew that they had to work hard again next day, and many wished to return home to put in an hour or two in their own fields before dark. At that time of year, too, grain was seldom plentiful enough to permit the brewing of large quantities of beer. Yet the beer was important; a man and his wife were at pains to provide some, even when grain stores were low, and no participant in the work-party would leave without taking a drink The standard reference to a work-party was *kulima ujimbi*, literally "to cultivate beer". The beer was more than just refreshment, though it was in no way a payment for the service rendered. Payment was made by return labour or some other assistance in the other men's work-parties. To sit, relax, and drink together on this as on many social occasions (such as the successful end of a moot) symbolised good neighbourliness and mutual trust. It signified also that the convener was satisfied with the work accomplished and his neighbours' share in it, and that all were glad to have done it together. One old man went further than this, explaining that the beer they were drinking had been made from the crop taken at the previous harvest in the field which they had helped to cultivate the year before. "In the same way we shall drink beer next year made from the maize we just planted today", he told me. To him, and probably others, the beer-drink symbolised the continuity both of planting and harvesting and of cooperative effort by the same body of neighbours.

Some agriculturalists have held that these kinds of work-party are inefficient: time is wasted, and the work often done cursorily as slower workers try to keep up with the faster ones, and as men try to get it over as quickly as possible; men feel little responsibility for other men's fields and crops, and there is more concern for the beer-drink than for the agricultural work. There may be some technical truth in this argument, but the criticism is scarcely legitimate otherwise. Perhaps outside critics, especially those trained in a more technically developed agriculture, do not allow for the relatively low technical level of efficiency in shifting, hand-hoe agriculture, irrespective of the kind of social organisation of labour. To an anthropologist, such criticism disregards the essential way in which this kind of organisation meshes into the total social system, gaining strength from and reinforcing it.[5] Neither, I think, do the critics fully appreciate the human difficulties of intensive labour with a hoe at a time when food supplies are usually low, working conditions are filthy, and the long dry season has just ended with its absence of labour to maintain an active routine. This is part of the dilemma of shifting cultivation in the semi-arid tropics. Collective labour, with the encouragement of song, the tapping of sentiments of mutuality and concord, and the short beer-drink afterwards, lightens the burden and maintains incentive at a trying time.

Each household normally held one work-party during the cultivation season, though some larger households might try to arrange a second one if possible. But a household was not entirely dependent on that work-party for its cultivation. A man and his wife worked in their fields in the late afternoon after participating in a neighbour's party earlier in the day; and they worked there on days when they were not involved in another's party. Such work added to the area planted with maize, but it dealt also with all the secondary crops such as cassava, beans, and other crops.

Most households tried to weed their fields twice during the growing season. For first weeding, work-parties were arranged on the same lines as in the cultivation season, but without the pressures and tensions of that earlier time, Ndendeuli did not give the same importance or urgency to weeding; the second weeding was often desultorily performed by members of the household, or sometimes by women from the same hamlet working together. My field notes are inadequate for detailed analysis of this period.

The season for preparing new fields was a good deal longer than that for cultivation, so that work-parties were much more easily arranged. They were more relaxed affairs. The parties were usually larger as men took the opportunities to express rather wider loyalties than there was time for in the early wet season. Each party ended in a prolonged beer-drink, there being not only leisure to enjoy it but generally plenty of grain for brewing. These beer-drinks were major social events in the cycle of community life: attendance was not limited to members of the work-party, though they had prior attention. Commonly, as the beer-drink went on into the evening, the majority of household heads in the community (even in the larger communities) gathered together at those times. Intoxication was more or less expected, and for that reason alone work-parties were not held on successive days at that

[5] See Gulliver 1967.

time of the year. Work-parties for house building and major repairs were similar, being held later in the dry season when there was little other activity.

It would be difficult to assess the direct economic value of these leisurely work-parties, though Ndendeuli rated them highly. It is rather irrelevant, however, whether or not the work could have been accomplished more quickly or efficiently by individual men, for there was plenty of time available, the work was done, and economic advantage was not the major criterion. Those parties were more important in the general social life among neighbours, expressing the acceptance of mutual obligations, goodwill, and toleration.

In all these work-parties the heavier work was performed by the younger and middle-aged men. Women and children had their lighter tasks; elderly women and small girls looked after the babies. Elderly men were not expected to take on hard physical labour, but they assisted when they could, gave advice, and helped in supervision. Even if they were too infirm to do much of any consequence, if they were still able to get about they should, and did, attend the party in the field. Thus they could at least show their goodwill and claim in return the labour of those to whom they showed it. Unless there was good reason, the whole household should have turned out—men, women, and children. To do less than that was to suggest some lack of goodwill and could give genuine offence.[6]

AGRICULTURAL WORK-PARTIES IN LIGOMBA, 1953–1954

Figure 16 gives the actual composition of those men's work-parties that I was able to record for both dry season and early wet season tasks. It is, of course, a list of empirical action-sets. Without making a detailed analysis of the composition of these sets, it may be said that these data confirm the general principles of recruitment that have already been described in relation to dispute settlement. Members of an action-set were the convener's kin-neighbours and the close kin of those kin-neighbours.

---

[6] A rather differently organized work-party system among the northern Nyamwezi of central Tanzania was described in Abrahams 1965. Although the literature contains many references to such systems in Africa and elsewhere, detailed accounts of the mode of organization and its relation to the general social system are most uncommon. Agricultural records seldom give more than a casual reference, unfortunately: cf. de Schlippe 1956, Allan 1965.

FIGURE 16: The Composition of Work-Parties in Ligomba.

Dry season 1953: cutting and clearing new fields
Early wet season 1953–1954: hoeing and planting maize fields

Convener	Workers on both occasions	Workers in dry season party only	Workers in wet season party only
D1	C6, C7, D2, D3, D4	D5, D6, D7	—
D2	C6, D1, D3, D4	C7	D5
D3	C6, C7, D1, D2, D4, D5	—	—
C7	C6, C9, D1, D4, D5, D6	C17, D2, D7, D9	D3
D5	C7, D1, D2, D4, D6	C6, C9, D7, D8	D3
C9	C7, C11, D6, D7, D8, D9, D10, D13	C6, C12, D4, D11, D12	C13, D5
C11	C12, C15, D9, D10, D11, D13	C9, D12	C13
D11	C11, C12, D10, D12, D13	D9, D14	C13
C13	no dry season party		C9, C11, C12, C15, C17, C19, D9, D10, D13, D14, D15
C15	C11, C13, D13, D14, D15, D19	C17, C19, C21, D16, D17, D20	C12
C17	C19, C21, D15, D16, D17, D19, D20	C7, C15, D21, D23	C13, D14
D21	C21, D16, D17, D20	C17, C19, D15	D19, D23
D23	C21, D16, D17, D20, D21	C17	D19

NOTE: In wet season work-parties, most or all of a man's household accompanied him as all able-bodied persons joined in the labour. Almost all dry season work-parties comprised men and youths only.

In practice, certain potential members of an action-set re-cruited on this basis were in some cases absent from a work-party. Sometimes this was the result of conflicts of timing (in the short cultivation season) when men had to choose between two con-veners to both of whom they were linked and obligated in some degree. This problem and its significance is examined later in the

chapter. There were also purely personal factors that prevented
the ideal scheme being worked out completely in actual achievement. A few casual examples will illustrate this minor point.

Tanda (C13) was absent from Ligomba during much of the dry
season of that year whilst he worked as a foreman on government
road maintenance in that region. He himself did not clear a new
field and so convened no work-party, nor did he join the dry
season parties of his neighbours, with the exception of that of
Zadiki his brother-in-law and close friend.[7] Konga's son (D18)
was absent from Ligomba during the whole year as a labour
migrant and therefore participated in no work-parties; but his
father and brothers arranged both dry and wet season parties for
his wife who remained in Ligomba. Amadu (D6) should have
joined the parties of his second cousin, Malindi (D3), in both
seasons—or so his elder brother, Beni, said as he himself supported
Malindi. But Amadu and Malindi were personally hostile to one
another and did not work in each other's parties, although both
were prepared to work in parties convened by their common kin-
neighbours. Yasini (C9) doubtless would have joined the cultivation party of Beni, but he was ill on the day. Nevertheless, Beni
turned out with Yasini's party three days later.

In general, men who lived in the same hamlet tended to recruit
similar work-parties. This was partly because usually only close
kinsmen were co-residents of a hamlet, and their ranges of cooperation within the community largely overlapped. But Ndendeuli
would have considered it most anomalous if one household head
in a hamlet had been unable to recruit neighbours who, though not
directly related to him, were the kin-neighbours of his co-residents.
Indeed it would have been unusual if such men were not fairly
quickly assimilated as direct kinsmen and own kin-neighbours.
This was the case, for instance, with the two brothers-in-law,
Salimi and Faranz. Three years after establishing a joint hamlet,
Faranz was treating Meha (cousin and sponsor of Salimi) as
"brother" (that is, kinsman of one's own generation). Faranz and
Meha engaged in regular mutual assistance on the overt grounds
of kinship and brotherliness. Thus Faranz and Salimi recruited the
same kin-neighbours to their work-parties.

This was a case where the co-residents of the hamlet belonged
to the same generation. Difference of generation among co-resi-

[7] Tanda's work area was generally not far away, however, and he was
able to attend a number of the important beer-drinks which followed the
work-parties in the late afternoon and evening.

dents of a hamlet, even father and son, could make for divergent orientations of choice. For example, Tanda (C13) and his son, Musa (D13), had their households in a common hamlet. In 1954 their early wet season work-parties were composed as follows: members of both men's parties—C9, C11, C15, D14, D15 (and Tanda and Musa); members of Tanda's party only—C12, C17, C19; members of Musa's party only—D9, D10, D11. The generational difference is obvious here. Tanda, a man in his mid-fifties, had lived in Ligomba for about thirteen years. He had well-established conventions of reciprocal assistance with linked neighbours of his (the senior) generation in the community; Musa, married only a year or two previously, was establishing his own conventions as head of a household, and in this was, for his own advantage, seeking to strengthen links with neighbours of his own (the junior) generation. In the senior generation Musa maintained kin-neighbour relationships with his father-in-law, his father's first cousin (a notable, and therefore a valuable ally), and his father's sister's husband (the particular personal friend of his father); in the junior generation Tanda maintained similar links with the two sons of his sister's husband (that same friend). Musa was (I believe, on the evidence of comparable situations) looking to the future when younger men of his own generation would be of more advantage to him, and with whom he shared the same generalised distinction from the older generation of men.

The principal concern of this chapter, however, is to examine the problems that arose in the arrangement of work-parties in the short cultivation season. This allows further detailed analysis of the actual operation of the kinship network, and of an extension of the time scale of events in Ligomba. That cultivation season came immediately after the period in which the dispute cases occurred as described in the previous chapter. Some of the problems of work-party arrangements were, quite directly, connected with and affected by those cases.

Figure 17 gives the actual timetable of work-parties as it eventually worked out in the early wet season of 1953–1954. The entire programme of one party for each household in the community—the conventional norm—was completed in a little over three weeks, beginning a day or two after the main rains began in mid-December. Only two men—Yasini and Kabaya—convened parties on a second occasion. Both of these men had large households and were thus responsible for much larger areas of arable

FIGURE 17: Timetable of Work-Parties in Ligomba.

Cultivation work-parties in the early wet season, 1953–1954

Conveners of parties

Dec.	19	C6; C21
	21	C12; D16
	22	C7 x C11; D17
	23	(heavy rain)
	25	C15
	26	D5; D11
	27	D2; D12; C17
	28	D3; C13 x D21
	29	D1 x C9; D19
	30	D4; D13; D23
	31	(heavy rain)
Jan.	1	(heavy rain)
	3	D8 x D14
	4	D6; D18
	5	(heavy rain)
	7	D10; C19
	8	D9 x D15
	10	D7; D20
	11	C9
	12	C11

NOTES: x between two conveners denotes some conflict in the composition of work-parties, as discussed in the text.

The days noted on which heavy rain fell were those when work-party arrangements had to be postponed and/or altered. Rain also fell on other days, but not sufficiently to affect cultivation work.

land than most other men in Ligomba that year. One or two other larger households were able, by individual effort, to avoid the extra commitment involved in claiming further labour from their neighbours. If it could be avoided, most men preferred not to convene a second party, for it was not easy to reciprocate the additional obligations incurred.

On five days three work-parties were held simultaneously, and there were two parties on eight other days. The majority of these parties did not, in practice, raise problems of conflicting interests for potential participants, nor competition between conveners for the labour of their common kin-neighbours. For example, the

parties of D2, D12, and C17 on 27 December did not require, or
at least they could manage without, the labour of neighbours
participating in one of the other parties. In this and similar cases,
the conveners of the work-parties were far enough apart in the
network that, for this purpose anyway, their action-sets did not
overlap. The context of social action—cultivation work-parties—
must be emphasised here, for in other contexts the same conveners of action-sets might have discovered conflicts of interests
when simultaneously trying to recruit assistance. No doubt, even
on 27 December, there were men who might perhaps have worked
for another convener in different circumstances. Thus, for example,
Musa (D13) might have worked in C17's party had not D12's
party been held on the same day. Choices of that kind had to be
made, but the conflict of interests was not intolerable for the men
concerned, in view of the need to accomplish the hoeing and
planting as quickly as possible. It should be noted, too, that although those three conveners were structurally comparatively distant from each other in the network, they would on other occasions find themselves together in action-sets recruited by another
neighbour; or conversely they would be members of opposed sets
in their support of two other neighbours in dispute. The flexibility
and relativity of action-set formation according to the context was
an essential characteristic of social organization through the kinship network.

Unfortunately, I was not present in Ligomba during the whole
period comprising the very end of the dry season and the early
wet season, therefore a full record was not obtained of all the
discussions during which the programme of work-parties was
arranged and at which problems of conflicts of interests were
dealt with. During the three weeks or so when the cultivation
parties were held, there were five occasions on which particular
conflicts of arrangements and of neighbours' interests were recorded; there may have been other occasions of which no note
was made, but these five were probably the more important to the
people concerned. In the following analysis I deal with these five
cases as illustrations of the factors and processes involved. They
are indicated in the timetable of work-parties in Figure 17. Although they are deliberately dealt with in chronological order,
the first and the third were more important in raising matters of
wider implication.

Work-Party Case 1, 22 December:
Ali (C7) and Kabaya (C11)

This was the first conflict of dates during that cultivation season. It should, and certainly could, have been avoided, as several Ligomba men pointed out. Since it occurred so early in the season —on the third day of work-parties—one or other of the two conveners could have rearranged his party on another day without serious agricultural consequences. Ali might have held his party the previous day without raising undue difficulty for Bilali (C12), and none at all for D16, who held their parties then. Or he could

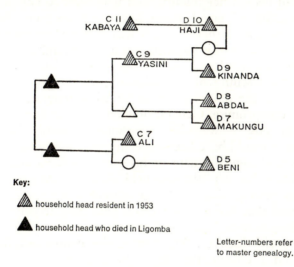

Key:

△ household head resident in 1953

▲ household head who died in Ligomba

Letter-numbers refer
to master genealogy.

FIGURE 18: Work-Party Case 1: Kabaya
(C11) and Ali (C7).

have postponed it for a day or two. The number of days of adjustment required for Kabaya (C11) would have been rather greater, but it was scarcely an insuperable problem for him either.

There is good, if not entire, reason to conclude that the conflict was largely deliberate. Both men sought to hold their work-parties early in the season, and neither pretended that he had no knowledge of the conflict of arrangements. As I have shown already, these two men were both notables: they were rivals for influence and leadership, and competitors for the allegiance of some of their neighbours. As the effective leaders of action-sets, or in the role of mediator, they had come into conflict a number of times—the most recent being only a few weeks before (Case 5, p. 172). Neither felt the need to give way in neighbourly toleration to the other; and both saw the opportunity to attempt to extend his influence at the direct expense of the other. In these circumstances, each feared the potential loss of prestige and of prior claim on certain neighbours if he were to give way.

A moot was held at the house of Yasini (C9) when it became fairly clear that the rains were to be sufficient to permit the start of hoeing and planting. Yasini himself initiated the moot since he was the principal neighbour affected by the conflict: he was close kin-neighbour, "brother", to both men. Each brought to the moot some of his kin-neighbours, men who were to comprise their work-parties; but Ali and Kabaya dominated the proceedings and the result was that neither of them was prepared to give way. If anything came out of this moot, it was a sharpening of the rivalry between the two notables. Their supporters, probably wishing to prevent any worsening of the situation, were agreed in letting things stand, to the discomfiture of Yasini, of course, who failed to gain any compromise. General opinion in Ligomba—the matter was common gossip—was that Ali should probably have given way because it would have been easier for him as a purely practical measure to rearrange the date of his party. Kabaya and his supporters claimed that Ali "always" held his work-party early in the season, thus getting the maximum agricultural benefit from it. It was argued that Kabaya had often held his party later in the season in the previous years, and this seems to have been correct as far as I could discover. Ali rejected this contention, however; "Why should I change the day?" he said to me later. "Does Kabaya think he is more important than me? Is he my friend? People will say that I am only an old man if he overcomes me in this matter". This expressed a part of his motivation; but it was not all. Ali wished to take the opportunity not only to contest with Kabaya in the general situation, but also to compete with him on a particular issue of importance to both men. His aim was to demonstrate that he had a superior claim on his cousin, Yasini, and on the latter's "sons" (D7, D8, D9) as against Kabaya, the affine of these men.

Both Ali and Yasini, and no doubt the other men, were clear on this issue. Ali wished to compel Yasini to declare and show primary allegiance to him, rather than to Kabaya. Competition between men not directly related for the allegiance of a third who is related to both was not unusual in the network system. In a jural dispute the third man could make a choice one way or the other, or he could attempt to act as mediator, or he could evade the dilemma by opting out.[8] In the context of work-party conflict it was less easy to avoid a choice, though men did make efforts to achieve this in an attempt to preserve both links. In this present case, the rivalry, with Yasini as third man, had arisen earlier in the year, in Cases 3 and 4;[9] Ali was now seeking to strengthen his claim and to weaken that of Kabaya. Ligomba men were more or less explicit about this. As one uninvolved man put it: "this is how big men fight".

In the end Yasini felt compelled to join Ali's work-party on the day. He was, of course, invited by both conveners. He explained to me that he could not properly refuse to work for Ali even though he held that Ali was at least partly responsible for raising and pressing the conflict of loyalty he faced. This was Yasini's personal decision; it was not suggested, let alone discussed, in the abortive moot. Yasini discussed the matter with his son and the nephews (co-members of his hamlet) and they agreed to demonstrate and maintain their by no means negligible relations with Kabaya. Whilst Yasini joined Ali's work-party, his son Kinanda joined the party working for Kabaya (father-in-law of Kinanda's sister). It was difficult for Ali to complain about this—in fact, he kept quiet—so that Yasini's solution was accepted. Yasini's nephews (sons of Ali's dead cousin) should most probably have worked for Ali, for their linkages with and obligation to Kabaya were comparatively much weaker. But they had a practical interest to develop mutual assistance with Kabaya's son through Kinanda, for all were members of the junior generation seeking to associate and create enduring links with their peers. Yasini suggested to them that they should absent themselves altogether on the day, and in a rather obvious manner by visiting kinsfolk in another community. Such visiting was not usual at that frantically busy time of the year. This they did, to Ali's public disappointment. Moreover, at Kabaya's party Kinanda let it be known that the others were away visiting and were not working for Ali; the implication, understood by everyone, was that the men put the blame on Ali.

Yasini's solution to this conflict was not an original one, though it was fairly satisfactory for him in the circumstances. Ali should have foreseen these tactics, and perhaps he did; but at least he

[8] See page 136.
[9] See pp. 159 and 166.

achieved a public demonstration of the prior loyalty and obligation of Yasini. This event and its result continued the general conflict and competition between the two notables. A similar situation between two other neighbours, where timetable rearrangement was not feasible, could have ended in the same sort of solution, but without necessarily threatening relations among the neighbours involved.

Work-Party Case 2, 28 December: Tanda (C13) and Hanju (D21)

This was merely an unfortunate error of practical arrangements, discovered only a day or two beforehand. The men affected by divided obligation to both convenors were Konga (C17), his sons, and his brother Mitedi (C19). On Konga's advice, no moot was held to try and rearrange the timetable. Konga and Hanju normally worked in each other's parties, as they had done for clearing and cutting in the preceding dry season. Hanju worked in Konga's cultivation party the day before. But for Konga he was a less important neighbour, especially in comparison with Tanda. More than this, both Konga and Mitedi were most anxious to maintain good working relations with Tanda—and vice versa—in view of chronic tension between Konga and his cousin, Zadiki (C15), the brother-in-law of Tanda, and the open dispute that had occurred a few weeks previously (Case 5, p. 172). This dispute had threatened to cut a rift in the network, that is, to sever or at least weaken indirect linkages between kin-neighbours of Tanda and Konga. These men therefore wished to lose no opportunity to express continued friendly relations by concrete action and assistance. Thus both Konga and Mitedi were quite deliberate in their decision to join Tanda's work-party at this time; and this may explain Konga's unwillingness even to have the matter publicly discussed in a moot. His sons, on the other hand, preferred to emphasise their links with Hanju and so they joined his party and did not accompany their father. The generational factor was significant here. Konga's sons, together with D20, D21, and D23 were all of the junior generation, concerned at this period in establishing and strengthening their own fields of linkages and mutual assistance, as against Tanda, Konga, and Mitedi of the senior generation.

Another man of the senior generation who might have joined with Konga in his expression of good relations with Tanda was Sedi (C21). He however was too closely associated with and obligated to his son-in-law, Hanju, to have real choice in the matter. Neither he nor any of the other neighbours involved were especially worried or incommoded by the situation and the necessary choices to be made. Both conveners were still able to assemble adequate work-parties for the jobs to be done, and no ill-will was caused. Men commented to me that complete avoidance of timetable clashes could not be expected, and here no one blamed anyone else for the conflict or the choices made. This was in some contrast with the course and results of the previous case.

Work-Party Case 3, 29 December: Salimi (D1) and Yasini (C9)

In origin, this case was merely the result of a failure of communication and organisation on the part of several men. In the event it raised a number of issues that are important to the understanding of the kinship network and community life.

This case presented Ali (C7) with conflicting obligations. He wished, as he told me, to maintain cooperation with Salimi, who lived in the same hamlet as Ali's son-in-law and could be expected to give support in Ali's action-sets. On the other hand, Ali could not possibly avoid participation in Yasini's party. Yasini, his first cousin, was a particularly valued kin-neighbour of his own generation; but only the week before Ali had (as already described) more or less deliberately constrained Yasini to join his own party. He was compelled to acknowledge the clear obligation to reciprocate. Yasini did not attempt to force the issue, but neither did he favour the idea of a moot that Ali proposed in order to attempt to make alternative arrangements. Ali was unable to use the same tactics that Yasini had employed against him earlier. Ali's sister's sons, co-residents of his hamlet, who might in other circumstances have gone to work for Salimi, chose unequivocally to join Yasini; they desired to maintain their reciprocal assistance with him and to express their association with his "sons" (D7, D8, D9), their peers, who were assessed as being more important to them than Salimi. In contrast, Ali's son-in-law, Faranz (D4), was obviously bound to give his labour to Salimi, who was his sister's husband and co-resident of his hamlet.

All that Ali could do eventually was to start the day in Salimi's party, and then, after a short while, move on to Yasini's party for the main work of the day and the following beer-drink. On the day Yasini expressed his satisfaction, and refrained from anything that might have exacerbated Ali's dilemma. No overt refer-

ence seems to have been made to the previous week's incident.
Yasini appeared to have no wish to take advantage of the situation.
He was a quiet, elderly man who did not, as he put it, "seek
troubles"; nor did he desire particular influence. His own legitimate
claims were met and this was sufficiently satisfactory for him.

On the other hand, Salimi fared less well. His work-party was
a small one, containing only five men and their households in addi-

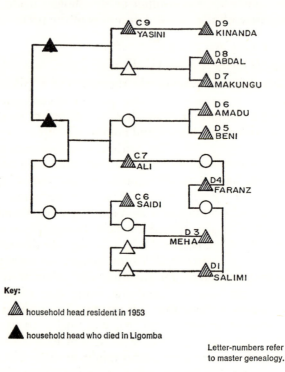

Key:

△ household head resident in 1953

▲ household head who died in Ligomba

Letter-numbers refer
to master genealogy.

FIGURE 19: Work-Party Case 3: Yasini
(C9) and Salimi (D1).

tion to his own. He was one of the two most recent newcomers
to Ligomba—settling there in 1950—and he told me that he had
had difficulty each year in convening satisfactory work-parties.
He had been sponsored in Ligomba by his only two kinsmen
there—Meha (D2) and Faranz. As usual in this sort of situation,
he could depend on assistance from these two neighbours, and
through them he offered his cooperation to their kin-neighbours
(Saidi (C6), Malindi (D3), and Ali), and through Ali to his peers,

D5 and D6. All these men were willing in principle to accept his offers for it was to their advantage, as Ali indicated, to increase the size of their work-parties and their range of neighbourly assistance and support. Thus in the conventional manner they had fairly clearly committed themselves to work for Salimi. He had, I think, some hopes of reaching similar arrangements with D7, D8, and D9, all of his own junior generation, and perhaps even with Yasini. These hopes had not so far been realised, although there was no hostility and he joined with them in the action-sets of other men. They were not averse to cooperation with him and willingly accepted his support in other matters. Yet they were not prepared to prejudice their relations with their kin-neighbours on his behalf; and, with numerous kin-neighbours, they had relatively little need of his labour since they could expect to assemble fairly large work-parties without him.[10]

Salimi was therefore at a disadvantage compared with Yasini. He had fewer neighbours on whom he could call, but, for men whose obligations conflicted, Yasini's claims were much superior—especially in the particular circumstances relating to Ali. Salimi was perhaps unwise to persist when the conflict of dates became obvious. He should have postponed his party to a later day, as both Faranz and Ali advised. Salimi rejected the idea; he said that in previous years (since settling in Ligomba) his cultivation party had been one of the last to be held, and this had brought him poor harvests. Like most newcomers, he had had to take his place at the end of the queue. This may have reduced his harvest yields; certainly it increased the risk of it. Therefore this year he had determined to cultivate and plant earlier, claiming the right to do this by the moral standards of equity in a community.

This man was in the relatively weak position of many new-comers to a local community who had few kin-neighbours and had not yet had time to establish reliable links with other neighbours. He had a strong incentive to attract and sponsor his own kinsmen as newcomers, but this he had so far been unable to accomplish, partly (it was said) because of the relative shortage of convenient land there.[11] He had been considering the possibility of moving away again to settle elsewhere where his disadvantage might be less. However, he had rather few kinsmen at all: no sibling of his mother had survived to adulthood, his father had

[10] D7, but not the other three, had in fact participated in Salimi's dry season work-party in 1953.
[11] See page 120.

had only one brother (father of D2), and other kin were scattered. After his father died, in 1949, he had hoped to benefit by moving to Ligomba where he had the two resident kinsmen. Of course not all newcomers found themselves so disadvantageously placed as that. For example, Ndoma (D23) had come to Ligomba in the same year as Salimi, but he had several reliable kin-neighbours by this time.

In this particular case there were further disadvantages for Salimi and others. By Ndendeuli norms, a man expected to obtain the assistance of all those neighbours whom he himself assisted. Obligation reciprocated benefit of right. People expressed this as a clear general rule; and it lay at the heart of community life, indeed social life as a whole, in a society where there were very few sanctions on a man's behaviour. Corporate groups were insignificant and authority was equivocal. The insistence of Salimi in holding his work-party, despite the conflict with Yasini's party, meant that some neighbours could not reciprocate assistance they had received or expected to receive from either Salimi or Yasini. Faranz's work-party was still to meet, and Faranz wished to have Yasini (and D7 and D8) join it, as they had done in previous years. Faranz and Yasini had been members of each other's work-parties in the preceding dry season, and Yasini had since participated in a house-repairing party for Faranz. Yet, because of Salimi's insistence, Faranz was virtually compelled to join Salimi's party rather than Yasini's. At the moot to discuss the conflict, Salimi and Faranz almost quarrelled when the latter strongly advocated a postponement by Salimi. The conciliatory intervention of Saidi and Ali prevented this, and Faranz duly worked for Salimi.

As we have seen, Ali was able to make no more than token participation in Salimi's party, whilst D5 and D6 simply gave their assistance to Yasini. None of these men wished to lose cooperation with Salimi if that could be prevented; thus they urged postponement on him. They expressed some resentment that he should force on them the conflict of obligation otherwise engendered. None of them seemed to expect Yasini to postpone his party. The onus was on the unfortunate Salimi. He remained stubborn. By Ndendeuli standards he acted both foolishly and wrongly towards his neighbours and towards his own best interest. It was possible that in the future he might find it more difficult to obtain the assistance and support of some of these neighbours, as D5 declared in the moot. Relations between Salimi and his brother-in-law were strained. Salimi's reputation in Ligomba deteriorated. Ali commented, "Yes, I went to work in his field for a time, but perhaps I shall not go and hoe for him another time. If he disputes with Yasini again, I shall go with [support] Yasini for truly he is my brother, a good man, a man who helps. But Salimi is only a youngster and he should not quarrel with men who have lived here for a long time and are big (senior, influential). Neighbours ought to talk together and listen to one another so that they can make arrangements properly".

So Salimi attempted, with limited success and potential disadvantage, to ignore the realities of his relatively weak position. The actual work-party that he did assemble was small in numbers. It could, then, either accomplish less work than the larger parties of neighbours, or perform the work less efficiently. Members of the party complained that he asked too much work of them. Although Ndendeuli did not want very large parties for cultivation work, they disliked small ones. When there were more people the work was likely to go more easily and, they said, the additional camaraderie made it less arduous. There was one compensatory factor in this instance. Salimi's household had only two adults (himself and his wife) and one small child to feed, and therefore he had a smaller area of cultivation than, for example, Yasini. Though the latter could assemble a larger work-party, he had to feed himself, two wives, a widowed sister, and six children (three adolescent). His fields were more than three times the size of those of Salimi, and in 1953 he had to convene a second party. The other newcomer, Ndoma (D23), was better off than either of these: he had two adults and two small children to feed, and could rely on a fairly large work-party.

Work-Party Case 4, 3 January:
Abdal (D8) and Misawa (D14)

In this case the conflict was not severe. It concerned Musa (D13) and possibly his father, Tanda (C13). Abdal had only a weak claim, if any at all, against Tanda, an older man of the senior generation, nor had Abdal joined Tanda's party the week previously. Musa, however, was husband of Abdal's first cousin, they were both members of the junior generation, and they had been engaged in developing mutual assistance in recent years. The primary obligation of Musa was to Misawa, his first cousin; in fact this was so clear that perhaps Musa had not properly considered his conflicting obligation to Abdal. When in the end Abdal did discover the problem he did not see sufficient reason to make

a last-minute rearrangement at that advanced stage of the cultivation season. He had already worked in Musa's party—it was on
that occasion that the problem came to light and was discussed.
So he forfeited the labour of Musa and his household, but was
still able to assemble a satisfactory work-party from among the
remainder of his kin-neighbours.

This was, then, a quite minor conflict, easily solved and not
calling for a moot. The burgeoning relationship between Abdal
and Musa was still so much at the edge of each man's field of kinship and neighbourly cooperation that difficulties would often arise
where stronger interests and obligations prevented one or the
other rendering assistance, as happened in this instance. Men experimented, as it were, with potential relationships at the edges
of their range of cooperation in attempts to extend them where
possible and to discover whether obligations to another neighbour
could be made to fit into the current pattern of obligations to
existing kin-neighbours. It might prove possible to make a fit,
perhaps involving adjustments in relations with others; or it might
be shown that conflict of obligations occurred too often to allow
the development of a reliable association in a certain direction.
Much would depend, of course, on changes in the community as
some men moved away and newcomers arrived. It is important to
note that Ndendeuli did experiment in this way, probing the potentialities of the network available to them, finding an advantage
here and a frustration there. For example, Tanda (C13) and Sedi
(C21) had in the past attempted to establish regular cooperation
but, baulked by too frequent inabilities to meet each other's
legitimate demands because of other, prior obligations, they had
tacitly agreed to acknowledge the overriding difficulties. As Case
5 (p. 172) showed, both men were concerned to maintain the
possibility of present friendliness and future association. The
problem was again made evident in Work-Party Case 2.

Work-Party Case 5, 8 January:
Kinanda (D9) and Rajabu (D15)

This conflict primarily involved Tanda (C13) and Musa (D13)
in divided obligations. By this time it was some three weeks since
the rains had begun and those men who had not yet held a work-
party were, with good reason, beginning to be anxious about their
harvest prospects. Both conveners of the two parties on this day
refused to consider postponement, nor was it seriously urged by
their neighbours. No moot was held.

Kinanda and his father Yasini talked informally with Tanda and Musa. Yasini, by his own account, complained of the failure of his son-in-law, Musa, to be on the alert for conflicts in his obligations. Yasini pointed out that in this, as in the previous case, Musa had apparently not noticed the impending difficulty, or at least he had done nothing about it. Yasini also referred to the dispute he had brought against his son-in-law some weeks ago, when the latter had failed to fulfill normal obligations to a senior affine (Case 6, p. 173). It appeared that Musa, in his middle twenties, was proving to be an irresponsible young kinsman; certainly Yasini thought so. As a result of pressure by Yasini and Kinanda, it was agreed that Musa should join Kinanda's party. And, perhaps in some acceptance of partial culpability, Tanda spent a token half hour or so in Kinanda's field, although the bulk of his time was given to Rajabu, his sister's son. There was no question that Tanda would ignore his primary obligation to Rajabu, and neither Yasini nor Kinanda attempted to persuade him to do that. Afterwards Kinanda explained to me that, "Tanda is a good man, a neighbour, and we are kinsmen. But look; it would not be good if he ignored his own sister's son in the fields. So he went there. But we are still kinsmen and I shall help him another time". Dispute in which neither side's interests would have been helped was equally avoided, and no real damage was suffered.

These five cases of conflicting arrangements and obligations could be taken merely as apt illustrations, selected to support analytical conclusions already reached. They were, however, arbitrarily recorded in the field as those which came to light when I was present in Ligomba during that period. Not only do they illustrate the operation of the kinship network system in a particular context of vital importance to the people, they permit an advance in the analysis by a more detailed examination of the problems of choice and of organisation. These problems occurred by the very nature of the system, and they were treated without benefit of superimposed control from within or without the community.

One cannot simply state that an Ndendeuli called on his neighbours, kin-linked or indirectly linked, with whom he maintained reciprocal rights and obligations of assistance. It is essential for discriminating analysis, in order to understand how social action was effectively organised in a network of complex, convolute relationships, to examine how far and in what ways a man was limited in the demands he made and acceded to. No doubt the organisation could have been made to work more efficiently by better communication and perhaps some centralised supervision, rather than by the informal techniques of the Ndendeuli. A computer could, for instance, produce a timetable of work-parties in which conflict of obligations would be reduced to a minimum, just as a busy college's timetable of lectures is so drawn up to prevent conflicts for teachers and students. But the Ndendeuli were near-subsistence farmers with meagre techniques. In essence, a man's claims were subject to equally legitimate claims of those who in some degree were linked with him through the network. Men were concerned to prevent a situation arising in which they would be compelled to neglect obligations, for such neglect limited or weakened the claims they could make afterwards. Inevitably these situations did arise, however, and choices were made that had greater or lesser effect on future relations, future liabilities, and abilities to make claims. I have remarked on the way in which men experimented in the attempt to develop cooperative relations with neighbours: the potentialities of the developing network were not clear to men involved in it unless they tried out apparent possibilities. I have also shown how a newcomer might find difficulties in developing a viable field of cooperation—and much the same applied to the newly married man who became a household head and a new focus of relationships. The problems occurred here not because the new man was rejected as such, but because there were real difficulties of fitting him into existing patterns, or of adjusting patterns to the changing requirements (cf. Work-Party Case 3). Earlier, in Chapter Four, it was shown how men developed new cooperative relations, and how others were allowed to die away because they could no longer be successfully accommodated to the evolving patterns. I emphasize again that this was a dynamic system and not a static situation.

There was a practical morality of reciprocity. A man sought to build up, strengthen, and develop credit and reputation by turning up to work in his neighbours' fields. Men were, Ndendeuli sometimes said cynically, less zealous of their labour obligations when their own work-parties had successfully met and their own cultivation was accomplished. This might have been true in a very limited way, but it could not have been so to any marked degree—and no disputes on this score arose in Ligomba. The whole pattern of reciprocal assistance was largely self-reinforcing for each individual involved in it. Social life and its requirements continued, weeding season succeeding hoeing and planting season, whilst the composition of the local community, and thus the opportunities offered, changed relatively slowly. A man remained dependent on the fund of goodwill and reciprocal privilege born of accomplished obligation. Some men did acquire a work-shy reputation, but they found it less easy to be sure of the assistance of their neighbours when needed. They might be compelled to accept a late date for their cultivation parties, for instance, or to be the ones to postpone a party when conflict of dates occurred.

Of course there was no direct accounting of mutual assistance. A neighbour might be ill, or absent in labour migration or for other good reason; this was no cause to refuse to assist him when he properly required it. Some men were better workers, physically stronger, more efficient, more conscientious, and others were less so. These considerations were scarcely relevant to the operation of the system. Vital though agricultural work obviously was, intimately affecting the livelihood of the people, it concerned only part of the totality of cooperation in the ongoing social life of a community. A poor worker might have been an excellent man to have on one's side in a dispute, and at very least he might be hindered from joining an opponent's side or unfavorably influencing intermediary neighbors. He might have been an otherwise congenial neighbour, perhaps skilled in ritual knowledge or a good raconteur at beer-drinks. Even beyond these practical considerations, which Ndendeuli understood well enough, they said that it was worth some disadvantage in order to maintain a reasonable cordiality among neighbours. These points are raised here in order to counteract any tendency to perceive too mechanical an operation of relationships and activities throughout the network. Sociological analysis can too easily give that erroneous impression because of the necessary abstraction involved in it. But there was in practice a good deal of give and take, of toleration, and, I believe, of generosity, in relations between neighbours that tempered the formal appearance of reciprocal rights and obligations.

VII

Kinship and Cooperation

The object of the three preceding chapters has been to examine in detail some of the empirical facts in the organisation and mobilisation of men for social action, and the ways in which that action was carried out, in a single (but not necessarily typical) local community. It has been shown that social action was not undertaken by the community as a whole, nor on behalf of it as a whole, for it was not a corporate unit in the sense of having rights, interests, and activities shared and pursued in common. Nor did a local community stand in structural or practical opposition to other communities. Social action occurred in the interests and needs of particular individual members of the community, and for these purposes a member required the assistance and support, material and moral, of his neighbours—or rather, of some of his neighbours. Had the empirical data been collected more systematically and comprehensively, it would have been possible to give additional evidence on the organization and performance of other kinds of cooperative action, and on the recruitment and operation of action-sets under these conditions. Especially important is the omission of information on ritual cooperation, in life crises and in misfortunes that affected individuals and households, for which action-sets were mobilised in the same way as described for agricultural cooperation.[1] Despite this defect, I would claim that sufficient data

[1] As far as my knowledge goes, it appeared that the recruitment of action-sets for ritual purposes closely paralleled that for dry season work-parties for the clearing and preparation of new fields. That is, such sets were recruited at times when there was usually no competition from other neighbours who simultaneously wished to arrange collective action. Therefore, on these occasions, a man could expect to mobilise virtually all those neighbours who acknowledged cooperative relations with him. Action-sets at these times were the largest in size that Ndendeuli mobilised within a community, and they tended to reveal the total ego-focussed sets of relations of each convener.

have been presented to illustrate the principles and processes involved.

With this evidence in mind, it is now possible and necessary to examine more closely the sociological factors concerned in the organisation of collective action. The object of the present chapter is to consider the nature of the social relationships involved—social relationships that were primarily subsumed under the rubric of kinship.

For an Ndendeuli, the explanation of collective action, indeed of almost all significant interaction between neighbors, was quite straightforward. It was invariably said that kinship established a moral right to claim assistance of all kinds and a moral obligation to provide it. When a man had need of assistance of some sort beyond the means of his own household, he expected to obtain it from those neighbours who were his acknowledged kinsfolk.[2] When he came into dispute with another neighbour he expected his own kin-neighbours to support him and to help in the prosecution or defence of his case. In each instance a man's expectations were, he might have said, based on accepted assumptions about the inherent, moral, categorical character of kinship, and its universal, automatic applicability. Ndendeuli expressed this idea not merely in response to the general questioning of an ignorant, western outsider, but in actual social situations in which assistance was required and rendered. As Ndendeuli expressed it, the rule that (1) "You must help a man because he is your kinsman" had the same imperative quality as (2) "You must cultivate because you must provide food for your family". Both were perceived as unavoidable, moral requirements. Both were accepted as axiomatic, and as having the same constraining quality as (3) "You must cultivate because you need food to live": that is, all three statements had an inescapable, natural, and practical quality. They were self-evident truths for the people, scarcely calling for explanation or justification. They were part of the natural order of things, inherent in the process of living.

"Who else can I ask for help?" said one man, discussing this with me. "We cannot do everything by ourselves and without help. But we do not pay people to work for us and to do things for us, as you Europeans do. We do not have a chief or wealthy

[2] A man similarly expected and claimed assistance from his kinsfolk who lived in other communities—that is, who were not neighbours at the time. This aspect is considered later. Here I am only concerned with interaction among co-neighbours of the same community.

men to go to for help, as the Ngoni do. No, we help each other, kinsman with kinsman. I cannot ask any man to help me—only kinsmen. But kinsmen cannot refuse. Look! they would not be kinsmen if they refused".

In the light of these commonly expressed principles and attitudes, I have examined the kinship network that enveloped the local community. It has been shown how that network provided both opportunities and limitations on men's actions and interaction. The first hypothesis I wish to explore is that the network of kinship linkages provided an established, recognised, and acceptable system within which a man could operate with reasonable confidence, with reliable expectations, and in which his rights and claims, and his obligations and involvements, comprised a fairly coherent whole. It was not an arbitrary system, as it might have been had it been based on a convention of ad hoc cooperation with those who happened to live near or to be congenial, for it emerged out of past experience and past commitments, and it was able to take account of the complex inter-relationships and cross-cutting ties that naturally arose within it. It was a fairly flexible system that men could to some extent manipulate and within which they could make choices in their own self-interest. As we have seen, in the recruitment and operation of action-sets, the system did not by any means rule out all conflict, but it did a great deal to permit limitation of conflict by establishing the "rules of the game": rules that were fairly clear and fairly easy to follow, and that had the additional advantage of being underwritten by accepted moral principle. In short, rights and obligations, the lines of social action, were systematised and rationalised but with flexibility.

From the evidence presented, it is obvious that the concrete social reality, as might be expected, was a good deal more complicated and less straightforward than would be suggested by the simple equation of kinship and the imperative to give assistance and support. There were a number of factors that tended to override a simple adherence to the kinship ethic in particular contexts. There were also problems in practice over the definition and determination of kinship itself.

First, I note an essential vagueness about who were and were not kin. In the widest sense of the word, all Ndendeuli could be classed as *akarongo* (s. *nongo*), "kinsmen", either in emphasized contradistinction to those non-Ndendeuli of whom they were markedly aware, or to stress inclinations towards particular friendliness and helpfulness. Certainly at times any neighbour could be brought within the simplest classificatory system of "father", "brother", or "son" to emphasize the association of being neighbours, co-members for the time being of the same community. Even in the more limited sense of "close kinsman", *nkuru* (which in its most limited sense meant "brother") Ndendeuli were sometimes disinclined to be limited to known genealogical linkages. Moreover, there was little or no emphasis on the idea of kinship stemming from common blood or physiological connection. Affines were just as much kinsfolk as were cognates, both in the wider and narrower frame of reference. Indeed the nuclear quality of Ndendeuli kinship, and especially close kinship, when stripped of its various detailed manifestations, resided in a potentially advantageous and cooperative relationship rather than in biological facts. As I shall suggest, it is almost possible to reverse the Ndendeuli ethic, but without distorting the empirical facts, and to say that people who regularly exchanged assistance were kinsmen *because* of that regular assistance. That is the second hypothesis to be examined here.

Ndendeuli genealogical knowledge was not particularly extensive, and was quite often vague in its details. The limits of knowledge varied from person to person, not only, I think, because of the varying capabilities of memory but in response to quite definite social facts and the social position of a person at a particular time. Briefly, and a little oversimplified, a man remembered where it was of advantage to him, and forgot where there was no advantage, as no doubt is the case in very many societies. Many, and perhaps all, men knew of some genealogically related persons (cognates and affines) with whom they neither cooperated nor expected or wanted to. Memory held knowledge of some kin who were no longer "useful", although such people were scarcely referred to unless occasion made it relevant. When recording genealogies I repeatedly found that the cut-off point in acknowledged memory tended to coincide with the point at which active relations ceased. After reaching a certain kinsman—perhaps a cousin of some degree—I was told that I should enquire of that cousin if further information were required. Quite often I was told of a vaguely known cluster of kinsfolk whose names, whereabouts, and exact linkages were forgotten. Under pressure of questioning the informant was often able to give me more information; but it was usually declared to be irrelevant and was given unwillingly and with expressed impatience. Whilst not denying the admitted genealogical facts, informants would deny that such men were "really kin". As one informant put it: "We are no longer kin for we do not know and help one another".

Let me examine this connection between acknowledgement of kinship and the empirical facts of cooperation. First I cite some illustrative cases from the material already presented, and then I shall seek to generalise from these.

The nephews of Ali (D5 and D6) admitted under questioning that there might be some kind of genealogical link between themselves and the sons of Konga (D16 to D19). They were in fact third cousins (MMFZSSS), though the most that they would agree to was that since Ali and Konga were kinsmen ("brothers"), then they and Konga's sons must also be connected. They were certain, nevertheless, that Konga's sons were not their kinsmen. Beni (D5) told me: "It is a matter of long ago, perhaps in our grandfathers' time. I do not know properly. There is no reason to know. They are not my brothers [kinsmen]; they are just neighbours". He had no expectations of assistance and cooperation from these neighbours, and there never had been any between them.

Ali (C7) readily acknowledged kinship with his second cousin, Konga (C17) (MFZSS); but he denied that Zadiki (C15) or Mitedi (C19) were his kin, though both were genealogically related to him in the same way (through the same intermediaries) as Konga. Ali's first cousin, Saidi (C6), was linked with all three men in the same way as Ali, but he denied kinship with any of them. Both Saidi and Ali disclaimed the genealogical knowledge but were later able, at my insistence, to give me the correct connections. These were older men who had been living as co-neighbours in the same community for two decades.

Musa (D13) and Rashidi (D12) acknowledged each other as kinsmen ("brothers") although neither was able to trace the precise connection. They were in fact second cousins of second cousins—from Musa (FMBWBSS). Musa described the linkage as "the sons of brothers", but he was unable to explain the linkage between their fathers, Tanda and Bilali (who were first cousins of first cousins). When I pressed him further, he justified his assertions by appeal to the practical facts: "We help one another. We cultivate in [each other's] fields. So are we not brothers? It must be so. Do you think we are not brothers although we help each other like this?"

Both Zadiki (C15) and Bilali (C12) could, with difficulty, explain their genealogical linkage although each of them, separately, preferred to explain the connection by asserting that they were "brother" to Kabaya (C11).[3] On the other hand, both were reluctant to commit themselves to clear affirmation of kinship with the other. "We are like brothers", was as far as Zadiki would go. He implied a relationship closer than that of mere neighbours, but not quite acknowledged as kin-neighbours. Almost certainly some years previously these two men had regarded each other as only the kinsman of a common kinsman, but the degree and reliability of mutual assistance had developed at least to the point where they had become "like brothers". Formerly their sons, Misawa and Kasim, had not counted themselves as kinsmen either, but through their achievement of fairly regular cooperation, and their mutual desire to emphasize this, they had come to acknowledge themselves to be now "brothers" and kinsmen. It is significant to my argument that these men operated within a cluster of comparatively high inter-connectedness in the kinship network, involving a number of other young household heads (D9, D10, D11, D14, D15) and their fathers, and the leadership of the notable Kabaya. Thus they could, even without exact genealogical knowledge, assert kinship without difficulty.

Changes in the acknowledgement of kinship resulted from changes in the practical possibilities of mutual assistance and in the configuration of the network of neighbourly relations. I have already shown, with specific reference to the case histories of Ali and Konga,[4] that at an earlier period men may have cooperated regularly with certain kin-neighbours, so acknowledged, with whom later there was neither cooperation nor expectation of it, and no claim to kinship. This change was not necessarily the consequence of animosity or conflict at an inter-personal level, though sometimes it may have worked out that way. More importantly, with or without hostility, men "moved away" from each other over a period of time as their interests, advantages, and commitments diverged, and as it therefore became increasingly difficult to meet their obligations to each other because of prior obligations to different neighbours. New neighbours moved into the community, new household heads became established, and new affinal ties were created. All these offered new linkages, new opportunities for co-

[3] Note the use of Kabaya as the common reference. He was the notable to whom both men looked for leadership in their cluster within the community network. In fact, Bilali was first cousin of Kabaya, whilst Zadiki was brother-in-law of another first cousin of Kabaya.

[4] See page 112 ff.

operation, and fresh commitments. Some of the older commitments, more peripheral ones that were less consistent with the total pattern of a man's obligations, would have been gradually dropped. Indeed they *had* to be allowed to atrophy if in practice they began persistently to raise conflicts of obligations that could not easily be reconciled. Ali was able to explain this kind of process in respect of his second cousin, Mitedi (C19). He related how it had begun to be difficult to meet his obligations to Mitedi because of the priority of the growing claims of other kin-neighbours whom he (Ali) considered now to have become more important to him (and whose claims he could reconcile with one another fairly well). Ali noted that Mitedi's assistance to him became less reliable as Mitedi became increasingly involved with his own newer kin-neighbours. Neither man resented the change or blamed the other, though I believe that both regretted its necessity. Their evolving ranges of commitment had become too separate from each other, so that expectations of cooperation ceased. At the same time, acknowledgement of kinship began to lapse. Even though, obviously, genealogical memory had not disappeared in 1953, neither man was willing to admit to this at first. It seems to be a fair assumption that admission of the inactive kinship link raised inconsistency in the working model that each man held in his mind, and by which he was able to orient and systematise his expectations and obligations.

Thus although the objective facts of genealogical connection continued, actual practical relations changed, and the claim to be or not to be a kinsman changed correspondingly in the working model. This occurred gradually over a period, seldom suddenly as far as I could discover. Selective memory could easily cope with this transformation, whilst a man could at the same time retain the working principle that kinship ascribed the unavoidable moral basis of rights, obligations, and cooperation. Without an inquisitive anthropologist to ask awkward questions, the Ndendeuli could ignore the contradiction. Certainly it caused them neither confusion nor discomfort. The anthropologist, of course, pursues his enquiries (or at least I did) in the light of formalised genealogical diagrams, synthesised and recorded on paper, with a kind of existence of their own, independent of actual social life. An Ndendeuli had no such diagram on paper, or even in his head, to act as a blueprint or to disclose inconsistencies. Instead he knew a range of kin-neighbours with whom he enjoyed fairly regularly, fairly reliable cooperation of many kinds. These were his "fathers", "brothers", and "sons". If and when necessary he could explain his particular genealogical connection with each. But he did not perceive, or need to perceive, all the connections in a single, comprehensive, consistent genealogy.

These illustrations and considerations suggest some general conclusions that summarise the discussion so far. First, a known genealogical link did not of itself necessarily establish acknowledged kinship. Second, of men genealogically linked in the same way, one or more might have been acknowledged as kin whilst others might not have been. Third, acknowledged kinship could exist although the proper genealogical link was unclear to the men concerned. Fourth, neighbours may have been genuinely uncertain whether or not they were kinsmen, but this was a matter of uncertain practical expectations and not of uncertain genealogical knowledge. Fifth, acknowledgement of kinship might change through time, for neighbours who were once accepted as kin became no longer so, and some became acknowledged who had not been so before.

Another factor—that of generation—affected the determination of those neighbours with whom a man regularly cooperated and had reliable expectations of assistance. There was a tendency to develop and maintain cooperation with one's peers in preference to one's seniors or juniors. This affected the junior generation of household heads more than the senior generation, and it applied principally to more distantly related kin-neighbours rather than to close kin. This factor can easily be over-emphasised, for there was no institutionalized separation of the generations to set them into structural opposition or contradistinction. Men of the junior generation were to a limited extent dependent on individual "fathers" (own father, WF, MB, and FB, in particular) because of their superior experience or special knowledge, and also because such a father's position in the community was often more stable and more reliable. Men of the junior generation were expected to show a degree of respect and deference to their seniors; generally this was the case, as for instance when senior men were attended to first at beer-drinks or allowed priority in speaking in a moot. As shown in Chapter Five, some younger household heads were prepared to allow a father, particularly an own father, to take the initiative in the recruitment of action-sets and the prosecution of a claim in dispute situations. This seemed seldom to occur, however, with men of the junior generation who were older and more experienced, nor was it in any way mandatory.

The main point of relevance here is that younger household

heads consciously and deliberately sought to develop their own fields of reciprocal assistance and cooperation. They neither wished nor were they bound to adopt a father's field intact; they were able to express their autonomy as household heads by independent action in this connection. No less importantly, they were inclined to take account of future probabilities. From that point of view there was advantage in establishing close working association with peers, which could be expected to endure, rather than with older men of the senior generation, who would die off. Thus for example (and reverting to a previously used illustration), it was likely to be more advantageous to Misawa to have a firm association with Kasim, his peer, than with Kasim's father—or for Hanju (D21) to build regular, reliable cooperation with the sons of Konga rather than with Konga himself. These younger men were prepared to associate with more distantly linked neighbours, and to acknowledge expressed kinship with them. This was partly, or perhaps mainly, an effort to keep the options open at that early stage of a man's career, until he could see who were likely to offer the more stable and reliable relations in the longer run. Older men tended to narrow their fields of cooperation with a preference to more closely linked kin-neighbours, as experiment and experience showed the more advantageous relations. For older men, distant "brothers" were replaced by married sons, daughters' husbands, and the fathers of children's spouses. Thus younger men commonly acknowledged second and third cousins, and the cousins of cousins; but men did so less and less as they grew older, as the case histories of Ali and Konga indicate. This was rather a matter of age than of generation, of course; but the developmental cycle worked out in the context in which attitudes and expectations among "brothers" differed from those between "fathers" and "sons".

It must be added, however, that the range of choice open to a man of the junior generation was limited by the logic of entailment within the network. A younger man's range of commitments had to mesh reasonably well not only with the commitments of his "brothers" but also with those of such "fathers" as he wished to or had to acknowledge. For example, Musa was in no position to ignore his "fathers", Tanda (own father), Zadiki (FZH), and Kabaya (FMBS): they were too important to be neglected, and the three "fathers" were intimately committed to each other. What Musa could and did do was to give less emphasis to his association with Bilali (another "father") and more to Bilali's sons; and he had experimented in developing cooperation with the sons of Konga, whilst more or less ignoring Konga himself. That kind of development produced the logically discrepant situation in which a man cooperated closely with a peer, acknowledging him as a "brother", whilst he scarcely recognized that peer's father as a kinsman and exchanged assistance with him far less regularly. Thus a "brother's" own father might not have been recognized as a "father" by ego. But this is discrepant only if we, as outsiders, insist on the formal logic of genealogical ties and the primacy of kinship.

To return directly to the rationale of cooperation and commitment, and the Ndendeuli assertion that a man recruited his kinsmen to his action-sets because they were kinsmen, and that they responded because of the moral imperatives of kinship as such. It hardly requires emphasising that in actuality men joined action-sets for a variety of reasons, only one of which, if at all, was the straight kinship tie. Men supported a neighbour because he supported them previously, and in the desire to assure his support in the future. The support and assistance was essentially a part of a whole series, a stream of transactions between the men concerned. Support was given not only to help a kin-neighbour when he became a principal in a dispute, but also directly to express or implement opposition or hostility to the other principal and/or one of his supporters. A man might wish to demonstrate association with a fellow-supporter of his own principal (for example, Ali vis-à-vis Yasini in Case 4). Sometimes a supporter had marked personal interest in the outcome of the matter concerned (as Yasini in Case 2, p. 148), or he might take the opportunity to gain influence through the demonstration of ability and leadership. A man might not respond to the demand for his support in an action-set because of the probable disadvantage that could result for his own interests (for example, Kabaya in Case 6, p. 174), or to express some dissatisfaction with the principal's actions (for example, D7 and D8 in Work-Party Case 1, p. 205). Obviously the reasons for giving, or not giving, support were numerous, and they varied in combination and importance from situation to situation, and from neighbour to neighbour. It would indeed be simplistic to think that Ndendeuli joined an action-set purely to meet a moral kinship obligation. Ndendeuli did not think that either. They were prepared to concede that other factors were involved and they found an interest in discussing what these were in particular cases. The kinship ethic was not sufficient in itself. In so far as it was important—which it undoubtedly was—it was as a dogma, and as a simplified symbol for other factors.

Often the grounds for a claim to support or assistance were intrinsic in the relations between two men: they were not and had no need to be overtly stated each time a claim was made. In cases of reluctance or refusal to accede to demands, the claimant might have referred to the acknowledged kinship link. More certainly, and also more emphatically, he referred to past services rendered, the established practical association, and the prospects of future reciprocity. In making this point there is no need to ignore the fact that men were, at the same time, moved and motivated by their accepted moral standards. Although seeking preferential advantages for themselves, they did not abjure moral requirements —even to the point of immediate disadvantage sometimes. On the whole, moral and practical requirements coincided in general over a period: if they did not, then adjustments occurred of the kind already indicated, so that the moral dogma of kinship obligation applied to those with whom regular, reliable, reciprocal assistance was practicably possible. Of course men's decisions were by no means all well calculated, much less were they invariably wisely made. The motivations of a man in making his decisions were almost invariably mixed. Neither he nor an external observer could properly unravel them and weight them comparatively. It is sufficient to my argument at this point, however, to indicate that motivations and decisions were not confined to the "automatic", moral requirements of kinship per se.

There are, then, crucial reservations that must modify the Ndendeuli contention that it was kinship which produced cooperation and which involved an inherent obligation to give assistance. Yet two unavoidable considerations remain; they are vital and demand explanation. First, a man's neighbours in his local community who regularly cooperated with him were his acknowledged kinsmen. Indeed, as we have seen, there seems to have been a need to create an acknowledgement of kinship where that had not been previously recognised, as a response to the new development of active cooperation. Secondly and more importantly, virtually all nearer kin in the community did in practice come into the category of a man's regular and reliable supporters and associates. It was the more distantly related kinsmen who were mostly affected by the kind of reservations I have previously raised. The question arises therefore: for nearer kin (cognates and affines), the more important kin on the whole, are we compelled to accept the Ndendeuli axiom that kinship was the primary motivating force and a basic, irreducible factor in social life?

In consideration of this matter we must take account of the second general principle of the Ndendeuli, one that they themselves coupled with the dogma of kinship obligation. This was the principle of reciprocity. You had to give assistance to a neighbour because he had assisted you earlier; and you could claim his assistance now because you had supported him in the past. Obtaining assistance was something like a debt that had to be repaid; though Ndendeuli did not use the concept of debt explicitly in this matter, they were quite firm on the necessity of reciprocating assistance. But it was more than merely transaction A being balanced by transaction B in the reverse direction; that simple reciprocity would have suggested to Ndendeuli a tentative relationship only, without particular past or future. They perceived reciprocity as operating within a long series of transactions, a persisting relationship between two men in which not one but many acts of support and assistance merited the claim for continued return support. Reciprocity was not only a moral principle, though that it definitely was; it was essentially a practical mode of conducting social relations. As one informant (Beni) put it in reference to his third cousins: "We do not help one another nor go together [support each other, act in unison], so how can we be kinsmen?" [5] That is, the kinship bond was only acknowledged when it was demonstrated in the practical, persisting interaction of actual mutual assistance, in a stream of reciprocation.

Nevertheless, this consideration, valid enough in itself, still does not explain the fact that cooperation seems to have been expected and was generally regular and reliable with a man's closer kinsmen who were also his neighbours. By "closer kinsmen" I refer to the category identified as *akuru* by the Ndendeuli,[6] which, though not entirely clear cut, included cognates up to first cousin, and father-in-law and brothers-in-law among affines. True reciprocity informed the relationships here, of course, but seemingly as a derivative of the kinship bond. Ndendeuli in effect put it that way. The kinship ethic made sense: it explained, justified, and maintained men's expectations of the relationships. But we must take note that in reality the appeal to kinship was not made

[5] Very many similar statements were recorded in the field. Cf. the end of the informant's remarks quoted at page 218, for example.

[6] *Akuru*, s.*nkuru*, in its limited sense referred to brothers (sons of the same parents) and in its wider sense to kinsmen of the same generation. In its widest sense it referred to closer kinsmen, irrespective of generation. The usage seems to be comparable to that of the Swahili term *ndugu* in some (though not all) Coastal communities.

primarily on the grounds of biological links or common blood or similar metaphor. There was little symbolisation of kinship, and little development of a mystique.

The fundamental reason why these close kinsmen were almost invariably regularly cooperating associates came from the men's involvement in the kinship network. Inherent to the logic of a network is the principle that actual, operative relations must have a fairly high degree of common consistency. The commitments of A to each of his kin-neighbours, B, C, D, . . . must be consistent *both* with each other *and* with the commitments of those kin-neighbours to one another. If this were not so, then conflicts of obligations become so great that expectations cannot be reliably realised: there would be continual interference in the practical efficiency of "getting things done", to the point of virtual breakdown. Social life, here as anywhere else, required reasonable certainty of expectations and reasonable fulfilment of them. Consciously or not, Ndendeuli sought to develop and maintain this double consistency of their commitments.

This is more easily seen, perhaps, with respect to agricultural work-parties and the developments that followed the introduction of a newcomer into the local community: for example, the experience of Salimi (D1) to which reference was made in Work-Party Case 3 (p. 209). A newcomer such as Salimi joined the community already bearing commitments to those kinsmen there who sponsored him. Some kind of working relationship must have existed previously, for otherwise those resident kinsmen would have been unlikely to have assumed sponsorship. The newcomer incurred heavy obligations to his sponsoring kinsmen for the very considerable assistance they gave him in the first year. But they also offered the prospect of continued neighbourly cooperation and dependable support long after the initial stage of establishing the new household and farm. They for their part were willing to sponsor and assist him in the expectation of gaining normal reciprocal assistance from him after he settled in.[7]

Salimi, however, required more assistance and more supporters than his two sponsoring kinsmen alone could provide. A successful work-party required more than three men and their households. Through the intermediation of his sponsor-kinsmen (D2 and D4),

[7] In this connection, note the cases of sponsorship by Luinga (B4) and Ali (C7) in the early years of Ligomba (p. 89 ff.), and by Zadiki (C15) after his unsuccessful dispute with Konga in 1939 (p. 99 f.).

Salimi was able quite successfully to establish working relations and cooperation with some of their kin-neighbours—C3 and D3—to whom he promised a useful extension of their own ranges of reciprocal commitment that could be rendered consistent with their existing obligations. In the fourth year after his arrival in the community, these neighbours virtually accepted him as kinsman, whereas before they had not done so. By that time Salimi was actively endeavouring to establish the same advantageous relations with Ali (C7) and with the latter's nephews, D5 and D6. This was proving less easy to accomplish with reasonable reliability, as Work-Party Case 3 indicated. These men were more indirectly linked to Salimi and his sponsor-kinsmen: they had commitments to other neighbours that could not readily be made consistent with a new commitment to Salimi and a reinforced commitment to his sponsors.

In extending his relationships and his commitments in this way, Salimi had to integrate his operations into the already existing pattern of commitments of all those neighbours. His claims on them and his ability to render assistance to them needed to be so arranged that they did not conflict in themselves or with theirs to each other. This was not difficult with closer kin because commitments were mutually consistent among the same set of men; but it was less easy with more distant kin since there were fewer mutually consistent obligations and more inconsistent ones. Had Salimi wished to establish working cooperation with some other neighbour—say, one who arbitrarily happened to live nearby, or an influential notable who might seem to have offered particular advantage—it would in practice have proved impossible to make consistent his already existing commitments with the already existing commitments of that other, unrelated neighbour. Practical arrangements would most probably have become too complicated within the organisational means available. Moreover, the wider the range of a man's commitments throughout the community, the greater the likelihood that he would find himself in a conflicting position with loyalties to both sides in a dispute case. Therefore the newcomer (and similarly the new household head) allowed himself to be guided by the pattern of inter-relations and cooperation—the mesh of commitments—that he found already in operation. Later he would experiment, as already described,[8] to discover what extensions might work within the pattern and how far the

[8] See page 212.

pattern itself might be modified. Ndendeuli referred to all this when they said that in those circumstances men sought cooperation with the kin of their own kin-neighbours.

Thus in the case of Salimi, he was able to undertake regular co-operative commitments with the closer kin-neighbours of his own two kin-neighbours; but he began to explore the possibilities of establishing cooperation with others within the range of his two sponsors. This he was engaged in during the period of my research. He was finding some difficulty, as the particular case (Work-party Case 3) indicated. When faced with the necessity of choice, Beni and Amadu (D_5 and D_6) deliberately decided to give their preference to another kin-neighbour whose work-party was being held on the same day in the cultivation season. They both said, doubtless rightly, that they wanted to assist Salimi, and they would have joined his party had he been prepared to postpone it until a later date. Clearly, Salimi could not yet entertain reliable expectations of the support of those two neighbours. Possibly he never would unless the circumstances altered for those two men; yet there was probably some advantage to both sides in persisting to seek co-operation whenever possible, even on a second-best basis, since they might in the future require each other's support in an action-set in a dispute situation.

The potentialities were to a large extent unknown to a new-comer. They were not necessarily clear for an established member of the community as circumstances changed over time. The possibilities were explored and re-explored by each man as he experimented with work-party recruitment, and as new conflict cases raised new opportunities or cut off others. As a result of this more or less continuous experimenting, men discovered what would work, what was unreliable, and what would not work at all.

At the purely practical level of efficacious organisation it was more advantageous and reliable to cooperate regularly as far as possible with those neighbours who also cooperated with one another. It amounted to more than organisational convenience, however. Firstly, if a man's commitments were congruent, they were thereby positively reinforced as the participants regularly came together in all, or rather very many, of their action-sets. Secondly, commitment included support in dispute situations and in moots; and there was likely to be less conflict of obligation and loyalty, and support would therefore be more effective, if commitments articulated together. Thus, starting with a few kin-neighbours, as every man did at some point in the life of the community, it was both impracticable and unwise, if not absolutely impossible, to ignore their commitments and their closer associates.

On the other hand, there is no justification in assuming a condition of fine harmony in a community and its kinship network. The argument of logically inherent consistency only operates up to a point, fundamental though it obviously is. Certainly I have no wish to suggest some kind of necessary equilibrium. Empirical data alone rule out such an idealistic model. In the first place, close kin-neighbours could, and did, develop competition, animosity, and conflict between them. The chronic conflict between Zadiki and Konga is one excellent case in point: here it was not only a matter of structural incongruity, for there were strong interpersonal undercurrents. As I showed in the account of their case history,[9] it was not merely relations between the two antagonistic cousins that were threatened by the conflict between them, but also the enveloping set of relations and commitments among and between their closer kin-neighbours. Working consistency and useful cooperation were endangered, and thus considerable efforts were made to prevent a decisive rupture between the two men. Had there been such a rupture, then the commitment of, say, Tanda (C13) with Zadiki would have conflicted with Tanda's desire to continue cooperation with Konga and others. Even for Zadiki and Konga themselves, self-interest favoured the continuation of some cooperation that would allow them successfully to maintain commitments with their other neighbours involved. Konga, for example, was quite aware that it was to his own advantage to continue cooperation with Tanda and others; but he could not, so to speak, have Tanda without also having Zadiki. It might have been possible, at least for a time, for Tanda to participate in each of these men's work-parties although they themselves refused to cooperate; but even so, the two men would have had to come together in Tanda's own work-parties if they were to reciprocate Tanda's assistance to them. Before long, however, his divided loyalty—that is, his inconsistent commitments—would have raised conflict in the obligations relating to many kinds of social activities and requirements.

Patent inconsistency could sometimes be tolerated temporarily. For instance, in 1953–1954, Malindi (D4) and Amadu (D6) quite deliberately refrained from participation in each other's work-parties, although both joined in parties of their common kin-neighbours. The situation arose entirely out of personal animosity be-

[9] See Case 5, page 167 ff.

tween those two younger household heads: it had no structural basis at all. Their idiosyncratic behaviour was much less significant to their neighbours than that between Zadiki and Konga. Their continued cooperation was less essential because the linkages they provided were less critical in the network. Their neighbours could afford to refuse to give importance to their capriciousness. Nevertheless, men considered the situation to be at least embarrassing and anomalous, and one that ought not to be condoned or allowed to continue. Both men were subject to general censure and to informal pressures to resolve their personal animus toward each other. One or the other was in danger of losing support if a crisis situation arose, when their kin-neighbours would have been forced into some choice disadvantageously. But that crystallisation of the issue had not yet occurred at that time.

It will be clear from the various case histories that there were a number of unresolved problems in the sets of commitments of Ligomba men. Many, though not all, disputes left difficulties and doubts about men's future commitments. Partial failures in work-party arrangements raised questions of reliability of cooperation thereafter. Any nice balancing of all the men's commitments and the elimination of problems and conflicts was not likely to be attained; at least, it never was empirically, especially with the conditions of cooperation and inter-dependence changing as the membership of the community itself changed.

Conflict between kin-neighbours might be irreconcilable: that is, it could not be worked through and removed, nor could the men involved afford to ignore each other and each other's kin-neighbours. The result then was often that one or the other eventually shifted away from the community and sought more reliable, less problematic, cooperation elsewhere. These structural conflicts were often expressed or exposed in the context of a specific dispute, as I have shown previously. For example, Kindabi (B3) left Ligomba fairly soon after his marked failure to obtain much support in his conflict with Ali.[10] C18 left in 1950 after conflict with his elder brother, Konga, in which he obtained little support from their common kin-neighbours in the community. Kasudi (D22) was virtually forced to move away after his remaining supporter (his cousin Hanju [D21]) was compelled to neglect him in favor of other kin-neighbours (Case 1, p. 142 f.). In these and similar cases, the neighbours involved were constrained to make choices, when put to the test in crises, that left one or the other of the two ir-

[10] See page 92 f.

reconcilables comparatively isolated. But in these circumstances men were not simply choosing one kin-neighbour in preference to another; they were also choosing a pattern of congruent commitments, free of difficulties of conflict as far as was possible. This sort of solution seems to have been the more common one; but very occasionally the conflict separated the neighbours into two distinct, identifiable segments between which cooperation ceased. This cut the network, for although kinship links crossed the line of cleavage they were no longer operative. The community then was liable to separate into two parts as effective relations ceased. This kind of process and its results are examined in Chapter Eight.

In actual practice, then, two close kinsmen could not consistently refuse cooperation and reciprocal assistance with each other because both were linked with and desired to continue reliable cooperation with their common kin-neighbours, all of whom wished for continued cooperation with one another. A recalcitrant, estranged kin-neighbour was subject to considerable pressure, partly overt and conscious, to conform or to leave: either way, conflict of commitment was removed. The pressure was brought to bear by such a man's kin-neighbours seeking clarification of the reliability of his assistance to them. Where, however, two kin-neighbours had few kin in common (as second cousins might, though not of course necessarily), the lack of congruence was less troublesome since the inter-linkages they provided might be less crucial because they involved few co-neighbours. Collective pressures were then likely to be less persistent and less effective. The acceptance of commitment diminished, or lapsed altogether, and the acknowledgement of kinship came to atrophy. But—and this is the important point—it was not simply a case of the degree of moral implication contained in the relative closeness, genealogically, of the kinship link. Rather, what was crucial was the degree of involvement of the commitment between two kin-neighbours in the articulated network of linkages and operative cooperation in the community. On the whole a genealogically closer link did involve, or entail, a larger number of other inter-linkages. This was not inevitable, for a genealogically remote link might have been effectively significant in its entailment. A single example can illustrate this. In Ligomba, Meha (D_2) and Faranz (D_4) were genealogically linked in a way that was scarcely acknowledged as such by Ndendeuli: FBSWB. In that case the linkage entailed the inter-linkages of such neighbours as D_1, D_3, C_6, C_7, and others. Those men would have been put into serious conflict had Meha and Faranz refused to cooperate. What is important is not the degree of genealogical closeness per se, but the significance of the link within the mesh in a particular sector of the network. The links between brothers, first cousins, or uncle and nephew, might be equally significant, or insignificant, depending on the configuration of which they were part. But in general, genealogically closer links would have entailed a larger number of common kin-neighbours, a large number of inter-linked commitments that could not readily be ignored.

Complete and stable articulation of commitments was, of course, impossible. Firstly, neighbours changed as newcomers established themselves and former residents left.[11] This required adjustment of the pattern of commitments and cooperation. A link with a kin-neighbour came to entail less, or more, or different, inter-linkages. The sociological implications of the changes in the members and genealogical inter-connections in Ligomba were most complex during the two decades or so up to 1953. Secondly, and quite apart from positive changes in neighbours and the entailments of inter-linkages, two neighbours who were closely linked might well have had slightly different ranges of commitments. One brother might be more strongly committed to his wife's father or brother, and the other brother to his affines. A father might be more committed to members of his own generation than to those of his son's generation, and vice versa.[12] In those circumstances lay the need to work out work-party timetables so that kin-neighbours could fulfill those obligations that were diverse, and to secure their separate claims to assistance, without preventing fulfilment of their common commitments with the kin-neighbours they had in common. Given goodwill and adequate exchange of information about plans, these requirements could be dealt with and arrangements revised where necessary. Without goodwill, with animosity, rivalry, and ambition, the arrangements could founder in conflict. Then readjustment of commitments was required to meet the fresh circumstances. Between kin-neighbours whose linkage entailed few other common linkages, the conflict of obligations was often less easily avoidable. Those links were more fragile and tended to be abandoned first in case of difficulty. New situations continued to confront neighbours as disputes occurred and demanded treatment by a moot. A man would find himself compelled to choose between

[11] Cf. Figure 10 (C).
[12] For example, the case of Tanda (C13) and his son, noted at page 200.

competing commitments; and such choices, as we have seen, directly affected subsequent commitments and possibilities.

The importance of a particular kin-neighbour relationship was, then, largely determined by the extent to which it entailed other, inter-linking relationships. This is not necessarily quite the same thing sociologically as the degree of closeness of a genealogical link. The correlation between the two was likely to be considerable, or otherwise the kinship ideology and ethic would have been blaringly inadequate. But the degree of entailment was the decisive factor, and not genealogical closeness per se. Entailment also concerned the degrees of inter-connectedness in different clusters within the network, and that aspect is taken up in the following chapter.

In concluding the present chapter I revert directly to the connection between kinship and cooperation. We have seen the general necessity for the congruent articulation of commitments among men involved in the kinship network. That network, as far as it was acknowledged by individual men, provided a system of guide-lines they could follow—a model with which to work in real life. In so far as men were willing or compelled to abide by it, they were given a common pattern, an operational basis, and a moral system, by which commitments could be adjusted, made more or less compatible, and thus fulfilled. This is the real significance, analytically, of kinship to the Ndendeuli. It established a coherent, understandable system of linkages that were used to obtain, more or less, consistency of expectation and behaviour. In the Ndendeuli case, it did not have to be followed rigidly. This was as valuable as it was necessary. There was room for manoeuvre and manipulation. Desirable, workable relations with other men could be brought into the system and designated in kinship terms if they were made congruent with the entailments.

No doubt a computer could work out many patterns of working, cooperative relationships that would eliminate, or rather that would reduce to a minimum, conflicts of commitment among thirty or more household heads living as neighbours and seeking certain kinds of assistance from each other. This could be accomplished on the purely objective basis of ensuring that each man could be reasonably sure of enough neighbours for his work-parties and adequate support in his other action-sets. The computer might then determine the choices to be made by particular men when, as inevitably occurred, they are faced with conflict of commitment to two neighbours who simultaneously require their support. The Ndendeuli, however, used the one system they had, in the absence of any other organisational mechanism: their kinship system with its moral rationale.

There was little evidence that the Ndendeuli fictionalised their genealogies, consciously or unconsciously, in order to make them fit the empirical facts by some process of "structural amnesia".[13] There was little or no need of this: a man found no advantage in pretending that a second cousin was, say, a first cousin, or that an affine was a cognate, and so on. Men merely ignored those genealogical links that were irrelevant and inconvenient, and they emphasised those which were relevant and advantageous. To a considerable extent—and this is most significant—the precise nature of asserted genealogical links was rather unimportant. There was a notable laxity of "rules" as to who should and who should not be acknowledged as kinsmen. As I have pointed out earlier, an Ndendeuli did not hold in his mind a single comprehensive genealogy. Particular kinds of genealogical relationship only marginally ascribed kinds or degrees of cooperation and assistance. My persistent efforts in seeking to work out precise and formal genealogical links were frequently met with impatient irritation. They tended, as I now think, to raise conflicts in the simple, home-made models with which the people themselves worked. The Ndendeuli were content to operate their model without too much concern for logical inconsistency; and in doing this they preserved a most valuable flexibility that would have been denied to a more "correct", formal model. Adaptation was easily possible to meet various kinds of circumstance and gradually changing conditions. The model had the advantage of seeming to express intrinsic moral principle and obligation beyond purely practical considerations. In analysis, however, it was the practical considerations of what would fit and what would work fairly reliably that was the principal determinant. The moral principle entered in to justify and reinforce that; but, like perhaps all moral principles, it had an autonomous force of its own in men's minds and motivations, for it was often less trouble, as well as more ethical, simply to follow the approved line when in doubt or confusion.

The anthropological study of kinship has been at something of a watershed for some time. Such study has nearly always been at the forefront of monographic analyses and will probably continue to be so in the future. For Africa especially, a great wealth

[13] See Barnes 1947:52–3; also Gulliver 1955(a):113 ff.

of detail and sophistication of analysis was developed in the lengthy concentration on unilineal descent and the corporate groups founded on that. But it is no longer novel or heretical to suspect that the segmentary descent group systems are not quite what they have been held to be. They began to look more like idealised patterns, the products partly of the folk models of the various peoples themselves, and partly of the models of anthropologists oriented to structural-idealism. The systems appeared not to work in concrete practice; great distortions and modifications and manipulations were necessary which in the end almost destroyed the patterned models. Men and women did not almost automatically follow the rules of the unilineal descent system; the corporate groups were not neatly composed of people with the correct descent designation.[14] Some anthropologists have become so sceptical that, with Leach, they have concluded that "it might even be the case that 'the structure of unilineal descent groups' is a *total* fiction; illuminating . . . but still a fiction" (Leach 1961:302). Furthermore, the concentration on unilineal descent produced the unfortunate neglect of cognatic and affinal kinship, and it almost forced an artificial and unhelpful contradistinctive categorization of non-unilineal kinship systems as a special, separate type.

It is, however, not merely the over-concentration on unilineal descent that is troublesome, but also the strong tendency "to isolate kinship behaviour as a distinct category explainable by jural rules without reference to context or economic self-interest". To a considerable extent kinship structure has been "treated as 'a thing in itself'; indeed a very superior sort of thing which provides a self-sufficient and self-maintaining framework for all that we observe" (Leach 1961:305–306). This, bluntly stated by Leach, was perhaps not so novel an idea as all that. Worseley had suggested something similar in his critique of the Tallensi material in 1956; and I had tentatively suggested the primacy of practical relations in respect of property (domestic livestock) over the ideology of kinship with reference to the Turkana nomads.[15] For a number of both empirical and theoretical reasons, therefore, there has been a recognition of inadequacy in kinship studies. There has been an increasing desire to examine what lies behind the complex kinship systems, and in what ways kinship is effectively important.

Leach declared: "I must insist that kinship systems have no 'reality' at all except in relation to land and property". This is a

[14] See, for example, Forde 1963.
[15] Worseley 1956; Gulliver 1951 and 1955(a).

somewhat characteristic overstatement, and one that is too limited
if we desire to apply it more generally, and beyond an economy
based on a strictly limited supply of water. It should be obvious
that, for the Ndendeuli, neither land nor property are what
"really" lie behind kinship. Land was plentiful and other property
negligible, unless some very special definition is given to that term.
In Undendeuli, the kinship system was, however, a way of "talking
about" practical relations of cooperation, reciprocal assistance, and
support, in the everyday business of making a livelihood. But in
addition to that it was a flexible, manipulable means of ordering
those relations not only for economic purposes but also for other
considerations such as dealing with disputes, competing for influence and prestige, performing rituals, and just participating in
human company. The fact that there was such a close correlation
between those essential relations and the formal ones of kinship
is important and is capable of satisfactory explanation.

Perhaps it should be emphasised that in dealing only with one
local community, I have been dealing with only a part of the total,
or rather of the wider, open-ended, kinship system of these people.
In fact a man did not necessarily, or even usually, maintain close
relations with all of his genealogically close kinsmen. It was always
possible for Ndendeuli to avoid and neglect those close kin with
whom for one reason or another a man did not wish to cooperate
or found it inconvenient to do so. Brothers, for example, in inter-
personal or structural rivalry could, and did, live in different
(oftenly widely separated) communities, preserving either a
muted relationship or none at all. A man could shift his residence
when his neighbourly relations, expressed in kinship terms, were
unsatisfactory or downright harmful. On the other hand, as will
be discussed later, a man deliberately was at pains to maintain
many of his kinship links outside his current local community,
and for two reasons. First, he never knew when he would need
supporters in another community (for example, if he came into
dispute with some member of that community); and second, it
was considered necessary "to keep the options open", to have
kin in other local communities to which a man could shift his
residence if and when he desired to leave his present one. Ndendeuli
were always potentially mobile, and in fact a good deal of residential movement occurred in each early dry season, for a variety of
reasons. But the kinship options were kept open *not* to afford
access to land and property, but to afford access to the system of
cooperation and assistance operative within a local community.

Such assistance was the only means an Ndendeuli had for promoting his interests, defending them against encroachment, and reliably getting a livelihood.

As we have seen already, there was no particular pattern to the structure of the kinship network of a local community, nor to the set of kinsmen associated with individual men whether in the closed or open networks. There was, however, discernible patterning of the inter-connected relations of cooperation and assistance: but that pattern could be described in terms of, and explained by, a wide variety of kinship links. It will be seen later that, similarly, there was no standard pattern to men's "universes of kin" or to the sets of kinsmen with whom they were associated in active, practical relations. This is why an Ndendeuli could so commonly simplify his kinship system to the basic referents of "father", "brother", and "son", and why, in seeking assistance and justifying his own action, he appealed not so much to the ethic of kinship as to the past record of transactions between himself and other men. Most usually the genealogical facts were known, but these were clearly of secondary importance.

VIII

Clusters, Segments, and Leaders

CLUSTERS AND LEADERS

The Ligomba network constituted a continuous, convolute, mesh of kinship linkages and of practical relationships and inter-action among the limited range of neighbours in the community at any period. Clearly, however, the mesh of the network was not of equal scale throughout, so that the nodes (that is, the neighbours) were not spaced equally apart in the network. Instead there was (to persist with the metaphor) a bunching or clustering of nodes in certain parts of the network, giving a small mesh within such a part and a larger mesh between those parts. Three such "clusters" of neighbours were evident in Ligomba. Their significance was latent in the analysis of inter-action, cooperation, and conflict, given in Chapters Four, Five and Six. Having examined the actuality of the social relations underlying the ideology of kinship, I now consider more closely the nature of these clusters within the total closed network.

Clusters were identifiable in two inter-dependent ways. Firstly, a cluster comprised a number of neighbours amongst whom there was a relatively high degree of inter-connectedness, as this was shown in collective action over a period.[1] It might appear, *prima facie*, that it was the comparative closeness of kinship ties that separated one cluster from another; and indeed this was the expla-

[1] Barnes has defined a cluster as "a set of persons whose links with one another are comparatively dense" (1968:118). He proposed means to measure degrees of density, but I do not see how these could be applied to the Ndendeuli material (or, for that matter, to other concrete cases from real life). It is not necessary, however, to measure degrees of density in order to distinguish the clusters in Ligomba, or in other Ndendeuli communities, for they were clear enough both to the people concerned and to the external observer.

nation favoured by the Ndendeuli, though it was only an ideological approximation to the concrete facts. Many of the men in a cluster were, it is true, closely linked by formal kinship: but others were no closer than second or third cousins (whilst other such cousins were excluded), and some were only indirectly linked. Moreover, almost all the members of a cluster had individual close kinship ties with other neighbours outside the cluster. Such a cluster of neighbours was more realistically distinguishable by their high degree of inter-connectedness and inter-dependence in terms of practical interaction and cooperation. With considerable regularity over a period they were recruited to almost all of one another's action-sets. There was, as they arranged their action-sets for various purposes, a good "fit" in their mutual commitments and claims.

Secondly, a cluster was identifiable in terms of an informal leader, a "notable", who occupied a focal position in terms of social action though not necessarily in purely genealogical terms. A cluster gradually emerged in the evolution of the community with fairly explicit reference to the man simultaneously becoming acknowledged as a notable. The process was reinforced by rivalry between notables.[2]

Thus, to summarise, a cluster emerged over a period as an identifiable part of the network in which there was both focal leadership and considerable, though not complete, overlap of the members' sets of kin-neighbours. There was at least a greater overlap than existed among neighbours who did not comprise a cluster; and members were at pains consciously and continuously to make such arrangements as to avoid conflicts of commitments in action-set recruitment. The explanation of the specific membership of a cluster lay in the processes of sponsorship of newcomers, the marriage of bachelor sons, and the practical utility of coordinated collective action on as reliable a basis as possible. Part of the role of the notable was to maintain this coordination and so to further the interests of his associates.

Before considering the role of the notable in more detail, I wish first to emphasise that these clusters within the community's kinship network were not altogether clearly defined. Ligomba people did refer to "the people", or "the neighbours", or "the kinsmen", of Ali or Konga or Kabaya. Although fairly common, this usage was ambiguous out of context for it could also refer to an action-

[2] The emergence of the Ligomba clusters was described in Chapter 4, p. 87 ff.

set recruited or led by one of those men.[3] In any case, men were not restricted to their clusters for this would have meant that they would have had to forfeit the valued support and assistance of other kin-neighbours (not involved in the cluster) that were available to them according to the context of collective action. There was no overriding loyalty to the cluster per se, nor to the notable. The composition of the various action-sets in dispute cases and for agricultural purposes demonstrates this adequately.[4]

The membership of certain individual men was uncertain, since they were closely associated with members of two clusters by virtue of their sets of kin-neighbours and their regular patterns of cooperation and reciprocal assistance—for example, Yasini (C9) and his son and two nephews; but he had also become closely associated with Kabaya, and later with Tanda (an associate of Kabaya), by close affinial ties. Rajabu (D15) as the son of Zadiki was strongly inclined to belong to Kabaya's cluster, as did his father; but Rajabu was also son-in-law to Sedi, and therefore he was fairly closely associated with Konga's cluster. Conflicts of obligations for such men were demonstrating the uncertainties of their alignment in a cluster, and these conflicts were more crucial than the more commonplace clashes of commitment that could, in particular contexts, affect any man in the community. The time might come when such men would have to make a fairly decisive choice between the available alternatives in order to reduce effectively the continuous incongruity. That had been the case in the earlier years of Ligomba when Saidi and Ali, on the one hand, and Mitedi and Sedi, on the other, had to forego previous reciprocal assistance as the new clusters developed within the community and set them further apart.

Summaries of the participation of Yasini (an older man) and Rajabu (a younger man) may point up the argument here. These summaries are necessarily simplified from the details of action-set formation given in the previous chapters.[5]

[3] Note the use of the phrase by Ali and Saidi (Case 7, p. 177) when denying their own involvement in what they considered to be the purely internal affairs of another cluster in Ligomba.

[4] Note the anxiety of men of opposed action-sets from separate clusters, in Case 5 ("A Cousins' Quarrel", p. 172) lest the outcome of the dispute should jeopardize relations of reciprocal assistance which cross-cut the clusters. Many of these men seized the opportunity in the following case to join in a common action-set that ignored the membership of the clusters ("An Errant Son-in-Law", p. 175).

[5] For simplicity in these summaries, only the leadership of notables is referred to, although in most cases a notable shared the lead with the convener of the action-set, as previously described.

Yasini (C9)

Case 2: He participated in the action-set in which Kabaya shared the leadership, though here a major consideration was that Yasini stood to gain personally if the defendant were successful.

Case 3: He did not join either action-set; but as mediator between sets led by Ali and Kabaya he appeared slightly to favour the latter.

Case 5: He chose to opt out of the situation in which he had weak loyalties to both sides, but where there was little personal advantage as both principals were linked with him only indirectly.

Case 6: As plaintiff himself he needed the support of Ali's cluster against a member of Kabaya's cluster. (Kabaya opted out of this case.)

Case 7: He was excluded from participation in the hurried moot limited to Kabaya's cluster.

Work-party Case 1: He chose to support Ali in the latter's conflict with Kabaya, although through his son he was able to show continued association with Kabaya.

Work-party Case 3: He gained the support of Ali in the conflict with another member of Ali's cluster.

His cultivation work-party contained men of *both* Ali's and Kabaya's clusters.

Rajabu (D15)

Case 2: As defendant he needed the support of Kabaya's cluster against a member of Konga's cluster.

Case 3: He did not participate in the moot, although the defendant's action-set was comprised of members of Kabaya's cluster.

Case 4: He deliberately opted out of the moot in which opposing sets were drawn largely from the clusters of Kabaya and Konga.

Case 5: Again he deliberately opted out in similar circumstances (although his father was plaintiff).

Case 6: He participated in the defendant's action-set comprising members of *both* Kabaya's and Konga's clusters.

Case 7: He participated in the hurried moot limited to Kabaya's cluster. His cultivation work-party contained men of *both* Kabaya's and Konga's clusters.

On the one hand, then, men were both unwilling and unable to give unreserved loyalty to a particular cluster, because each fresh occasion of dispute and conflict raised something of a fresh problem concerning the recruitment of neighbours to the action-sets. It was not in men's immediate or longer term interests to allow certain useful neighbourly cooperation to be cut off merely to enhance the unity of the cluster or the influence of a notable. On the other hand, it remains fairly clear that over a period members of a cluster tended to cooperate with one another in collective action more than with other neighbours. To put it another way, there tended to be a common core to those men's action-sets, though these usually also contained other neighbours. Clusters were, therefore, inductively recognised by the people themselves, as well as by the external observer.

It might have been useful to designate these clusters as quasi-groups, thus distinguishing them analytically from corporate groups and from ephemeral action-sets. Such otherwise useful reference seems to be prevented, however, by the two criteria established by Mayer. He has defined quasi-groups, first, as "ego-centred, in the sense of depending for their very existence on a specific person as a central organizing focus. . . . Second, the actions of any member are relevant only in so far as they are inter-actions between him and ego or ego's intermediary. The membership criteria do not include interaction with other quasi-group members in general".[6] The emphasis on the focal ego is too strong for this Ndendeuli case, important though a notable was; but the rejection of interaction between members themselves, and not through the focal ego, is not applicable to the Ndendeuli circumstances. I am not, in this context, inclined to contest Mayer's useful definition. It is perhaps better not to introduce even so mild a term as "quasi-group" into an analysis of an Ndendeuli community. It is easy to overemphasise the unity and coherence of a cluster, and so to distort the analysis. This I wish to avoid, lest inadvertently the impression is conveyed that a local community—or the Ligomba one in particular—was clearly and decisively segmented. This was certainly not the case empirically, nor in the perceptions of the Ndendeuli. On rather few occasions did a cluster operate as a distinct unit in that all or virtually all members were involved whilst other neighbours were excluded. Neither was the leadership of the notable inevitably clear, and it was usually shared with the current convener of the action-set.

Notables were *wandu wakurungwa*, "big men" in literal translation. A man gradually acquired the reputation of being a big man over a period of years of taking, and being allowed to take, a leadership role. He had to be an able man, capable of giving good advice, tactically perceptive, and well spoken and shrewd in argument (especially in moots). As far as my records go, notables seem to have been rather ambitious men, at least by Ndendeuli standards —ambitious to gain influence over their neighbours and to join in competition with other big men, though not so ambitious that they sought to acquire authority. For a notable to attempt that was

[6] Mayer 1966:97–98.

almost certain to defeat his own ends. He could not directly compel some of his neighbours to particular courses of action, for no such means were available to him. His neighbours would have reacted strongly against the suspicion of authoritarianism, or pretension to it, on the part of a notable. Ndendeuli were inclined to be somewhat cynical about the notables in their communities, perceiving that those men were operating at least partly in their own interests and to their own advantage, sometimes even at the expense of those they purported to help and advise.[7]

Deliberately, I do not in the present context use what is the literal translation of the Ndendeuli descriptive reference term, "big man", and for two reasons. One relates to the Ndendeuli circumstances per se, and the other concerns established usage in other, quite different socio-cultural contexts. Among the Ndendeuli, many men were described as "big men" in some social situation or other when they were the acknowledged senior or temporary leader of one or more other men. For instance, there could be a "big man" in a dyadic kinship context (for example, WF vis-à-vis DH), on a ritual occasion (the principal performer, or an especially knowledgeable or spiritual person), in a moot (action-set leader, a persuasive mediator, or one who won a point of argument), in a work-party (the convener, a song-leader, a skilled builder or thatcher), the host at any beer-drink, and so on. The term *mundu mukurungwa* could, then, be more freely translated as "leader", "senior", "more important person", with the emphasis varying slightly according to the context. The men I call "notables" were, however, "big men" in many contexts, although especially in politico-jural ones, and were acknowledged in a general sense by their neighbours even without specific context. They were also important as advisors and counsellors to those with whom they were particularly associated. To limit the term "big man" to them alone, or to limit them to that term only, would do injustice to the Ndendeuli idiom and its significance.

The term "big man" has also been used for a long time in Oceanic (particularly Melanesian) ethnography, and with certain

[7] The men who led the Ndendeuli in their successful attempt to gain independence from the Ngoni in 1952–1953 were not beyond these aspersions. They were sometimes described sardonically as "being like Ngoni". The stereotype of the Ngoni, in Ndendeuli eyes, was an authoritarian person always seeking power over others in order to compel them to do as he wished for his own advantage. Significantly enough, Ndendeuli did not see these leaders attempting to gain economic advantage. I never heard that charge made against them.

attributes that did not apply to the Ndendeuli. To be sure, Melanesian big men were political leaders, and they held focal positions around which political groups or factions clustered and operated. But the political element seems to have been generally much stronger than in the Ndendeuli case, and it was commonly associated closely with economic entrepreneurship. Sahlins wrote on this point: "Typically decisive is the deployment of one's [the big man's] skills and efforts in a certain direction: towards amassing goods, most often pigs, shell monies and vegetable foods, and distributing them in ways which built a name for cavalier generosity, if not compassion".[8] Similarly Scheffler has referred to "the common Melanesian pattern of the acquisition of prestige through competition and public exchange"; and he noted that "prestige and proprietary rights were . . . closely intertwined and both were sources of conflict".[9] This is all quite contrary to the role and goals of an Ndendeuli notable. The latter was not necessarily, or even usually, more wealthy than his neighbours. He did not receive gifts from his associates, nor did he seek to amass wealth. Indeed in this poor, near-subsistence economy, with virtually no domestic livestock, little wealth of any kind and annual shortages of foodstuffs for eating, and still a most limited circulation of money, it is not easy to see how economic entrepreneurship could have operated. In Ligomba itself, Ali was, if anything, a poor man and with only one wife; Konga was no more than run-of-the-mill economically, and he too had one wife. Kabaya, however, was rather better off with two wives and a small flock of goats—but these were the results of his wage-earning before he lived in Ligomba. His continued comparative affluence since residing in Ligomba had come from his personal enterprise as a tobacco grower. Neither Ali nor Konga had wealth with which to attract associates, but Kabaya did not (as far as I was aware) use his slight affluence to that end, though perhaps his admired life-style had helped him in becoming a notable. The other men of a little above the low average standard of living were Meha (D2), Yasini (C9), and Zadiki (C15), none of whom were notables nor did they, I feel sure, aspire to be. No one, including these men themselves, suggested any such ambition on their part, or alluded to past endeavours of that kind. Their slightly better standard of living was the result of modest success as tobacco growers.

A second feature of the Melanesian big man was his embodiment

[8] Sahlins 1963:291.
[9] Scheffler 1965:130–131.

of the notion of "strength". "He is a person who is aggressive, a warrior, a man inclined to swagger and boast, who displays a marked awareness of his individuality and is jealous of his self-importance", as he has been described by Read.[10] That author went on to describe him (in the Central Asaro Valley of New Guinea) as an orator and able debater, and also as one who appeared not to dominate and who was able to judge the appropriate opportunity for self-assertion without this seeming to overbalance into overt aggression. So, in that region at least, the man of "strength" did not become a big man without other qualities. Yet there, and I think elsewhere in Melanesia, the man who did not have "strength" was unable to achieve that favoured role. The Ndendeuli did not at all associate their notables with that kind of more or less aggressive self-assertiveness, either in ideal or practice. Doubtless their notables had inner springs of personal motivation that fed their ambition to become influential and to have prestige; but whatever the inner constitution, display of aggressiveness was not approved, nor did it produce acknowledged attainment of influence. Indeed the New Guinea type of ethos, embodying aggressive assertion, was conspicuously absent from Ndendeuli life altogether. Moreover, I should reiterate that the degree of influence and prestige a notable could gain was meagre. Notables were seldom if ever so outstanding that they could, at any time, directly influence the community as a whole, let alone become its accepted leader. The narrow range of the cluster, the associates of a notable in Ligomba, was not untypical of other local communities in that region. It was virtually certain that a cluster which increased in size would become too large for the kind of cooperative advantages of inter-dependence it offered. It would then generally drift into two or more clusters just as the original Ligomba community had, without special conflict, developed into two clusters with Luinga and Nchinda (later Ali and Konga) as the notables. Essentially a notable could only emerge and operate when there existed a cluster of highly inter-connected kin-neighbours in the context of the need for regular, reliable cooperation and mutual support.

Although in a sense the cluster could be identified by reference to its notable, yet at the same time the notable himself was precipitated and identified by that cluster of inter-linking neighbours of whom he was one. Those neighbours required a leader in their own interests, and partly because they did not wish to be caught

10 Read 1959:427.

up in the sphere of influence of another notable whose principal concern was the interests and working relations of another cluster of neighbours. The emergence of Kabaya as an accepted notable in Ligomba is a clear example of this. The rivalry between notables tended further to identify the clusters to which they belonged, though at the same time this rivalry could also demonstrate the absence of any precise definition of a cluster as notables competed for the support and involvement of intercalary neighbours.[11] If a notable stood to gain in prestige by appearing or being more able and successful than a rival on some occasion, it was also usually a gain for one or more members of his cluster, for principally it was in the context of protecting or promoting their interests that the notable operated at all. The notable who was so intent on belittling a rival and augmenting his own prestige at the expense of what his kin-neighbours considered their own true interests would begin to forfeit their confidence and support. Without their confidence and support he had little or no influence.

In the nature of the system and because of the small numbers of men in the average cluster, there was not room for two notables in it. There was need for one, but disadvantage or worse in two. If two men did have concurrent ambitions to be the notable within a single cluster, their rivalry would lead either to the dissolution of that cluster or to the support of one and neglect of the other aspirant by their common kin-neighbours. The latter seems to have been the more common. It was the case, for instance, between Ali and Kindabi after the death of Ali's father in 1938, and probably between Konga and his FFZH (A5) after the death of Nchinda in 1937. In each case the unsuccessful aspirant moved away from Ligomba since his expectations of future support were unreliable.[12] The precise kinship status of the successful notable was of little importance, as might be expected in this sort of system. A notable's position in the network was more important: he needed to be accepted as kin-neighbour by each member of the cluster—to have reliable, reciprocal obligations with each. Nevertheless, in the rivalry between Ali and Kindabi, their respective sets of kin-neighbours were virtually the same. Probably Konga was rather more focally placed than his rival, A5, although this was not quite

[11] E.g., the competition between Ali and Kabaya concerning Yasini, and his three sons.

[12] After leaving Ligomba, Kindabi later achieved the role of notable in another local community and among a quite different cluster of kin-neighbours.

clear to me. My data from Ligomba, Namabeya, and other local communities suggest that, given adequate and effective direct linkages with other members of the cluster, the success of a notable in becoming the leader of his kin-neighbours was partly a matter of his individual character and ability, but more importantly it was a matter of the inter-personal confidence he could engender. The established notable who failed to maintain such confidence, and whose ability waned, was either replaced, or his kin-neighbours moved away from the disadvantageous situation to seek more reliable leadership elsewhere.

In this analysis I use the often-vaguely applied terms "prestige" and "influence" to refer to both the tools and the goals of notables. In this usage it is necessary to keep distinct the notable's associates, on the one hand—those with whom he largely shared common ends —and his opponents, on the other hand—those with whom his ends were not common but in conflict, so that a gain for one was likely to be a loss for the other.

Scheffler, following Nadel (1951:171), has defined prestige as being "visible in the deference shown to an individual in the readiness of others to support him in varying ways, to take his advice, imitate his example, or merely express their admiration or approval".[13] I would add to this an emphasis on the marked subjective quality in seeking and being accorded prestige. I would also note that an Ndendeuli notable was allowed prestige even among those who did not support him and have common ends with him. Thus the notable not only gained support of his associates because of his prestige, and gained prestige because of that support, but he was able to use both in seeking to gain his ends over his "opponents" who, in varying degrees, were susceptible to the strength of his prestige. If the concept is used essentially as Scheffler has defined it, then it can still be useful and it can escape the common fate of being a cliché capable of "explaining" almost anything.

By "influence" I intend here a quite deliberate contrast with "authority" and "power". As Parsons has written, "influence is a means of *persuasion*". That is crucial to the idea and to the social processes through which it operates. Parsons continued: "It is bringing about a decision on alter's part to action in a certain way because it is felt to be a 'good thing' for *him*, on the one hand independently of contingently or otherwise imposed changes in his situation, on the other hand for positive reasons, not because of the

[13] Scheffler 1965:182.

obligations he would violate through non-compliance".[14] Here
Parsons was in effect concerned only, or at least mainly, with
situations where the wielder of influence and the other person(s)
have ends in common; though even there, for the Ndendeuli, there
could sometimes be rather more than that purest form of persuasion. In these situations there was, however, as Coleman noted,
the important question of "the investment that a person makes in
another which permits the other to have influence over him".[15]
This is most pertinent to the way in which a notable's associates
submitted to his influence and to his leadership. But his associates
imposed burdens on him at the same time. They wished to take
advantage of his particular, personal ability, energy, and willingness to give advice and take a lead (even if only to save themselves trouble); but they were in a position to bring pressure to
bear on him should he fail them. That is, they could withdraw
their support from him, or threaten to do so, for he was also
dependent on them. There was a feed-back effect here: the more
successful a notable was, the more his kin-neighbours would trust
him, allow him influence, and depend on him, and thus the greater
his prestige. But to lose their confidence was to forfeit influence
and prestige in the converse way. The degree of inter-dependence
between a notable and his associated kin-neighbours was therefore
probably greater than if he had had authority over them.

When influence and prestige were used against neighbours
with whom, in a dispute situation, there were not (by definition)
common ends, then a gain for one (for example, receiving compensation) was a loss for the other (for example, paying compensation). In that case something more than pure persuasion was required, and used, by a notable. Argument appealing to ethics and
emotions, special pleading, confusing and twisting the issues and
introducing irrelevant ones, making use of personal weaknesses,
invoking past favours, all these rested largely on the informal sanctions of approval and disapproval. But there were more particular
inducements: offering or withholding advantages and disadvantages, or involving interests of other neighbours who then sought
to protect them. These inducements were at least as crucial, and
sometimes more so. There cannot in concrete reality be any
clearly defined line between authority and power on the one hand,
and influence on the other, whatever the niceties of theoretical

[14] Parsons 1963:44.
[15] Coleman 1963:67.

argument in this field. To some sociologists the kind of practical inducements to which reference was made above smack of power rather than of persuasion. Parsons described power as "the threat of negative situational sanctions",[16] but that would seem to be too broad a definition. Surely power relates essentially to the ability to *compel* a person to do or not to do some act, on pains of avoiding a probable disadvantage that the power-holder may impose.[17] Influence, in distinction, seeks to *induce*, by offering approval and positive advantage as well as threatening disapproval and disadvantage, but without the final ability to compel, whatever means are used. In the Ndendeuli context, a notable needed to take care not to seem to be attempting compulsion: this was not only culturally disapproved but it was hollow in practice. Even the imposition of disadvantage upon an opponent could not necessarily effect compulsion.

Notables tended to be more or less seeking to extend their prestige and influence, although it would be incorrect to emphasise this too greatly. Extension of prestige and influence was in large degree at the expense of another notable, since notables were in opposition, as rivals, in situations where these attributes were to be acquired and increased. But, rivals though they were, the competition was intermittent and in low key. The prizes were scarcely sufficient to stimulate it intensively, and too great a rivalry could threaten, or at least appear to threaten, interests of their associated kin-neighbours who maintained some degree of cooperation across the loose boundaries of the clusters. Even notables did not allow themselves to be limited purely to their own clusters in recruiting action-sets. It was almost always useful to enlarge action-sets as much as possible. Not to do so would have reduced the potential effectiveness of the set for the particular purpose in hand in its context within the network, as well as depriving neighbours of the opportunity to extend reciprocal assistance. Apart from action-sets mobilised for a notable's own interests, however, he himself seldom made the final choice of whom to invite; this was the pre-

[16] Parsons 1963:90.

[17] Here I am following Weber, who defined power (*Macht*) as "the probability that one actor within a social relationship will be in a position to carry out his own will despite resistance, regardless of the basis on which this probability rests". For Weber power was closely associated with "imperative control" (*Herrschaft*), which is "the probability that a command with a given specific content will be obeyed by a given group of persons" (Weber 1964:152).

rogative of the man for whom the set was to operate, and the choice in part depended on his range of cooperation in the community.

So long, therefore, as inter-linkages between neighbours of different clusters were considered to have persisting value and were actively utilised, the identity of the clusters remained ill-defined. The influence of notables was thus restricted, even though they might perhaps entertain the idea of its expansion. In Ligomba, to the best of my knowledge, a major and persistent cleavage between clusters, led by their notables, had never developed. This could perhaps have occurred—not necessarily because of positive conflict—as the emergent clusters, led by Ali and Konga respectively, became less and less inter-linked—that is, as individual members discontinued cooperation with kin-neighbours in the other cluster. The degree of inter-connectedness might have intensified within each cluster, and the leadership of each notable could have become less ambiguous. This trend was, however, directly affected by other developments. The conflict between Zadiki and Konga in 1939 led more or less directly to Zadiki's sponsorship of his brother-in-law, Tanda, and the latter's sponsorship of Kabaya and Bilali.[18] Thus the nucleus of a third cluster was established. Through inter-marriages, men of this cluster developed important kin-neighbour linkages and active cooperation with men of Ali's cluster (specifically with Yasini and his sons) and with men of Konga's cluster (specifically with Sedi and his son). That was the particular historical evolution in Ligomba. Essentially the same sort of effect might have come about in innumerable other and quite feasible ways: by other residents sponsoring other newcomers, by other intra-community marriages, by men deciding not to move away. To give some random examples: in 1947 Kasoro (B1) and his three "sons" might have stayed in the community and have sought to rectify their demonstrated weakness vis-à-vis Ali by sponsoring newcomers who would have become their own associates and supporters—just as Zadiki in fact did. Sedi (C21) might have sponsored his cousin (MBS) who was, it so happened, also the first cousin of the father of Saidi (C6). The fathers of Faranz (D4) and Hanju (D21) were second cousins, and either might have settled in Ligomba, or the common first cousin of both, thus offering potential linkage of those otherwise very distantly linked neighbours (distantly linked within the pragmatic network of Ligomba as it actually developed). Those are but casual examples

[18] See page 98 ff.

of the possibilities that might have occurred; but a member of Ligomba men had common kinsmen of this kind elsewhere, or they had kinsmen who themselves had kin in common. The settlement of such men in this local community could, and probably would, have stimulated some development of active, neighbourly cooperation that would have cut across and inter-linked clusters, or even would have started new clusters. Who did come to live in Ligomba —who was, and who was not, sponsored and by whom—depended on a great variety of factors, many or most of which lay well outside Ligomba itself: the desire or need of a kinsman to shift from some other community, the actual relations of that man with his kinsmen in Ligomba and with his kinsmen in other communities, his assessment of probable advantages in Ligomba and in alternative communities. The potential consequences raised by a newcomer were even more complex. Had such a man decided to settle in Ligomba, he may or may not have stayed on, he may or may not have sponsored other newcomers. Empirically Zadiki did sponsor Tanda, and not some other kinsman from outside; Tanda stayed and he sponsored others, and so a whole new cluster and a wide range of inter-linkages emerged. These were consolidated as Kabaya, without harmful competition, developed as the acknowledged notable. The pattern of evolution was not entirely fortuitous, and there was conformity to a general pattern and to the principle of entailment. But there were inevitably and quite logically important elements of adventitious contingency in the actual flow of events and the development of social relations. These elements were, of course, the direct and indirect results of the individual freedom of action that Ndendeuli exercised within the non-unilineal framework of their kinship system. There were neither corporate groups nor powerful roles occupied by individuals; nor were there crucial interests and rights that could extend control and impress their patterning on the dynamic processes of development.

A major consequence of all this was that, despite the emergence of de facto clusters of highly inter-dependent neighbours, it was unlikely that alignments and their practical relations and social actions would crystallise into discrete, virtually autonomous sets. Each new situation calling for collective action and mobilising individuals' interests tended to produce new ephemeral alignments—action-sets. Goals and interests, and operative relations and interaction, were too diverse from individual to individual in the community. There were no positions of authority, nor common rights, that might have provided foci of competition and conflict for their control. Sufficient concrete evidence has, I think, been provided to support and justify that conclusion.

To put this into more general sociological terms, factions were only weakly developed, they were continuously cross-cut and even ignored, and they were unable to crystallise on either side of a major cleavage such as might have produced persistent segmentation and even fission. Leadership was also, logically, weakly developed.

Following Firth (1957) and Nicholas (1966) and others, factions may be defined as persisting, non-corporate conflict groups in a society. A faction clusters round a leader. It is involved in competition to protect and promote a succession of interests of the leader and its other members; its leader in particular is in competition with the leaders of other factions for power within the total community within which the factions operate. The model of factional conflict would seem most usually to be a zero-sum game.

The Ligomba clusters had, therefore, the characteristics of factions, but with certain reservations. A cluster focussed round a leader—the notable—who was partly responsible for its persistence; but he was in large degree precipitated as the cluster emerged, in order to serve the growing interests of the members. The clusters were non-corporate and they persisted over time, without necessarily becoming permanent. There was competition between leaders, but this was not competition for any general power or control in the community as a whole. It is, however, straining the facts beyond the analytical weight they will bear to suggest that these clusters themselves were in competition and conflict with each other. Members of a cluster were intimately concerned with their own interests—the maintenance of reliable cooperation and support—rather than controlling or limiting the interests of other neighbours. Furthermore, the individual interests of particular members—their operational relations with kin-neighbours—invariably extended beyond the cluster, and so therefore did the actual action-sets they mobilised. This was the case also for the leaders themselves.

NAMABEYA: SEGMENTATION, FACTIONS, AND FISSION

In the Ligomba local community the faction-like clusters never developed the discrete segregation of multiplex social relations and inter-action to the point of segmentation of the whole group. Not that a more or less stable equilibrium was ever attained either, for membership and therefore contingent inter-linkages gradually changed. The people themselves expressed, and the observer could perceive, a mild degree of unity within the local community; but this must not be emphasized. If the community did not segment or separate into autonomous parts, this was also because there were rarely significant interests of common concern on which conflict could focus to produce persistent groups in competition.

It could happen, although rarely, that the faction-like clusters became distinct enough to be established as opposed segments, and that such segments could generate sufficient conflict to produce ultimate fission of the community. By "segmentation" within a social group I intend to mean a state of internal division with fairly clear lines of demarcation, such that the interests of members of a segment are more or less contained within and catered for by that segment. Inter-dependence among individuals of different segments is slight or nonexistent. By "fission" I mean the process of division of a group into two distinct, autonomous parts, usually accompanied by some territorial separation.[19] In order to examine this kind of process, and thereby to throw further light on the nature of the closed network within an Ndendeuli local community, I am compelled to abandon my concentration on a diachronic study of one group of inter-acting people (Ligomba) and to resort to an "apt illustration".

It so happened, fortuitously during the period of my field research, that this actual process of segmentation leading to fission did in fact occur in a local community only a few miles from Ligomba. This was in Namabeya, as will be described in the present section. It is not suggested that this sequence of events was in any sense typical of Ndendeuli local communities. Indeed, it seems to have been most uncommon. Some sketchy information was obtained about two earlier cases of the same sort of process. These latter two seemed to be generally known about, at least in eastern Undendeuli, because of their unusual character. Each had been a *cause célèbre*, judging by the fact that informants in different areas referred to these same two cases, though one had taken place in about the mid-1930s. Whether the pattern of events and inter-action leading to segmentation and then to fission was in principle the same in those two cases as in Namabeya, I do not know. Adequate data were obtained only for the Namabeya case. This case developed as a major issue during 1952 and 1953, with its culmination in 1954.

A brief description of the Namabeya local community was

[19] Cf. Barnes 1955.

given in Chapter Three.[20] It was founded in about 1940 by thirteen
pioneers; their genealogical connections are shown in Figure 3. In
approximately a dozen years this community had grown from
thirteen to forty-two households which, in 1953, were grouped
into eighteen hamlets, containing something over two hundred
people scattered over about three square miles of woodland. This
may have been a comparatively rapid growth, but I do not have
adequate data from enough local communities to compare rates of
growth. Certainly the rate was higher than that for Ligomba. Unlike Ligomba, where most newcomers had arrived singly, in Namabeya there were two (and probably three) cases where four newcomers had arrived together, already having well established
working relations amongst themselves. This possibly rapid growth
did, I think, have some influence on the subsequent events leading
up to fission. At all events, the kinship network was less convolute
in 1953 than that recorded for other communities, including
Ligomba. That is to say, although there was a single extended network in Namabeya, there were significant numbers of men who
(being far apart in that network) were scarcely involved, even
indirectly, with one another except as adventitious neighbours.
On the other hand, as events and alignments of 1952–1954 demonstrated, no great emphasis can be given to this. Developments and
processes in the network clearly showed the inter-dependence of
neighbours who were, nevertheless, far apart in its mesh.

Data with the detail and time depth comparable to that for
Ligomba were not obtained for Namabeya.[21] To that extent my
analysis and conclusions are restricted and impaired; and for that
reason my account here is limited almost wholly to the period of
about two and a half years from early 1952 to the middle of 1954.
For brevity, and not to tax the reader's tolerance further, the
account is principally a summary version of the major events and
without detailed analysis. The object of the account is not to

[20] See page 73 ff.

[21] At no time did I reside in Namabeya during my field research, although I was able to visit frequently from Ligomba and to hear of the
occurrence of major events through my Ligomba informants. It was, however, impossible to devote the time and effort required for the meticulous
accumulation and checking of data, in the way that this was accomplished
in Ligomba. Moreover, the actual field situation in Namabeya was much
less favourable to me personally. The notable, Lihamba, was persistently
unwilling to accept my enquiries, and I had no good informant amongst
his associates; whilst the notable, Amiri, persisted in maintaining strictly
formal relations only.

repeat the kind of analysis of network dynamics already attempted in respect of Ligomba, but to add a further and different dimension.

In Namabeya, by early 1952, there were four acknowledged notables. None of these was the "owner of the land" (Q12) who had by that time lapsed into premature old age. Referring to the genealogical diagram of the Namabeya kinship network, in Figure 4 (*facing* p. 74), those notables and their approximate clusters were as follows: [22]

Q4, Kambi—Q5, R1–5 (7 household heads)
Q8, Lihamba—P2, Q6–8, R6–15 (14 household heads)
Q16, Amiri—Q12–14, R16, R18–20, R22–27 (14 household heads)
R29, Mohamedi—Q18, R28–33 (7 household heads)

It must be emphasised that this is a crude categorisation only, for purposes of simplified exposition. The clusters were much less clearly defined than the above data suggest. Just as in Ligomba community, there were some men in ambiguous statuses because of their important kin-neighbour linkages that cross-cut the clusters.

The principal stages of development in Namabeya during the two years 1952–1954 were in chronological order as follows.

June 1952: The Dispute between R14 and R16. R14's wife died suddenly, with severe stomach pains. R14 alleged that R16 had committed adultery with her whilst she was pregnant, and that this was the cause of her death. This was flatly denied by the accused. There had been a series of disputes earlier between those two men: formerly R14 and his sister's husband, R15, had shared a common hamlet with R16, but the latter had shifted away and now his household lived alone. The former close kin-neighbour relations between the men had deteriorated, although they had not been severed altogether. In this dispute R14 consulted with the notable Lihamba (Q8) (his MB), whilst R16 sought the advice of the notable Amiri (Q16) (father-in-law of his WB), whom he acknowledged as his kin-neighbour.[23] A moot was arranged in which

[22] Letter-numbers refer to men's positions in the master genealogy in Figure *facing* p. 82. Apart from the four notables, Namabeya men are referred to by these symbols for simplicity of exposition.

[23] Whilst R16 had shared a hamlet with R14 and R15, he had been a member of the cluster focussing on Lihamba. With his estrangement from those two kin-neighbours he had also become estranged from Lihamba and others in that cluster. He had increasingly associated with his affines (wife's kin), and this had brought him into the cluster focussed on Amiri.

the two notables took over the leadership of the respective action-sets. The approximate composition of these action-sets is given below; it should be noted that men of the clusters of the other two notables, Kambi (Q4) and Mohamedi (R29), were not involved as participants in this moot.

Action-set of R14	*Action-set of R16*
Q8 (MB—notable Lihmaba)	Q16 (WBWF—notable Amiri)
R15 (ZH)	R20 (WBWB)
R12 (MBDH)	R22, R24 (WB)
Q6, Q7 (MMZS)	R25, R26 (WMZS)
R6, R8 (MMZSS)	R27 (Q16's ZS)
R10 (MBDHB)	
(9 men)	(8 men)

The moot was held at the house of Q14. The latter might well have joined R16's action-set in support of Amiri and other kin-neighbours, but he seems to have chosen to assume the role of mediator in an attempt to limit the conflict between Amiri and Lihamba. Q14 was not a notable.

There was general consensus that relations between R14 and R16 had long been strained, but there was no agreement as to the cause or the remedy. R14 continued to demand compensation from and ritual purification of R16, whilst R16 persisted in his denial of any responsibility for the woman's death. Much time was taken up with mutual and increasingly hostile recriminations. The two notables firmly supported their respective principals, and eventually they began to accuse each other of wilful obstructionism. (Each was probably correct in his accusation, for notables would resort to these tactics; but this was not normally a matter for recrimination unless, as here, rivalry between notables was intense for some other reason.) Attempts at mediation by Q14 were quite unsuccessful. In the end Q14 openly censured Lihamba when the latter failed, indeed refused, to dissociate himself from an indirect imputation by R14 of witchcraft against R16. Q14 thereupon ostentatiously went and sat with Amiri and other members of R16's action-set. This virtually ended the moot, with no agreement on the settlement of the dispute.

A second moot was held some days later, being convened at the instigation of the notable Mohamedi (R29), and held at his house. No adequate record of the composition of the action-sets was obtained, but it is certain that they were both larger than on the preceding occasion. Almost all the men of Lihamba's cluster and of Amiri's cluster participated, whilst Mohamedi as potential mediator was accompanied by some members of his own cluster. Members of Kambi's cluster did not participate, however, though some attended the moot as "neutral" spectators. Mohamedi emphasised to me afterwards that only a few Namabeya men were not present: this was an indication of both their and his assessment of the importance of the moot. In the interval between the moots R14 had not reduced his demand for compensation nor withdrawn his insinuation of witchcraft against the defendant. All this was well known to the Namabeya people.

Amiri began the moot by directly referring to and condemning the insinuation of witchcraft, saying that it implied that the dispute could not be settled and that R14 and R16 could not remain neighbours in the same community, although formerly they had acknowledged a tie of kinship.[24] Amiri denied that R16 was a witch and declared that R16 would not be driven away from Namabeya because of such calumny. R16 said that his opponent, R14, had raised the issue in order to draw attention away from his own faults. (According to Mohamedi, this was a counter-insinuation of witchcraft.) Lihamba continued his full support of R14, and Amiri directly accused him of trying to break the community. With this kind of recrimination and open bitterness, the second moot also failed to find a settlement of the dispute. Mohamedi apparently made little attempt to mediate, though whether deliberately or not I do not know. "What could I do?" he explained, "they wanted to fight". There was little negotiation on the dispute, and little or no narrowing down of the area of disagreement. Instead, the sharpness of conflict and absence of willingness to compromise had set the two clusters and the leaders openly in opposition to each other.

Soon after this moot, R16 shifted his single household hamlet away from its site not far from the hamlet of R14 and R15. He rebuilt near to the hamlet of his wife's brothers, and was assisted in the task by work-parties that included many of the men of Amiri's cluster, not all of whom were R16's acknowledged kin-neighbours. At the following beer-drinks these men were joined by Mohamedi and several of his kin-neighbours—signifying their friendliness—whilst men of Lihamba's cluster did not attend, although they could have been expected to under other circumstances.

[24] On Ndendeuli ideas about witchcraft charges, see also page 160 f.

August, 1952: The Question of Tobacco Cultivation. Amiri
had been canvassing the idea of starting the cultivation of tobacco
as a cash crop in Namabeya. The community was, apparently,
well located with respect to soils, but the people had not grown
much tobacco because of the problem of transporting their crop
some eight miles to the nearest buying centre of the local Cooperative Society. An official of the central Union of Cooperative
Societies visited Namabeya to hold an open meeting. He told the
men that, if they wished to grow tobacco for sale, it would be
necessary for them to clear a track about six miles long to the
nearest existing road and capable of taking a lorry that could
transport their produce. This was normal policy at that time; the
Cooperative Union provided supervision and some tools. Amiri and
Mohamedi both supported the proposal and urged their neighbours
to participate in the necessary voluntary labour. They spoke of
the value of earning cash at home so that their young men need
no longer go away as labour migrants. Lihamba was, at best, luke-
warm about the idea, and in the end he opposed it. He took the
conservative view that Namabeya and similar communities had
managed in the past without a road, and he foresaw danger in
becoming involved with the Cooperative Society which, he persisted, was merely a branch of the Government. How far his
opposition was engendered by his antagonism to Amiri, I could
not determine. In the meeting the two men verbally attacked each
other personally. Not all of Lihamba's associates supported him
in his expressed views; but many did, and none of them spoke out
against them.

Later that month Amiri travelled to Songea to arrange for the
construction of the track. This was done in September. Most men
of the clusters of Amiri and of Mohamedi gave their free labour
for some ten days; it was not an unduly difficult undertaking. R1
and R2 of Kambi's cluster also participated regularly, saying that
they wanted to cultivate tobacco. Amiri had previously been a
foreman and labour clerk on a sisal estate in central Tanganyika,
and it was he who largely took charge of the work. He kept a
record of daily participation, and publicly pointed out the failure
of Lihamba and many of his kin-neighbours to contribute their
labour.

November 1952: The Mosque Affair. Q18, the community's
mwalimu (Moslem teacher), raised the matter of the repair of the
small hut that served as a mosque in Namabeya. It was in very
poor condition. Usually, in this as in other local communities, the

mwalimu himself convened a work-party to undertake the task, but this year Amiri and Mohamedi called a general moot to discuss arrangements. Lihamba and his associates, and also Kambi and his associates, refused to attend—though almost all were professed Moslems. The eventual work-party included men only of the clusters of Amiri and Mohamedi. Amiri said at the time that "the neighbours of Kambi and Lihamba should not use the mosque afterwards. This did not become an issue, however, probably because in part the people were not deeply involved in Islam and few men attended the mosque on Friday mornings. My own inference is that Amiri, supported by Mohamedi, had sought to force the issue deliberately. But deliberately or not, this affair did emphasise two points: the alliance of Amiri and Mohamedi, and, in the actual work-party, the cooperation of men of their clusters in distinction from the men associated with Kambi and Lihamba.

Wet Season, 1952–1953: Tobacco Growing. Most men in the clusters of Amiri and Mohamedi and some (R1, R2, Q5, R5, R8, R9) of the other two clusters cultivated tobacco. Before the wet season began, Amiri and Mohamedi had been to Songea together to attend a short course on tobacco cultivation. They made their knowledge and advice available to their own kin-neighbours but, reportedly, avoided giving assistance to other Namabeya men. Probably as a result, the men associated with Amiri and Mohamedi obtained fair yields and managed to sun-dry their crops moderately well. Three of the other men had almost complete failures in the novel task of caring for the seedlings, and the remaining three partly spoiled their crop in the curing process.[25] Public comments by Amiri and others on this invidious result, at a beer-drink, led to some fighting.

Next day R16's new house caught fire, though the damage was not serious. R16 accused the young kinsmen of R14 and R15 as the culprits, and this revived the earlier witchcraft accusations on both sides. Amiri himself declared publicly that the alleged arson was linked with the fighting the previous day and with the unsettled dispute between R16 and R14. The incidents did not lead to a moot, which in itself was some indication of the cleavage between the men in the community. Undoubtedly these matters sustained, and perhaps strengthened, the developing antagonism and division.

May, 1953: The Issue of Ndendeuli Autonomy. The process of

[25] I depended on the opinion of Cooperative Union officials in this matter.

segmentation was also continued and quickened over the then current issue of the political separation of Undendeuli from the Ngoni chiefdom.[26] Local meetings were being held in various parts of Undendeuli at this time to keep people informed and to gain their support. When such a meeting was held in Namabeya, Amiri claimed to be spokesman for the community in advocating and declaring support for an autonomous Undendeuli with its own local government. It was generally known that he had connections with Ndendeuli leaders, and it was generally believed that he had hopes of becoming an official, paid headman (*jumbe*) if autonomy was achieved.[27] Lihamba, supported by his associates as they sat in the meeting, was scornful of Amiri's pretensions and aspirations. Amiri was accused of supporting the Europeans' Government, of seeking authority for himself, and of being "like an Ngoni" and seeking merely to take their place. Lihamba said: "We are all right here. The Ngoni, and the Europeans too, are a long way away. There is nothing to worry about. Let us stay as we are and let the Government stay away. Who wants to bring the Government? They will increase the tax, and they will bring new laws which we shall have to obey". On this occasion Kambi supported Lihamba, opposing what he said was Amiri's attempt "to be a big man over all of us. But he is not my big man, nor am I his kinsman".

August, 1953: A Bridewealth Dispute. The effective crystallisation of opposed segments in Namabeya occurred in connection with a dispute between Kambi (Q4) and his son-in-law, R25, over outstanding bridewealth. When R25 had returned from labour migration towards the end of the previous year he had, apparently, brought back only tiny savings from his earnings abroad. But it had become known that he had money in a post office savings account. This disclosure occurred when R25 began to make arrangements to build a small shop in Namabeya. This would be the first shop in that area and was likely to be a more practicable proposition now that the new lorry track was available. R25 hoped to augment petty retailing by engaging in some trade—buying maize and other local produce to sell in bulk to

[26] See page 34.
[27] In fact his hopes were ill-fated, since there was little political reorganization, at least at first, when later that year Ndendeuli autonomy was realised. Former headman remained in office and no new ones were appointed. Namabeya continued, like Ligomba, with no official representative of government among its members.

Songea traders. The claim by his father-in-law for one hundred and thirty shillings in bridewealth would, of course, have seriously interfered with his intentions; but so far he had given only fifty-five shillings to Kambi. According to his savings account book, he had a total capital of two hundred and eighty shillings.

Amiri supported R25's plan to open a shop in Namabeya, for it fitted his idea of local economic development. Amiri was also kin-neighbour of R25 and notable of their common cluster. According to Mohamedi and other informants, Amiri went to much trouble to recruit neighbours to R25's action-set. In the moot R25's set was a large one, containing fourteen men, comprising most of the members of the clusters of Amiri and Mohamedi. On the other hand, the plaintiff, Kambi, gained the active support not only of his own kin-neighbours but also of most of Lihamba's associates. His set contained seventeen men. He also had the strong personal support of Lihamba who largely pre-empted the leadership of the action-set in the moot. As a notable himself, Kambi must (I presume) have considered Lihamba's leadership and prestige to be valuable to him. In the moot there was, in addition to consideration of the bridewealth demand, lengthy discussion of the projected shop and its possible benefits. This developed into a more general argument over tobacco cultivation and the advantages and disadvantages of economic development. In each matter Lihamba and Amiri were the principal spokesmen, each acting on behalf of a more or less distinct segment of the whole community. The only significant men who were not clearly aligned were Q12 (the "owner of the land") and Q13; these men made some attempt to mediate between the two sides, but with little success other than to persuade R25 to promise to pay another fifty shillings in bridewealth to his father-in-law. No payment was made at that time, however, so that the specific dispute was left virtually unsettled.

It was clear, and the men themselves recognised it, that Namabeya had separated into two distinct segments, focussing on Lihamba (with Kambi) and on Amiri (with Mohamedi). This second, virtually unsettled dispute had highlighted the division as social action and persisting conflict had followed its alignment. Overtly pervading the whole development was the conflict between the two leading notables, each seeking to consolidate and extend his influence and prestige. Each, as the result of the other's opposition, had been able to achieve this at the expense of the community's loose unity, and to some extent at the expense of the

other two notables. They had, however, made no effective encroachment on the sphere of influence of each other.

This unusually clear-cut segmentation of the local community
was demonstrated in the following season of work-parties recruited for clearing woodland and preparing new fields. In almost
none of these work-parties (though my reliable evidence is unfortunately limited) were previously acknowledged ties of neighbours
activated across the line of cleavage. This was in marked contrast
with the more vaguely defined, open-ended clusters that had
previously operated, comparable to those in Ligomba. Moreover,
men recruited to these work-parties neighbours of their own segment who before had not been available. There were separate
time-table arrangements within each segment, and beer-drinks
after work-parties (normally almost pan-community affairs) were
similarly limited to the segment. This condition was repeated for
later house-repair work-parties and on ritual occasions throughout
the remainder of 1953. There were no further public disputes,
however. The only particular event of note was another attempt
by Q12 to act as a mediator between the two segments. He was,
of course, closely related by kinship to both of the principal
leaders: half-brother of Lihamba, and MZS of Amiri. His plan of
inviting his kin-neighbours from both segments to his work-party
in late August was a complete failure. The party on the day was
composed of only his brother-in-law, Q13, and their sons. It
seems doubtful, even had Q12 been a more active and able man,
that he could have succeeded as mediator in the circumstances.

In the following wet season most of Amiri's segment continued
with their tobacco cultivation; but only R1, R2, and R5 in
Lihamba's segment attempted this for a second season. During the
rains, part of the new lorry track was washed away on a hill slope.
Repairs were out of the question without outside assistance, for
much of the hillside was gone and a wholesale realignment of the
track was required. Namabeya men had great difficulty in transporting their tobacco crop (by head loads) to the market store-
house. They were advised that money would not be available to
construct a new and more circuitous track in the place of the
earlier one. Tobacco cultivation was therefore, at least for the
immediate future, no longer a ready possibility for residents of the
community.

The men of Amiri's segment decided to move away from
Namabeya and to resettle near to the Government-maintained road
that ran through eastern Undendeuli. I did not obtain an adequate

account of the discussions that led up to this final act of fission in the Namabeya local community, but it seems to have occurred without further overt conflict between the two segments.[28] After fourteen years of existence the community broke up, although a large rump remained to continue their residence there. The former residents became dispersed as follows:

(i) Remaining in Namabeya: Q8 (Lihamba), Q4–7, P2, R3–15 (19 households)

(ii) In a new local community near to the main road: Q16 (Amiri), Q14, Q18, R16, R20–23, R32, R33 (16 households)

(iii) In another, already established community, X: Q12, Q13, R18, R19

(iv) In another, already established community, Y: R1, R2

(v) In another, already established community, Z: R31

Analysis

The outlines of this process of factional segmentation are, it is hoped, clear enough to show the development that led ultimately to the fission of that local community. The process must have had its genesis much earlier than I have been able to show, however. There is reason to believe that it began with the establishment of the community when, I was told, Lihamba and Amiri competed for influence over Q12, the "owner of the land" and original leader, in the making of pioneer decisions. Both men had been active in sponsoring newcomers and in building up clusters of kin-neighbours amongst whom cooperation was encouraged and conflict minimised. This did not, of course, make the later developments inevitable, but it laid a potential basis for segmentation and conflict. The existence of established and patterned conflict by 1952, where my narrative begins, is clearly demonstrated in the dispute resulting from the sudden death of R14's wife and the accusation of adultery against R16. This was the latest in a series of disputes between those two men, and it was in large part an announcement and a public expression of their hostility and the rupture of their kin-neighbor relations. The mutual accusations of witchcraft, though made indirectly, signalled the decisiveness of that rupture. But such accusations would have been quickly repudiated and squashed from both sides in the moot, whatever the state of relations between the principals in the actual case, had

[28] My field research was completed before that time, but I was still in the Songea District and was able to learn the bare results of the fission.

the leaders and members of each action-set seriously wished to minimise conflict and to maintain cross-cutting, cooperative inter-dependence. This is what had happened in Ligomba in Case 3 when the hinted suggestion of witchcraft was immediately and firmly repudiated by members of the accuser's action-set and by the mediator. In this instance, to the contrary, each notable (Lihamba and Amiri), effectively leading his action-set, chose instead not to repudiate his principal's charge; and so, by implications well understood by the participants, each notable condoned and supported the charge. Thus the declaration of hostility, of non-neighbourliness, was extended beyond the particular dispute and disputants to the burgeoning factions led by these two notables. The declaration was overtly upheld by their respective followings in the failure of other members to deny the witchcraft accusations. This, then, was not the beginning of established conflict and the taking of sides, but only the beginning of the end.

Segmentation thereafter crystallised through the issue of tobacco cultivation and the construction of the lorry track, the mosque affair, the production of tobacco and its one-sided results, the fighting at the beer-drink, the alleged arson, and the issue of Undendeuli autonomy. It culminated in the bridewealth dispute where the membership of the factional segments was made clear in the formation and confrontation of action-sets in the moot, led by Lihamba and Amiri respectively. By that time the two smaller clusters and their notables had aligned themselves with the larger groupings. Thus the community was almost completely divided into two segments, operating autonomously of one another in day-to-day life in the community. There remained only the small, intermediary cluster of neighbours focussing on the enfeebled "owner of the land". These men were more or less rejected, or ignored, by both segments, and they were ineffective mediators. The reality of segmentation was evident in the recruitment of agricultural and house-repair work-parties, in participation in beer-drinks, in ritual gatherings, and in social intercourse generally during the year preceding the eventual fission of the community. That is to say, in diverse interests and activities, in matters of inter-dependence, men had come to operate only within the limits of their own segment. Co-activity between individual members of different segments virtually ceased, where before the original clusters had had no such narrow limitations.

In exploring the implications of the concept of network through the analysis of local community organisation and inter-action within the closed network, what is of primary importance here, and must be given especial emphasis, is that the emergence of autonomous segments necessitated the severance of the mesh of inter-linkages and inter-dependence. To develop and maintain the cleavage, men had to ignore a number of cross-linkages with kin-neighbours and with the kin of kin-neighbours that had previously been utilised in advantageous, cooperative activity. Where, as in Ligomba, these cross-linkages persisted, it was impossible for clusters to consolidate into clearly and decisively separate segments. In Namabeya the cross-linkages were broken. In some cases the break came from positive conflict: as between R16 and both R14 and R15, and between Q4 and R25, and their kin-neighbours entailed by their former relationships. In other cases the break came from deliberate and effective neglect of relationships as men chose not to activate them: the links of Lihamba and others on the one side, and of Amiri and others on the other, with Q12 and Q13. The lines of cleavage in the emergence of factional segmentation are shown diagrammatically in Figure 4 (*facing* p. 74), and they indicate the number and variety of the severed or neglected linkages. In formal genealogical terms, these included every kind of closer kinship tie—full- and half-brothers, first and second cousins, classificatory "fathers", brothers-in-law—as well as more remote but, in context, also actively important ones. It will be remembered, too, that a break in relations between two acknowledged kin-neighbours meant also a break in the relations between some of the kin-neighbours of these men (that is, the kin of kin). All of these now severed relations had been useful and utilised, and they all held the potential of practical, advantageous, social relations between neighbours. This is the measure of the seriousness of segmentation, and explains the rarity of such development in Ndendeuli local communities. In brief, men had to eschew otherwise valuable relationships if segmentation were to occur and to persist. The single, continuous network therefore disappeared, being replaced by two separate networks.

The emergent groupings of neighbours in Namabeya have been referred to as "factional segments". Each focussed on a principal leader; they were persistent (though not necessarily permanent), unlike the ephemeral action-sets; they operated in a variety of contexts and interests; and they were conflict groups. What, then, were they in conflict about? What was the rationale of their distinctiveness?

Neither Namabeya men nor their leaders were in competition

for the use or control of land or of other scarce resources. Nor were they striving for political domination over one another: this was not possible within the institutional structure and practical opportunities afforded by an Ndendeuli local community, and there is no evidence of any attempt to seek such atypical power. What men were seeking, there as elsewhere, was reliability of cooperation and reciprocal assistance among neighbours. In certain key instances such reliability was seriously threatened by genuine conflict (dispute) between particular individuals—conflict that in practice could not be, or was not, resolved or sealed off. This conflict threatened the reliability of useful and essential cooperation, not only between those particular individuals themselves but between other neighbours linked with them, and through them with each other, in the context of network inter-linkages and inter-dependence. Failing some reasonable resolution of these conflicts and therefore reasonable continuity of reliable cooperation, it was preferable to cut the linkages altogether. Or, to put it in another way, it was preferable to concentrate on those other linkages that remained reliable and that could be further consolidated and also extended to other neighbours in the network. Intersegment conflict was, therefore, a means of announcing and reiterating these essential aims. This was true not only for the men more or less directly concerned, but also for those apparently more remotely concerned. Men of Kambi's (Q4) cluster sought to ensure and strengthen their valued cooperative relations with men of Lihamba's cluster. They were, of course, expected to honour their reciprocal obligations in supporting Lihamba's cluster. In the final dispute situation—Kambi's bridewealth claim, the eventual catalyst—Kambi and his kin-neighbours had clear need of the support of Lihamba and his associates. Similarly men of Mohamedi's cluster sought these same ends and their own interests by alliance with Amiri and his associates. Wholesale repudiation of acknowledged linkages and accepted reciprocal obligations was in no one's interests and would only have led to dangerous fragmentation of the community, i.e. of the means of reliable co-activity. Instead there was a consolidation of the segments of the old single network.

The search for reliability of cooperation and reciprocal assistance—essentially the Ndendeuli framework of social action— might be put in another way, though one the people themselves did not use as far as I know. The fulfillment of kinship obligations may be seen as forms of investment and accumulation of capital: these were expected to produce and hopefully to guarantee returns, that is, assistance and support of various kinds in due course in times of need. Men therefore attempted to invest where it was most likely that the returns would be adequate and reliable. A kinsman (neighbour or not) who could not give the appropriate return when required was a bad risk, and assistance given to him was a poor investment. He might be unable to make that appropriate return because of conflicting obligations that he judged to be more important to him; and where a sequence of conflicts developed with the two men on opposite sides, then their investments in each other would have been seriously threatened or, as in Namabeya, rendered more or less valueless. In making their decisions, Namabeya men had to take account of this. Members of each cluster, and gradually of each developing segment, increasingly invested in other members of the same cluster and the same segment. In this way their investments were more secure, their return more reliable, as they reinforced one another. Earlier investments in members of the opposed segment had to be written off or, at best, held in abeyance. For the notables, their decisions were also moves, or investments, in a more political game in which they sought the prizes of increased influence and prestige. But in the Ndendeuli cultural context they were unable to invest heavily or to expect high returns.[29]

Conflict was therefore emphasised between the segments in order to strengthen the reliability of relations within each one separately, and in order to announce implicitly what was being done. Analytically one may say that the sequences of conflict were in the interest of both sides, once the segmentation process developed. Similarly, those sequences were advantageous to each of the principal leaders of the segments, though I do not suggest that they necessarily perceived it that way, let alone that they were in collusion. It was, in effect, the function of each leader to promote advantageous conflict and to polarise the loyalties of their respective supporters. But each leader separately took the opportunities to consolidate his influence and prestige. Amiri, but not I think Lihamba, perhaps had some idea of seeking more than the normative influence and prestige of an Ndendeuli notable, for he saw something of the modern possibilities of a role of authority

[29] This tentative conceptualisation was suggested to me by the "self interest" model developed by Scheffler 1965 and Keesing 1967(*a*).

under the new system of local government and administration. For the first time since the Ndendeuli moved out from the Ngoni authoritarian regime, such a role was at least a possibility.

There was an ideological element in the inter-segmental conflict, though this was not the basic issue at stake and it only served as a secondary rallying point in the total process. The two segments, and the two leaders themselves, were sometimes identified as "conservatives" ("those who stay [remain, sit, not change]") and "progressives" ("those who go on"), by themselves and by each other. Lihamba was an elderly man who had never had formal education and who had expressed himself as content with "the old ways". He had apparently travelled little outside eastern Undendeuli since his labour migration as a young man over thirty years previously. Amiri, and also Mohamedi, perceived advantages in new opportunities beginning to become available. Probably this was partly the result of their own, more protracted careers as labour migrants, which had been more successful and stimulating than those of the vast majority of Ndendeuli who went as unskilled labourers to the distant, alien estates. Both men had attained lower supervisory jobs.

The issue of tobacco cultivation was largely ideological, and gave a good pretext for engendering conflict and strengthening leadership. Men of the clusters of Amiri and Mohamedi were perfectly able to grow and to market tobacco despite the opposition of Lihamba and his associates to that enterprise. The lorry track would have been constructed more easily and quickly had Lihamba's men participated, but it made little difference to the eventual achievement. Few, if any, men were opposed to Undendeuli political autonomy from the Ngoni chiefdom, though many perceived little positive advantage in it to themselves. But, true to Ndendeuli values, there was genuine resentment at Amiri's apparent pretensions to gain influential ascendancy over the whole community (cf. Kambi's remark on p. 262), which threatened the other notables and suggested new, undesired authority.

Yet it is important to note that Namabeya men did not take sides specifically as "conservatives" and "progressives", but essentially as kin-linked supporters of a notable and in terms of their interdependence within the network. The ideology was, in fact, only weakly developed, although it did come realistically to represent some of the burgeoning differences of interests of a secondary kind (cash crop cultivation). Not all of the men of Lihamba's segment were opposed to tobacco cultivation—a few actually took it up—and some disagreed with Lihamba's stance on Undendeuli autonomy. Nor did all members of Amiri's segment altogether support his "progressive" views; some did not, at that time, grow tobacco, and some were apprehensive of Amiri's apparent ambition for authority. Such men, in either segment, were nevertheless induced with little or no difficulty to follow their leaders because of their involvement in positive linkages with fellow-members of the cluster and of the segment.[30]

Most probably, effective segmentation of an Ndendeuli local community could not have developed without factional conflict. The essential severance of normal cross-linking, kin-neighbour relations would seem to have required persisting hostility. Let me reiterate, and emphasise, firstly, the rarity of the development of cleavage, segmentation, and fission, in local communities; and, secondly, that its occurrence in Namabeya was *not* merely the result of the sheer size of the community nor of the extended nature of its kinship network. There were other, larger communities in the same part of eastern Undendeuli that had not segmented during a longer period of existence, although their kinship networks could probably have been no less extended. It is possible—it can be rated no higher than this—that the Namabeya network was rather less convolute than those of some other communities: thus there may have been rather fewer strands in the network to be cut when segmentation occurred. I do not see how this factor can be assessed, as between Namabeya and Ligomba for example, for the variables were too inchoate and situationally determined for quantitative calculation.

It was not possible, in these local communities, to achieve segmentation at one level, in one field of social activities, or in one kind of social relations, whilst leaving other kinds of cooperation and interaction more or less intact. Those crucial relations between kin-neighbours were multiplex, concerned with a wide variety—indeed virtually the totality—of interests and activities of men living together. It was impossible, ideologically or practically, for men to separate the various strands in those relationships. And, of course, the multiplex character was powerfully symbolised, ethically justified, and rationalised by the all-embracing idiom of

[30] Note that two non-conservatives in Lihamba's segment, R_1 and R_2, took the opportunity to move away from Namabeya at the time of fission. They did not, however, join Amiri's segment in its new location, but went as newcomers to another existing local community where tobacco cultivation was already established.

kinship. The rarity of the Namabeya case of segmentation and fission is ultimately explicable by the nature of the particular kind of network, identified in terms of kinship, and operating in linking sequences of inter-dependency in cooperation, reciprocity, and support.

Whether the ultimate form of fission of Namabeya was an inevitable culmination is problematical. The two autonomous segments could have merely regrouped geographically and residentially, so that fission would have occurred without the migration of one segmentation. Each segment would still, however, have reconstituted itself as a new, separate local community. It seems fairly certain, on the other hand, that effective segmentation engendered and maintained through a conflict sequence must have produced some kind of fission. The *raison d'être* of a local community was destroyed by segmentation, for there was no over-arching common interest or mutual advantage that remained, unless the two segments could later establish or re-establish inter-linkages between individual members. In this particular case of Namabeya there can be seen an instance of what, at that period, was a general trend among the Ndendeuli: a slow development of cash crop cultivation and a drift of settlement towards lines of communications along which agricultural produce could be transported away and consumer goods be brought in, and along which both people and news could travel. Nevertheless, and despite the eventual outcome of this particular case, there was no suggestion (as far as I was aware) by Amiri and his associates that they should move their residence before the new lorry track was washed away and thus the transport of tobacco was made extremely difficult. Men then chose, presumably, to continue cultivation and cash earning, although it necessitated residential movement.

From the rather unsatisfactory evidence at my disposal, it would seem that the end of the large majority of Ndendeuli local communities was far less dramatic and far less conflict-laden than that of Namabeya. What seems to have occurred was a gradual exhaustion of adequate, cultivable woodland conveniently within reach of the hamlets and their water supply. As I indicated in an earlier chapter (p. 45), Ndendeuli disliked to have their hamlets far from domestic water supplies or more than a mile or so from their fields under cultivation. Perennial water supply was relatively scarce and most communities focussed on one or two points in stream beds where water-holes could be successfully dug in the second half of the dry season. Thus, after about a couple of decades (but depending on the size of the community and the proportion of cultivable land in the area), available untouched woodland for new fields became, by Ndendeuli standards, too far from the hamlets and their water supply. It was a subjective opinion when that stage was reached, and some people were prepared to be more tolerant than others. But gradually newcomers ceased joining the community and there was a trickle away of households as men sought more advantageous conditions. The first to go were likely to be those for whom the state of neighbourly relations and the reliability of cooperation was least satisfactory. To the best of my knowledge, a cluster of neighbours, with their leading notable, did not migrate away together. This is a good indication of the relative weakness of the solidarity of a cluster. Households departed in ones, twos, and threes, as their heads individually sought to join other local communities already existing or just being started. In any case, household heads sought to move to where they had acknowledged kinsmen to sponsor them, and where expectations of kin-neighbour cooperation were good. Each man had his own individual range of kinsmen scattered irregularly in other communities; thus his opportunities for migration were different, often quite different, from those of his kin-neighbours. The cluster really only had viability and consistency within the particular context of the network of the local community in which it emerged and operated. Thus an old community gradually dispersed during a period of a few years but without conflict, factional segmentation, and fission.

Part Three

The Open Network
in the Wider Society

IX

The Kin-set:
The Individual's Orientation

In Part II of this book it was shown that a local community in eastern Undendeuli comprised in effect a group of neighbours who were all linked genealogically, directly or indirectly. The majority of household heads were linked only indirectly—many so indirectly that the links were not overtly recognised—and the community did not operate explicitly as a kin group. For the great majority of household heads (and thus the dependent members of their households), most of their acknowledged kinsmen lived elsewhere, scattered irregularly in a number of other local communities. Ndendeuli kinsfolk did not aggregate into kin groups of any kind. There were no descent groups, unilineal or otherwise, neither in ideal conception nor empirically in terms of actual social behaviour and interaction. No recognition was given to lines of descent, or to categories based on descent as such. For most practical purposes, as well as in ideal perception, the people scarcely distinguished between cognatic and affinial kinsfolk: they were not different categories of associates.

In his society, each household head stood, as it were, and operated from, the centre of his own peculiar set of active kinship relations—his kin-set—comprising both cognates and affines. Empirically each man's kin-set was in total specific to him alone, so that neither father and married sons, nor brothers, had quite the same set or the same range of social interaction expressed in kinship terms. But, of course, kin-sets overlapped in varying degrees, for many of the kinsmen with whom a man was related were at the same time also related to one another. Thus a man's association and interaction with his kin was always and inevitably affected by their association and interaction with one another. Men's kin-sets intermeshed in an open-ended web of kinship relations comprising an unbounded, convolute network that extended *de facto* to include presumably all Ndendeuli and others beyond.

In this chapter the principal concern is the examination of the nature and extent of ego-oriented kin-sets. This, however, is a convenient analytical procedure only, although it is one that Ndendeuli would have understood since they themselves tended to perceive society (the social field) from that individual point of view. Nevertheless this was a limited point of view that must be seriously modified in due course of exposition and analysis by a full recognition of the implications of the complex inter-linkages of kin-sets within the unbounded network. These impli-cations will sometimes necessarily be explicit in the following account of kin-sets; but they must always be implicitly accepted.

THE GENEALOGICAL NORM OF
ACTIVE KINSHIP: A STATISTICAL MODEL

Before considering the quality and operation of Ndendeuli kinship relations in the open network of the wider social field, or the nature and implications of variations in individual men's kin-sets, I first seek to give an indication of the empirical norm of the range of active kinship. The people themselves gave no verbal or other particular cultural recognition to the effective range. They were much inclined to assume, in so far as it seemed a significant matter per se, that a man maintained privileges and obligations with all of his genealogically known kinsmen, *akatani*. Certainly there was some tendency for the universe of kin to be limited to that range of persons with whom a man was more or less actively related by practical interaction. But the congruence was very seldom, if ever, exact. That, however, tells nothing about the actual range of interaction involving rights and privileges, obligations and responsibilities, and cooperation in mutual interests.

In this section I attempt to give an approximate, first stage, descriptive model of the empirical norms by fairly simple, un-sophisticated means. For each man in a sample of eighty-three household heads,[1] I enquired whether or not he had visited or been visited by each of his acknowledged kinsmen since the end of the preceding dry season. This date provided a quite definite time that both the men and I could understand and clearly remember.

---

[1] These eighty-three men were among 107 household heads whose genealogies were comprehensively recorded in Ligomba, Namabeya, and two other local communities in eastern Undendeuli in 1953.

My enquiries were made between nine and ten months after that date, in the middle of the following dry season. It would have been preferable to have based my survey on a complete twelve months, for there remained two to three months of the dry season at that time, during which period visiting was continued. Field research necessities made this impracticable, and there was no clear, firm date twelve months prior to the time of the survey that could have been used as a proper base-line.

Visiting a kinsman's home was a good indication of an active relationship with him. There was, of course, more inter-visiting between residentially near kin than between those who lived at a distance; but if a man went for more than nine months without visiting, or being visited, it is not unreasonable to suppose an absence of active relations, for whatever cause. Ndendeuli agreed with his argument. They considered it important, as well as pleasurable and perhaps immediately profitable, to visit and exchange hospitality, news, and opinion. There were often more cogent reasons for visiting—to obtain or give some positive kind of assistance, or to obtain information on some matter of concern; but when there was not, for the moment, it was thought important to make the visit in order to prevent the atrophy of the desired relationship that neglect might foster. Failure to visit indicated either a conscious willingness to allow active relations to lapse, or a disregard for the potential value of the relationship. Therefore men did visit their kinsmen, even when there was no special purpose, simply to express continued friendliness and to maintain communication. Consequently it was of genuine sociological significance if a man visited one kinsman, but not another. It is no less significant if a marked proportion of men visited certain kinds of kinsmen and failed to visit other kinds.

Before presenting the results of this survey, there are certain limitations and considerations of presentation that need to be made clear. Firstly, it did not seem possible to distinguish, in the results, between visiting one, several, or all kinsmen of a particular kind (for example, mother's brothers' sons). To make these distinctions would have given superior results, no doubt, but it would have made straightforward presentation impossible. Secondly, no account was taken of either the frequency or purpose of visiting with particular kinsmen. The problem of obtaining the information reliably in the field (without a team of research assistants) would have been formidable and probably self-defeating in the matter of retaining informants' cooperation in what was already a most tedious business. I was more concerned with maintaining goodwill in the field context than with obtaining seemingly impeccable statistical data.

Thirdly, my enquiry and the results referred only to kinship relations between male household heads. In this I was concerned with the more significant aspects of the total kinship network. Kin links with females were fully recognised, of course. A man visited his mother or sister, perhaps even female cousin, in her own right; but he visited their husbands at the same time. Women played little overt part in the social arena of public life in which kinship relations were most dominant, however much they privately influenced their husbands and sons. They and their unmarried children were held to be represented by the head of their household. Questions of residence, areas of cultivation, the organisation of work-parties, the treatment of disputes, the arrangement of rituals, and the exchange of information and opinion were monopolised in public by men and male relationships. These relationships were not only between men, but between their households as units.

The presentation of the data raised two main problems. Firstly, in every case among the sample of eighty-three men there were instances where there were no kinsman of a particular kind (for example, the mother had no brother). To meet this problem, the raw figures for each type of kinship link were transformed into percentages: the proportion of men who, acknowledging a kinsman of a particular degree, had visited with him. For example, whilst only fifty-one of the men visited with a brother, this represented 93 percent of all the men who had and acknowledged a live brother, head of his household, and living at home during much of the period.

Secondly, the raw figures showed that a large majority of the eighty-three men had not, or at least did not acknowledge, a kinsman of certain degrees. For example, only one sixth (fourteen men) acknowledged a third cousin of any kind; the rest of the sample expressed either unshakeable ignorance or complete refusal to acknowledge such a kinsman. Often only a small proportion had visited with these kinsmen, even when the link was admitted, but in some cases this was not so. For example, of three men in the sample who did acknowledge one kind of third cousin, two had actually visited with him: a proportion of 66 percent. Clearly, to have used the percentage figures alone would have given a false impression in this instance as compared with, say, the twenty-three men who visited with a ZHB out of forty-three who acknowledged that kinsman—a proportion of 53 percent. It is not insignificant, where a particular kind of kinship link was acknowledged by so few men, that a high proportion visited with him, but to establish a general descriptive pattern of empirical norms, these special cases have to be ignored. This problem has been met by taking only those kinship links that were acknowledged by at least one third of the sample men. This is somewhat arbitrary, but it was chosen in fact because there was a fairly clearly marked distribution of the data at about that point. Almost all the links acknowledged by less than one third of the men were recognised by less than one sixth of them. This means that there was a high degree of empirical agreement in the point of cut-off in the men's genealogical reckoning.

It has, therefore, proved possible to present the results of the survey by reference to two dimensions: both acknowledgement of kinship links and inter-visiting. To be sure, there was a scatter of other kinsmen with whom the informants visited, but the pattern and proportion of such kin were quite irregular. Thus the simplified data presented here show those kinds of kinsmen (at least one in each category) who were acknowledged by at least one third of the informants and visited by at least one half of them.

Finally, without intent and unfortunately through failure to take account of the matter, the majority of my informants in the sample were between the ages of about thirty and fifty years. This meant that most of them were not old enough to have adult, married grandsons and yet were too old to have surviving kinsmen in the grandparental generation. Older men over about fifty years of age did sometimes have active relations with kinsmen two generations below their own, and younger men, of less than about thirty years of age, reciprocated. It is now only possible to give an impressionistic account of the importance of kinsmen two generations apart, for the numbers of older and younger men were too small for statistical significance. Doubtless the age distribution of my informants reflected a field research bias on my part; on the other hand, that bias agrees with the Ndendeuli model of their kinship system, and it relates also to the fact that in any case the majority of household heads were between the approximate ages of thirty and fifty years. There appears to have been a rapidly rising death rate over about fifty years of age.

Bearing these considerations in mind, and taking visiting as the criterion, the general empirical model of the range of active kinship relations is shown in Figure 20.

FIGURE 20: The Range of Active Kinship Relations. (Based on a sample of 83 household heads)

Grandparental *generation*	FF MF	FFB FMB		
Parental *generation*	F(84)	FB(87) MB(73)	FFBS(74) FMBS(60) MFBS(64)	WF(88) ZHF(48) WFB(56) FZH(71)
Ego's *generation*	B(93)	FBS(89) FZS(68) MBS(80) MZS(61)	FFBSS(73) FFBDS(51) FFZSS(65) FMBSS(68) MFBSS(49)	WB(88) ZH(87) SWF(76) DHF(71) BWB(47) ZHB(65) WFBS(65) FBDH(61)
Son's *generation*	S(82)	BS(84) ZS(86)	FBSS(74) FBDS(62) FZSS(57)	DH(89) SWB(52) BDH(55) WBS(73)
Grandson's *generation*	SS DS	BSS ZSS		

NOTE: The figures in brackets after each kinship category give the percentage of men in the sample who, having a kinsman in that category, had visited or been visited by him during the period between mid-December 1952 and late September/early October 1953. Cases are ignored where less than about half of the men had visited with a particular kind of kinsman. No account is taken of either the frequency of visits, or of the common cases where there was more than one man in a particular kinship category. See text for a fuller discussion of the sample and presentation.

Let me be clear on one important point. These data do not, however approximately, inform us about the actual composition of the kin-sets of individual men. Rather they provide a simple model comprising those kinsmen who were most commonly included in men's kin-sets: a kind of highest common factor. This model is not, nevertheless and quite deliberately so, the equivalent of those ideal models that anthropologists have sometimes reported for societies with a non-unilineal kinship system: for instance, that the kindred comprises all ego's kinsmen up to third, or fourth, or fifth, cousins. This model for the Ndendeuli is based directly on empirical facts of some diagnostic significance. Actual kin-sets were considerably more variable than this simple pattern, as will be seen presently.

This model suggests, then, the genealogical character of the core of men's kin-sets. It reveals a pattern of which the Ndendeuli were not aware and that was no more than dimly perceptible to me during actual field research. There is shown a comparatively narrow lateral range of cognates, which excludes all of ego's third cousins and all of his parents' second cousins. Included within the model are ego's first cousins, his siblings' sons and his parents' brothers. Beyond that range there is a notable asymmetry. Only five of the sixteen logically possible second cousins are included, only two of ego's father's four first cousins and one of his mother's first cousins, and only three of his son's second cousins. This pattern indicates a definite patrilateral bias among cognates. The comparatively narrow lateral range is more pronounced among affinal kin. The range is restricted, first, to the male spouses of the sisters of father, ego, father's brother's son, and of ego's daughter and his brother's daughter. And secondly, it contains the close patrilateral kinsmen of the spouses of ego and his own closest kin.

This model, then, provides a descriptive basis from which to develop an account and analysis of actual, active, kinship relations in concrete social life. It is, I emphasise, to be taken as no more than that. Its particular characteristics and their implications are considered in the following sections of this chapter.

THE UNIVERSE OF KIN

The Ndendeuli universe of kin was shallow in depth and narrow in lateral range. Cognatic memory did not usually go much beyond the grandparental generation and the second cousins of mature men. In the genealogies of 107 household heads, 68 percent of those men asserted that they knew nothing beyond the grandparental generation, or at least nothing that added to the lateral spread of genealogical memory and the numbers of men included. Fairly frequently, men recalled the name of a father of one or more grandparents, but without knowing anything of that person's siblings or siblings' descendants. In 23 percent of the genealogies, men knew of one or more siblings of a grandparent and some (but probably not all) of their living descendants. In those cases the lateral spread was increased to include some third cousins. Many informants were, on the other hand, openly perplexed or scornful

that I seemed to expect them to know of third cousins. Some informants, particularly younger ones, knew the names of men
whom they thought were father's second cousins, but without
being able to trace complete genealogical linkage. It was generally
specifically denied that such men were "really kin", and (with
few exceptions) they were not visited during the period covered
by my survey. The presumption must be that earlier kinship relations in the father's time had since atrophied. Accidents of residential movement leading to proximate residence did sometimes
encourage a re-activation of such relations, and a few cases of this
occurrence were recorded.

Only 8 percent of the men in the sample knew, even by name,
anything of a grandparent's grandparent. In only a single case did
that knowledge involve a member of the informant's kin-set, and
in that instance the cognatic link was secondary to a closer, more
recently established, affinal relationship. At the other extreme,
every one of my informants was unable to trace collateral links
through one or more of his four grandparents.

One important explanation of this shallowness of genealogical
knowledge lies in the history of the Ndendeuli since the middle
of the nineteenth century and the Ngoni conquest. Many of the
recent forbears of modern Ndendeuli—parent, grandparent, great
grandparent, male and female—were abducted from distant homes
in Ngoni military raids during the second half of the century, in
the region stretching from the Indian Ocean to Lake Malawi. The
kinship links of those war-captives were generally abruptly cut
off, although occasionally captives later found kin who had also
been seized by war-parties. Inter-marriage between autochthonous
Ndendeuli and war-captives probably began more or less immediately, and it has continued ever since. No Ndendeuli was discovered in 1953–1954 who had not at least one war-captive among
his forbears, and thus automatically certain areas of genealogical
extension were closed. The most extreme case was represented by
an elderly man whose father and mother had both been war-
captives (one Ngindo, one Bena), of whose antecedents nothing
at all was known. This man had no cognatic kin other than his
parents (now deceased) in generations preceding his own. This
factor operated arbitrarily in producing irregularities in genealogies. On the other hand, genealogical knowledge was also fairly
shallow in areas where this cut-off had not been imposed. That is
to say, the shallowness was a function of the particular operation
of the kinship system. Whilst I cannot suggest that the Ndendeuli

positively could not operate with a larger range of kinsfolk than they in fact had, at least it would seem that a man did find more or less a sufficient number of kin to meet his social requirements. Had this not been so, it is reasonable to suppose that greater care would have been taken to remember and to maintain active relationships with, say, third cousins.

The universe of kin, and also the kin-set, of a particular individual was commonly given an erratic character by the inclusion of one or two kinsmen with whom precise genealogical relationships were not fully known, or with whom the links were rather indirect. This was almost always the result of the development of kin-neighbour relationships within a local community. There, through the inter-meshing of common kin-neighbours within a cluster in the network, two otherwise "unrelated" men were able to establish regular and reliable relations with each other. This point will be taken up more fully later on.

KIN-SETS

A man's kin-set—the collection of kinsmen with whom at any period he maintained active relations—neither comprised the whole of his universe of kin, nor did it conform in detail to the kind of statistical norm given in Figure 20. The nature and causes of these divergences are important to an understanding of the network within which, as it were, men operated in their actual social lives.

The highest incidence of indicated, active social relations was with brothers and father's brother's sons. Even here, roughly one man in ten had not visited with such a kinsman during the survey period, although he had acknowledged genealogical connection. For other kin the apparent absence of active relations was rather more pronounced, as the figure indicates. Even allowing for the crudity of the basis of the statistical model, these conclusions are clear enough. Men did retain knowledge of kinsmen, even genealogically close kinsmen, with whom they did not engage in social activity. This fact is, of course, unremarkable in itself, though it is inconsistent with the expressed ideal of the Ndendeuli. But an appreciation of how it came about and its implications are helpful to an understanding of the concrete reality of the kinship system. Furthermore, it suggests that the simple working hypothesis, that men were only concerned to acknowledge kinsmen with whom they had active relations, was valid only over the long run.

There were two principal factors that affected the actual composition of a man's kin-set. One was the particular membership of his local community, the other was the geographical scatter of kinsmen over the country.

Within his local community, at any time, it was virtually impossible to ignore a neighbour who was fairly closely related genealogically, as I showed in Chapter Seven.[2] Quite apart from the practical disadvantage of ignoring such a neighbour with whom there was a basis for useful cooperation, that neighbour would in all probability have been simultaneously linked with some of ego's other kin-neighbours. To have ignored him, therefore, would have introduced inconsistency, and sooner or later conflict, of obligations and loyalties into the operation of the network of interaction within the community. But in addition, a man was most likely to acknowledge as kin—that is, as kin-neighbours—some neighbours whose genealogical connections were remote, and who otherwise might have been regarded as the kin of kin. These were neighbours who were involved with ego (they had several kin-neighbours in common) in one sector of the network, and especially within the same cluster (within the same area of high inter-connectedness and inter-dependence). Examples were numerous in both Ligomba and Namabeya, a number of which have been previously cited. Some casual illustrations may emphasise the point here. In Ligomba, there was a mutual acknowledgement of kinship, as kin-neighbours, between Salimi (D1) and Saidi (C6) (Salimi's FBWB), and between Faranz (D4) and Saidi (Faranz's WFMZS). Saidi was "little father" to both men. Similarly there was mutual acknowledgement of kinship, as "brothers", between Bilali (C12) and Tanda (C13) (Bilali's FZHZS), between Tanda and Konga (C17) (Tanda's WBFBS), and between Hanju (D21) and Ndoma (D23) (Hanju's WFFBDS). It would be needlessly tedious to lengthen the list of examples. Every man had one or more such distantly related kinsmen in his kin-set.

These kinds of acknowledged, active kinship relations went much further genealogically than anything that Ndendeuli recognised outside their local community in the open network. Within the local community it was necessary, possible, and advantageous to recognise them. When such a kin-neighbour moved away (or when ego moved) to live elsewhere, the acknowledgement of kinship soon disappeared, for then the degree of mutual entailment in the wider, open-ended network was insufficient, in most cases, to sustain the relationship, that is, to make it advantageous and/or

[2] See page 232 ff.

necessary. The logic of this (the logic of the network) was borne out by actual cases investigated. A single case may suffice here. Five years after his departure from Ligomba, C22 was no longer acknowledged as a kinsman by Konga (C17) (Konga's MBWZS). Konga specifically stated this, although he also agreed that formerly C22 had been his kin-neighbour. While C22 lived in Ligomba, he and Konga had a number of kin-neighbours in common within the cluster of which Konga was the notable. Afterwards the two men had but a single common kinsman—Sedi (C21). Sedi had continued to acknowledge C22 (his MZS) as a kinsman and to maintain active relations with him; those two first cousins had several other kinsmen in common.

Atrophy of more distant or indirect kinship connections could also occur without residential movement and separation, as two (or more) kin-neighbours developed over time gradually divergent sets of kin-neighbours and fields of obligations and interests. Examples of this were revealed in the data given in Figure 10, and they have already been discussed in Chapter Seven. I briefly repeat two cases at this point for convenience of reference. This atrophy could occur where remote genealogical connections were involved —for example, Ali (C7) and Sedi (C21) (Ali's MFZSWBS)— and also where more direct and closer links were involved—for example, Ali and his second cousin, Mitedi (C19) (Ali's MFZSS).

In all these kinds of cases the crucial feature was the degree of entailment of the particular relationship within the network. Thus some kinsmen were acknowledged as such only temporarily, though often for lengthy periods. But these were, however, only special cases of the general processes by which a man's kin-set changed and developed over time. The process is easier to see, since it occurred more quickly, in the case of these "irregular" kin-neighbours who were highly indirectly connected. Nevertheless these are but particular kinds of instances of the general rule, already discussed in Chapter Seven, that kinship was defined by continued active relationship rather than by genealogical connection per se.

The second main factor affecting the actual composition of kin-sets was the nature of the geographical scatter of kinsmen. On the whole, a man maintained active relations, and thus in the longer run acknowledgement of kinship itself, only with men who lived within fairly easy reach. The survey results showed that a little over 80 percent of all kinsmen (with whom men had visited) actually lived within about twenty miles of their own hamlets.

This was, very roughly, something like an easy day's walk. It seems to have become too difficult for men to maintain active relations much beyond that distance, although presumably most Ndendeuli found that they had a more or less satisfactory number of kin within the acceptable geographical range. That range applied, moreover, both to genealogically near and to distant kinsmen.

Movements of residence were generally no more than about ten miles or less, and seldom more than about fifteen miles, on any one occasion. In making decisions about movements, men took account of the current geographical distribution of their acknowledged kin, in an attempt not to cut themselves off from advantageous relationships when settling in a new community. One informant described how he rejected the tempting possibility of moving to a local community in which his friendly brother and two other kinsmen already lived. It would have taken him thirteen or fourteen miles westwards and thus out of range of most of his other kin. Doubtless there were other considerations involved in his decision to move only about six miles, but other informants agreed with him that this socio-geographical factor was most important. Marriage similarly tended to be limited to that geographical range. Partly, no doubt, this resulted from limitations on acquaintanceship with marriageable girls and their fathers or brothers much beyond that distance; but men said that it was foolish to seek to establish new offinal links beyond a tolerable distance and with men who might also live beyond the range of other existing kinsmen.[3]

Not only did geographical distance between kinsmen engender atrophy of social relations, but to an unknown extent failure of active relations tended to engender geographical separation. It became less important to endeavour to keep within range, and possibly it was expressive of hostility to move apart. At least in some cases of chronic conflict between a man and his father, or his brother, the man had chosen to shift to a relatively distant community where there lived kinsmen on the periphery of the geographical range. In that case a man was then able to develop his own kin-set among people largely beyond the range of his father or brother. A later, second, move after ten years or more could completely separate those close kinsmen, leading even to a complete lack of their mutual acknowledgement of one another as kin. Cases of this kind were recorded fairly frequently. It amounted to the fact that, in making their decisions about residential movement, men could not only attempt to keep within range of those kinsmen

[3] On marriage choices, see below, page 308 ff.

who seemed advantageous to them, but they could seek to avoid those with whom relations were disadvantageous or fraught with hostility and conflict.

Special considerations could sometimes make it possible and useful to maintain active relations over greater than the average distances. Where motor transport was available along the main road through eastern Undendeuli, an appreciable number of men continued to maintain relations with kin in the Luegu region of western Undendeuli, some forty miles away.[4]

It was, of course, impossible, with this kind of loose cognatic/affinal kinship pattern, for a man to ensure that he remained within reasonable distance of all his kinsmen permanently. Both he and they periodically shifted their residence. Since each man's kin-set was at least slightly different from that of each of his kinsmen, there was no necessary congruence of geographical ranges. Individual movement was unrestricted as each man sought what he considered best in his own interests. Invariably a shift of more than a few miles was most likely to involve putting an increased distance between a man and at least some of his kin. This was certainly understood by the Ndendeuli: a man perceived that his most advantageous move could probably take him out of range of one or two (or more) otherwise valued kinsmen. This was inevitable in the circumstances, and it was accepted by the people; but it gave irregular patterns to men's kin-sets. Some first cousins, say, remained within range over the years, whilst others did not. This affected both those who had moved comparatively frequently —say, once a decade—and those who had remained in one community for a long period, such as those long-term residents of Ligomba (for example, Ali, Yasini, Konga).

Empirical data on kin-sets were derived from the sample survey of visiting by the eighty-three men. Figure 21 indicates an average and mean size of kin-sets of a little over thirty kinsmen, of whom approximately two thirds were cognates and one third were affines. The range was between thirteen and fifty-seven kinsmen. These figures are probably underestimates, because of the somewhat arbitrary conditions of the survey, although it has been possible to take account of each individual member of each kinship category (for example, each FBS of an informant). There were also a

---

[4] Many older men living in eastern Undendeuli had formerly, in early colonial times, lived in western Undendeuli. They had second cousins who had not shifted eastwards—or who had moved back again—and who still lived in the western area.

FIGURE 21: The Composition of Kin-sets. (From a sample of 83 men, as
for Fig. 20.)

(A) *The sizes of kin-sets*

Number of kinsmen	Number of men in sample
Less than 20	10
20–29	21
30–39	29
40–49	17
over 50	6
	83

(B) *The constitution of kin-sets*

	Cognates			Affines			Total for 83 men
	I	II	III	I	II	III	
Total	334	457	926	346	383	241	2687
Average	4.0	5.5	11.2	4.2	4.6	2.9	32.4

Cognates:

I F, B, S
   FF, MF
   SS, DS

II 1st cousins
    parents' brothers
    siblings' sons
    sons of BS, ZS

III 2nd cousins
     parents' 1st cousins
     others

Affines:

I WB, WF, ZH, DH

II F, B, S, of category I, and of SW,
    and BW
    BDH, FZH

III others

number of men not included because of absence (probably temporary in most cases) from home during the survey period. The data
are, then, no more than approximate indications.

The sizes of kin-sets were not particularly large, and the genealogical cut-off is again demonstrated here. It is not possible, nor
perhaps necessary, to give full details of the survey data here; but
the full composition of the kin-sets of three Ligomba men is given
in Figure 22. The idiosyncratic character of kin-sets is apparent,

FIGURE 22: Three Examples of Kin-sets, as Measured by the Criterion of Visiting.

	Cognates			Affines		
	I	II	III	I	II	III
Ali C7						
(aged c. 55)	1DS	1FBS	3FBSS	2DH	1DHB	1WFBS
		2FZS	2FFBSS	1ZH	1DHF	1DHZH
total		2MZS	1FMBSS	1WB	1ZHB	1ZSWF
32 kinsmen		4ZS	1FZDS		1WBS	
			1MZSS			
			1MMBS			
			1MMBSS			
			1MFZSS			
Konga C17						
(aged c. 60)	2B	2FBS	3FBSS	1DH	2WBS	1FBSWB
	4S	3FZS	3FFBSS	1ZH	2SWF	1MBDH
total		2MBS	1FFZS	2WB	3SWB	1MZDH
42 kinsmen		1ZS	1FFZSS		1BWB	
			1FMBDS		1BDH	
			1MBSS			
			1MBDS			
			1MZSS			
Salimi Di						
(aged c. 30)	1B	2FBS	2FFBSS	2WB	1FZH	1FBWB
		1FZS	1FFBS	2ZH		1FBWBS
total		1BS	1MFBDS			1WBWF
19 kinsmen		1ZS				1WZH

NOTE: Categorization of kinsmen is explained in Figure 21.

and also the limited numbers of second cousins and parents' first cousins who were included.

There was some tendency for older men to have rather larger kin-sets than younger men, though this was not at all inevitable. The small size of the kin-set of Salimi (D1) (Fig. 22) was at least partly the result of the scarcity of his cognates. His mother had no siblings who reached adulthood, and his deceased father had one brother and one sister. These three illustrative cases are not presented as "typical", but they are given here for the tentative picture they can provide.

DIFFERENTIATION WITHIN THE KIN-SET

The range of men's kinship relations contained a fairly large number of genealogically defined linkages, and the genealogical structure of kin-sets showed a good deal of irregularity. The pattern of actual social relations was, however, very much simpler both in ideal and in practice: the pattern of expectations and the realisation of rights, privileges, obligations, responsibilities, modes and degrees of cooperation and reciprocal assistance. I start first with the folk-model, which is the simpler pattern, and thereafter consider actual variations from that model. The folk-model was an essentially static one, and thus it makes some sense both in exposition and logic to start with this, and then to proceed to "set it to work" in order to analyse the dynamic reality.[5]

The Ndendeuli model appeared quite clearly and unambiguously in their general statements of right behaviour and expectations. They worked with a two-generational model—ego's own generation and that of either his father or his son. Older men perceived kinsmen as those of their own generation, "brothers", and of their sons' generation; younger men perceived kinsmen as "brothers" and "fathers". Thus overall there were three basic kin terms for adult males: "father", *tati;* "brother", *nkuru;* and "son", *mwana.* These three terms allowed for the reciprocal terms of reference and address within the two-generational model. That model could be extended if necessary: younger men could include "grandfather", *hukuru,* and older men could include "grandson", *mchuku,* though this happened rather infrequently. These generational categories of kinsmen could be further divided into primary and secondary: "big, senior", *kurungwa,* and "small, junior", *kepa,* or sometimes "near" and "distant", respectively. These terms referred principally to adult men who were heads of their own autonomous households, for it was relations between such men that were principally important. There were separate terms for more specific genealogical categories of kinsmen, but these were infrequently used.

---

[5] This procedure was followed by Bailey (1960) in a quite different ethnographic and theoretical context. Then Bailey was primarily concerned with the analysis of radical social change. His methodology is, however, equally applicable to the study of social dynamics in a case where radical change is not particularly marked.

They were, in a way, unnecessary to the conceptual model, and perhaps men did not wish to make the finer discriminations which conflicted with that model, and, indeed, with actual practical social relations. There was a similar generalisation of kinswomen (essentially, for the model, wives of kinsmen) into "mother", *amaje;* "sister", *numba;* and "daughter", *mchikana;* with "grandmother", *ambuja*, and "granddaughter", *mchuku*, added when necessary.

This generational model has been referred to earlier in this book.[6] Briefly, a degree of respect and superiority was given by "sons" to "fathers", so that expectations between them tended to be tinged with reserve and restraint. Relations between them were perceived as slightly asymmetrical: a "father" could, with caution, make greater or less easily avoidable demands than a "son", and a "father" recognised rather more responsibility towards "sons". Kinsmen of the same generation were "brothers" and equals, treating one another with cordial familiarity and ease, and making roughly equal kinds of demands on one another.

The ascription of kinsmen between "big" and "small" (primary and secondary) categories within a generation was less definite, but in ideal at least it was sufficiently clear. Primary kin were as follows:

> "big father"—own F, FB, MB, WF
> "big brother"—own B, first cousins, WB, ZH
> "big son"—own S, BS, ZS, DH

whilst secondary kinsmen comprised all others in the relevant generation.

All this provided a most simple and straightforward model. It was less straightforward in actual application, but even then the modifications required were such as to allow greater flexibility in the use of terms and of corresponding expectations and fulfillment of behaviour, rather than fundamental modifications of the basic model itself. That model can, in its simplest elements, be illustrated diagrammatically as shown in Figure 23.

Empirically, both kin-sets and local communities usually contained members of only two generations. Although a minority of younger and older men included "grandfather" and "grandson" respectively in their kin-sets, this was generally uncommon. The majority of men included kinsmen of two generations only. This was the case also in the closed kinship networks of those local

[6] See pages 223 ff.

communities that were sufficiently investigated for this purpose.
Ligomba and Namabeya seem to have been representative in
that sense.[7] Nevertheless, a three-generational model was required
to cover these two situations adequately, since the recognition of
"father" logically prescribed the reciprocal term and behavioural
expectations of "sons" and vice versa.

It is important to note that this two/three generational system
was not especially institutionalised or given ritual and symbolic
identification, nor was it rigid in practice. Only to a minor extent
did men perceive themselves as members of one generation vis-à-
vis an older or younger generation, and there was no unambiguous
form of reference to the generic concept of generation itself. Kinsmen who, though of a different genealogical generation, were
roughly the same age as ego tended to be treated as if they were

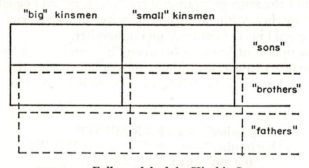

FIGURE 23: Folk-model of the Kinship System.

"brothers"; similarly, a large age difference between ego and a
man of his own generation tended, in ego's conceptions and behaviour, to push that man into an older or younger generational
category. This seldom raised problems of inconsistency, for the
purely genealogical link was held to be of minor importance.

The vertical, non-generational feature of the model—distinction
between "big" and "small" kinsmen—served to limit the purely
generational feature in relevant conformity to actual expectations
and behaviour between kin. That is, in terms of reliability and
regularity of cooperation and assistance, there were stronger expectations towards *all* primary kinsmen as against all secondary
kinsmen; such expectations were, I think, more consistently ful-

[7] Cf. the master genealogies of these communities. In Namabeya there
was, however, a single exception: P2, who was MF of R13, and acknowledged as "grandfather" by R10, R11, and R12.

filled. In a conflict of loyalties and obligations, a man felt compelled, indeed for his own advantages he was compelled, to give priority to any primary kinsman in preference to any secondary kinsman. A man acceded more readily and more frequently to the demands of primary kin (whether "father", "brother", or "son"), and likewise made greater and more frequent demands on such people. In concrete practice this categorisation commonly overrode the generational distinction, making it only subordinate.

The principal flexibility in the application of this model was evident in the allocation of kinsmen to the categories of "big" and "small". So far I have followed the scheme of the people themselves when they were prepared to generalise about it. I may have tended to make the folk-model more rigid than the Ndendeuli did, although informants were certainly able to ascribe kinsmen to those categories on the standard genealogical basis. Nevertheless, purely genealogical linkage was rather unimportant for the Ndendeuli. It was clearly important, however, that a man's own father, brothers, and sons were "big" kinsmen *par excellence*, and never "small" kinsmen: though in some cases, such a person might be effectively excluded altogether from a man's kin-set when, usually quite deliberately, a marked geographical separation of their residence had been established by one or both of the men concerned. Most usually, other kinsmen of the model-ascription category of "big" were so treated in actual practice, but not always and not necessarily. For example, a mother's brother or a first cousin who lived near the geographical limits of social intercourse might in effect be relegated to the category of "small" kinsman, and this would have been confirmed by terminological usage. Similarly, and sometimes applicable to the same kinsman, a man with whom experience had shown cooperation and reciprocal assistance to be unreliable or niggardly was also relegated to the secondary category. On the other hand, kinsmen ascribed in the ideal model to the secondary category might be treated as "big" kinsmen, for reasons the opposite of those given above. For example, a second cousin or a sister's husband's brother who lived in ego's local community and was a member of the same cluster within its kinship network was most likely to be treated as a primary kinsman: he would have been referred to and addressed as "big brother". Clearly in both types of variation from the model it was actual behaviour in practical interaction and cooperation that was decisive and that men were recognising in their verbal usages.

Thus far I have been giving priority to expectations and actual performance of assistance and cooperation. Important though they obviously were, they were subject to and in many ways a product of the network within which they occurred. To oversimplify slightly, primary kinsmen were in an important sense those with whom the relationship entailed many other inter-linking relationships. Or to put it in another way: the kin-sets of primary kinsmen tended to overlap to a greater extent than those of secondary kinsmen, as the former had more acknowledged kinsmen in common and, therefore, a wider area of inter-dependence. The primary kinsmen were more or less continuously involved, not only in each other's affairs and interests, but together in those of many common kinsmen. This degree of inter-dependence and co-activity tended to strengthen expectations and to raise the level of performance. A man was very likely to be induced to perform adequately by the totality of interacting expectations, and by the persuasive pressures of many kinsmen, not merely by those of the particular kinsman who was currently in need of assistance.[8]

Genealogically, other things being equal, the primary kinsmen of the model category should each have entailed a larger number of other, common kin than should a secondary kinsman. But of course other things were very seldom equal. The actual configuration of the kin-sets, of the network, was more significant. A mother's brother might have been rather unimportant in this way if a man had few other kinsmen whom he traced through his mother: the two men might therefore have become "small" kinsmen of each other, especially if they lived rather distant from each other. But with a different configuration, a MMBS might entail a significantly large number of other, common kinsmen, and then that man would have probably been ascribed to the primary category.

The matter was rather more complex than this, however, for the same kinsman could be ascribed as "big" or "small" according to the changing context of social action. Thus the wife's father's brother living in some other local community would generally have been a "small father", if he were acknowledged at all. But it might have happened that ego came into dispute with some other member of that community and that he then obtained the principal assistance in the matter from his wife's father's brother. On that occasion the latter would certainly warrant the designation of "big father"—not merely in flattering deference (though that was relevant), but because that man was in the particular context the principal kinsman working on ego's behalf. He was in the

[8] On the social control aspect of close-knit networks, see Epstein 1961.

circumstances the "big man".[9] As a result of this situation (especially if successfully concluded), the two kinsmen might thereafter have maintained closer and more regular cooperation in other matters. Ego would have assumed a debt of reciprocal obligation that could have flowered into a series of transactions above the level formerly established. This was not necessarily the case, and on a succeeding occasion the two men might equally have resumed the expectations, practice, and ascription of "small" kinsmen. A great deal depended on how far the two men could have assumed greater obligations to each other without raising undue complications and inconsistency in each of their existing kin-sets. One could not generalise about this, and neither could the men involved: it required a detailed knowledge of their kin-sets and a knowledge of the context of situations of interaction that occurred later. This would typically have been a case where Ndendeuli would have experimented to see if a change in expectations and obligations were practicably possible. This was a matter of empirical testing by the men concerned rather than ideology.

Similar contextual variations in the actual application of "big" and "small" were fairly common within a local community. A single example may be sufficient to make this point clear, important though it is. In Ligomba, in Case 5 ("A Cousins' Quarrel"), Tanda (C13) was definitely on the side of his sister's husband, the plaintiff Zadiki (C15)—his "big brother". As the case developed in the moot, Tanda showed increasing determination to prevent a decisive rupture of relations between Zadiki and the latter's first cousin, Konga (C17), who was acknowledged by Tanda as his kin-neighbour. Tanda consistently addressed Konga as "my small brother", thus affirming his kinship link and his desire to retain cooperative relations with Konga, but at the same time showing that Zadiki continued to be the more valuable kinsman for him personally. This was a most useful application of the terminology, and it conveyed in brief shorthand Tanda's desired expectations: to support Zadiki, but to remain friendly with Konga. A little later, in Case 6 ("An Errant Son-in-law"), Tanda, Zadiki, and Konga were all co-members of one action-set, with Konga as its effective leader. On this occasion Tanda and Konga addressed and referred to one another as "big brother", partly to emphasise their common cause (Tanda's son was the defendant), and partly to show the success of their continued friendly expectations of co-operation after the conclusion of the previous dispute.

It is unexceptionable that for flattery and persuasiveness a

[9] On the contextual significance of "big man", see page 245.

"small" kinsman was addressed as "big", just as in some other kinship systems a first cousin is addressed as "brother", or a half-brother as "full-brother", for the same sorts of reasons. This is a commonplace phenomenon. Sometimes, both in general and in the case of the Ndendeuli, it was assumed to be something of a deliberate slight if a kinsman were addressed by the lesser category of terminology. It might be discourteous, at the very least, to remind a kinsman of his implied lesser importance when he was fulfilling the demands legitimately made on him. Nevertheless this was not inevitably the case, and again the context was all important. It could have been flattering or indicative of genuine appreciation of services rendered, punctiliously to address a "small" kinsman as such and thus to acknowledge that the secondary kinsman *was* fulfilling his obligations properly, or even doing more than was minimally expected of him. For instance, in Case 6 just cited, Tanda addressed Sedi (C21) as "my small brother". Here no slight was, I believe, intended or received. Tanda was being complimentary to a neighbour (kinsman of a kinsman—ZSWF) who was a member of the action-set on behalf of Tanda's own son. Similarly, Faranz (D4) commonly referred to Saidi (C6) as his "small father", indicating (as I understood it) that despite their genealogical distance (WFMZS) he and Saidi acknowledged each other as kin-neighbours. In fact, Saidi was, apart from Faranz's wife's father, the only "father" he had at that time in Ligomba, and was therefore a highly valued kin-neighbour. The use of "small", reciprocally, suggested however that their relationship was produced primarily from their common involvement in a single cluster in the community's network. Before Faranz settled in Ligomba, he and Saidi had not acknowledged kinship at all; and quite possibly in later years, when one or both had moved elsewhere, the active relationship would die away as they lived in different communities.

On the other hand, an ideally "big" kinsman might for some reason not have been fulfilling the expectations of that category. To be referred to in that situation as "small" was then an expression of the speaker's opinion and disappointment. It was also an announcement to other involved men of the perceived failure, with the possible intention of gaining their support to persuade the kinsman to perform more adequately. And it could also have been an announcement that the speaker himself would not feel bound to strong reciprocal assistance in the future. That is, it was a statement about active expectations and behaviour, rather than about genealogical linkages.

Thus the nuances of meaning, of statements about actual relationships and expectations to each other and to other men, were variable and could be crucial to the transaction between the men, and even to a whole enterprise concerning several men. The particular meaning, the message conveyed, the acknowledgement of assistance or lack of it, and the intention to persuade, depended inherently on the particular context. A whole and even complex situation could be illuminated, tersely but clearly, by appropriate usage. My example of Tanda's references to Zadiki and Konga in Case 6 was such a case: it was selected for that reason, for it made clear not only the relationship between him and the two disputants, but the similar circumstances of several other neighbors involved in the dispute.

With their simple system of categories, the Ndendeuli had only a most limited range of expressiveness in communication. They seemed to use it to full effect. It must be admitted, frankly, that while in the field I was not properly alert to this contextual character of their kinship terminology, and therefore did not direct specific attention to this cultural feature. It is possible that some aspects of it went unrecorded in consequence. Nevertheless my case records are, in retrospect, abundantly clear so far as I have described the matter here.

Let me reiterate and emphasize two points in this connection. Firstly, the Ndendeuli placed more weight on actual relations, practical assistance, support and cooperation than on purely genealogical connections. To be sure, ego's own father, brothers, and sons were invariably "big", if active relations existed with them at all. Usually, but not inevitably, FB, MB, and WF were also "big", and similarly very close kinsmen in the other two generations. But a close genealogical link (however defined precisely) was pretty useless to an Ndendeuli if concrete interaction was absent. The close connection presupposed that it would be present, but this was not inevitably the case. Genealogically more distant kin would quite commonly be as reliable, regular, and generous in their assistance as nearer kin, sometimes more so. Thus Saidi was more advantageous at that time to Faranz than was his own father's brother who lived fifteen miles distant. Saidi was his "father" not because of direct kinship connection, but because in the context of the Ligomba network the two men became strongly inter-dependent within a cluster of inter-dependent kin-neighbours. The genealogical connection was in its details unimportant to either man. As I have noted earlier, Ndendeuli did not carry a comprehensive genealogical model primarily in mind, but rather a set of expectations based on past experience and sequences of transactions in the context of either the closed or the open network, as was relevant. This set of expectations ascribed acknowledged kinsmen to the simple categories. If these expectations were not fulfilled—or indeed, even if they were—the reference was not primarily to genealogical connection but to those previous transactions and the possibility of their extension into the future.[10]

Secondly, and also to reiterate earlier analysis, this contextual application of terminology operated in a social mode where rights and obligations associated with kinship were all of a common, generalised kind. There was exceedingly little of rights and obligations that was specifically prescribed to any particular kind of kinsman. Assistance, support, cooperation were required for economic enterprises, for ritual participation and performance, in dispute cases, for communication of news and opinion, for advice and sympathy. All kinsmen gave, and were expected to give, the same kind of assistance; only the degree of reliability, regularity, and extent varied. And that variation was encompassed by the fairly broad categories of "big" and "small", and of generation.

DYADIC RELATIONS

The emphasis throughout this book is principally on collective social action and the implications of the collective organization of social activities in a society without specialised roles and institutions of social control, and without kin groups or, indeed, organized corporate groups at all.[11] As I have argued already, and shall further exemplify later, interaction between two kinsmen was inevitably affected by the fact that they were enmeshed in a whole network of kinship relations. Men appreciated this fact and took account of it to a considerable extent, although the sociological implications, the effects on individual behaviour, and the limitations and compulsions on a man's decisions were more pervasive than they could altogether perceive.

[10] See Chapter Seven, page 220 ff.

[11] The local community can scarcely be considered a corporate group, for although it had a bounded membership and some sense of separate identity, it never acted as a unit. With the peripheral exception that members of a community could, in extremis, effectively exclude a man and his household from membership (that is, from participation in the pattern of cooperation, but not from the use of land), the community controlled no rights and interests.

Nevertheless, of course, a good deal of the active relationship between any two kinsmen (whether they were neighbours or lived in different communities) occurred overtly in a dyadic context, rather than in the collective context of action-sets. This is perfectly obvious, no doubt, although it has been under-emphasised in my analyses; but accounts of kinship systems have often tended to over-emphasise this feature as though pairs of kinsmen operated and maintained expectations in a vacuum.

There were many and recurrent situations of social need in which a man turned directly to an individual kinsman. His household might have been short of food in the early wet season; he may have required contributions of grain to provide beer and porridge on some ritual occasion; he may have been short of seed or have desired to modify his seed stock. A man could have been in need of money, to pay tax or a court fine, to repay a debt, or to pay compensation or a bridewealth instalment, or with which to buy some essential commodity (clothing, a tool, medicines). A man needed a sympathetic listener to his problems and perplexities, with or without advice; and he needed to obtain information relevant to his problems and interests, as well as news of a more general kind. He needed advice in ritual and religious matters. Much of a man's visiting was for these and similar purposes; but in any case, visiting involved a man in giving hospitality to his kinsman, and usually some small gift on his departure.

It is significant that an Ndendeuli turned to his kinsmen on these occasions. Conceivably he could have established conventions of reciprocal assistance, through a sequence of transactions, with unrelated men—neighbors who lived nearby in the same community, or a congenial acquaintance elsewhere who became a trusted friend. The extent of socially significant friendship was not easy to investigate. It had been hoped to enquire systematically on the visiting of friends during the survey of visiting with kinsmen, but this was prevented by the difficulty of defining "friend" and "visit". Neither a casual "dropping in whilst passing by" kind of visit, nor one for a single, isolated purpose (for example, to an official headman to pay tax, to a man to buy medicine) could be included. Instead I fell back on the inferior device of merely asking the men in my sample who their unrelated friends were. From this information I endeavoured to eliminate casual acquaintances and also atrophied relationships with youthful companions (such as co-migrants to an employment area years previously). Co-neighbours in the same community were also eliminated if they were the kin of kin, though that was a more doubtful procedure. The results for what they are worth—almost certainly some underestimate—are as follows:

Number of Unrelated Friends	Number of Men in Sample
0	17
1	39
2	15
3	4
4	1
	76 men

Thus a fifth of the men claimed no unrelated friend at all, and half claimed only a single friend. Only a small minority had more than two friends.[12] These results confirm what the Ndendeuli said in a general way, and also my own impressions during field research: that unrelated, personal friends were few and that they were rather unimportant to social life. The Ndendeuli explanation of this was that whereas a kinsman could be trusted and had to accede to requests for assistance *because* he was a kinsman, an unrelated man was unlikely to be so concerned, could not be trusted, and had no need to entertain obligations nor right to make demands. The sociological explanation follows the general argument of this book: an unrelated man would be involved in interdependencies in his own sector of the kinship network, and not in the sector involving ego. The inclusion of such an unrelated person among ego's close associates was likely, therefore, sooner or later, to raise problems of inconsistency and conflicts of loyalties and obligations in which that unrelated person would be the obvious man out. It is significant that, although there might be affection and trust between unrelated friends, such non-kinsmen were seldom expected to give of their labour or their goods, or to participate in a man's action-sets.[13]

Most commonly, as far as I could discover, when Ndendeuli men developed inter-personal friendships, these were with men with whom they were already associated in the kinship network.

[12] The man with four friends was Amiri, the notable in Namabeya community (cf. page 261 f.). At least two of those friends appeared to be political associates in the campaign that year for Undendeuli autonomy.

[13] An exceptional case where a close friendship produced relations tantamount to kinship was noted at page 63.

Typically a man's friends were made amongst his "brothers", kinsmen of about the same age and generation. In Ligomba the outstanding example was the friendship between the brothers-in-law, Tanda and Zadiki, who spent a great deal of their time together and invariably assisted and supported each other in their enterprises. But most, perhaps all, Ligomba men had one or two kinsmen, both within the community and elsewhere, with whom they were especially friendly in an inter-personal sense. The two notables, Ali and Konga, had a long-standing friendship going back at least to the founding of Ligomba; but in that case there was an added element of mutual advantage in their common antagonism to the third notable, Kabaya, and in their willingness and efforts to maintain toleration and cooperation between their respective clusters of kin-neighbours. That is, in this case friendship was associated with political alliance.

PATRILATERAL BIAS

The empirical mean demonstrated by the survey data on active kinship relations (Fig. 20, p. 282) and the examples of actual kinsets (Fig. 22, p. 291) show a degree of patrilateral bias in the Ndendeuli cognatic/affinal kinship system. This calls for some comment.

Among cognates, there was a tendency for links through the father to be more emphasised than those through the mother. To a lesser extent, links through a brother (in any generation) were more common than those through a sister. This is most clearly seen among second cousins. Here, among the five second cousins occurring in the statistical model, four were patrilateral, and three of those were linked through the father's father. By contrast, of the eleven types of more disregarded second cousins, seven were matrilateral and only one was linked through the father's father (that is, FFZDS). Second cousins tended to be on the periphery of the range of active kinship relations, but the cut-off was much greater for matrilateral than for patrilateral cousins. Similar bias was indicated also by the rather higher frequency with which men visited with patrilateral kinsmen than with the directly comparable matrilateral kinsmen (for example, *cf.* FBS and MZS).

Concerning affines: in the statistical model these were the nearer agnates of spouses. Pre-eminently they were fathers and brothers of spouses, but also included were WFB (but not WMB), and

WFBS (but not WMBS). Other kinsmen of a spouse were most likely to be regarded and treated only as the kin of kin—for example, the mother's brother or a sister's husband.

A man's property, it was generally said, should be inherited by his sons or brothers. The significance of this was its expression of orientation and attitude, rather than its material content and its effect on social relations directly. The amount of heritable property was limited to meagre personal effects such as a little clothing, a few tools and ornaments, and perhaps a little money. Ndendeuli technology and production allowed little accumulation of wealth from year to year, even when tobacco was cultivated as a cash crop; though by their prevailing standards these small amounts were not altogether negligible. Land rights were entirely ephemeral under the shifting cultivation regime, so it was seldom worthwhile for an heir to move to the dead man's hamlet and fields. If he lived in the same hamlet he could, however, take over any unexhausted field and usable buildings or building materials.

Inheritance of rights over widows and unmarried children were also generally said to be the privilege of brothers or sons. The ideal norm was not altogether clear, but perhaps most Ndendeuli would have agreed that these rights should go to a brother, failing him a son, and failing him a patrilateral cousin.[14] There was rather little to constrain a widow, if still fairly young, to accept the ideal heir if she preferred another man. Without systematic data, my impression was that a widow's choice was decisive, and that she tended to choose a man who had no wife. Nevertheless, from evidence culled afterwards from my genealogical records, twenty-nine out of forty-six younger widows were inherited by near agnates of their late husbands—brother, patrilateral cousin, father's younger brother. This again suggests a certain strength to the patrilateral connection.

The patrilateral bias directly related to two factors in Ndendeuli social life. One is that we are dealing with a range of social action between male household heads. In the activities and interests with which they were concerned, men logically gave greater weight to relations with other men; but also they stressed relationships established through other men (rather than through women). In part, the patrilateral bias was a masculine bias.

---

[14] Polygyny was uncommon and therefore cases of a son inheriting a young co-wife of his mother were rare. A son could, however, inherit rights over and responsibilities to his own immature siblings. His mother, especially if elderly, would then occupy her own house in his hamlet and become a dependent of his household.

The second and more important factor derived from the actual norm of residence after marriage. As described earlier (p. 56), a man was free to choose his place of residence when he became head of his own autonomous household, unless he was engaged in suitor-service obligations with the necessity of uxorilocal residence for some years. Without suitor-service, as the majority of men were, there were no direct restrictions on choice, although there were certain advantages of a generalised kind that induced a high degree of consensus among newly married men. The large majority chose to remain and live in their father's hamlet, if the father were still alive. This not only represented the younger men who had fairly recently married, but perhaps as many as half of the then middle-aged men (that is, most of those who had in their youth given bridewealth rather than suitor-service). But even among those who had engaged in suitor-service, there were many who had nevertheless returned to their father's hamlet after completion of uxorilocal obligations. In Figure 2 (p. 59) it was shown that 44 percent of multiple household hamlets comprised a man and some of his sons. My data are regrettably vague, but perhaps as many as two thirds of young household heads began their careers in such a hamlet. An examination of the Ligomba and Namabeya data well supports this assessment.

Why should this have been so? Household heads had no property rights of consequence to safeguard, neither were they subject to the legal or ritual superiority of the father.[15] Ndendeuli expressed the ideal expectation that sons should remain with the father, but certainly it could not in any sense have been prescribed and enforced. On the other hand, a young household head had need of a "father" whose experience, knowledge, and skill he could use as he began to develop his potentialities and to seek reliable cooperation in his new enterprises. It was advantageous and convenient for him to plug into the already existing set of kinship relations, especially kin-neighbour relations, of a "father"—and most convenient of all to look to his own father in this matter. The young man's kin-set would have been, in the first instance, virtually the same as that of his father, particularly within the cluster of kin-neighbours. His father would most usually have developed a

[15] The Ndendeuli case may be compared with, for instance, that of the Arusha of northern Tanzania. There sons of whatever age and extra-familial status were legally and ritually minors, dependent on their fathers whilst the latter remained alive. Fathers retained control over both land and livestock, although allocations were made to married sons (Gulliver 1964).

moderately consistent set of kin-neighbours with whom his reciprocal obligations worked fairly well in concrete practice. By
the kind of experimenting previously described, and by recognising
the priorities of those relationships that entailed several or many
others, the father by experience knew what worked and what on
the whole did not work in reciprocity within the closed network.
The young man could move into the father's cluster within the
community's network, with access to its leading notable. All this
offered advantages in contrast with the possibility of starting from
scratch in a new community among neighbours whose potential
was comparatively unknown; it was easier to start off, as men
pointed out, in the community where one knew and was known
by the neighbours and the father's associates. A young man could
(and some did) plug into the existing set of kinship relations of
some other "father" in another community, but this was less
advantageous unless father-son relations were personally of a
hostile kind from which the young man was seeking escape.

A young man soon began to develop his own idiosyncratic set
of kin-neighbours, emphasising those of his own generation rather
than those of his father's generation,[16] at least partly as a means of
expressing his own individual autonomy in his own field of social
action. But many of his father's kin-neighbours remained valuable
associates to him. Like his father, they were able to give advice,
information, and assistance; some at least were likely to be important members of his action-sets in cases of disputes because of their
forensic skill and experience.

The decision about residence was made easier by what were
generally non-authoritarian, even indulgent, relations between
father and sons. Fathers had little opportunity to domineer over
adult sons, and many informants spoke of the necessity to be
lenient and to retain filial goodwill. The socio-psychological aspects
are not my concern here, but I note that Ndendeuli fathers were
much more tolerant and easy-going with even their non-adult sons
than was the case in so many East African societies where fathers
controlled property rights and other social potentials of decisive
concern to their sons.[17]

It was, of course, to the advantage of the father that his son
should elect and remain content to live in his hamlet. He gained
valuable, reliable addition to the labour potential on which he
could draw. He gained, to a limited extent, a follower for whom

[16] On this matter, see page 223 ff.
[17] Cf. Gray and Gulliver 1964, *passim*.

he often acted as spokesman in the community, thus enhancing his prestige and influence. He gained a man who would succour him in his old age. Therefore he was generally prepared to make it worthwhile for his sons to remain with him.

All this meant, first, that a man remaining with his father tended to give emphasis to the kinship relations established by his father. And, second, it meant that brothers, at least in their earlier adult years, tended to live together and to develop much the same range of kinship relations. This was afterwards interrupted as, at least in middle age, brothers separated—certainly by the time of their own sons' adulthood—and often came to live in different communities. Nevertheless those earlier adult years had sufficient formative influence that the patrilateral bias was commonly established. Brothers were likely to have markedly overlapping kin-sets, and so would their sons in turn, looking back to the father's father's brothers' descendants. Had the social necessities and advantages induced each man to live with, say, his wife's father, then brothers would have been separated from the start of married life and it is most probable that no patrilateral bias would have occurred.[18]

It should be noted, however, that there were exceptions to early virilocal marriage residence. Some sons lived with the wife's father (usually, though not invariably, connected with suitor-service); some went to live with another "father". As far as I could tell, these were (apart from cases where the real father was dead) instances in which there was some inter-personal animosity between father and son, or between brothers. Young married men then considered it more advantageous to seek an alternative "father", or to join "brothers" elsewhere and to seek to establish kin-neighbour relations through them. In these kinds of cases men's kin-sets showed much less patrilateral bias, even none at all.

Finally, I note that the patrilateral bias did not lead to patrilineal

[18] This raises the question: when suitor-service and uxorilocal residence in the early years of marriage were the most common practice—at least as late as the early part of this century, according to informants—was the patrilateral bias largely absent? I can give no answer to this, for the data were not collected or, perhaps, collectible. Logically I would assume this to have been the case. The growing use of bridewealth during the first half of this century is likely, therefore, to have produced a change in the pattern of kin-sets. On the other hand, the essential principles of the network and the cognatic/affinal system, and the factors involving decision making, have themselves probably not changed much as a direct result. More significant changes probably came from the territorial expansion of the Ndendeuli into new eastern areas, and their autonomy from Ngoni overrule.

groupings beyond those of father and sons, as Figure 2*b* indicates. Brothers did eventually separate, and their sons eventually separated in the succeeding generation. Patrilateral kin were irresistibly divided in the long run by the diversity of their kin-sets—by the advantages of cooperation and interaction with other cognates and with affinal kin.

One other feature may be conveniently mentioned here, to complete the ethnographic record. The Ndendeuli had patronymics, the generic term for which (*Ibongo, s. kibongo*) clearly derived from the patrilineal praise-names (*chibongo*) of the Ngoni. The evidence is that Ndendeuli were compelled to adopt these patronymics for identification purposes by their Ngoni overlords. This usage was taken over by German and then British colonial authorities for bureaucratic purposes in tax collection and court records. Some of the patronymics were brought in by war-captives who became absorbed among the Ndendeuli. Some appear to be of matrilineal, Yao or Makonde, origin. Others, more truly local, derived from what seem to have been the names of localities in which the autochthonous Ndendeuli lived at the time of Ngoni conquest. Because of official requirements, every man (but not all women) knew his patronymic, though it was of no interest to him otherwise. I do not recall hearing these names used in non-official contexts. Certainly a common patronymic ascribed no kind of relationship or expectations between men. The same phenomenon, and some of the same names, also existed among other former subject peoples of the two Ngoni chiefdoms in the Songea District, where they appeared to be similarly unimportant.

MARRIAGE

Most Ndendeuli would state in general terms that marriage with a kinswoman of any known degree of genealogical relationship was wrong. This was often phrased in the form: "A man cannot marry a sister". It would also be explained that sisters of acknowledged affines were similarly excluded. Nevertheless a few marriages did occur within those limits, and apparently without especial concern or ritual repercussion, even between first cross cousins. No case was recorded, even by hearsay, of marriage between first parallel cousins. From my genealogical records, less than 3 percent of all known marriages were between cognatic or affinal kin.

Although Ndendeuli men recognised and condemned incest,

they were—but I report impressionistically—rather little concerned about it, at least overtly. By contrast, considerable importance and interest were commonly given to a more practical issue. Marriage was regarded, inter alia, as a means of establishing new, valuable, kinship ties, especially with the wife's father and brothers who would probably become "big" kinsmen. It was a means, that is, of enlarging a man's kin-set, and in a secondary sense those of his own father and brothers also since they thereby acquired additional "small" kinsmen. Many informants emphasized that, as it was often put, "a man can choose his own affines"; and moreover he could seek to choose congenial ones and ones who would, if he so desired, improve the geographical distribution of his kin-set and give access, or better access, to other local communities. The implication here was, inter alia, that a man's cognates were ascribed, though this was in fact true only up to a point in a system like that of the Ndendeuli. The general argument was perfectly sound, however. It was considered foolish and wasteful of opportunity to marry the daughter of a man with whom there was already an active, acknowledged, kinship relationship. One of my most perceptive informants (Ali of Ligomba) explained the matter as follows. "Can one of your fathers become your father-in-law? He is already your father, and so you cannot make him your father a second time. But you want another father, yes, and new brothers also; and that is good for then you obtain other big kinsmen who will help you". As previously explained, a father-in-law was, or at least could be, equivalent more or less to a man's own father. By "father" at the beginning of that quotation, Ali explained that he meant father's brother and mother's brother in particular, but also "any kind of father, whether he is big or small".

The father and brother of a man's wife were regarded as particularly important to him because in a sense they were peculiar to him alone. Their relationship with his own father and brothers was commonly less close and less reliable. Thus to some extent a man's social identity, the individual divergence of his kin-set from those of his nearest cognates, was gained and expressed through these affines. That was again the case when his daughter married. This was less important, probably, than the aspect of increasing the size and range of a man's kin-set through marriage; but it was nonetheless not unimportant. It may to some extent explain the slightly emotional character of a man's relations with his father-in-law in contrast with those with a father's or mother's brother, and likewise the rather special camaraderie so common between brothers-in-law.[19]

Intra-community marriage was also uncommon. It is impossible to be sure what proportion of marriages had occurred between neighbours, because of the problem of sorting out the complexities of residential movement over a period of time. I neglected to record whether spouses were, at the time of marriage, members of the same community; and my field notes are confused by the numbers of men who joined the wife's community at marriage. My impression is that only infrequently was intra-community marriage advantageous by linking together men who had previously been only neighbours. This kind of marriage could create difficulties greater than the advantages offered, and for that reason at least some informants were opposed to them. The creation of new, potentially close, kinship links between hitherto "unrelated" neighbours could raise very difficult problems of conflicting obligations. The husband and the wife's father, along with some of their existing kin-neighbours, had to make the new obligations of assistance and cooperation reasonably consistent with those they already had in the community. In most cases, considerable readjustment of kin-neighbour relations was required, and this could leave tensions and conflict. There might be serious conflicts between the existing clusters in the kinship network. In Ligomba this had occurred pre-eminently as a result of the marriage of Zadiki's son and Sedi's daughter. Inherent conflicts of obligations and interests between Zadiki and Sedi, and between Sedi and his son-in-law, underlay the disputes, processes settlement, and resultant consequences in Cases 2, 4, and 5. The marriage of Yasini's daughter and Kabaya's son was probably made at least partly on Kabaya's initiative in order to widen his range of kin-neighbours in Ligomba at a time when he was still a comparative newcomer. It had raised a number

[19] Most of the interest among anthropologists in the running debate on marriage and alliance seems to have focussed on alliances between *groups* and which are maintained by marriages between men and women who are already kin (that is, some preferential rule operating). Rather less attention has been given to alliances between individuals (for example, husband and WB; WF and HF) that are deliberately sought by marriage choices, and that are often preferentially between non-kin, in order to extend the range of advantageous connections available to the individual. This can happen where there are no groups that can come into alliance (as among the Ndendeuli), or where groups are weak (as among the Turkana; Gulliver 1965(a):226); but it may occur where there are important corporate kin groups (as among the Northern Somali; Lewis 1962:24).

of problems since that time, and put Yasini and his son in recurrent conflict situations: Work-Party Case 1 provides an excellent example of this (p. 203).

In summary then, marriage was seen as a most important means of extending a man's kin-set, and dislike of inter-kin marriage is chiefly traceable to that fact. Intra-community marriage was also disliked since it could raise acute problems of conflict amongst neighbours in the closed network, though it could occasionally be practiced as a means of extending the range of kin-neighbours.

At the time of field research, a majority of marriages were being established by the transfer of bridewealth in cash. The size of bridewealth was not fixed, not even ideally, but depended on negotiations between a man and his son-in-law. It was almost invariably given in instalments over a period of years following the wedding and a first payment. The wife's father or brother sought to obtain further instalments as and when he could, whenever it was thought that the husband had acquired money: on receipt of payment for crops (especially tobacco) or of bridewealth for a sister; on return from local employment or labor migration; and so on. There was not only no fixed amount of bridewealth, but no fixed period for its completion. In many cases demands ceased as the marriage became well established and affinal relations became reliable and mutually advantageous. But there were more disputes over bridewealth (the major transfer of wealth among these people) than over any other matter. Several cases are described in this book.[20] A son-in-law could seek to obtain a public declaration by his wife's father of the final completion of payments—usually when new demand was made, as in Case 2. Completed bridewealths in the decade prior to the research period ranged between 100 and 300 shillings, as far as reliable evidence could be obtained in what was a difficult matter of research. The average was, roughly, rather less than 200 shillings.

It was generally agreed by informants that bridewealth was formerly uncommon, and that it was not original Ndendeuli custom. This is probably true, for similar information has been reported from the related Ngindo peoples to the north-east of Undendeuli. It was said that the institution of bridewealth was introduced by the Ngoni, among whom it was essential, since the chiefs refused to recognise marriage without it. Bridewealth became prestigeful among Ndendeuli; but far more importantly, it provided a welcome alternative to traditional suitor-service. Under that system, a

[20] Cases 2, 6, and 9, and at page 262.

suitor, on acceptance by the girl's father, gave labour services—
on an occasional basis before marriage (following pre-adolescent
betrothal of the girl), and more continuously after marriage, with
compulsory uxorilocal residence. Service consisted of labour in the
fields, building and repair work, and a general obligation to carry
messages, accompany the father-in-law when he was visiting or
engaged in public affairs, and attendance to his domestic comforts.
The period of suitor-service, like the period of bridewealth payments, was indefinite. Informants suggested that three or four years
were typical.

Younger Ndendeuli were unanimous in resisting suitor-service
by the middle of this century. It was explicitly likened to slavery.
A principal incentive for labour migration has been the desire of
unmarried men to obtain money for bridewealth and thus to avoid
service. But money remained scarce relative to the size of bridewealth demands, and neither labour migration nor tobacco cultivation was certain to produce sufficient cash after other kinship obligations to give shares had been met. Consequently some cases of
full suitor-service still occurred in the nineteen-fifties, and there
were others in which a combination of bridewealth and service
occurred.

Despite the stereotype epithet of "slavery", suitor-service was
not invariably harsh and onerous. In a number of cases, obviously
a perceptive man had refrained from requiring too exacting and
arduous services from his son-in-law, and had concentrated on
developing a mutually advantageous relationship that would endure
beyond the period of service. The aim was to gain a reliable "big"
kinsman, hopefully a "son" who would agree to remain in the
man's hamlet or local community afterwards. Ali had succeeded
in this with his son-in-law, Faranz, and so had Sedi with Hanju, in
Ligomba. Ali's success was achieved in competition with Faranz's
own father; but Hanju had neither father nor father's brother and
was, I believe, contented to have gained a "big" father in Sedi. It is
most probable, however, that with the majority of men paying
bridewealth, fewer men will become residentially associated with
their father-in-law.

X

Cooperation and Conflict
in the Wider Society

As we have seen, each household head had at any time a range of cognatic and affinal kinsmen—his kin-set—some of whom were his kin-neighbours, whilst others (the majority) lived scattered in various local communities within a radius of about twenty miles from his hamlet. These were men with first degree linkages to ego. A man also engaged in active social relationships with some non-kinsmen who were acknowledged as kin by one or more members of his kin-set: the kin of kin. He had contact and joined in common enterprises with the kin of kin on behalf of the common kinsman; and through the latter's intermediation he could sometimes obtain the assistance of such men in his own enterprises. These were men with second degree linkages to ego. In addition there were third degree linkages—with kin of the kinsman of a kinsman —with whom a man might occasionally be actively associated, say, in some enterprise on behalf of a first or second degree man.

This third degree level was virtually the limit of the kinship system and the kinship network for a particular individual. Beyond that, other men were (apart from particular, idiosyncratic acquaintanceship) largely an undifferentiated mass of unrelated persons of whom a man had only the generalised expectations of an Ndendeuli. The periphery of the kinship network was vague and shifting, but for the individual man it was not an infinite network. From the observer's point of view, however, the network was unbounded, for kinship linkages continued to extend outwards to include, presumably, all Ndendeuli and people beyond. There is no reason to suppose that this network was limited or bounded in any direction, although Ndendeuli themselves did not know this, nor was it of concern to them. In so far as they perceived connections with people beyond about the third degree level, it was in terms of common language, common culture, common social conditions and problems, and a degree of geographical contiguity. It is unlikely, in view of the smallness of scale of economic and political action and interests, that the effects of decisions and arrangements and their results spread very far through the network from one area to another. The ripples on the pond soon died down, or at least they became so attenuated that they were no longer readily perceptible.

The open network was not, of course, a linear phenomenon, for it stretched away indefinitely on all sides for each individual. It was also convolute, so that linkage with another man of first, second, or third degree range was not usually single stranded. That is, linkages could be, and often were in particular contexts, traced by more than a single route through the network. Beyond the second degree range, linkages were very often more or less unknown by the men involved until particular situations evoked and activated third degree or even more indirect range of linkages. For instance, where two men were linked in potential alliance as the kin of kin (say, the first cousin of a first cousin), they would occasionally have been directly associated in common activity. On a particular occasion they could have found themselves on opposite sides in a dispute where the principals had first or second degree linkage with each man respectively. Those principals would then have been connected by fourth or fifth degree linkage in a manner significant both to them and to their associates. Indeed this is not merely suppositional, for something like it not infrequently occurred and was intelligible and manageable—to the Ndendeuli by contextual operation, and to the observer through the concept of the open network.

In this chapter I am concerned with the further sociological implications of this open network of kinship linkages for the behaviour and interaction of men who were associated together directly or by a sequence of links. Attention is directed to the potential opportunities and to the limitations bearing on individual choice. Two aspects of social need and of interaction are considered, both of which involved men beyond their own local communities. Firstly, I deal with the processes that occurred when disputes arose between men residing in different communities—between men who were not constrained within the closed network of a single local community. Such disputes could occur between men who were related by known, acknowledged kinship linkages, or between men whose linkage was not known to them and perhaps was highly indirect. Secondly, I examine the phenomenon of residential movement. This was clearly bound up with but not entirely subsumed by the requirements of shifting cultivation. Residential movement, as indeed the cultivation regime, was also a social phenomenon subject to and organized through the open kinship network.

PROCESSES OF DISPUTE SETTLEMENT
BEYOND THE LOCAL COMMUNITY

In many ways these processes were similar to those operating within the closed network of a local community, as described in Chapter Five. A plaintiff, unable to obtain acceptable satisfaction by private negotiation, sought to put the matter into the public arena by having it openly discussed in a moot, with some of his kinsmen and kin of his kinsmen as supporters and advocates. Within the same local community, it was seldom a major problem to secure the agreement of the defendant and to convene a moot, for their neighbours were so inter-linked that a defendant was scarcely able to withstand the demand to defend himself and to state his own case. Moreover, each principal had kin-neighbours, and also the kin of kin, who were his automatic supporters; and so there was little problem of gaining supporters, although the allegiance and responsibility of certain neighbours might be ambiguous. Where the defendant lived in a community different from that of the plaintiff, the problem was for the latter to recruit supporters in that other community who, he hoped, could utilise that community's network, bring pressures to bear on the defendant, and achieve a settlement of the issue in dispute. In such a case, the plaintiff was an outsider in the defendant's community, so that he could not himself directly manipulate the closed network in his own interests. If the plaintiff had kinsmen (members of his kin-set) in that community, he had the possibility of exerting leverage —though how far he could be successful depended on who those kinsmen were and what their position was vis-à-vis the defendant. Of course, the defendant might in any event have been willing to have the dispute considered in a moot; but then the plaintiff still had the problem of recruiting an action-set for the moot.

The extreme situation was that in which the plaintiff had no kinsmen or kin of kinsmen who were resident in the defendant's community. His case was then likely to go by default, even if he could convene a moot, since his action-set would have been composed of outsiders with weak ability to bring pressure to bear on the defendant. His main hope then would have been to find men who were related to both principals, even though living elsewhere, who might act at least as mediators. The more widely the members of a man's kin-set were distributed among other local communities, the more fortunate he was in having entrée to those communities in the event of a dispute arising with one of their members. There was, however, little that a man could do to influence the distribution of his kinsmen, other than by his choices in marriage.[1]

By accident, or through highly complex residential movements and kinship relations over the years, most men had kinsmen living in nearby communities—that is, communities with whose members they were more likely to have social intercourse and thus the possibility of dispute. But for most, perhaps all, men there were other communities in which they had no resident kin.

In the event of a dispute, the plaintiff therefore sought to activate kinship claims upon certain men: those who were neighbours of the defendant, and those who through other inter-linkages might be able to exert some influence directly or indirectly against the defendant and his more important supporters. If the plaintiff were able to reach the stage of a moot, the negotiations there were essentially the same as in an intra-community moot. Action-sets were, however, more heterogeneous and sometimes less easily managed. Some or many of the participants in the moot were "unrelated" or only indirectly linked, and so the kinds and strengths of pressures and counter-pressures tended to be rather different and to be less reliable than within a single community.

The following cases are those which, in 1953, concerned Ligomba residents. Previous accounts of Ligomba dispute cases and other organizational matters, in Chapters Four, Five, and Six, were given chronologically in order to demonstrate the effects and after-effects of a phase of interaction on later phases. This was a deliberate device of exposition for obvious analytical purposes and advantages. In the present argument, however, I have chosen to present the cases in the order that will best bring out and illustrate the analytical features to be emphasised, rather than in purely chronological, developmental succession. The date of each case is given, and where it is relevant I relate details of a particular case to dynamic relationships and developments within the Ligomba community (and, in one instance, with Namabeya community). Thus, whilst the principal interest here is the analysis of extra-community

[1] See page 309.

processes, it remains possible and useful to fit these cases and their implications into the ongoing continuum of the Ligomba kinship network, with its continually evolving relations, conflicts, and co-operation. On the other hand, I have deliberately avoided giving merely apt illustrations and have limited my exposition to events concerning Ligomba residents as those happened to arise during the arbitrary period of field research. The positive advantages of this continued procedure seem to me to outweigh the admitted defects: certain aspects of extra-community processes could per-haps have been better demonstrated by apt illustrations from quite different communities. Such illustrations, however, would have been (or might seem to have been) liable to selective bias in my research and analysis, and they would not have related to a known context of neighbours and network.

Case 8: A Marital Quarrel (October)

The wife of Beni (D5) left him because of alleged ill-treat-ment and, taking her two children, she went to live in the hamlet of her brother, X_1, in Liwanda local community about seven miles from Ligomba. Beni denied ill-treatment, but he wanted his wife to return home. He went to see his brother-in-law, X_1, but the latter refused to try and compel her to return until she, and he, were assured that she would obtain redress of her grievances and promise of better treatment in the future.

Beni was in a fairly good position to exercise influence in Liwanda and to bring pressures to bear on his brother-in-law through inter-linking kinsmen. Firstly, he acknowledged as kins-men and maintained active relations with X_2 and X_3, his FFBS and FFBSS respectively. Both of these men acknowledged X_1 as their kin-neighbour (X_2's WBDH). Secondly, another resident of Liwanda was X_5, father-in-law of Amadu (D6), the younger brother of Beni. X_5 was also acknowledged kinsman of notable Ali (C7) of Ligomba: Beni and Amadu shared a common hamlet with Ali (their MB) in Ligomba. Ali did not, however, ac-knowledge X_2 as a kinsman: he was recognised as the kin of kin.

After consultation between Ali, Beni, and Amadu, it was decided that Beni should appeal to X_2 for assistance in the matter, whilst Ali and Amadu should discuss the affair with X_5. Both of those Liwanda men expressed willingness to try and arrange a moot. X_2 and X_5 were not kin-neighbours, but they recognised each other as the kin of kin, having a second cousin in common—X_4. They were therefore friendly: they periodically participated together in the action-sets of X4, and of other common neighbours, and occasionally joined in each other's action-sets, although they were oriented to different clusters with the Liwanda kinship network.

It was not difficult for X2 and X5 to consult together and to agree to a moot, to be held at the house of X2. X1 had no objections to this. Action-sets in the moot were as follows. The wife was not present, and she took no overt part in the proceedings.

In the moot Beni's action-set was led by X5, who was a Liwanda notable, whilst X1 was the leading spokesman for his

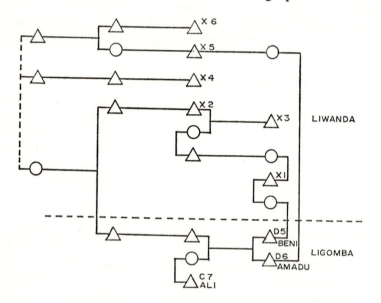

FIGURE 24: Case 8: A Marital Quarrel.

own action-set. The mediator was X4. He was not an acknowledged kinsman of either principal, but appears to have been invited to participate by both X2 and X5. X2 himself was also intermediary between the principals, but he chose initially to ally himself with X1, though without becoming leader of the action-set (thus leaving himself freer for his role in the moot). The dispute was not a difficult one to settle: there was a marked inclination to reach agreement. Beni made it clear that he wanted his wife to return; X1 explicitly denied that his sister wished for a prolonged separation, let alone divorce, although he insisted that Beni's behaviour had been the true cause of his sister's desertion.

Action-set of Beni
  from Ligomba:
      Beni D_5
     Amadu D_6 (B)
       Ali C_7 (MB)
     Yasini C_9 (MFBS)

                                    (6 men)

  from Liwanda:
          X_5 (Amadu's WF)
          X_6 (X_5's MBS)

Intermediary
  from Liwanda:
          X_4 (second cousin of both X_2 and X_5)

Action-set of X_1
  from Liwanda:
         X_1
         X_2 (WFZH)
         X_3 (X_2's S)   (7 men)
    four other kin-neighbours of X_1

X_2 gradually joined with X_4 in urging reconciliation, but X_1 demanded concrete demonstration by Beni of his good intentions. Finally X_4 said that Beni's alleged parsimony was the cause of all the trouble. There was no overt denial of this statement of the apparently general opinion of the moot; instead, X_5 and Ali urged Beni to agree to give his wife money to buy cloth for herself and her children. After some demur, Beni eventually agreed. X_5 then mildly criticised X_1 for encouraging his sister's complaints, and urged him to persuade her to return to her husband's home in Ligomba. X_2 advised Beni to be more generous in the future. These admonitions were given in what may be described as muted and friendly form—older men, "fathers", speaking to their "sons". Neither Beni nor X_1 made reply, thus indicating their acquiescence. The moot ended as all the men drank a small quantity of beer provided by X_2 and X_5.

    The moot was conducted by pre-arrangement between the two Liwanda men, X_2 and X_5, both of whom had valuable kinship relations with the Ligomba men. X_2 could not, however, operate as a mediator (at least not initially and overtly) since in terms of his status and interests in Liwanda he had to give support to X_1. The Ligomba men—"strangers" in Liwanda—were able to play a lesser part, leaving the initiative to the Liwanda men. Even Ali, the Ligomba notable, who in his own community was seldom content to take such an inactive role, was here willing to do this. He explained later that a man should be restrained in another community and not behave as if he were a "big man" there, possibly antagonising people. That view, though commonly approved, was also somewhat stereotyped and not always followed in actual cases. But, as Ali also pointed out to me, the matter was clearly going well in the hands of X_2 and X_5, and there was no need for him to intervene and possibly interfere with their successful handling of the moot. It should be added that a "stranger" was comparatively ignorant of the precise nature of the community network and therefore he was liable to misjudge the potentialities and problems it offered: it was preferable therefore to allow a "friend at court" to conduct the actual operations if at all possible.

This was a simple, straightforward case. The dispute itself was not difficult to resolve since essentially both husband and wife wished for reconciliation. Beni, the husband, was fortunate in being able to take advantage of the particular convolution of the Liwanda kinship network, and of his own relations with particular Liwanda men. He was also fortunate that his two Liwanda kinsmen, X_2 and X_5, were friendly towards each other, although they were not kin-neighbours nor in the same cluster within the community's network. The dispute itself, and the network relationships involved, were not such as to raise particular problems for the social relations of the men. That is, they were not required to endanger their own sets of relations: indeed, it is possible that X_2 and X_5 would thereafter have been more inclined to cooperation with each other, and with X_4, than they had been hitherto, as the result of this eminently successful resolution of the dispute. It is probable (though I gained no direct evidence) that X_2 and X_5 were aware of this, and that it influenced their willingness to act in the particular context.

Case 9: Bilali's Bridewealth (July)

Bilali (C_{12}) claimed a further instalment of bridewealth from his daughter's husband, R_{13} of Namabeya local community. His claim was instigated by the marriage of R_{13}'s sister and his receipt of a first instalment of bridewealth from her husband. R_{13} made a token payment of three shillings to Balili, but refused to give more than that. In Ligomba, Balili consulted with the notable Kabaya (C_{11}), his cousin (FZS) and kin-neighbour. Kabaya agreed to take up the matter and went to see his cousin (FBS),

Q5 of Namabeya. Q5 had previously lived in Ligomba, between about 1944 and 1948—he is marked on the Ligomba genealogy as C10—and he was also acknowledged kinsman (FZS) of Tanda (C13). Tanda was recognised as kinsman by Bilali, and both were members of the cluster in which Kabaya was spokesman and principal leader. Q5 had continued to acknowledge both Kabaya and Tanda as kinsmen, and was therefore disposed to assist in the matter. He himself was a member of the cluster led by the notable Kambi (Q4) in Namabeya; but he was also brother-in-law of Q6 and Q7, members of the cluster led by the notable Lihamba. R13 was a kin-neighbour of Lihamba and a member of his cluster.

Q4 and Kambi approached Lihamba and persuaded him to convene a moot at his house. Action-sets were composed as follows:

Action-set of Bilali
  from Ligomba:
    Bilali C13
    Kasim   D11 (S)
    Kabaya C11 (FZS)
    Tanda   C13 (Kabaya's FZS)
  from Namabeya: (7 men)
              Q5   (Kabaya's FBS)
              R5   (Q5's S)
    Kambi   Q4   (Q5's MBDHB)

Intermediary
  from Namabeya:
    Q6 and Q7 (Q5's WB; R13's MFBS; Lihamba's MZS)
    R6   (Q6's S)

Action-set of R13
  from Namabeya:
              R13
    Lihamba Q8   (MZH)
              P2   (MF)
              R14 (Lihamba's ZS)   (6 men)
              R11 (Lihamba's DH)
              R10 (R11's B)

This dispute occurred in July, 1953 at the time when the influence and leadership of Lihamba was growing in the process of segmental conflict within the Namabeya community. Lihamba was becoming accepted as the leader of one of the two burgeoning segments there—that segment comprising his own cluster and that

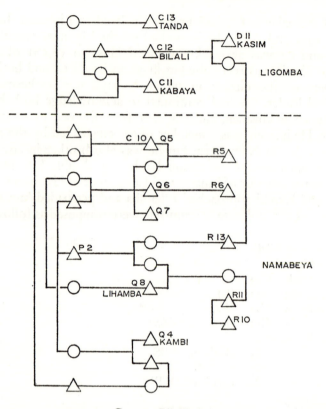

FIGURE 25: Case 9: Bilali's Bridewealth.

of Kambi. Lihamba was, of course, concerned to protect and consolidate his position: he was therefore inclined to be sympathetic to
the interests of Kambi and of Q5 and certainly wished to avoid
alienating their alliance with him. The crystallisation of the segment had yet to be fully accomplished, so that it was a critical
period for Lihamba.[2] On the other hand, Lihamba was compelled
to look to the interests of R13, his kin-neighbour (WZS). Thus he
accepted the moot as a convenient procedure. Q6 and Q7 were
prepared to act as mediators, being linked by acknowledged kinship with Q5, R13, and Lihamba. Possibly, though it was not
clear to me at the time, this was at Lihamba's suggestion. In the
moot, Q6 and Q7 fairly soon supported Q5's demand that some

[2] See Chapter Eight, page 257 ff. This dispute arose in the period between
stages 5 and 6 in Namabeya developments: page 262.

additional bridewealth should be given to Bilali. Q5, on behalf of Bilali, based this demand on the grounds that R13 had so far given only 160 shillings (this was rather below the average size at that period), and that he had the means of making a further instalment because of receiving bridewealth for his sister. Lihamba scarcely disputed this at all, but concentrated on reducing the amount to be given. The final settlement was reached with little difficulty, and R13 handed over a sum of thirty-five shillings to his father-in-law in the moot.

The defendant was, in the circumstances, the disadvantaged person, for he might have avoided any further payment at that time had his father-in-law not been so well placed to exert pressure. The plaintiff, Bilali, found himself in a fortunate position, as Q5 (advised by his cousin, Kabaya) was able to exploit the particular situation in Namabeya at that time. The main discussion in the moot was, in the event, monopolised by Namabeya men—Q5, Q6, Q7, and Lihamba. The "strangers" from Ligomba were able to remain largely passive, as preferably they should have done.

From Lihamba's point of view (as I understood it) the outcome was satisfactory. He had shown readiness to recognize the legitimate interests of men in Kambi's cluster whom he sought as allies in the segmental conflict then in progress within Namabeya. He showed himself a fairly adroit notable, yet without seeming to be unduly neglectful of the interests of his own kin-neighbour, the defendant. Although overtly Lihamba, and Q5 and Kambi, were in opposed action-sets, with Q6 and Q7 as active intermediaries, in effect these senior men were operating a kind of cooperation, demonstrating friendliness and mutual trust and toleration. It would, of course, have turned out very differently had Bilali's principal supporter in Namabeya been a member of the segment that was in conflict with Lihamba. In that case, the chances of a satisfactory settlement of the dispute in the prevailing circumstances would have been very slight.

Finally I note that Bilali, the plaintiff, was able to achieve his end although he himself had no acknowledged kinsman in the defendant's community. Similarly, the defendant had no kinsmen (other than the plaintiff and his son) in Ligomba, and he had (as far as I knew) no means of exerting counter-pressures against his father-in-law. Thus although in principle the development of support was similar in Cases 8 and 9, the means of that development and its social context were somewhat different.

Case 10: The Frustrated Creditor (September)

Abdal (D8) was visited by Amali, a member of a community about fourteen miles from Ligomba. Amali was at the time visiting his kinsmen in Njaheka local community, about seven miles from Ligomba. He alleged that Abdal had borrowed money from him the previous year when both were working in the same Public Works road gang in western Undendeuli. He now wanted to be repaid the loan. Abdal admitted to the loan, but said that he had repaid the money when he received his last wages before returning to Ligomba. After some argument, Amali left Ligomba without gaining any satisfaction and, as I was told, in some indignation.

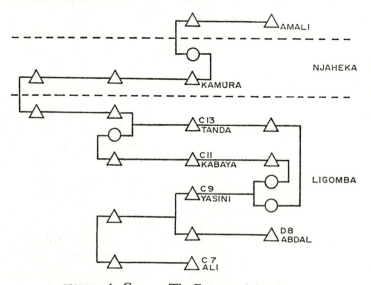

FIGURE 26: Case 10: The Frustrated Creditor.

Amali had no kin in Ligomba; but his kinsmen in Njaheka, Kamura (FZH) and his son, were acknowledged kinsmen of Tanda (C13) of Ligomba: Kamura and Tanda were second cousins (FFBSS—"small brothers"). On Amali's behalf, Kamura visited Tanda to explore the possibility of some further action in the matter of the alleged debt. Tanda took Kamura to discuss the affair with his (Tanda's) kin-neighbour, the notable Kabaya (C11). As a result of this, Tanda and Kabaya went to talk with the alleged debtor, Abdal, and his father's brother, Yasini (C9). Yasini was father-in-law of sons of Tanda and Kabaya. Abdal continued to deny the charge of debt. He and Yasini refused to agree to a moot at which the matter could have been considered, though Tanda urged this on behalf of Kamura and Amali. The notable Ali (C7) was aware of Amali's earlier visit and his allegation, and had already advised Abdal (Ali's FBSS) to refuse further negotiations. After the visit of Tanda and Kabaya, Abdal and Yasini consulted again with Ali (who had not been present). Ali reaffirmed his advice to them.

At a beer-drink the next day, Ali made public the advice he had given, spoke of "strangers" bringing troubles to Ligomba, and declared his support of Abdal. How far this was premeditated (as I suspected) and how far it was the result of a tongue loosened by beer, I could not determine. Kabaya, who was also at the beer-drink, spoke of the need to help kinsmen who lived in other communities. He also remarked that he was a "brother" of Yasini, and that Abdal was his "son". Little more was said on that occasion; but neither Kabaya nor Tanda attempted to persuade Yasini and Abdal again.

Thus, whatever the truth about the debt of money, Amali was frustrated in his attempts to bring the matter to open discussion in a moot. Presumably Tanda advised Kamura of the impossibility of further action. Amali was from the beginning in a weak position with no kinsman in Ligomba. Tanda was, however, prepared to make an attempt to meet Kamura's reasonable request on behalf of Amali; and Kabaya agreed to assist his kin-neighbour in this attempt to bring influence upon Yasini and Abdal. Yasini appreciated the comparative weakness of Tanda and Kabaya in the context, and he was able to accept and act on Ali's advice. The notable Kabaya had no wish to come into open conflict with his rival notable, Ali, in a context where Ali was clearly in the stronger position. These events occurred not long after Case 4 ("A Creditor's Claim", p. 163) when the relative strength of Yasini's kin-neighbour association with each notable had been partly at issue. To have persisted in pressing this outsider's claim would—at least as Ali perceived it—have resulted in emphasising the dependence of Yasini, and Abdal, on Kabaya rather than on Ali. Indeed, as Yasini said, Kabaya was perhaps unwise to have taken up the matter at all. But presumably he felt compelled to make some show of support for his kin-neighbour, Tanda, and he may have over-estimated his influence over Yasini. This abortive case had, I believe, some bearing on the decision of Kabaya and Tanda not to include Yasini in the hurried, semiprivate moot effectively comprising neighbours of their own cluster, about three months later.[3]

This case demonstrates an inherent weakness in the Ndendeuli processes of dispute settlement and the limitations on effective action through the kinship network. To achieve a moot to deal with a matter in dispute, a claimant needed supporters to assist him in the defendant's community—supporters who were able to exert significant influence on the defendant and his supporters within the context of the closed network of kin-neighbours and neighbours. Amali failed in this as a result of the distance between himself and Abdal in the open network: they were linked only at the fourth degree level. As far as I know, Amali had no other kinship linkages through which he could have initiated influence in Ligomba, though there could have been some of which he was not aware. It was his misfortune that the one connection available to him was intrinsically weak because of the rivalry between the notables Ali and Kabaya, and thus Kabaya's inability in practice to press effective influence for fear of damaging his own interests. It was to no one's advantage and interests to bring pressure firmly and unambiguously upon Abdal, the defendant. It might possibly have turned out rather differently had Amali's connection via Kamura been with some other Ligomba neighbour who was not in conflict with Ali's interests. Even so, the influence that could have been exerted was likely to have been weak because of the indirect mode of its operation.

The disagreement over the alleged debt never, therefore, became a public dispute and no agreed settlement was achieved between the two parties. There was, however, a settlement—by default—since the self-styled creditor failed to take effective action, whilst the alleged debtor paid no money. The contrast is marked with the more fortunate, influential position of the plaintiffs in the two preceding cases in their social contexts.

This case is the only one, of the four here described and concerning Ligomba men, that involved disputants who were not acknowledged kinsmen. This absence of kinship, of positive interaction and mutual concern, itself tended to weaken the influence that a complainant could exert in his own interests. But it was not inevitably decisive. In other recorded cases, not concerning Ligomba men, where the disputants were inter-linked as kin of kin (second degree linkage), the complainant was able to achieve the

[3] See Case 7 ("A Refusal to Lend Seed to a Kinsman"), page 176. Action-set formation in Case 6 was also affected by events in Case 10.

arrangement of a moot. I recorded no case where this occurred when the disputants were linked at the third degree level, though conceivably it could have happened if circumstances were favourable. On the whole, disputes seemed much more likely to occur between men who were acknowledged kin or the kin of kin. These were the people who were in contact with each other, who had rights and obligations against each other, and who were involved in common interests and activities. They were, therefore, more likely to discover disagreements in expectations and realisations of their interaction.

Case 11: The Disgruntled Grandfather (September)

Mugaya (C22) had lived in Ligomba for several years previously. He had been sponsored by his MZS, Sedi (C21), and they had shared a common hamlet. In 1947 his wife died, leaving him domestically dependent on Sedi's wife. In 1948 it was learned that Y2, Mugaya's cousin (FBS), an absentee labour migrant for over ten years, had married a local woman and settled in her village in the Tanga region of northeastern Tanganyika. Y2's deserted wife, still living in his hamlet in the Luenga local community, agreed to accept Mugaya as her husband. Her brother, Y1, agreed to this also. Mugaya's elder son, Y6, already lived in Luenga, having remained there in the hamlet of his father-in-law, Kalanda (Y3), after completing suitor-service some years before. Kalanda now suggested that Mugaya should go and live in Luenga. This apparently seemed advantageous to Mugaya for he moved there in 1949. Although he was, and remained thereafter, on friendly terms with Sedi in Ligomba, yet he had gained rather few kin-neighbours there and perhaps felt himself not to be entirely secure in neighbourly cooperation. The move to Luenga gave him, as a man in middle age, the opportunity to live with his elder son and therefore to try and ensure support in his elderly years. When he shifted to Luenga he was joined by his younger son, Y5, and together with the elder son they established a common hamlet. These three men had at least four immediate kin-neighbours of whom they could have reasonable assurance: Y1, and Kalanda Y3 and his two sons.

For some reason, Mugaya and his "brother" (SWF), Kalanda, failed to develop friendly relations. My data are unclear, but there seems to have been some conflict over the priority of the loyalty of Y6, as well as some personal incompatibility. In 1952, Y6 died in an accident and Mugaya demanded that his young

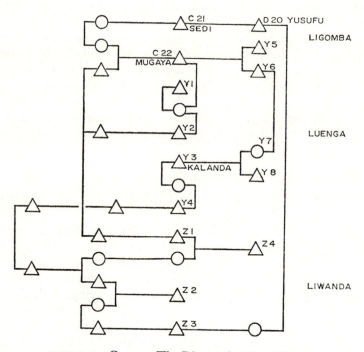

FIGURE 27: Case 11: The Disgruntled Grandfather.

widow, Y5, should be inherited by the younger brother, Y5, whose own wife had deserted him earlier. The widow refused and was supported in this by her father, Kalanda, and her brothers. An open quarrel resulted, with Mugaya and his son on the one side, and Kalanda and his sons on the other. A moot was arranged by the notable of their cluster, Y4, but it failed to reach an agreement. The widow insisted that she would live with her father and brothers and would not remarry. Mugaya suspected, no doubt wisely, that she wanted to marry some other man. Kalanda refused to consider any payment of compensation for the effectively broken marriage, pointing out that no bridewealth had ever been given by her dead husband.

As a direct result of this impasse and the generally poor relations among the two parties, Mugaya and his remaining son moved from Luenga to the Liwanda local community. There he was sponsored by Z1, his FBS.

In September 1953, a little over a year later, the granddaughter of Mugaya underwent initiation. This girl, Y9, had remained with her mother in Kalanda's hamlet in Luenga where the ritual was performed. Despite invitations from Kalanda and Y8, Mugaya refused to attend the initiation rituals. This was generally held to be ritually dangerous to the girl concerned. It was, however, tantamount to a repudiation of kinship with her by her grandfather, and a denial of persisting kinship relations and thus of cooperation between Mugaya and his late son's affines. Kalanda did not wish to accede to either implication, as Mugaya had surmised, for this seems to have been Mugaya's gambit according to information from Sedi. Kalanda consulted with his brother-in-law (ZH), Y4, the notable of his cluster in the Luenga network, and the formerly acknowledged kin-neighbour of Mugaya. This notable was a kinsman of Z2 (FFBSS), the notable of the cluster in Liwanda with which Mugaya was now associated. Y4 and Z2 agreed to convene a moot to consider and attempt to reconcile relations between the two disputants. Sedi informed me that this was their intention; but it appeared that Mugaya, at least, saw himself as the plaintiff in the matter of his son's widow. I did not learn what Kalanda's perception was. The two notables, each acting on behalf of one of the disputants, took the lead in assembling participants to the moot, which was held at the house of Y4 in Luenga. The participants were:

From Luenga —Kalanda Y3 and his son, Y8
(7 men)   Y1 (WB of Mugaya)
            Y4 (notable—ZH of Kalanda)
            three other kin-neighbours of Kalanda

From Liwanda—Mugaya C22 and his son, Y5
(8 men)   Z1 (FBS of Mugaya) and his son, Z4
            Z2 (notable—WMBS of Z1; FFBSS of Y4)
            Z3 (MBS of Z2; WF of Yusufu of Ligomba)
            two other kin-neighbours of Z1 and Z2

From Ligomba—Sedi C21 (MZS of Mugaya)
(2 men)   Yusufu D20 (S of Sedi; DH of Z3)

From two
other local
communities —one kinsman of Mugaya and Z2
(5 men)   one kinsman of Mugaya and Kalanda
            one kinsman of Kalanda and Z3
            two kinsmen of Kalanda and Z1

This collection of twenty-two men was an ad hoc set of men who were acknowledged kinsmen of Mugaya or Kalanda, or of both. They were men who were interconnected around the focus of the two disputants. They came from five different local communities, all within three to ten miles of each other. There was not the encounter of action-sets typical of most moots. This was, I believe, because so many of the participants were linked with both principals, and also with one another, that sides could not easily be taken. The notable, Y_4, gave overt support to Kalanda, and similarly the notable, Z_2, supported Mugaya. But they did not act as the leaders of opposed sides. They each made it clear at the outset of the moot—before either principal spoke—that they themselves were kinsmen, friends, and virtual allies, with no dispute between them. They spoke of helping Mugaya and Kalanda to become friendly again, and there were direct references to the web of kinship relations in which they were involved. These themes were taken up by other participants who had no clear unilateral status in the context. The whole character of the moot was thus established—deliberately, as it seemed—of a group of men with a common purpose: to resolve the problems between Mugaya and Kalanda, and to achieve their reconciliation. This was indicated by the way the men sat in a more or less compact group, rather than in physically distinct sets as was the usual practice in Ndendeuli moots. It might therefore be described as a "reconciliation moot" rather than a "confrontation moot".[4]

The organisational roles of the two notables were crucial in all this. It seemed clear that a good deal of preparatory groundwork had been accomplished beforehand by these notables among their participatory kinsmen. Certainly Sedi of Ligomba had been visited by Z_3 as a kind of emissary of the notable Z_2; and Sedi had visited a kinsman in one of the other communities who was also a kinsman of Kalanda. "Everyone has visited his kinsmen and talked with them", Sedi explained in pardonable exaggeration. How far the principals were aware of this activity is unknown, but they could not have been entirely unaware, and they probably acceded to these preparations. Neither made any protest or comment in the moot itself.

In the moot it was, therefore, some time before either principal

---

[4] These two terms are not altogether satisfactory, for reconciliation may have been at least one aim of a confrontation moot, whilst there was at least an element of confrontation in a reconciliation moot. But they may serve here to distinguish broadly between the two general kinds of moots.

spoke. When at last they did, the moot settled down to a thorough review of the relationship of the two men. Although one or the other, or both, were censured for certain inadequacies of behaviour, repeatedly the moot returned to the theme of reconciliation and to the importance of their relationship to the principals. After more than four hours a settlement was agreed. The culminating negotiations were largely conducted by the two notables, and each eventually urged the settlement upon both principals. The latter specifically agreed to it, rather than (as was more usual in moots) merely acceding tacitly, and this itself indicated the success of the reconciliation (I was told) since both men signified their positive willingness to put it into effect rather than a half-grudging acceptance of necessity and *fait accompli*. The widow, Y7, was to become the wife of her late husband's brother, Y5, who himself was to become the father of the initiated girl, Y9. It was agreed that Y5 should give a small bridewealth to Kalanda (as a token), and twenty shillings was handed over on the spot to this effect. Mugaya was persuaded to contribute to that payment, to provide a cloth for his granddaughter, and to promise a gift of food to Kalanda. At the conclusion of the moot the men joined in consuming porridge and a little beer provided by Kalanda and Y4.

This case—or rather, the social context in which it developed and was treated—is given here although it has minor significance in the continued analysis of the Ligomba community. It is one of the best illustrations of the way in which the potentialities of the open kinship network could be used by Ndendeuli. The totality of social relationships expressed in terms of kinship was complex. The skill in manipulation of the potentialities was considerable, particularly by the two notables from separate local communities. The acquiescence of the two principals was less important than it may seem *prima facie*. The reconciliation process was eased, of course; but had the principals insisted on a confrontation moot, it is most probable that the two notables, as leaders of explicit action-sets, would have sought to minimise conflict and to work in collusion towards the same end. The notables' roles would, however, have been more delicate; and they virtually ruled out confrontation by their manipulations before the moot began.

However hostile and aggrieved the principals may have felt, they were almost inevitably restricted in their freedom: they were enmeshed in a web of interlinking relations and interdependence among a larger collection of people. The participants in the moot, and in pre-moot discussions, were concerned for the reconciliation of the principals, but they were also concerned for their own relations with one another. Essentially the situation was quite similar to that previously noted in reference to Case 5 ("A Cousins' Quarrel", p. 172). Continued breach of relations between the principals seriously threatened the interconnected relations between the other men. Moreover, in the successful operation in the case, men were able to express and perhaps to reinforce the strength of their relations with one another. The two notables were not in competition with each other, and they had no desire to be so nor advantage in becoming so. They were kinsmen living in different but nearby local communities, and their continued friendliness was especially valuable to them, without being a threat to the interests of either. Each acquired, I think, added prestige in his own cluster of his own community.

In Cases 8 and 9, the moots were of the common confrontation type, for there the principals and their supporters were less closely interconnected in the open network. The mesh, metaphorically, was looser. In Case 11, the high degree of interconnection caused the men to avoid a confrontation that would have put them into opposed action-sets. It might even have been impossible for the men to have determined their prime loyalty to one of the two confronting sets. It was more useful tactically for the two notables to increase the pressures on the principals by inviting and obtaining the participation of men from the three other communities where neither principal lived (such men as Sedi and Yusufu of Ligomba).

In the end, reconciliation was achieved and a settlement agreed; and, with the social relationships clarified and consolidated, it was possible for the participants to give emphasis to the symbolic idiom of kinship: the moral value of the principals' kinship and thus of kinship in general; the obligations of affines, of a grandfather to his son's daughter, and of a widow to her late husband's brother. Ndendeuli ethics were justified whilst practical interests were taken care of. The general expression of euphoria during the commensality at the conclusion of the moot was particularly marked.

This case was peripheral to Ligomba affairs and relations, affecting only Sedi and his son, Yusufu. It had no immediate or direct repercussions within Ligomba. It may perhaps have affected subsequent kinship-based relations of each of those two men: only later circumstances and their requirements could show this, and I had no further relevant data. In retrospect, I think that similar situations may have arisen, unknown to me, affecting the relations of other Ligomba men in the open network of their wider social field. It did not seem possible to check the reason and significance of every visit of a kinsman to Ligomba, and every visit elsewhere by Ligomba men. Such systematic enquiry would perhaps have revealed similar cases in which Ligomba men were involved during the period (although neither principal was a Ligomba resident). It so happened, partly by chance, that this particular case involving Sedi came to my notice and that it was possible to investigate it.[5]

Unfortunately, therefore, it is not possible to assess the frequency with which kinsmen in third communities were brought into dispute cases and moots. Neither, for want of an adequate number of cases, is it possible to assess the comparative frequency of reconciliation moots and confrontation moots. Within the closed network of a single local community, confrontation moots involving action-sets were certainly more common. There, reconciliation moots seem to have occurred when the principals in a dispute were both associated within the same cluster, as in Case 7 ("A Refusal to Lend Seed", p. 176). In the open network beyond the single local community, however, it is possible that reconciliation moots, without specific ego-focussed action-sets, were proportionally more common. Yet I would think that confronting action-sets continued to be the more frequent, as in Cases 8 and 9 above. As I have suggested already, a critical (but not the only) factor was the closeness of the mesh in that part of the open network involving the principals and their supporting kinsmen: the greater the degree of inter-connectedness the more likely was the probability of a reconciliation moot.

Ultimately, however, the kind of moot and the tactics employed depended on the decisions of the leading men concerned in the context. They were much influenced by the factors I have noted and that, indeed, I learned from such men and their behaviour. But there was no rule, not even a rule of thumb, and it would be forcing the facts and the cognitive appreciation of them by Ndendeuli to seek to deduce anything quite so specific as a rule.

[5] Konga (C17) first told me about it in conversation, partly fortuitously. My field assistant was able to persuade Sedi to allow us to accompany him to the moot in Luenga. Sedi was not a principal informant in Ligomba, but on the walk of several miles to and from Luenga my assistant was successful in encouraging him to discuss the case in detail.

Men certainly attempted to adopt the course that seemed to them most likely to be successful, as was made obvious in pre-moot discussions that I was able to overhear. "Successful" meant reaching an agreed settlement that was put into effect, and a degree of reconciliation where that was possible and necessary, in controlling the after-effects, and in taking care of the interests and relationships of the other men involved and concerned. Although it seems to me that Ndendeuli showed a good deal of sophistication and self-awareness in making these decisions and in carrying them through, it would be misleading to suggest that they always made the "correct" decision in the circumstances. Perceptions and judgements could be at fault, or based on inadequate knowledge of the situation and its implications. It is important to recognise that sometimes the decision that was made, and the tactics that were employed, were not necessarily the best for all participants, or even for anyone. Compromise, and the ability to recognise the necessity of compromise, were valuable qualities. A principal might, for instance, be constrained to acquiesce in a decision that was not in his best interests, though it might suit those of other participants—as the defendant, R_{13}, was compelled to do in Case 9.

In Case 9 ("Bilali's Bridewealth") it might have been possible for notable Lihamba ($Q8$) and for Kambi ($Q4$) with Q_5 to have arranged a reconciliation moot that perhaps would have favoured the defendant by getting his case more adequately presented and argued. However, the plaintiff, Bilali, was not enmeshed in the network relations of the Namabeya men (cf. Fig. 25, p. 322); or, to put it in another way, the other participants were not themselves highly involved in the continued relationship between the two principals, but they *were* highly interconnected among themselves. My own conclusion is that notable Lihamba had, and saw that he had, to make some show of supporting the defendant (his own kin-neighbour, WZS), a show less for the defendant than for the other members of the cluster Lihamba led. Moreover, at a time when the clusters of Lihamba and Kambi were becoming increasingly allied as a single segment in the Namabeya community in opposition to a second, similar segment, it may have been (or thought to have been) preferable to mark the identities of the two clusters by their distinction in the moot itself. Each notable, Lihamba and Kambi, needed to reassure members of his own cluster of the continued reality and viability of the inter-dependencies that made the cluster. Then the effective collusion of the two sides was a practical demonstration of their alliance together and their ability to cooperate. Kambi in particular was in this way able to show a degree of unthreatened autonomy. This is supposition, initially suggested in my discussions with notable Ali and my field assistant, without sufficient information on the perceptions, motives, and choices of Lihamba and Kambi. But it is supposition in line with my general understanding of Ndendeuli behaviour in such matters. That is, Lihamba and Kambi, and probably also the mediators Q6 and Q7, were in the circumstances markedly concerned with their own interests as well as or even prior to those of the two principals.

It is clear, however, that in an extra-community dispute involving a confrontation moot, the plaintiff sought to mobilise support in the defendant's community. Preferably the plaintiff left the initiative to those supporters. They were not only *persona grata* in the defendant's community, but more importantly, they better understood the nature and potentialities of the closed network within that community, in a way not possible to a stranger. Secondly, the plaintiff and his supporters sought to discover (for it was not necessarily known offhand), and to make use of, kinship inter-connections between the two sides. Thus pressures could be brought to bear on the defendant, and mediators might be determined and influenced. Although it did not happen in Cases 8 and 9, it was of course also possible for the defendant to mobilise support of his own kinsmen in the plaintiff's community for similar purposes. Each principal and his leading associates sought to take what advantage they could of the complex inter-linkages of the open network. Men made decisions in the light of their knowledge and perception, always more or less limited, of those inter-linkages. The potentialities were fairly extensive and were not necessarily exhausted in any particular situation. That is to say, the actual inter-linkages that were activated and kinsmen who were mobilised were not necessarily the only relevant ones in the context. They were the ones best known and considered to be the most advantageous to the participants at the time. My exposition could perhaps give the impression of a finite set of relationships obvious to the participants with something like perfect knowledge, since I have largely described (after the fact) what in effect happened and who were mobilised. The actuality was far less clear cut than that. If a first attempt to gain a settlement (a first moot, or negotiations for a first moot) were unsuccessful, the plaintiff and his associates, and perhaps the defendant also, sought to mobilise other inter-linking men and thus to use other resources, other portions and potentialities of the open network, in an attempt to achieve more influence and better success.

Kinsmen acceded to these requests for support, assistance, and intermediation, said Ndendeuli, because they were kinsmen. This was but partially true as men acceded to normative expectations and moral standards. More crucially, they acceded to such requests as part of their advantageous involvement in a continuum of reciprocal transactions, and in order to ensure support and assistance in their own interests at another time. They acceded also because it was, or could have been, advantageous to operate in cooperation not only with the principal but with his other supporters as well. And at least sometimes those kinsmen had vested interests in the relationship between the principals in the dispute.

RESIDENTIAL MOVEMENT

The wider the distribution of a man's acknowledged kinsmen among other local communities, especially the geographically nearer ones, the stronger his position was likely to be when his interests and activities took him beyond his own home community. As we have seen in the matter of dispute settlement, a man needed kinsmen to act on his behalf in the community where his opponent lived. Ideally, therefore, a man needed kinsmen in every community in which he might become involved. On the whole, the more kinsmen he had in a particular community, the stronger his support there would have been; although a great deal depended on the inter-connection and state of relations between his kinsmen and those of the man with whom he had the dispute.

To some extent a man could extend the distribution of his kinsmen by his choice in marriage—his own marriage, and that of his sisters, daughters, and sons—and the acquisition of new affines.[6] In Case 8 ("A Marital Quarrel"), it was to the husband's advantage that his younger brother's father-in-law lived in the same community as his own brother-in-law (though the two affines were not themselves kin-neighbours). I do not know to what extent, if at all, the younger brother's marriage had been deliberately planned with that kind of advantage in mind.

It is reasonable to suppose that the continued acknowledgement of kinship with some men in particular communities was influenced by the geographical distribution of his other kinsmen: that is, there was some incentive to maintain active relations with a man in a

[6] On marriage choice, see page 308 ff.

community where no other kinsman was resident. This factor was not properly investigated in the field, but circumstantial evidence supports the hypothesis. On the other hand, as men shifted their residence periodically, no individual was able to do much about influencing the distribution of his kinsmen as time went on. His kinsmen attempted to choose their new residence in their own interests, not his; and their various interests were only partly coincident. A man could, therefore, find that he had no kinsmen in some other community when his kinsmen shifted away from it for their own purposes.

This usefulness of a good distribution of kinsmen was not limited only to occurrences of disputes. It was demonstrated in any of his dealings beyond his home community. For example, he was better able to obtain news and opinion—not altogether a trivial matter in such a society. Most importantly, however, the more communities in which he had kinsmen, the more communities there were to which he might move when he wished or was compelled to shift his residence. He required a resident kinsman to sponsor him and to give him much practical assistance during the first year's residence. If he had several kinsmen resident in the new community, then he was likely to have several kin-neighbours at the outset with a most favourable start.

To the best of my knowledge, no man in eastern Undendeuli remained in one community permanently. Some stayed in one place longer than others, but every man had to take account of the accepted inevitability of residential movement, sooner or later. Apart perhaps from a few long-time, well-established residents such as Ali or Konga of Ligomba, Ndendeuli could not, and said they could not, be sure when they would wish or be more or less compelled to move. Some poorly established residents had to bear this in mind fairly deliberately; most other men had the matter in mind, even if less acutely. In saying this, I am following men's own statements and opinions; but these fitted well with the facts of the situation.

Data on the frequency of residential movement are not as clear as they should have been. Problems of dating were not entirely resolved for the period before 1939, a period during which my middle-aged informants had been household heads. The best that my records yield refer to eighty-seven men of all ages, though they are little more than rather rough estimates. For these men, the average time between moves (including the time in their current residence) was about twelve years. The range of average periods of residence was from about five years to about eighteen years. These results suggest, tentatively, that an elderly man would have made about four shifts of residence—at least one and perhaps as many as seven. There appears to have been little difference between the earlier years of men who had since become elderly and men who, at the time of research, were still fairly young. Thus the average figure seems not to have changed much since the gross upheavals of the abortive Maji Maji Rebellion of 1905–1907.

More reliable data are obtained from residence records in three local communities in eastern Undendeuli, made in 1953.

Average length of residence in the community

	Men still resident	*Former residents*
Ligomba	9 years (32 men)	8 years (20 men)
Namabeya	6.5 years (39 men)	. . . .
Njaheka	10 years (44 men)	8.5 years (14 men)

The Ligomba figures are taken from the information previously given in Chapter Four.[7] The lower figures for Namabeya were of course a result of its shorter period of existence. Njaheka had been in existence for about twenty years and was, therefore, comparable with Ligomba.

The range among current Ligomba residents was from about twenty-two years (four men: Ali, Konga, Mitedi, Sedi) to one year (two newly married household heads). Nineteen of the thirty-two Ligomba household heads had been resident there for nine years or less. Of the fifty-seven household heads who had lived in Ligomba since its founding in about 1931, only six had resided there for more than fifteen years.

A precise calculation and analysis of the frequency of residential movement, though preferable, is not essential for present purposes. It should be sufficient to take a general assessment that on the average men had tended to move their residence from one community to another as often as every twelve years or so. A small minority of men remained in one community for as long as two decades at a time, but seldom much longer than that. This corresponds with a conclusion that local communities existed for little more than two decades, and that during that period there was a flow of households through each community.

[7] See pages 87, 97, and 103.

In Chapter Two the ecology of Ndendeuli shifting cultivation was briefly examined. To summarise: the people would not have needed to shift residence on agricultural grounds, and with their current technology, if they had lived at a density of not more than thirty to thirty-five persons per square mile. At that maximum density, they could have merely shifted their arable cultivation focussed on a stable residential base, but with sufficient land to cover the period of natural regeneration following loss of fertility as a result of cultivation. In practice, however, Ndendeuli congregated in local communities with densities up to twice that figure. Even so, and because of stretches of untouched woodland between communities, it would have been possible to obtain sufficient land if the people had been prepared to cultivate fields more distant from their hamlets. This they were not willing to do, little more than a mile being the limit of what they were prepared to tolerate as maximum. There was a certain amount of intra-community movement as men shifted their households nearer to untouched woodland on the periphery of their community. This was not very common: once immediately available land became scarce, men chose to shift completely to another community.[8]

It is fairly clear that among former residents in Ligomba (who had lived in that community for an average of eight years) there were many who must have moved away well before land exhaustion set in, even within the immediate vicinity of their hamlet. Indeed, I can dogmatically assert this to have been the case. A number of references in case histories, particularly in Chapter Four, have indicated some of the sociological factors involved in residential movement.

First, I reiterate that there was no authority controlling the time or direction of residential movement, nor was there restraint of movement because of men's rights and obligations in land-holding or other corporate groups of any kind. In empirical fact as well as in ideal expectations, a household head could choose to move or to stay, depending on his own assessment of relative advantage and disadvantage. Obviously he had to move when available land for new arable fields became scarce; but many, and perhaps most, moves were made before that time and for social reasons. However, one factor that a man might consider was the future availability of woodland for fields. It was, in Ndendeuli opinion, fairly easy to move over distances up to about a dozen miles. There was little to be transported other than food stocks.

[8] On Ndendeuli shifting cultivation, see pp. 39 ff. and especially 47 ff.

The practical issues were, first, that the old house had to be abandoned, since building timber and thatch could not be carried. Second, on arrival in a fresh community, completely new fields had to be cleared without the labour-saving advantage of the use of existing fields for a second or third crop. These factors seemed to be rather unimportant—at least I seldom heard men mention them when discussing a move. The cooperative work-party system largely took care of those problems. Movement itself occurred in the cool season and early dry season, May to August, when the last harvest had been taken and whilst there was time to clear new fields in the new community.

In brief, a household head decided to move his residence if he considered that in his present community he was not obtaining, nor likely to obtain, the security and reliability of cooperation that he required; and if he considered that he could obtain more advantageous conditions elsewhere. Under extreme circumstances, the disavantages of staying might have been irresistibly pressed on him—as in Case 1 ("The Persistent Thief") where Kasudi (D22) was effectively cut off from all neighbourly cooperation. Such an event was undoubtedly rare; it was more common that a man was impressed by the unreliability of cooperation and the probability of conflict where he himself was in a relatively weak position. With the changing composition of a local community, and with new kin-neighbours being recognised and old ones being relinquished, a man's position, his expectations of cooperation and of conflict, could all change gradually or even fairly rapidly. Defeat or relative disadvantage in the outcome of a particular dispute or conflict could persuade a man of his weakness in the community, and induce him to move. Several examples in Ligomba history have already been described: Kindabi (B3) after his unsuccessful dispute with Ali (C7) (p. 93); Kasoro (B1) and his "sons", after gaining poor support in their dispute with Yasini (C9) (p. 94); Abram (C25) after his dispute with Bilali (C12) (p. 105); C18 after chronic animosity with his elder brother, Konga (C17), who monopolised the support of their common kin-neighbours (p. 101); and others.

Such conflict did not necessarily result in a change of residence, for the alternative communities available might have seemed to offer no better advantage. Zadiki (C15), after humiliating failure in his dispute with Konga in 1939, chose instead to sponsor new-comers who would, and in fact did, provide him with new, co-operative kin-neighbours (p. 99). Salimi (D1) considered leaving

Ligomba in 1954 when his weak position was demonstrated in Work-party Dispute 3 (p. 209), but his available alternatives seemed to offer no more advantage than he already had. His kinsmen elsewhere were few and scattered, whilst he had at least four fairly reliable kin-neighbours in Ligomba.

The advantages sought in another community were an expectation of reliable cooperation and support, and an absence of conflict, with new kin-neighbours and other neighbours. This was inevitably uncertain; but if there were two or three kinsmen already living there and they themselves were kin-neighbours of each other, the chances might be good. If those kinsmen were already friendly and even actively inviting the move to their community, the prospects were even better. A man endeavoured to enquire about the circumstances in a community to which he might move: for example, whether his kinsmen were in serious conflict with other neighbours, so that he himself would probably be drawn into the matter; whether his kinsmen had a number of fairly assured kin-neighbours, and a successful notable in their cluster; where he might build his house; and the availability of woodland for fields.

The disadvantages of the current community might be so great that a man might be glad to become a newcomer almost anywhere. Or the probable advantages in another community might be attractive enough to draw a man away from his current community where his circumstances were no more than tolerable: for example, the move of Mugaya (C22) from Ligomba to Luenga to inherit his cousin's deserted wife, and to live with his two autonomous sons (p. 327). As a number of instances have demonstrated, men actively sought to attract their kinsmen from other communities in order to increase the number of their own kin-neighbours. This could have been in an attempt to build up a following by an ambitious, potential notable, as Luinga (B4) and Ali (C7) had done in the earlier years of Ligomba (pp. 89 ff.); or it could have been the strategy of a man who was in danger of having too few kin-neighbours to provide reliable and adequate cooperation and support, as in the case of Zadiki (C15) (p. 99), and as an alternative to moving away from the community.

With the comparative ease of movement and the fluidity of social relationships expressed in kinship terms, as kinsmen shifted their own residence, most men remained more or less alert to the changing possibilities of moving. It was therefore expedient to maintain good relations with kinsmen elsewhere and to maintain some knowledge of circumstances in their communities. A long-term resident and successful notable, such as Ali of Ligomba, had been too well established to consider seriously a shift of residence for many years; but by 1954 he began to see that the Ligomba community was probably nearing its end (due to growing local exhaustion of woodland) and that he would, sooner or later, have to move. Less well established men in Ligomba, particularly the younger household heads, gave more attention to a possible move. For example, although the elderly Yasini (C9) appeared to have developed a tolerable *modus vivendi* between his two kin-neighbours, the notables Ali and Kabaya,[9] his two nephews, who shared a hamlet with him, were less tolerant of the situation that produced recurrent problems and conflict, and they consciously considered the advantages of a move. Ndoma (D23) (a recent newcomer to Ligomba) told my field assistant that he had moved to Ligomba because four of his former kin-neighbours had moved away from his previous community. They had gone to live with their kinsmen elsewhere, but those men were not acknowledged kin of Ndoma. Therefore, after being deprived of previous reliable cooperation in his community, he chose to move to Ligomba where some of his own kinsmen already lived. He was not altogether settled, however (according to his own statement), and had been considering the relative advantages of shifting again. These are but casual illustrations drawn from evidence presented in earlier chapters. A quite common topic of conversation during extra-community visiting of kinsfolk was the possibilities of a move. My marked impression was that this was an interesting and important matter to both visitors and hosts.

Perhaps sufficient evidence has been given to make a convincing argument. The importance of a man's kinsmen should then be clear. They were the men who could make a successful move possible by sponsoring a man as newcomer, giving him invaluable practical assistance, and mediating his new relationships with potential kin-neighbours. But it was important, indeed necessary as the people perceived it, to have several possible communities to which to move, for this allowed choice of the most advantageous shift of residence. Conditions and membership of communities changed as residents moved and as interaction and neighbourly relations developed and changed. Men were quite aware of this, and the fortunate man was he who had a wide range of selection at the time when he wished or was compelled to move. Ali was

[9] See Work-Party Case 1, page 203 ff.

able to tell me of thirteen local communities where acknowledged kinsmen lived, and he considered that at least seven of these might offer acceptable conditions for him. Konga listed sixteen such communities, and seven or eight to which he could have contemplated a move. Salimi could name only six communities in which he had kinsmen, for his kin-set was small, as Figure 22 showed; he was unable to choose between them, for none was especially attractive in his opinion. The larger the potential choice, then (as Ndendeuli said) the larger the range of action if and when a change of residence became desirable. Normally a man would scarcely have chosen to move to a community where he had only one kinsman resident, nor would he have wished to join a community where his resident kinsmen were in a comparatively disadvantageous position.

A good distribution of kinsmen among other local communities was, then, most important: for potential shifts of residence, in extra-community dispute settlement, in the dissemination of news and opinion, and in general in obtaining assistance and support. In view of this, the question arises: why did not Ndendeuli men have larger kin-sets? Why did they not recognise a wider range of kinsmen, including a broader genealogical range? Associated with this problem is the question whether certain kinsmen were acknowledged as such partly because they lived in communities where a man had no other kinsmen. The data provide no ready answer, and the question did not occur to me during the research period. I have indicated that the genealogical range was comparatively narrow: it did not, in general, include even all second cousins or parents' first cousins. Third cousins were infrequently included in kin-sets. There may have been an optimum size to a kin-set within the Ndendeuli social context of the period. That is to say, too large a number of kinsmen in the kin-set was perhaps difficult to handle because of the possible conflicts of obligations and loyalties. In that kinship system, without corporate groups or lineal categories, there were inevitably recurrent conflicts since men's kin-sets (their linkages, rights, and obligations) only overlapped but never coincided. Men were able, as I have attempted to show, to cope with a degree of such conflict. They were also able to take advantage of the partial overlapping when they wished to bring pressure to bear on other men with whom they were not directly related, but only indirectly inter-linked. Yet there seem to have been limits to the toleration, and the advantage, of discongruity. It was, on the whole, more or less possible to operate where many or most of one's kinsmen were also kin of each other, and where the problem of numbers (one might say, the number of variables) was not too great. Men probably made no conscious decision about this matter, but rather they found it inconvenient, proportionally disadvantageous, to maintain active relations and to accept obligations towards kinsmen on the periphery—kinsmen who were not directly linked to several or many of the other members of the kin-set.

The principal context in which this conscious or unconscious limiting of the size of the kin-set occurred was that of fairly frequent residential movement. The kinship system was fluid in its socio-geographical sense. Even the man who remained in one community for a long period was affected by those of his kinsmen who moved more frequently. Without corporate interests, or ritual obligations, or political unity to provide the means or the expression of integration, men's individual abilities to maintain and fulfill dyadic relationships were weak. They were strengthened by inter-connection and inter-dependence among kinsfolk, but not extensively. My records suggest (it can be put no stronger than that) that, as they grew older, men tended to reduce the genealogical range of acknowledged kin. Younger men acknowledged second cousins more readily than did older men, whilst the latter tended to concentrate their attention, their responsibilities and claims on nearer kin and upon nearer affines (children's spouses and their fathers). It seems that they did this through a long period of experimentation and testing: with which kinsmen was cooperation more reliable, and which kin were more inter-linked with each other in the context of the ego-focus of the man himself? The evidence for this kind of development has been given previously.

A more satisfactory answer to this problem would require further investigation. A comparative approach might also be useful in suggesting the significant factors. Anthropologists have reported kindreds in southeast Asia that allegedly included cognates up to fifth cousins. Unfortunately the societies concerned have not been described at all well in their actual operation (as against vague and ideal models), so that it is not possible to discover the empirical range of men's acknowledged kin, nor to see what were the concomitant factors that were connected with a wider range of kinship. It might even be true that the apparently narrow range of recognition among the Ndendeuli is less atypical than appears at first sight.

XI

Conclusions

In considering my field research data on the Ndendeuli, and in working out the exposition presented in the foregoing chapters of this book, it seemed to me that the most satisfactory frame of reference, in a general sense, was that of "network". This is a term, along with similar, cognate ones (web, mesh, grid, reticulation, and the like), that anthropologists and sociologists have often used in the past, principally as a convenient metaphor or as a suggestive analogy rather than as a developed theoretical concept by which to order and analyse social data or through which to develop hypotheses. In his preliminary account of a Norwegian parish, in 1954, Barnes sought to give the term a more precise meaning, to make it an integral part of his analysis, and to give it theoretical potential. This, together with developing work by some sociologists, renewed anthropological interest in the possibilities of the concept and the approach it offered, and stimulated efforts to define and refine the term and to use it as a means of analysing ethnographic data.[1]

Unfortunately, despite the more serious attention given to it and its potentiality, "network" still retains a good deal of the metaphorical character: a general image of something difficult to grasp, an impressionistic reference to complex phenomena. It is still a somewhat elusive concept. In the opinion of at least some anthropologists with whom I have discussed the matter, it is considered likely to remain helpful, if at all, only at a very general level. Although I do not agree with that view, it must be admitted that it is not altogether unreasonable in the light of positive results to date. Moreover, and distressingly from any point of view, there seems simultaneously to have been an increasing use of "network" in a vague, jargonistic sense. Students, and others, have tended to

[1] Helpful surveys of the use, and suggested use, of the term and related matters are given in Mayer 1966 and Barnes 1968.

use it as a loose substitute for the sometimes suspect terms "structure" and "system", without giving it substance or significance:
indeed, as a substitute for genuine analysis. There is danger, therefore, that the term may degenerate into another meaningless cliché.

There has, however, been some value and success in efforts to
develop the term positively and constructively, even though there
is not yet general agreement in theory or methodology. There
have been some useful attempts to apply "network" to empirical
materials and to produce "actual, operating" networks based on
concrete social situations.[2] By "actual, operating" is meant, of
course, a first level abstraction of the real impingements of people
on one another (Barnes 1968:110–11); but also I mean that the
abstracted social relationships (inter-linkages) refer quite directly
and explicitly to actual people and to their actual behaviour and
interaction, and not to imaginary or experimental laboratory
situations. This, it seems to me, is essential if the concept is to
become genuinely significant and productive.

Perhaps the most obvious depiction of a network of social relationships is the production of a diagram giving the "actual" inter-
linkages of people and making up the mesh. This is undoubtedly
an extremely difficult task to accomplish with any clarity, and
without gross oversimplification, for one's diagram in two dimensions quickly becomes so complicated by the criss-cross of lines
that it becomes more or less incoherent and thus valueless as a
visual, explanatory device. Diagrammatic presentation also calls for
considerable detailed information, and it raises the problem of
determining and assessing the various kinds, strengths, and im-
portances of different linkages. My own attempts to construct
intelligible diagrams of various partial networks had reluctantly
to be abandoned, even with the limitations of a closed network
such as that of Ligomba or Namabeya local community. It is, of
course, impossible to give visual clarity to an open network where
the convolutions and ramifications are highly intricate and virtually
infinite. This failure to succeed diagrammatically is diagnostic of
the inherent difficulties of the theoretical conceptualisation. But
"network" is, or should be, ultimately an intellectual concept, and
as such should be valid and useful, despite visual deficiencies—just
as "structure" has been. Yet intellectually the convolute intricacies
often seem to be more than the mind can readily contain and
handle; this is because there has not yet been adequate develop-

[2] For example, see Bott 1957, Epstein 1961, P. Mayer 1961, Pauw 1963,
Parkin 1969.

ment of a theoretical framework, analytical categories within that framework, and working hypotheses.

Essentially the concept seeks to embrace the obvious facts that each person in social life is operationally connected in some more or less regular way with a number of other people: that is, that person is in active, direct social relationships with each of those others. And each of those others is similarly connected with a range of people; and each of the latter is connected . . . , and so on. It is less simple than that, however, for at any stage some of the persons connected with (in social relationship with) a common individual are also directly connected with one another. The circumstances are considerably simplified where sets of connections are in some way aggregated and given distinguishing character and conformity: that is, if the persons involved in such a set form a social group, or even a fairly well-defined social category. On the whole, such groups reduce the variety by giving the set of people a common (even a single) connection with other sets for one, some, or many activities and interests. Indeed, for many analytic purposes, anthropologists have been able (or at least, have been content) to concentrate on the examination of the aggregrated connections within and between social groups: for example, in a segmentary system of some kind. The network is still there—or, rather, the actual impingements of people on each other which comprise it—but it is simpler, and it has been possible, largely to ignore its persisting non-group features. Some considerable success has resulted, but at the cost of what is in effect but a partial analysis. Be that as it may, the problem is certainly different, and more intractable, when amongst a given population there are few or no groups, and few or no categories defined in terms of common interests and common action.

In this book, concentrating on those social relationships expressed in a kinship idiom, I have had to deal with circumstances in which there were few significant groups. The household and the hamlet were, of course, kin-based groups, and highly important in certain contexts. My chief concern, however, has been with the interaction and inter-dependence of people—the Ndendeuli—beyond their households and hamlets, as they sought and practiced cooperation and mutual assistance, and came into various kinds of conflict, in economic, politico-jural, religious, and other activities. In these contexts it seemed quite necessary to try and use the concept of network, even if it were little more than a metaphor or analogy.

It was necessary to recognize constantly the implications of the facts that: (1) A's relationships with B, C, D, E, . . . were very often, and perhaps always, affected by the relationships of B with D, and C with E, and so on; and (2) A was, in certain contexts, indirectly in relationship with (impinging on) P, who was directly in relationship with B; and with X, who was directly in relationship with P but not with B, and so on; where relationships were expressed, oriented, and morally justified in kinship terms. Those relationships concerned material and non-material interests, ranging from helping to hoe a man's field to giving recognition of his status vis-à-vis some other person.

That observation is fairly straightforward, put in that way abstractly. It is merely the common-sense observation of everyday life in many societies. Yet it is by no means so straightforward when the social anthropologist seeks to translate it into "actual" relationships, and the "actual" interaction and inter-dependence of real people in concrete social life. The variables become very numerous, and their inter-connection is complex. Moreover, it is not merely an act of description with which I am concerned, but with an analysis of the implications and effects of the inter-connections when social action occurs. To seek to understand the opportunities for and limitations on men's choices, and the results of their actions—among the Ndendeuli—it was necessary to go beyond description. Therefore, whether or not it was always explicit in my exposition, I always endeavoured to bear firmly in mind those implications of the network and to avoid over-simplifying or blurring the facts.

In the end-result, with my present account of the Ndendeuli completed, I remain uncertain whether or not I have been able to give more significant meaning, more objective "reality", and more theoretical potential to the concept of the network. Perhaps, in the end, it has remained only a powerful guiding metaphor, descriptive of the complex reality, and orienting my account of evolving situations, decision-making, interaction, and their results. This, for example, seems to have been Firth's opinion on Barnes's use of "network" (Firth 1954:4), and it seems to be one that many anthropologists would share. On the other hand, Mayer has suggested that the construct may be "important in so far as it is a *basis* for sets rather than as a means for describing them and . . . the two are distinct" (Mayer 1966:100). In this book I have attempted to demonstrate the validity, significance, and analytical utility of such sets—kin-set, action-set, cluster, faction—that derive directly from my conceptualisation of the network and that have been the means of analysing the particular empirical data. Those sets cannot properly be understood in isolation, but only as parts of, or emerging from, the enveloping network.

Perhaps the concept of "network" will only be fully developed, and its potential realised, by socio-metric treatment. I have no competence to assess the possibilities, but there seems to be an advantage in seeking to handle the obvious complexities mathematically, as a number of sociologists have been advocating in recent years. It would appear, nevertheless, that the techniques have still to be worked out to the point where they can be applied to real-life circumstances. There is not yet general agreement amongst the advocates of mathematical analysis of networks; furthermore, "the methods of analysis developed for the study of clearly delimited small groups of a dozen or less persons in the laboratory, or of thousands of neutrons lacking individuality" (Barnes 1969) are inadequate to cope with the far greater complexity of real-life. Even if they become more adequate, the problem will then arise of providing sufficiently valid data as required by such rigorous methodology. One wishes the socio-metric workers well; but there must be legitimate doubts whether in the near future they will provide the answers and insights we need. In the meantime the non-mathematical anthropologist can try to develop both research and concepts from which to obtain improved understanding.

To revert to the account of the Ndendeuli: it has seemed rather easier to employ the idea of network with reference to the limited and smaller number of people involved in what I have called the "closed network" of a local community. It was easier to handle the complexities involving the thirty-two household heads of Ligomba. To some extent, the single, synthetic genealogy of Ligomba (or, similarly, of Namabeya) is a representation of the closed network. But this is so only in an elementary way. The inter-connections and inter-dependencies (whether in cooperation or conflict) of the Ligomba men were very definitely *not* exhausted by that statement of the simple genealogical links. The data given in Chapters Four, Five, and Six adequately demonstrate that. The mere genealogical links told only a limited amount about actual relationships. They did not reveal the quality of the relationships and the dependent variables; they did not reveal all the indirect connections and the considerations that each man, in context, had to take account of, nor the many others that he did not altogether comprehend but that affected his decisions and his subsequent behaviour. The

"reality" of that closed network has only emerged—if it has—
in the course of detailed presentation of events, and of communications and interaction. Obviously not all the features of that network have been revealed, for only a proportion of the totality of
interaction has been described. Yet at the same time those events
and interaction could only be described and analysed in the way
I have done because of the underlying assumption of the reality
of the network and the implications of that assumption.

When it came to the open network, the far greater range,
variety, and complexity of inter-connections were much more
difficult to grasp in their application to real life. Although the idea
and assumption of network still persisted as the orientation, it has
seemed possible only to touch on it through illustration. The
intention has been to show how, in particular circumstances, men's
opportunities for action, the practical limitations on their choices,
and their actual decisions were all affected by their involvement
in the network.

The analytical value, as well as the practical research potential,
of the concept of action-set is clearer. For some purposes, and in
some cultural contexts, it may be necessary to distinguish different
kinds of action-sets, though this has not been attempted here. It
must be insisted, however, that whatever its value, the concept of
action-set can only be used through an appreciation of the social
complexity within which it occurs—the complexity that I have
called a network.

In this monograph the explicit concentration has been on
collective social action for certain purposes and interests of individual men. This was the result of my predispositions in the research field at the time and my subsequent theoretical interests. The
tool of the action-set was used to deal with this range of social
behaviour. It has seemed to me to be a serious problem to understand, in detail, how people could and did organize themselves and
take collective action where their relationships were not aggregated
into social groups, and where common action and interests were
not systematised by group affiliation and by specialised roles of
leadership and responsibility.

A network is not, however, comprehended only in terms of
collective action. Dyadic relationships are also integral to it: dyadic
relationships that are significantly affected by their involvement,
overtly or not, in the range of inter-connection and inter-dependence comprising the network. Little attention has been given here

to this aspect, therefore little attempt has been made to work out some of the necessary techniques and concepts.

There are a number of other questions raised by this analysis, two or three of which may be examined briefly. They may be of interest and assistance to other anthropologists concerned with comparable material and similar problems.

Among the Ndendeuli there was a single mode in which almost all significant social relationships were described, defined, and explained. That was kinship. A man's direct and personal relationships of most importance—to him and to the external observer alike —were kinship relations. But many of his other relationships were perceived as indirectly dependent on kinship: the kin of kin, and the kin of kin of kin. Moreover, even with declared non-kin, interaction was orientated in terms of kinship. In analysis I have shown how the indirect linkages of kinship sequences affected, almost controlled, men's decisions and behaviour, and their results. I have shown that kinship was essentially an idiom in which relationships were expressed—an idiom easily understood by the people, with an immediacy of its own, and one that had both moral strength and practical utility. Kinship provided a language of communication in agreed terms. It provided also a framework, a system one might almost say, by which to standardise expectations and to provide guide-lines of a kind everyone could (but not always did) follow. That the "objective" facts of genealogical connection could be ignored, blurred, or even altered did not diminish the real value of the kinship idiom. Indeed, it was this very flexibility that made it possible to use it so constantly, conveniently, and, above all, successfully.

It might be thought that the Ndendeuli network was of the simplest order, couched in terms of a single variable—kinship. From this, it might be thought that in other, more complex societies, the character of the network is far more intricate and far more difficult to comprehend within this frame of reference. Not only kinship relations, but specialised relations of an economic, political, neighbourhood, religious, or other kind, or concerning categories of stratification (class, caste, age, and so on), make the construction of network models, and understanding of them, a much more complex analytical operation. Up to a point this would seem to be true. The variables in such circumstances are more numerous, and the interaction of variables produces implications of considerable significance. Yet only up to a point, I think. The Ndendeuli only operated in terms of one explicit variable—more accurately, a coherent set of variables, since there were different kinds of kinship relations; and kinship relations were of a multiplex kind, rather than single-stranded or single interest. Yet in dealing with the Ndendeuli I have, of course, been dealing with economic, political, religious, neighbourhood relations, not with kinship for kinship's sake. Except perhaps in some philosophical sense, kinship does not exist in its own right, but only as a vehicle for other things. Thus the so-called kinship network was in fact a political, economic, and other network, and many of the variables of a more complex society were to be found in it. Indeed, in one sense analysis might be somewhat simpler where the variables are more overtly recognised and can to some extent be treated separately. Multiplex kinship relations made for a more complicated network continuum.

Secondly, in this monograph I have sought to avoid conceiving of a network of social relations as in any way forming a stable pattern. "At any one time" something like *the* network may be lifted out of the continuum of social life by analytical procedure and for analytical convenience. Even this procedure is, I would caution, introducing a danger that needs to be recognised and guarded against. In the first place, even "at any one time" the network of relations is much less definite than such procedures might suggest. Participating actors at the time would most probably be less certain. The network of relations is also one of expectations; and expectations may or may not be fulfilled. In the second place, the network "at any one time" must be viewed, and really can only be properly understood, as the temporary culmination of a great deal that has gone before; and what happens at that time will in some ways affect or alter the network.

We need (as others have pointed out before) a conceptualisation equivalent to a reel of movie film. The individual frame or picture is the "at any one time" part of the whole. It may have an internal consistency, a message, an individuality of its own; but its full significance emerges only as a part of the whole reel. Of course this is perfectly obvious, although it has not been so obvious in much of the work of anthropologists. There have been some excellent reasons for this, one of which is the undoubted simplifying value of limiting conceptualisation to the "at any one time" extract. The number of variables to be handled is reduced and important problems can be examined more easily in their absence. Certain less valid assumptions have also played their part. It has for some time now been fashionable to criticise these synchronic studies, and even foolishly to neglect the real value that lies in them; and yet still anthropology has scarcely begun to develop adequate techniques to take full and necessary account of the time factor and the constancy of change.

In a conscious attempt to study dynamic processes over a period, and to conceptualise networks as something like a continuous reel of film frames (the analogy is admittedly weak), I have tried to present the history of the development of the closed network of the Ligomba local community over more than two decades. In doing this I have wished to show that the network "at any one time" is the product of decisions made and interaction played out by people previously. Thus Ligomba as I first encountered it was an epiphenomenon of what had gone before; and it continued to change under my eyes as events occurred during that year of 1953.

It was not easy to obtain reliable data for the two preceding decades, and I was often (and still am) beset by serious doubts about the validity of those that I did obtain and that have been presented here. The problems of selective memory, post hoc rationalization, forgetfulness and plain dissimulation, and so on were all obvious in general, though often less obvious in detail. The ghost of Malinowski's history as myth and as a charter for the present was hard to ignore. I did not wish to ignore it altogether. Clearly, certain events (or versions of them) were well remembered because of the light they cast on the present; but then that, too, was one reason why I needed to know about them, while trying to penetrate behind any stylised facade. My informants were less clear about other events, other times, other people's actions that had undoubtedly contributed to the epiphenomenon. Often the bits and pieces were frustratingly fragmentary, or on the contrary they were too clear to be altogether credible. Furthermore, I sought if possible not to obtain merely a chronicle of events but an understanding of them, their significance, their interrelations, the reasons behind people's decisions and acts, and so on.

My attempt was, in the field at that time, begun principally as an interesting experiment: to see how far one could go, to test the problems, and try out methods, rather than a scientifically calculated, theoretically oriented piece of research. In the end, retrospectively, the results overwhelmingly justified themselves, even though a good deal more is obviously required. Ideally one needs an analytical record for each year of Ligomba's existence, equivalent at least to that which is given here for the single year of 1953.

It proved easier to handle the limited data of the closed network of the single local community than to deal with the virtually infinite, open network as a dynamic thing. Indeed, I am conscious that I have largely shirked the problem, for it is not clear to me how it could be handled. Yet the relationships and expectations that comprised that open network "at any one time" were also no less dynamic, impermanent epiphenomena.

In the analytical record for Ligomba in 1953, and more selectively for Namabeya from 1952 to 1954, the intent has been to demonstrate how decisions, interaction, and their results affected subsequent decisions, interaction, and results, among roughly the same collection of inter-connected, inter-dependent people. The most helpful stimulus for this approach was Turner's path-breaking work in *Schism and Continuity in an African Society* (1957). That work crystallised a good deal that was in my mind, but which hitherto had been rather inchoate; and it suggested further ideas of great utility for my analysis. The "social drama" of the Ndembu, as Turner presented and analysed them, were of a catalytic nature, however, whilst the cases I have recorded here were, individually, often much less dramatic. At least I wish to direct especial attention and give added emphasis to the cumulative effect of an endless series of incidents, cases, events that may be quite as significant in affecting and changing social relationships as the more dramatic encounters. Lesser events (if one may put it that way) also serve gradually to set the stage for the bigger encounters. In other words, I am advocating (and have tried in part to practice) that careful attention should be given to the continuum of interaction amongst the given collection of people. That continuum comprises "confrontations" (Bailey's term) and both major and minor encounters or contests. Furthermore, we must not concentrate so greatly on conflict situations that we neglect the equally important situations of cooperation—though the latter are likely to be less dramatic.

Turner's later concept of "phase development" (evidently replacing his "social drama") seems on the face of it less easy to apply generally (Swartz, et al. 1966:38). I find it difficult to identify the beginnings and conclusions of "phases" in many instances, for events merge into one another in real-life circumstances. Moreover, there is an implication of equilibrium assumptions in his "patterned sequence of events" that seems unfortunate and unnecessary. No doubt it depends on what Turner intends by the final event in his sequence: "restoration of peace". This is an ambiguous phrase, but suggests a degree of finality and a degree of restored stability even if at some new level. Probably there are a number of "patterned sequences" dependent on both the socio-cultural form and on the particular emphasis given by the anthropologist. I have not thought it particularly useful to seek to identify a common pattern of that kind in the sequences that occurred among the Ndendeuli. But, of course, it still remains to be seen how Turner can put his schema into actual analysis with specific empirical data.

Other anthropologists too have been stimulated by Turner's work, and I have certainly sought to build upon the foundations he laid. The concern is not with history for history's sake, nor primarily with the production of a reliable narrative account. Rather the intention is to use detailed historical data for overt analytical purposes. I would go so far as to say that without this kind of analysis, anthropologists' accounts of the social units with which they deal will be seriously incomplete, and therefore inadequate, for many things do change and not everything remains the same afterwards, even where radical social change is not in process.

Thirdly, especially in the analysis of action-set formation and performance, considerable attention has been given to decision-making. This I regard as fundamental to the understanding of any network and of any kinship context with a large optative element. Therefore there has been a consistent attempt to perceive and explain the options open to a man in context, and the limitations on his choice. And although I was not seeking to list a code of rules by which choice was made, the existence of something like such a code has been implicit. This raises two connected problems. First, how can one be reasonably sure what the options were in a particular instance? What were the dimensions of the range of choice, and how far could a man control or at least affect that range in his own interests? There is, doubtless, no ultimate answer to this, but the implications for research are important. Secondly, how can the anthropologist be reasonably certain about the individual's perception of the situation, and about the motivations behind his final decision? The individual may not have adequately seen all the (objectively) available options; he may have placed particular evaluations on them which affected his decision. He may not, often he scarcely could, have been altogether aware of his motivations. The anthropologist may not have been able to learn a man's reasons for his decision. Even if he did, they may not have been the real reasons. Men deceive themselves (as well as inquisitive anthropologists) about their motives; and some motives are so deep-seated as to be virtually unknowable. The idea of codes of rules by which decisions are taken presupposes that, in order to apply them, or even learn about them properly, we know all the circumstances in which they apply.

This kind of problem raises psychological issues that most anthropologists cannot, unfortunately, cope with. Here we need assistance from psychologists, if only they would be willing to muddy their shoes and observe people in so-called esoteric cultures. Anthropologists cannot supply adequate raw material: they do not know all the right questions to ask, and they are legitimately usually too busy asking their own sorts of questions and getting the answers. And anthropologists cannot obtain all the information in reply even to their own questions. In the majority of cases, to be pertinent, I did not and do not know why Ndendeuli made the decisions they actually did. I merely recorded the decisions, and went on to examine their effects as far as possible. In some cases, I could of course be pretty certain why a man had joined a certain action-set, or why two men had gradually come to acknowledge each other as kinsmen, or why a man joined the local community as a new-comer. The explanation was, or seemed to be, implicit in the context and the resultant action. In a few cases, better or more trusting informants were able to explain their motives and decisions; and I have tried to indicate this in my account of events.

The search for an individual's perception of a situation, for his motives, and for the reasons for his decision can be like the search for the end of the rainbow. And yet it is essential, and one needs to beware of ideal, stereotyped explanation. My own attempts among the Ndendeuli have been helpful, if not conclusive. They may perhaps stimulate more careful and perceptive research elsewhere. There is, on the other hand, it seems to me, some danger of over-concentration in the area of actors' perceptions and communication of perceptions, to the point where almost no action takes place at all, or at least it is not related by the anthropologist. By all means let us be much more perceptive about perception. It is badly needed. But let us continue to follow up and record and analyse the decisions made and the action and the results that follow.

This raises a fourth issue, and one that has perturbed me. In concerning ourselves with decision making, or indeed with the playing of roles and interacting of all kinds, we seem to be compelled to assume a rationality in men that we know by experience is often absent. Men can misconceive a situation and its possibilities;

they can be stimulated by high emotion, or by depression, to make moves and decisions that otherwise they might not; they can be stupid, obstinate, short-sighted, or they may be calculating, alert, intelligent, or something somewhere in between; they may be greedy or generous, intolerant or tolerant; and so on. Yet we have to a great extent to ignore these critical factors that affect role playing and decision making. Our abstractions, as social scientists, and despite our occasional protestations to the contrary, tend to refer to "sociological man" who, in given circumstances and with given values and interests, behaves in such and such a way. We induce regularities for that behaviour if we seek, for example, to produce a decision model or codes of pragmatic rules. We tend quite strongly to explain particular bits of behaviour, particular decisions for instance, in rational terms; and thus we impute to actual individuals a rationality that probably, almost certainly, they did not have. It is no complete answer to say that we are only concerned, as sociologists, with the regularities and generalities of social behaviour. It is true that we are, or should be; but we take our raw material from actual behaviour, and implicit in our argument is that from our abstract generalisation we could go back and explain (even foretell) what people are likely to do in actual instances.

If one is more concerned with ideal rules and roles, or with generalised ethnographic statements (for example, "fathers behave in such and such a way to their sons"; or "when we marry we do this and this") the problem may be unimportant. If, however, as in my own exposition here, one is concerned with the actual, concrete elements of specific real-life situations (as near as they can be recorded), then the question of irrational factors, and the problems of making valid abstractions and drawing logical conclusions, are relevant and difficult. I have been conscious of describing the behaviour of particular men of Ligomba or Namabeya as if they were craftily calculating individuals, wisely weighing up the possibilities and making their decisions, or contrariwise as if they were mere automatons directed by forces outside of them. I have sought to minimize both erroneous extremes by duly noting relevant aspects or occasions of human irrationality in the events described in this book; but I am not satisfied that I have been able to take due account of all this in presenting my analysis.

Important scientific and philosophical questions are implied in all this, the answers to which cannot be provided here. I feel it necessary, nevertheless, to note the general problem and to indicate my awareness of it, for it has for several reasons impressed itself upon me in the presentation of these data on the Ndendeuli. Pragmatically at least, Schelling's remarks are pertinent and helpful, though they may be unduly soothing. He wrote: ". . . the assumption of rational behaviour is a productive one in the generation of systematic theory. If behaviour were actually cool-headed, valid and relevant theory would probably be easier to create than it actually is. If we view our results as a bench mark for further approximations to reality, not as fully adequate theory, we should manage to protect ourselves from the worst results of a biased theory" (Schelling 1960:16).

It is to be admitted that my account of certain behaviour of certain Ndendeuli men has been no more than an "approximation to reality". Yet I have endeavoured to report as accurately as possible, and to make interpretations and to draw conclusions that are based on that report.

References

Abrahams, R. G.
 1965 Neighbourhood organization: a major sub-system among the Northern Nyamwezi; *Africa*, 25:168–86.
Allan, W.
 1949 *Studies in African land usage in Northern Rhodesia.* Lusaka, Rhodes-Livingstone Institute (Paper No. 15).
 1965 *The African husbandman.* Edinburgh, Oliver & Boyd.
Bailey, F. G.
 1960 *Tribe, caste and nation.* Manchester University Press.
 1968 Parapolitical systems; in M. J. Swartz (ed.): *Local-level politics.* Chicago, Aldine.
Barnes, J. A.
 1947 The collection of genealogies; *Rhodes-Livingstone Journal*, 5.
 1954 Class and committees in a Norwegian island parish; *Human Relations*, 7:39–58.
 1955 Seven types of segmentation; *Rhodes-Livingstone Journal*, 17.
 1968 Networks and political processes; in M. J. Swartz (ed.): *Local-level politics.* Chicago, Aldine.
 1969 Graph theory and social networks: a technical comment on connectedness; *Sociology*, 3.
Barton, R. F.
 1949 *The Kalingas: their institutions and custom law.* Chicago University Press.
Beattie, J.
 1964 *Other cultures.* London, Cohen & West.
Blehr, O.
 1963 Action groups in a society with bilateral kinship: a case study from the Faroe Islands; *Ethnology*, 2:269–75.
Boissevain, J.
 1968 The place of non-groups in the social sciences; *Man* (n.s.) 3:542–56.
Bott, E. J.
 1957 *Family and social network.* London, Tavistock.
Coleman, J. S.
 1963 Comment on 'On the concept of influence'; *Public Opinion Quarterly*, 27:63–82.
Conklin, H. C.
 1961 The study of shifting cultivation; *Current Anthropology*, 2.

Ebner, E.
1959 *History of the Wangoni.* Peramiho, Tanganyika.
Epstein, A. L.
1961 The network and urban social organization; *Rhodes-Livingstone Journal*, 29:29–62.
Evans-Pritchard, E. E.
1951 *Kinship and marriage among the Nuer.* Oxford, Clarendon.
Firth, R.
1954 Social organization and social change; *Journal of the Royal Anthropological Institute*, 84:1–20.
1957 Factions in Indian and overseas Indian societies; *British Journal of Sociology*, 8:291–5.
1963 Bilateral descent groups; in I. Schapera (ed.): *Studies in kinship and marriage.* London, Royal Anthropological Institute (Occasional Paper No. 16).
Forde, C. D.
1963 Unilineal fact or fiction; in I. Schapera (ed.): *Studies in kinship and marriage.* London, Royal Anthropological Institute (Occasional Paper No. 16).
Freeman, D.
1955 *Iban agriculture.* London, H.M.S.O. (Colonial Research Studies No. 18).
1960 Iban of western Borneo; in G. P. Murdock (ed.): *Social structure of southeast Asia.* Chicago, Quadrangle.
1961 On the concept of the kindred; *Journal of the Royal Anthropological Institute*, 90:192–220.
Geertz, H.
1961 *The Javanese family.* New York, Free Press.
Gluckman, M.
1955 *The judicial process among the Barotse.* Manchester University Press.
1961(*a*) Ethnographic data in British social anthropology; *Sociological Review*, 9:5–17.
1961(*b*) African jurisprudence; *Advancement of Science*, 74.
Goodenough, W. H.
1961 Review of 'Social structure in southeast Asia'; *American Anthropologist*, 63:1341–47.
1962 Kindred and hamlet in Lakalai, New Britain; *Ethnology*, 1:5–12.
Gray, R. F. and P. H. Gulliver (eds.)
1964 *The family estate in Africa.* Boston University Press (London, Routledge & Kegan Paul).
Gulliver, P. H.
1951 The development & amnesia of unilateral kinship relations. Kampala, East African Institute of Social Research (Conference Papers).
1954 *Administrative survey of the Ngoni and Ndendeuli of Songea District.* Tanganyika, Provincial Administration.
1955(*a*) *The family herds.* London, Routledge & Kegan Paul.
1955(*b*) *Labour migration in a rural economy.* Kampala, East African Institute of Social Research (E. African Studies No. 6).

1956 A history of the Ngoni of Songea District; *Tanganyika Notes & Records*, 41:16–30.
1963 *Social control in an African society*. Boston University Press (London, Routledge & Kegan Paul).
1964 The Arusha family; in Gray and Gulliver 1964.
1967 The case of the Ndendeuli shifting cultivators of southern Tanzania; Paper presented to Conference on Competing demands for the time of labor in traditional African societies, sponsored by S.S.R.C. and Agricultural Development Council.
1969 Dispute settlement without courts; in Nader 1969.

Kaplan, A.
1964 *The conduct of inquiry*. San Francisco, Chandler.

Keesing, R.
1966 Kwaio kindreds; *Southwestern Journal of Anthropology*, 22:346–53.
1967(*a*) Statistical models and decision models of social structure; *Ethnology*, 6:1–16.
1967(*b*) *Kwaio descent groups*. Santa Cruz, Center for South Pacific Studies, University of California.

Leach, E. R.
1961 *Pul Eliya*. Cambridge University Press.

Lewis, I. M.
1962 *Marriage and the family in Northern Somaliland*. Kampala, East African Institute of Social Research (E. African Studies No. 15).

Mayer, A. C.
1960 *Caste and kinship in central India*. London, Routledge & Kegan Paul.
1966 The significance of quasi-groups in the study of complex societies; in M. Banton (ed.): *The social anthropology of complex societies*. London, Tavistock (A.S.A. Monographs 4).

Mayer, P.
1961 *Tribesmen or townsmen*. Cape Town, Oxford University Press.

Middleton, J.
1960 *Lugbara religion*. London, Oxford University Press.

Mitchell, W. E.
1963 Theoretical problems in the concept of the kindred; *American Anthropologist*, 65:343–54.

Morris, H. S.
1953 *Report on a Melanau sago-producing community in Sarawak*. London, H.M.S.O.

Murdock, G. P.
1949 *Social structure*. New York, Macmillan.
1964 The kindred; *American Anthropologist*, 66:129–32.

Nadel, S. F.
1951 *The foundations of social anthropology*. London, Cohen & West.

Nader, L.
1969 *Law in culture and society*. Chicago, Aldine.

Nicholas, R. W.
1966 Factions: a comparative analysis; in M. Banton (ed.): *Political*

systems and the distribution of power. London, Tavistock (A.S.A. Monographs 2).

Ogan, E.
1966   Nasioi marriage: an essay in model building; *Southwestern Journal of Anthropology,* 22:172–93.

Paine, R.
1957   *Coast Lapp society.* Tromso, Tromso Museums Skrifter, IV.
1964   Herd management in north Lapp society; Wenner-Gren Foundation.

Parkin, D. J.
1969   *Neighbours and nationals in an African city ward.* Berkeley and Los Angeles, California University Press (London, Routledge & Kegan Paul).

Parsons, T.
1963   On the concept of influence; *Public Opinion Quarterly,* 27:37–62.

Pauw, B. A.
1963   *The second generation.* Cape Town, Oxford University Press.

Pehrson, R. N.
1957   *The bilateral network of social relations in Konkama Lapp District.* Bloomington, Indiana University Publications.

Read, K. E.
1959   Leadership and consensus in New Guinea society; *American Anthropologist,* 61.

Sahlins, M. D.
1963   Poor man, rich man, big-man, chief: political types in Melanesia and Polynesia; *Comparative Studies in Society and History,* 5:285–303.

Scheffler, H. W.
1965   *Choiseul Island social structure.* Berkeley and Los Angeles, University of California Press.

Schelling, T. C.
1960   *The strategy of conflict.* Harvard University Press.

de Schlippe, P.
1956   *Shifting agriculture in Africa.* London, Routledge & Kegan Paul.

Swartz, M. J., V. W. Turner, and A. Tuden
1966   *Political anthropology.* Chicago, Aldine.

Tanganyika, Govt. of
1945   *Agriculture in Tanganyika.* Dar es Salaam, Government Printer.

Turner, V. W.
1957   *Schism and continuity in an African society.* Manchester University Press.

Van Velsen, J.
1964   *The politics of kinship.* Manchester University Press.

Weber, M.
1964   *The theory of social and economic organization.* Trans., A. M. Henderson and T. Parsons. New York, Free Press.

Worsley, P.
1956   The kinship system of the Tallensi: a re-evaluation; *Journal of the Royal Anthropological Institute,* 86.

Index